B. Traven: Life and Work

B. TRAVEN
LIFE AND WORK

Edited by
Ernst Schürer
and Philip Jenkins

THE PENNSYLVANIA STATE UNIVERSITY PRESS
University Park and London

Library of Congress Cataloging in Publication Data

B. Traven : life and work.

Bibliography: p.
1. Traven, B. 2. Authors, Mexican--20th century--
Biography. I. Schürer, Ernst. II. Jenkins, Philip, 1952-

PT3919.T7Z573   1986   813'.52 [B]   86-12213

ISBN 0-271-00382-0

CONTENTS

PREFACE

Normally, a commemorative volume might be expected to begin with a sketch of the life of the author concerned. As we will see, this is not possible for the writer who published under the nom de plume of B. Traven. Indeed, a recurring theme of the papers included here will be the debate over exactly who this author was who succeeded so thoroughly in concealing himself behind a mask of anonymity throughout his lifetime. This element of mystery has naturally fascinated many. It may well be that this was its precise purpose, as designed by that odd amalgam of recluse and publicity man who lived for so long under the assumed names of Ret Marut, Traven Torsvan, Hal Croves, and many others. For other readers, it may appear only as a tiresome and rather childish masquerade. Why then does Traven continue to exercise such fascination?

Traven deserves commemoration for far more than the lengthy maze that was his life. His work survives, and has acquired a growing reputation in several cultures, because of its literary and artistic qualities. Different critics will place their emphases on different parts of his achievement. Some will note the energy, wit, and drive which characterize his work; others will mark the remarkably contemporary note of his novels of third-world peasants, the sensitivity and wide humanity which lend a prophetic tone to his Caoba Cycle. Traven is "modern" in being perhaps the greatest anarchist novelist, the writer who pioneered the modern stereotype of seeking a resolution of Western class conflicts in the struggles of the "wretched of the earth;" yet his fascination with death and the baroque allows us to seek him in far older philosophical and literary contexts.

We therefore encounter a paradox--one of many associated with the man. He apparently believed his work should stand by its own merits, and that interest in the creator of the novels was at best irrelevant, at worst prurient. Had he not emerged from a Europe where progressive art glorified the images of the impersonal machine and the factory? Yet his very attempt to place his artistic identity in the background has led to scholarly interest focusing on this identity to an almost grotesque degree.

One of the healthiest trends of Traven studies in recent years has been the emphasis on the novels as significant works of art in their own right, and not merely as a catena of hints and cryptograms to be unraveled in a "quest for B. Traven." That caveat must precede any attempt to place Traven in the context of his times.

The Works of B. Traven

Although we attempt to provide a biographical framework for the understanding of Traven, we have frequent cause to note the uncertainty which still prevails about details of his life. Will Wyatt has compiled a list of twenty-seven aliases which Traven used at some point in his life, and this is surely a minimum figure. It is therefore desirable to approach Traven's work in the opposite way from a normal biography. We will begin with the relative terra firma of his works and then tentatively approach such arcana as the precise dates of his birth and death.

The Traven story properly begins in 1925, when the Berlin Vorwärts, the newspaper of the German Social-Democratic party (SPD) started the publication in serial form of his novel The Cotton Pickers. The following year, the German book club Büchergilde Gutenberg published a new work, The Death Ship, and there began an intense period of productivity. The novels of B. Traven appeared as follows:

1925 - Die Baumwollpflücker/The Cotton Pickers (originally entitled Der Wobbly)
1926 - Das Totenschiff/The Death Ship
1927 - Der Schatz der Sierra Madre/Treasure of the Sierra Madre
1929 - Die Brücke im Dschungel/The Bridge in the Jungle
1929 - Die Weisse Rose/The White Rose
1931 - Der Karren/The Carreta
1931 - Regierung/Government
1933 - Der Marsch ins Reich der Caoba/The March to Caoba Land
1936 - Die Troza/The Troza
1936 - Die Rebellion der Gehenkten/The Rebellion of the Hanged
1939 - Ein General kommt aus dem Dschungel/A General from the Jungle
1960 - Aslan Norval

The dates given here are those of the original German editions. Subsequent editions and translations often differ considerably from these originals, and they provide an interesting field of research, which has hardly been tapped because of the unorganized condition of Traven's literary estate in Mexico City.

Besides the novels, other works include a travel book, Land des Frühlings/Land of Spring (1928); a number of short stories with Mexican settings, collected as Der Busch/The Night Visitor; and the curious mythical piece, Creation of the <u>Sun</u> <u>and</u> <u>the</u> <u>Moon</u>. Traven's last six Jungle novels, starting with <u>The</u> <u>Carreta</u> in 1931 and ending with <u>A</u> <u>General</u> <u>from</u> <u>the</u> <u>Jungle</u> in 1939, form the so-called Caoba Cycle.

As we can see, Traven's major period of activity fell between 1925 and 1939. The Büchergilde Gutenberg continued to be his publisher. It had been formed originally by the Educational Association of German Printers (Bildungsverband der Deutschen Buchdrucker) in 1924 to enable working people to buy good books at low cost. Its international authors included, besides B. Traven, Jack London, Martin Andersen Nexö, Vicente Blasco Jbañez, and many others. Since its books were indeed inexpensive, as well as attractively bound in hard cover, the book club's membership grew to 80,000 by the end of 1932. The popularity of Traven contributed a great deal to this rapid expansion in membership. When it was taken over by the Nazis in 1933, an independent branch was established abroad in Zurich, and Traven promptly presented it with the copyrights to his books.

Traven's books were quickly translated into Swedish, Danish, Norwegian, Russian, Spanish, Dutch, Hungarian, French, and many other languages. In 1934, the publication of <u>The</u> <u>Death</u> <u>Ship</u> in English began a series of translations which introduced Traven to the American audience, and at that point, there commences a quest which continues today. Who was B. Traven?

The Quest for Traven

Traven himself had been very definite about his origins. He was an American, born in the United States, and not--categorically not--a German. He had written in German because that was the only way to publish his work after it had met systematic rejection from American publishers. His books were thus translated into German. He had little detail to provide about his American origins, but some have seen the American hero of <u>The</u> <u>Cotton</u> <u>Pickers</u> and <u>The</u> <u>Death</u> <u>Ship</u> as an autobiographical alter ego. In the 1960s, Charles Miller used this idea of Traven's American origins to reconstruct a hypothetical biography of the writer.

Speculation was not quelled, however. By the 1970's, a remarkable complex of myths had assembled around the identity of Traven. He was really Jack London, Ambrose Bierce, President López Mateos of Mexico, an Austrian aristocrat, a leper, a poor American, black or white, a syndicate of writers who may or may not have been political exiles. And what of the name Traven? Was it a significant clue? Did it represent a derivation of the German word <u>Traum</u> (dream), or was it a variation of the author's real name? And is the "a" in Traven long and Germanic, or short and English? Even the most basic facts seem beyond our grasp.

Traven did his utmost to intensify confusion. In 1947, the writer transformed himself into "Hal Croves" in order to observe and supervise the filming of The Treasure of the Sierra Madre, which subsequently did much to contribute to spreading his fame. And in the early 1950s, Croves produced a series of newsletters, the BT-Mitteilungen, to create more false leads about the identity of Traven.

Some of the rumors and speculations could be dismissed with ease. Far more difficult was the question of Traven's life before the appearance of the first novels in 1925. The concept of "Gerard Gales" as an autobiographical figure was very tempting, so that Traven could readily be seen as an American of German or Scandinavian descent who had migrated to Mexico. But there was also the all but insurmountable obstacle of Ret Marut. Marut had been a prominent radical in Germany in the second decade of the century, and he was linked to Traven by evidence which grew stronger over the years. As early as the late 1920s, Marut's friend Erich Mühsam had seen close resemblances between the work and style of writing of Marut and Traven; and Traven's writings began to appear very shortly after the disappearance of Marut from European soil. The East German scholar Rolf Recknagel was able to argue an extremely strong case for the identity of the two men in his Beiträge zur Biografie of 1966.

But Marut seemed to be a purely German figure, whose origins--though not precisely known--presumably lay in Wilhelminian Germany. Traven's supposed American past located his origins in Chicago, or San Francisco, or Minnesota.... How could the two biographies be reconciled? After Traven's death in 1969, scholarship based on his work reached a new age of maturity, with major books by Chankin (1975), Baumann (1976), Richter (1977), Stone (1977), and Raskin (1980), as well as numerous articles and detailed research by Recknagel, Raskin, Goss, Richter, and others; while the B. Traven Buch of 1976 provides an extensive survey of the writer's life and times. But the question of Traven's origins seemed beyond resolution.

A major new direction in Traven research was provided at the end of that decade by the work of Will Wyatt and Robert Robinson, both of the BBC, in their research for a television documentary on the author which was broadcast at the end of 1978. They uncovered records of Ret Marut's arrest in Britain in 1924 and found evidence that Marut's real name was Otto Feige, born in Schwiebus, Germany, in 1882. It was thus argued that a definite continuity had been established--from Otto Feige to Ret Marut, and thus to B. Traven and Hal Croves; so we were dealing with one author, not several, and he was a German with no discernible American connections.

We may now be in a position to provide an attempt at a biography of Traven. What follows is subject to numerous qualifications and caveats, but it will serve as a working basis on which to proceed; and it will form a context for the debates in the chapters that follow.

B. Traven: A Life

The author was born on February 23, 1882, in Schwiebus (Pomerania) and was christened Hermann Albert Otto Maximilian Wienecke. As an illegitimate child, he was first known by his mother's name of Wienecke, but the subsequent marriage of his parents legitimized him as Otto Feige. He lived with his family until about 1904-1906, when he began an acting career as Ret Marut who surfaces in 1907. In the First World War, he emerged as a radical and peace activist, who published the journal Der Ziegelbrenner (The Brick-Burner). In 1919, he was involved in the anarchist Räterepublik in Bavaria, but the subsequent right-wing coup forced him to flee and go underground. After wandering through several European countries between 1921 and 1923, he arrived in England, where he was briefly imprisoned. In 1924, he left London by sea and arrived in Tampico, Mexico.

In the summer of 1924, Ret Marut became B. Traven, who soon began the frenetic burst of creative activity we have noted. For the remainder of his life, he would base himself in Mexico--often in Mexico City, though we also find him for a long period of time in Acapulco, and on expeditions to the jungles of Chiapas. "Traven" continued to metamorphose: In 1926 he was "Traven Torsvan," and in 1947 he became "Hal Croves." Throughout his life in Mexico, he would encounter the world through "fronts" and intermediaries--Esperanza López Matéos in the 1940s, and later his wife Rosa Elena Luján. In 1964, Croves and Señora Luján moved to a house on Rio Mississippi, Mexico City, where Wienecke/Feige/Marut/Traven/Croves died on March 26, 1969, at the age of eighty-seven.

This is essentially the Traven story as reconstructed by Will Wyatt. As we will see, there are very substantial objections to it. They may be summarized as follows:

1. The identification of Otto Feige with Ret Marut is not

universally accepted.   What are we to make of the
repeated claims by Marut between 1912 and 1924 that he
was a citizen of either England or the United States?   In
the First World War, Germans like John Heartfield
expressed their rejection of the Second Reich by the
ostentatious adoption of Anglo-Saxon names and culture.
But did Marut's claims reflect a genuine American
heritage?   There is evidence of strong English-language
influence in the German prose of Marut and Traven,
sometimes to the extent that passages became a strange
linguistic hybrid.   Rechnagel, an authority who cannot be
dismissed lightly, argues that "Marut" was the guise
adopted by an American of German descent who had earlier
been known as Charles Trefny.

2. In what sense was Ret Marut the same person as B. Traven?
Scholars like Goss and Baumann would point to significant
differences in the thought and the style of writing of
the two.   In support of this contention, they would note
the extremely short time which elapsed between Marut's
supposed arrival in Mexico (summer 1924) and the
publication of the first "Traven" stories in the
following year.   Was "Traven" a separate person, whose
life in Mexico long predated 1924?

3. Even if Marut became B. Traven, to what extent can the
Traven writings be said to be his?   Again and again,
students of Traven argue for the existence of an
Erlebnisträger, a "bearer of experiences," who lived and
wrote the life portrayed in the novels.   Did Marut become
the editor rather than the author of this work, in a
collaboration under the name "B. Traven"?

4. Is it still possible that our tentative reconstruction is
wholly wrong?   Other candidates for the identity of
Traven might still emerge, such as the Wladislav de
Bourba mentioned by Judy Stone in her chapter.   And what
are we to make of the story told by Will Wyatt of the
radical agitator and IWW organizer "Sletov," whose
career resembled that of "Gerard Gales" at so many
points, and whose real name was P.I. Travin?   It seems
that we have an ocean of red herrings to deal with.

It is the opinion of the editors that all the objections
listed above are incorrect, and that the identification of
Feige/Marut/Traven/Croves is substantially correct.   It
should also be made clear that neither of the editors would
be astonished if they were proved to be utterly wrong.
Whoever Traven was---German or American, individual or plural, author or editor--he spent four decades in the systematic dissemination of questionable and distorted informa-

tion. It may take at least that long to separate fiction from reality.

The latest research on Traven's biography, published in 1980 as Will Wyatt's The Man Who Was B. Traven, was the catalyst which led, ultimately, to this volume. Dating Traven's birth confirmed that 1982 would be the centenary year, which surely deserved some commemoration to celebrate and analyze Traven's achievement. The growing scale and maturity of Traven scholarship suggested the need for a survey volume to provide an overview of the field and to suggest directions for future research. A call for papers elicited an enthusiastic response, with the gratifying result that nearly all important and active academic Traven scholars are represented. Not all contributors are from the field of literary scholarship, however, since the nature of Traven's work appeals to many who have developed a private enthusiasm for his stories and novels. Among them are representatives of other academic disciplines: journalists and professional writers, such as Judy Stone and Charles Miller; and representatives of the worlds of publishing and the mass media, such as Heinz-D. Tschörtner and Lawrence Hill. They also reflect a wide geographical diversity, coming from both Germanies, Switzerland, Czechoslovakia, Sweden, Israel, and the United Kingdom; while the American contributors hail from thirteen states.

It would be inappropriate to list any "conclusions" arrived at in this volume. Opposing viewpoints are aired on a number of issues, notably on the question of Traven's identity, and consensus is impossible. Certain broad impressions may be recorded, however. First, the unity and coherence of the life and work of Marut/Traven are stressed more strongly than hitherto. Also, Traven emerges as a much more sophisticated character than he sometimes appears. His self-concealment appears less of a neurotic over-reaction, and more of a calculated ploy. Numerous anecdotes stress the extent to which he was a man of humor, humanity, sensitivity, and commitment. In the 1930s, for example, he was so far from being a demented hermit shut off from the real world that we find him expressing horror at the conduct of the Nazis in Germany, supporting anticlerical radicalism in Mexico and Sandino's peasant movement in Nicaragua, and aiding refugees of the Spanish Civil War. His reasons for anonymity were mixed and certainly included a warped sense of humor as one element, but they may also have been rational. If the NKVD could kill Trotsky in Mexico, could not the Gestapo have an equally long arm to reach German exiles, as Wyatt has pointed out?

Furthermore, Traven's use of disguise and pseudonym was so

common among radicals of his period as almost to be de rigueur. Apart from celebrated examples like Trotsky and Lenin, we need only think of the cosmopolitan leftist exiles who played such a role in the Comintern, like "General Kleber" of the Spanish Civil War. A particularly close analogue to Marut/Traven is provided by Willi Münzenberg (1889-1940), another former anarchist and veteran of the 1919 revolution. He did not adopt a pseudonym but spent many years in the systematic invention of myths, propaganda, and outright lies, and he has been called "a genius without rival in the creation and manipulation of front-organizations." The alias--no less than the web of deceit and fantasy which surrounded such men--was part of a commonplace reaction of leftists and anarchists against both political repression and the growing corporatism of state and society.

However, the most rewarding and illuminating tendency of most of the articles in this volume is their move from the "quest for Traven" to the evaluation of his literary works. Several essays make a vigorous and successful attempt to give Traven's novels their proper place in the world literature of the twentieth century. And this is a significant place, in at least three cultures: German, Anglo-American, and Hispano-American. To ignore the work of Traven is to leave a wide gap in one's awareness of the "Third World" novel, of political fiction, of the "proletarian novel," and, perhaps most important, of the literary encounter between European and Latin American cultures. To study Traven is to gain new insights into other authors of his time who dealt with the same or similar themes and locales: Manuel Azuela and Graham Greene, Franz Kafka and Ignazio Silone, Joseph Conrad and Ilf-Petrov. It is in this direction that future research should move, with special attention being given to Latin American literature at that time.

In conclusion, we would like to express our hope that this volume will provide a survey of the current state of knowledge about Traven and Traven scholarship, a foundation on which to build, and a departure point for new directions in research. The articles presented prove that the ideas espoused in the works of B. Traven are still sufficiently relevant to cause intense debate about literary, historical, sociological, political, philosophical, and religious issues. They might even be more revealing today than they were half a century ago. Most certainly, they are stimulating and rewarding material for readers in all walks of life and for scholars from many disciplines.

PART ONE: THE ENIGMA OF B. TRAVEN'S LIFE

THE B. TRAVEN I KNEW

Lawrence Hill

The ghost of the Traven mystery is like Banquo's—it refuses
to be laid to rest. But I will give it another try.

My first awareness of Traven came in the early forties
when I went to work for Alfred Knopf as a junior salesman.
The Knopf list included The Death Ship and three other books
by a mysterious writer said to be hiding somewhere in Mexico
and using the pen name B. Traven. Even then his books were
known and admired by only a few "insiders" and left-wing
intellectuals. Even Treasure, which later became a bestseller in paperback because of the Humphrey Bogart film, at
that time had sold only a few thousand copies.

Many years later, at Hill & Wang, a sunburned young man
named Charles Miller appeared in my office and said, "I come
from B. Traven." He was looking for a publisher for a
manuscript, "The Night Visitor and Other Stories." He had
come to the right place, since I was one of the few editors
in New York at that time who knew and admired some of B.
Traven's books.

We published The Night Visitor—with an introduction by
Charles Miller that derided the Ret Marut theory and other
"wild guesses" about Traven's identity. The book received a
front-page review in the New York Times Book Review. The
enthusiastic reception for The Night Visitor revived enough
latent interest in B. Traven to lead us to sign a contract
to publish all of his novels, some of them in improved
versions. Nearly all of the negotiations were with Rosa
Elena Luján, Traven's wife. We received no letters from
Traven himself, but some of the contracts, as I recall, were
signed by him. Some of the novels we published for the
first time in the United States were improved or re-edited
versions of the original British editions. Where these
versions came from was always a secret, but some were apparently corrected in English by Traven himself.

In 1967 I visited Mexico City to work out the details of
publishing the illustrated edition of The Creation of the
Sun and the Moon, and there I met Traven. What follows is
an excerpt from an account of the meeting which appeared in
the New York Times Book Review.

9

In the summer of 1967 I made a trip to Mexico City to discuss with Rosa Elena Luján the details of our publishing program for Traven's books--no mention was made of meeting the author himself; so I was pleasantly surprised when at the conclusion of my first visit to their attractive townhouse apartment in the heart of Mexico City, B. Traven appeared as if from nowhere and greeted me cordially. He was a man of shorter than average stature with strong features; a large, prominent nose and an air of profound seriousness. He seemed much younger than his 77 years. We exchanged a few words about the jacket proof of our new edition of The Treasure of the Sierra Madre which he liked. He spoke with a slight German accent and appeared to be slightly hard of hearing.

A few days later my wife and I were invited to luncheon at Traven's house. The other guests were William Johnson, the U.C.L.A. professor who had reviewed a number of Traven's books; his wife, a former bookseller from Texas; and an Israeli artist who had been sponsored and befriended by Traven. The luncheon was an elegant affair--drinks on the attractive walled patio and then a beautifully served meal of chicken mole, rice salad and a delicious rose wine. Traven was very much the gracious continental host. His wife Rosa Elena, a charming and beautiful woman in her mid-forties, stayed close beside him to repeat in his ear remarks he missed.

Later in the afternoon Traven and I discussed his forthcoming book, The Creation of the Sun and the Moon, with the artist Alberto Beltran. Traven revealed considerable discernment and understanding of the problems of illustrating this retelling of an Indian folk legend which we later published as a juvenile.

Although the first time I met Traven he introduced himself as "Croves," this pose was soon dropped and he became Traven to me and my wife and the other guests at the luncheon. And he was obviously not a "stand-in" when he worked with me and the artist Beltran on Creation. Even though to the end of his life he was Croves to most visiting foreigners, to the many Mexican friends of Rosa Elena and Traven, he was known as B.T. or "The Skipper." These friends included Diego Rivera, David Alfaro Siqueiros, and top-level Mexican politicians, writers, and professionals. But none of us knew him well enough to ask him why he attempted to maintain anonymity and shunned all publicity. So even though the basic facts of his life are now known, the mystery of his secretiveness remains to occupy those who feel they need to continue the search for the secret of B. Traven.

But I think the time has come to turn our attention to another Traven mystery: Why, in spite of millions of words that have been written about Traven, does the reading public for his books remain so small? Some of his key books are again out of print; only one--<u>Treasure</u>--has achieved major sales, and that is due in large part to the Humphrey Bogart film.

Is it possible that Traven's work as a creative writer has been overshadowed by the attempts to penetrate the veil of secrecy which surrounded him? Have critics been so concerned with searching out his identity that they have failed to properly convey the full impact of his work? Try to remember when you last saw an analytical, appreciative review of one of Traven's books. There are certain honorable exceptions--William Weber Johnson and Allan Cheuse, for example--but most reviewers spend more time discussing the man than his books. I often run into self-styled Traven "experts" who have not read even his key books, but they can talk learnedly about the latest rumor concerning his identity.

It was Traven's hope that he be judged by his work. He urged his readers not to be concerned with who he was or how he lived. He said, "My personal life would not be disappointing but it is my own affair, which I want to keep to myself." Now that the problem of Traven's identity has been solved, it is hoped that people will concentrate on his writings and open the way to a wider appreciation of his works.

WAS THERE ANOTHER MAN?
B. Traven as Author of His Own Works

Karl S. Guthke

When I first read Traven, in the original German editions, I was struck by the fact that there were as many Anglicisms in his German as there are freckles on that all-American face that smiles at us from our cereal boxes. In a way, this linguistic feature was quite as familiar as the cereal face, of course: Most German professors in American universities write that way. But, then, Traven--while many things to many people--was surely not one of them, of us. In any case, his freckled German was written in a Spanish linguistic environment, and even with my smattering of Spanish, I knew that words like "Zahldreck" (paydirt) couldn't possibly have come from the language of Cervantes.[1] So, how were the Anglicisms to be accounted for?

Afflicted with insomnia as I was, I got it into my head one night that surely these German novels must have been translated from the English, from someone's else's English naturally, but whose? Who done it in the first place? You see, during those bouts with insomnia, I was reading detective stories, and that night the would-be Sherlock Holmes in me, pleased as Punch, had gotten hold of an idea that kept asserting itself against the most potent sleeping aids, both pharmaceutical and literary. Needless to say, when I consulted Watson--that is, when I turned to Travenology--I discovered that my idea had been anticipated by others, several others in fact, including those who claimed that they themselves were the original Traven, the sought-after "other man," the real (English or American) author of those stories (or some of them), and that they claimed this status much like that professor of philology who was asked by the House un-American Activities Committee, "Who is the most original philologist?" and answered, "I am." (When his colleagues asked him afterwards if that hadn't been a trifle "thick," he said, "You must remember, I was speaking under oath.") These would-be "real" Travens, or some of them, then implied that Marut/Traven had merely translated their work into German, and somewhat shoddily and hastily at that. After all, didn't he leave those telltale Anglicisms like so many smoking pistols for the academic police and professorial paparazzi to puzzle over? This mystery man, I discovered, had in fact been haunting Traven studies ever since the 1940s--so I discovered, and got sleepy at last.

But then I began thinking, with that well-meaning arrogance that is attributed to professors of a certain university, that if my idea was so popular, then it had a fair chance of being wrong. Maybe the time-honored assumption of "another man" was based on the logic of nursery rhymes which (don't you know) can be so charming in their fanciful way, as in: "As I was going up the stair, I met a man who wasn't there...."

Or was he? How are we to imagine it all came to pass, anyway? Did Ret Marut, German Expressionist with first-rate literary credentials and Death Ship coal-drag with dubious identity papers, get off the boat in Tampico and just stroll into the jungle of Tamaulipas after siesta one day and chance to encounter there—in a rickety shack that was standing only because the termites were holding hands—a seedy, down-and-out Anglo, sitting on a stack of moldy manuscripts of stirring novels about life in the Sierra Madre...a sort of Dr. Wilshed who just happened not to have torn up his manuscripts yet and who entrusted them to that probably unshaven and certainly "Tsherman shpeakink" newcomer and then most obligingly disappeared into the bush during the "happy hour," never to be seen again (except in the wish-fulfilling nightmares of some of us)? And perhaps he had even assured the gringo that he would never claim authorship of all those bestsellers-to-be? Was that how it was? Or maybe he didn't willingly disappear into the underbrush at sunset, but was instead shoved there, with a Krupp steel bullet in his head or a Bavarian horn-handle hunting knife in his heart? That scenario, slightly spicier as tropical fairy tales go, would explain beautifully why Ret Marut would spend the rest of his life hiding his real identity so successfully.

There is something for the armchair detective, surely, in all this: cherchez l'homme for a change instead of cherchez la femme (since Esperanza López Matéos is out of the running by now, as is the unforgettable Slovak shepherd with the stubby fingers, not to mention the leprous nun, from Honduras, was it?).

But why bring this up now since I said the "other man" was a time-honored assumption and possibly a time-honored canard at that? I bring it up not because I think that any season is wild goose hunting season (or wild canard hunting season); I bring it up because it is timely—timely because of Mr. Wyatt, or rather because of some of his reviewers who are among the more enterprising of stay-at-home adventurers. For they have indeed revived the "other man" hypothesis. These reviewers, to be sure (and to be fair), much like Mr. Wyatt himself, do not confess to knowledge of German, or, by implication, to expertise in the pertinent stylistic matter of the Anglicisms in Traven's German on which the "other man" hypothesis primarily hinges. Instead, they latch on to Mr. Wyatt's important and undeniably correct discovery that Ret Marut arrived in Mexico in the summer of 1924: that is to say, more than a year, perhaps a year and a half, later than he was generally believed, up to 1978, to have set foot on Mexican soil; in other words, just barely one year before his first Mexican novel, The Cotton Pickers, began to be serialized in the Socialist newspaper Vorwärts.

Why was this discovery of Mr. Wyatt's so significant? Well, it was like a strong breeze in the sails of that other argument that--apart from the Anglicisms--had given rise to the notion of the "other man," especially in the mind of one of the most distinguished of Traven scholars, whose writings, by the way, do not by any means stand or fall with the "other man" hypothesis. This argument goes like this: Traven's early Mexican novels (which allegedly show an intimate familiarity with the country)--the novels, that is, from The Cotton Pickers of 1925 up to The White Rose of 1929, as well as most of the stories of Der Busch of 1928--all appeared so shortly after Marut's arrival in Mexico that Marut couldn't possibly be the author or the only author. Why not? Because it would have taken years, it is believed, to have all those experiences that are described in the books, and it would have taken more years afterwards to write about them so knowledgeably. Consequently, Marut must have gotten hold of someone else's--an old-timer's--English manuscripts, which he then translated into German. Hence the Anglicisms (to come back to the first argument). For he must have translated without the benefit of either a dictionary or patient attention to stylistic detail or both, fighting off mosquitoes all the while. Now, when this argument was first made, and when it was last repeated before 1978, the time span (between going ashore in Tamaulipas and serialization of The Cotton Pickers in Berlin) was believed to be about two years. Thanks to Mr. Wyatt, the time span is now barely one year. You see what this implies: It is now even more likely than before that Marut was not the original author of Treasure and all the other early works; it is all the more likely that he translated hastily, letting the "other man's" English slip into his German in the form of Anglicisms, which are undeniably there. This is what several of Mr. Wyatt's reviewers have thought, thus reviving the old "other man" hypothesis.

Well, what about this argument? The underlying view of literary genesis--that you first experience, for a certain period of time, and then write, for a certain period of time (and can write only of historical occurrences that you have

witnessed yourself)--is not universally shared. Marut was a
skilled journalist who was used to speedy writing, who was
used to living from hand to mouth as it were, or from experience to typewriter. (We know, for instance, that when he
took part in the Palacios expedition in 1926, he spent hours
every evening jotting down the day's events and thoughts,
which later became Land des Frühlings.) So, one year from
arrival in Mexico to the serialization of the first--and
very short--Mexican novel seems plenty of time, really,
especially if we remember that what Marut writes about in
The Cotton Pickers is more or less his own experiences set
down in chronological order, as we know from his diaries of
that time. No need, therefore, for someone else's original
English manuscripts.

But if we are reluctant to believe in the "other man" on
the basis of the time factor (which was given new importance
by Mr. Wyatt's reviewers), how do we account for the other
argument for the "other man": the Anglicisms? That is the
real crux of the matter.

I'll start out with a fact that is curiouser than Alice
could have foreseen. The proponents, old and new, of the
"other man" hypothesis did not see it either. For they have
always focused on the Totenschiff and the early novels about
Mexico, not on the later novels about Mexico (the Mahogany
series of the 1930s). In other words, for the Mahogany
series no "other man" has ever been postulated as the real
or original author who wrote them in English. And yet I
find that (as BT would have said) "fact is," they, too, are
teeming with Anglicisms, just as much as in the early Mexico
novels.

How do the aficionados of the "other man" hypothesis
explain this curious fact? They could say that Traven was
American-born, that English was his native tongue, and that
when writing German he got the languages mixed up a bit,
hence the Anglicisms in the later novels. But if they argue
that way (and they have), they saw off the branch on which
they are sitting, for then you don't need an "other man"
hypothesis at all. That is, if the Anglicisms got into the
later novels by way of Traven's native language, then why
shouldn't they have gotten into the early Mexico novels the
same way, without "another man"? The Anglicisms, in both
instances, would simply be his own--no need to trace them to
someone else's English originals. But, of course, Traven's
American birth and English mother-tongue have become most
unlikely recently, especially in the light of Mr. Wyatt's
investigations. Whether Traven was Otto Feige or not, he
must have grown up in Germany, speaking German as his native
language. The very fact that Traven himself, speaking En-

glish with a German accent, claimed that English was his native language seems to prove that it was not; in this case, there is simply no truth in the wisdom of Gilbert and Sullivan that "It's greatly to his credit for he himself has said it." Traven's written English, as we all know, is full of Germanisms of all sorts. On the other hand, the German he wrote before he came to Mexico is absolutely innocent of Anglicisms of any kind, even though his Ziegelbrenner articles were often written in haste. So much for one line of defense that the "other man" or Erlebnisträger theorists might choose.

"Other man" enthusiasts also might argue that Anglicisms were sprinkled in on purpose in the later novels to give the texts some American flavor. This might be true of the occasional "Well" or "Good-bye" that crops up in the speech of some of the Americans in the novels. But beyond that, this argument becomes patently absurd, for many of the Anglicisms are to be found in the speech of Indios and Creoles, as well as in the prose of the narrator, and they are often very inconspicuous and, if you will, "unconscious," like "wo werden Sie verlangt" for "where are you wanted," "für lange Zeit," and so forth. That sort of Anglicism is surely anything but deliberate. On the contrary, it is the occasional avoidance of Anglicisms that is deliberate: for in Traven's revisions of his novels, there are instances of his cancellation of Anglicisms ("ich strollte" becomes "ich strolchte," for example), and these revisions indicate that Anglicisms were not originally put in deliberately, but that they slipped in, with the author correcting his error later. This entire defense is just as self-defeating as the other one, however. For if the Anglicisms in the later novels are deliberate, why aren't the Anglicisms in the early Mexico novels deliberate as well? Which is to say, why bother to postulate English originals written by that fabled "other man"?

To sum up this sorry state of affairs: The Anglicisms which have been taken as the prime evidence of the presence of "another man" as the "real" author crop up also in those novels that have not (as yet) been attributed to such an original English or American author. It stands to reason that the Anglicisms got into all the novels in the same way. The two supposed ways I've discussed--one, Marut as a native speaker of English; two, intentional Anglicizing--are impossible. At this point, however, the "other man" theorists might have a brainstorm: Since there are Anglicisms in all the novels, perhaps the later novels are translations from someone else's English originals as well, just like the early Mexico novels. But isn't that much like saying that if you cannot prove to most people's satisfaction that this or that Shakespeare play or scene was really written by Bacon or Marlowe, then you simplify matters considerably by assuming that all of Shakespeare's plays were written by Bacon or Marlowe? Not a shred of evidence, of course, in the case of Traven.

Or is there? Well, yes, of course there is--nothing less than a confession in fact. For who is the real originator of the "other man" hypothesis? It is--you guessed it--Traven himself. That, needless to say, is the former Ret Marut engaged in mythmaking, and I can imagine the good time he had doing it, raising mystification to the level of a fine art. The time was 1948: Traven--Torsvan at the time--was interviewed by Luis Spota in Cashew Park in Acapulco. In that interview he said that the supposed author of all those best-sellers was in fact using reports and information from someone else; needless to add, he said this in order to fob off a bothersome journalist at the very moment when he came close to his secret. The "other man" therefore enters into the picture as a patent fabrication of the author himself, as a ruse to throw someone off the track who must have been a particularly irritating specimen of that species of critic that Lord Tennyson called the lice in the locks of literature.

But still, as long as people, not knowing all this, read Traven in German and are struck by the Anglicisms of his texts, they will continue to jump to the conclusion that there must have been another man. So maybe Traven/Torsvan/Croves said the truth after all, in the perverse manner of what psychoanalysts call the Minsk-Pinsk phenomenon: Conversation on a railroad platform: "Where are you going?" "To Minsk." "Oh, I know you are a liar. You tell me you are bound for Minsk so that I will think you are really going to Pinsk, while in fact you _are_ going to Minsk!" (There, in fact, was "another man," Traven said so himself, hence the Anglicisms....)

There is only one way out of it: It has to be shown that the Anglicisms, which are widely thought to be evidence of the presence of "another man," got into all the Traven novels (from The Death Ship to the Mahogany series) in a way (one and the same way) that makes the assumption of another man unnecessary or credible only in the sense of Oscar Wilde's "I can believe anything, provided it is quite incredible."

The solution is this, and I state it as a fact, with a suitably (if only temporarily) bad conscience about this methodological caprice, rushing in where professors fear to tread: When Ret Marut escaped from Germany to England, he decided that, as a high traitor on the most-wanted list, with a death sentence hanging over his head, he did not have much of a future as a writer if he continued to write in German; so he immersed himself in English. He tried his hand at writing fiction in English--in England first and in Mexico later, during the early months of his stay in that country. (He even tried his luck with Popular Mechanics.) He failed to find a publisher in England or in the United States (in spite of all those books on how to place English manuscripts that I found among his papers). Thereupon, he returned to German as his writing language (while English remained, throughout his life in Mexico, his spoken language, with Spanish obviously entering into the picture as well). Therefore the Anglicisms that are ubiquitous in Traven's novels would be Marut/Traven's own Anglicisms, innocently enough. No need, then, for "another man" (who, by the way, his aficionados admit has never been "documented"--they actually used this particular term before the Immigration Service did).

This is a hypothesis, of course, but should it seem fanciful or absurd simply because Traven himself mentioned here and there during his early years in Mexico that he had written some of his novels and stories in English first? Or is this scenario the historically correct one, nonetheless? I think so, and "I've got a little list" of points that can be made to support this view.

My first five points have to do with Marut/Traven's English--with the fact that it is the English· of a non-native speaker and that it reveals that his native tongue was German. This is not the stirring stuff that insomnia is made of, and so I shall be brief.

(1) By the time Marut edited Ziegelbrenner, he knew English, but not very well. Anybody who translates (as Marut did in his German rendering of Shelley) "murder" as "Mörder" and "starve" as "sterben" (while at the same time giving evidence of his perfect command of idiomatic German) must be translating from a language that he is not thoroughly at home in, from a language that he learned either in a Wilhelminian high school or in the school of seafaring life (as some instances of globetrotterly namedropping in Ziegelbrenner might suggest). But no matter where Marut may have acquired the first smattering of the language of Shakespeare and Sir Arthur Conan Doyle, it was during that period spent in England in 1923/24, which Mr. Wyatt has discovered in the biography of Marut, that his command of English must have grown into full bloom like roses in the British rain. What could be more natural, then, than that his written German should deteriorate somewhat, from 1924 on, if only in the

sense that Anglicisms creep into it, which definitely had not been the case when Marut wrote Ziegelbrenner and the early stories. In any case (unlike Thomas Mann, who had nothing much to say that Nietzsche had not said before), Marut/Traven was always too preoccupied with what he had to say to bother all that much about how he said it. He had never been a fussy stylist, and the mosquito-infested cottage in the jungle of Tamaulipas was not quite as conducive to stylistic polishing as the soigné bourgeois ambience of Thomas Mann's villa in Munich's Poschingerstrasse. Hence the Anglicisms--like mosquitoes, you never catch them all.

(2) In Mexico, from 1924 on, the influence of English on Traven's spoken and written language by no means came to an end. On the contrary, as far as we know Traven moved primarily in English-speaking circles--English and American oil companies and, possibly, American Wobblies--during those early years in the country of his choice. He moved in the milieu, in other words, that his early Mexican novels present, with Gerard Gales as the American narrator and Americans as protagonists. And, as in England, there was every motivation in Mexico to avoid the German language like the plague, or the measles, rather. "The Bavarian of Munich is dead," Traven noted in his unpublished diary of 1924, meaning that Marut was dead, at least linguistically--that Marut who was being sought as a traitor by the gun-toting tonton macoute Bavarian-style who had brutalized political conditions for years, so much so that as early as 1918, Marut daydreamed in print about submerging himself in a remote tribe of non-Teutonic blood. Also, of course, having claimed American birth when he entered Mexico, "in spite of all temptations to belong to other nations," Traven had every incentive to deny any connection with anything German, as a simple matter of self-preservation. So, German was dead for him, except, of course, in the Traven novels. Small wonder, under the circumstances, that elements of his English, his spoken language, show up in the German of these novels, in the form of those telltale Anglicisms.

(3) For this reconstructed biographical and linguistic scenario we have the most personal and private of evidence: Traven's unpublished Mexican diaries of the 1920s. They are written in English--not in yours or mine (well, mine, maybe) but in a strongly Germanized English--and sprinkled with German words for which he didn't know the English equivalents.

(4) Among Traven's papers in the Calle Mississippi there are typescripts of essays written in English and dated 1925/26, into which he has corrected conspicuous Germanisms in longhand--proof positive, by the way, that after leaving

Germany Ret Marut tried to establish himself as a writer in English, as I suggested. (One of these essays, incidentally, makes much of the Volstead Act--the Prohibition Act--which is mentioned rather prominently in The Death Ship of the same year, somewhat to the puzzlement of German readers, I daresay, to whom this makes no sense, whether they drink of not.)

(5) The Germanized English, the English of the non-native speaker of English which we found in the diaries and the essays, also crops up in the novels, i.e., in those rare instances when entire English sentences are included in Traven's German novels. In The White Rose, for example, a newspaper headline is quoted as saying, "President of big corporation seen with dancer of the Vanity Theatre only with stockings on", never mind which of the two is wearing the stockings--linguistically this is a Germanism: "nur mit Strümpfen bekleidet." Or think of the surprising motto on the desk of another linguistically unfortunate American in the same novel; it says, "Smile, work and give the poor"--impeccably Teutonic.

To sum up these five points: After he left Germany, Marut/Traven lived, as a writer, in an English-German linguistic symbiosis, and this symbiosis shows up as Germanisms in his English. The following two points will prove what was suggested in some of the five earlier points: that the same linguistic symbiosis results in Anglicisms in Traven's German--which would then be his own Anglicisms. There is no need to claim someone else's original English manuscripts to account for them.

(6) Traven stated more than once that some of his works published during his early years in Mexico had first been composed in English and then translated into German after he failed to find an English or American publisher. Like everything else that Traven said about himself, this statement was received by most critics with polite disbelief. But as I said, there are good psychological, practical, and political reasons for such a switch from German to English after Marut escaped to England. And there is concrete evidence for this switch: The manuscript drafts (fragments) of The Death Ship are preserved in Calle Mississippi 61, and these drafts are in English, they are in Marut's handwriting, and they are, as I have determined, the antecedents not of the 1934 American edition but of the German text published in 1926; they are Traven's own English original Death Ship which, he wrote to the Büchergilde in 1929, he had translated into German in 1925, right after The Cotton Pickers. (And it was this German text that was in turn retranslated into English for Alfred Knopf in the early

1930s--without recourse to the original English manuscripts of the 1920s, as far as I can tell.) The English of these earliest manuscripts of the Ur-Death Ship (written, according to Señora Luján, in Brixton Prison, which Marut rather liked because the supply of paper and pencils was unlimited), is not bad, but it is clearly the English of a German and is full of Germanisms like "dead sick," "the Spaniard are so nice people," "water was not to have," "are you sailor?" and "to pell off the paints." On the other hand, the German text of 1926, based on this English version, is full of Anglicisms, revealing the other side of Traven's linguistic symbiosis. And while the translation into German is, for the most part, a free rendering into idiomatic German, there are a good many passages which contain Anglicisms that can be traced neatly to the English text which Traven translated in great haste ("auf einen Ruck" as he said in that letter of 1929), e.g., "der ganze Rahmen des Schiffs," which is meaningless in German (and not only to German landlubbers) but easily explained by a glance into the original, which says "the frame of the ship"; or take "anzeichnen" instead of "anmustern"--I suspected this would have to be "sign on" in the original, and there it was; or, finally, "rotblütiger amerikanischer Junge." (No comment.) What happened was that Marut/Traven fell victim to the linguistic symbiosis that most of us are familiar with, although it is a lot easier to spot other people's Anglicisms than one's own Anglicisms (or sins; and I am no specialist in either). The Anglicisms, then, are traceable to Marut's own English, not someone else's: not only in The Death Ship, but, by implication also in the other texts originally written in English and then translated into German. Furthermore, Anglicisms also appear in those sections of the German Death Ship which were not translated from the original English but were composed in German in 1925 as additions or interpolations, without an English counterpart. Here the Anglicisms stem from Marut/Traven's linguistic symbiosis as well, quite clearly; and the same is true, we may infer, of the Anglicisms in those novels which were written in German in the first place. In all cases, the Anglicisms in Traven's German are his own, as are the Germanisms in his English. No need for "another man": The portrait of the other man is (as Hazlitt said about the paintings of Turner) a "portrait of nothing--and very like."

(7) Such Anglicisms do not appear only in those novels which have been suspected of being translations from someone else's English originals, but also in Traven's German letters from the mid-1920s on (which, I think, have never yet been thought to have been translated from "another man's"

original English). The implication is clear. These Anglicisms appear, moreover, in Traven's occasional little essays published in the publisher's journal Büchergilde and in the Typographische Mitteilungen in the twenties and thirties, in the BT-Mitteilungen, and in all the late novels and stories right up to the "Wahrhaft blutige Geschichte" written in 1951--for all of which no Erlebnisträger has even been claimed. Also, when Traven revised Macario for the 1961 edition, the new wordings occasionally included Anglicisms-- and I have seen these in Traven's own handwriting, interpolated in the margins of the first version. And finally, to clinch my argument if that should really be necessary, there is Land des Frühlings of 1928, Traven's uniquely personal travelogue (with his genuinely original reflections --some familiar from Ziegelbrenner days, some rather "far-out," some only recently taken very seriously, such as Traven's notion that America is not a continent of Indian immigrants from Asia, but instead the cradle of the world's population, an idea recently revived by Geoffrey Goodman and others who make this claim for Southern California, if not Chiapas). The supposition that Land is not an original Traven work in every sense of the word is patently absurd for biographical reasons we all know, regardless of whether it was, as Traven claimed, originally composed in English. And, of course, the German of Land is studded with the Anglicisms that are familiar from the other Traven works. If they got into Land without the benefit of "another man" as they clearly did, and if they got into the letters and essays and revisions of Macario without the benefit of "another man" as they clearly did, then they must have gotten into all the novels in the same way. The Anglicisms are as much Traven's own as his German accent. No need for an "other man," although, of course, the author of the novels may have relied to some extent on stories told or reports made to him by others (to such influences and suggestions only a Trappist monk would be immune, or maybe Robinson Crusoe, and even he had Friday, eventually).

The conclusion is manifest to the point of embarrassment (by now I feel like I'm selling refrigerators to Eskimos): There is no need for "another man," dead or alive, most wanted though he is in some quarters.

But suppose for a moment that he had existed; suppose for a moment that the edifice of the "other man" hypothesis (that castle in the air constructed in the style of cloud-cuckoo baroque) were real. Don't you think that in that case (i.e., if there really had been something rotten in the state of Tamaulipas, if Marut/Traven really had plagiarized an English or American author) Marut/Traven would have had

22

enough sense to cover his tracks? And that would have been the easiest thing in the world. He could have easily weeded out the most obvious Anglicisms. But he didn't. He left the smoking pistol right on the bloody body for even Watson to see. Why? Because there was nothing to hide, and because perfectionism, as I said, wasn't Traven's cup of tequila. In The White Rose, for example, he writes "am Telephon" (correct) and "bei Telephon" (a glaring Anglicism) right on the same page, not to mention other instances of stylistic sloppiness, whether they involve Anglicisms or not. Traven felt he had more important things to do, and to say, and he said them—and we understand them, even through the network of his Anglicisms. That's what mattered to him—and, I think, to us. So, the Anglicisms remained in their glorious innocence. As a matter of fact, they—or some of them—became a kind of stylistic signature unique to Traven; that is, certain Anglicisms occur again and again in all types of his writing as a kind of literary signet: "vertwisten," "flimsig," "bulkig," "wissen" instead of "kennen," "lernen" instead of "erfahren," "auf der sicheren Seite," and others. All of them are more or less unintelligible in German and fully understandable only with a knowledge of English, although one German investigator (who shall remain unnamed) claimed to have located one or the other of these in a certain German dialect dictionary which, it seems, has done a complete vanishing act since.

I conclude with apologies and thanks to those scholars who have made us think harder about "The Mystery of B. Traven" by theorizing about "another man" and thus making him a "talking point." For no matter how successfully or unsuccessfully I may have de-mystified the "other man theory" (which I tend to think of as a chain composed of so many missing links, or a fata morgana in search of support in a desert), the mystery of Traven, or rather the mystery of Ret Marut, remains. Who was he really? Otto Feige? Someone who knew Otto Feige? A Hohenzollern? An American theology student expelled from Freiburg University for indecent behavior in 1903? In an unpublished letter of 1935, Traven says he wished he could answer the question "Who the hell are you," but "Fact is I myself don't know it." And whoever he really was, why did he plunge into the anonymity of the mask? Why this adventure of total abandonment of identity that is so appealing to Romantics and Rationalists alike? The mystery remains, as fascinating as ever. It's a bit like Rimbaud in Abyssinia, or T.E. Lawrence in the Royal Air Force. But perhaps some readers will agree with me in thinking that the hypothetical "other man" (who has added considerably to the mystery) has a good chance of being a ghost, and in thinking that I may have exorcised the ghost, even though he appeared, alive and well, as ghosts go, as late as 1981 in the Dictionary of Literary Biography (as ghosts will, you know: when Madame du Deffand was asked whether she believed in ghosts she said, "No, but I am afraid of them").

On the other hand, if you think it is too early in the day, too early in the history of Travenology, to talk about ghosts, you might think that my attempt to exorcise the ghost, my exercise in Rationalism, reminds you (or that even I myself remind you) of Jeremy Bentham, the very exponent of this kind of Rationalism. The body of Jeremy Bentham, professionally embalmed and professorially dressed, for many years after his death was wheeled into faculty meetings of the University of London, with the beadle solemnly intoning, "Mr. Bentham, present, but not voting."

Note

1. Full documentation is provided in the much longer German version of this essay in my book Erkundungen. Essays zur Literatur von Milton bis Traven (Frankfurt am Main, Bern, New York: Peter Lang, 1983), also published in book form as "Das Geheimnis von B. Traven endeckt"--und rätsel-voller denn je (Frankfurt am Main, Wien, Olten: Büchergilde Gutenberg, 1984).

SOME PROBLEMS WITH THE WHITE ROSE

Michael L. Baumann

I

Before B. Traven scholars and critics can even begin to do their work, they must decide which of the innumerable editions of Traven's works, in German or English, they will focus on and explain why. So far, they have done nothing of the kind; the question of which Traven edition may be the most authentic has never occurred to many of them. Yet in the case of no other writer I can think of is the answer to such a question more important. The texts of the German Traven editions vary a good deal; the texts of the British and American editions vary widely. How, under these circumstances, can we determine what Traven's intention may have been with any particular story or novel? With other writers we often find solutions to textual problems in their lives; with Traven we don't have that recourse. Earlier Traven critics depended on misinformation or erroneous assumptions about his life and thus were led into blind alleys. And we still run headlong into a nightmare the moment we try to unravel apparent textual clues to Traven's life or attempt to make sense of the clues he strewed so abundantly into his letters and essays and, late in life in Mexico, baffled reporters with, while proclaiming his right to absolute personal privacy. Every such clue, we now know, hides more than it reveals. If Traven wanted it that way, scholars and critics cannot. In 1928 Traven called literary scholars "that class of men for whom a special hell ought to be created."[1] He certainly created it for Traven scholars; our job is to try to find a way out. And our first step has got to be the attempt to come to some agreement on which Traven edition, in German or English, contains the most essential "B. Traven." Our second step must be to justify our choice.

Of the Traven novels and stories not told in the first person by an American protagonist, The White Rose well illustrates the difficulties we encounter with respect to the author's intention, when we compare editions. In this paper I shall compare the 1929 Büchergilde Gutenberg and the 1965 Robert Hale editions, because both versions were ostensibly written by the same man, the first in German, the second in English. Or so we have always been led to believe; no one so far has doubted that Marut-Torsvan wrote the German and Torsvan-Croves the English version, or that the two men were one and the same. I shall not question that identity either. I shall assume that whatever differences exist between the two versions are accounted for by shifting interests that the thirty-six-year span between dates of publication brought about, as well as by persistent language problems that those years were unable to erase. Actually, as we shall see, we don't know when either version was first composed. A few passages in the 1965 Robert Hale edition may be linked to probable dates of composition—of those passages; the internal evidence of when, historically speaking, this "realistic" novel might have taken place remains sketchy and contradictory in both versions and appears, in fact, to have been deliberately obscured in order to mislead readers. And that makes it impossible for us to tell exactly when the book was written.

Although one part of me respects Traven's overall intention of confuting the bourgeois critical-scholarly establishment with his work and life, as Wolfgang Essbach recognized several years ago,[2] because I sympathize with Traven's philosophical anarchism, it is the other part of me, the bourgeois critic and scholar, that will here be doing the bloodhound's dirty work, quite against Essbach's unstated but certainly implied injunction.

II

The White Rose deals with the conflict between an American oil company, with headquarters in San Francisco, and a Mexican hacienda in the state of Veracruz. The hacienda is one of the few Mexican haciendas actually owned by an Indian, though the Indian, whose name is Jacinto Yañez, does not feel he owns it; he feels that he manages it for the good of all other Indians living on it and that his is a sacred trust which he must pass on to future generations. The American oil company wants the hacienda, called the White Rose, because it already owns all the land surrounding it, and all that land is producing oil. Yañez, however, refuses to lease or sell the White Rose, not even for hundreds and thousands of pesos—or dollars. No amount of silver or gold piled up on a table in front of him can tempt him, for money means nothing to him or his people. Money will be gone tomorrow, he reflects, whereas the land will be there always and will always nourish him and his family and all the other families living on it. But a minion of the American oil company finally lures him to California and has him murdered there. Yañez's signature is then forged on a bill of sale, and the White Rose becomes the property of the American oil company—to begin producing oil almost immediately. In the 1929 Büchergilde edition of the novel, nearly all the men who used to live on the hacienda end up working for the American oil company, including Yañez's own son; they earn good money and come to know and accept a new way of life, and, what is more important, they find a new brotherhood that is worldwide rather than hacienda-wide.

This extremely significant theme conflicts with another theme that dominates the novel. It is the notion that the ancient, agricultural way of life and the hacienda-wide brotherhood represented by the White Rose are superior to life elsewhere, particularly in the city, and to the alienation from the land and from other human beings that industry and technology have brought about in the Western world. In the 1929 edition, the greater brotherhood theme which results from the take-over of the White Rose by the American oil company is inserted towards the end of the book and occupies not quite three pages (189-92). Those three pages begin by mentioning a teller of the story: "Der Erzähler dieser Geschichte hat nicht die Absicht, falsche Sentimentalitäten zu erzeugen..." ("The teller of this story does not intend to create false sentimentalities...") The impression this makes on the reader is that a second writer is suddenly intruding into the novel that has been told by a first writer who had something very different to say. Yet it is possible to reconcile the two themes. The style of those three pages is not different from the style of the reflective passages of the rest of the book. The book itself makes a powerful statement about the white man's greed and about how far he will go to satisfy it. It also explains what makes the president of an American oil company tick, as well as what binds a happy Mexican Indian to the land that has nourished him and his family for hundreds and perhaps thousands of years. One feels that even if some of the characters are representative rather than individualized, the novel works the way Traven presumably wanted his novels to work: It makes us think about social, cultural, and cross-cultural problems, and it arouses our indignation.

If the intruding teller of the story takes a stand against false sentimentality towards the end of the novel, he reminds us that there is what we might call permissible sentimentality in the novel. One aspect of it is the fact that we get to love the only thoroughly good person in the book, aside from Yañez, and to hate the only thoroughly bad person. The thoroughly good person is the governor of Veracruz, who, because his own Indian blood and heritage allow him to understand Yañez and his way of life on the White Rose, does what little he can to fight for his cause. The thoroughly bad person is a double-faced mestizo who introduces the minion of the American oil company to Yañez and figures out a way of getting him to leave the White Rose voluntarily and travel to California. Evil characters in Traven are few in number; they are evil because they are malicious and enjoy harassing and torturing other human beings. Most of mankind--and this includes American oil magnates and weak-brained minions of American oil companies, even when they go so far in their cupidity as to murder--is the product of its society and of its time, and most of mankind isn't either very good or very bad, although, by and large, Mexican Indians are both more human and more humane than white men. Mr. Collins, the American oil magnate, is a wheel in the machinery, as Traven repeatedly points out, an almost unconscious particle playing its foreordained role in a social system that Traven of course condemns; but Collins is not innately evil.

In the 1929 edition, Marut-Torsvan clearly meant to contrast two societies: the white man's industrial-technological, disspirited, and perpetually dissatisfied one, and the Mexican Indian's agricultural, spirited, and contented one. The impending clash, the reader intuits, will most assuredly lead to the destruction of the agricultural idyll in Veracruz, yet the ideological world-brotherhood theme threaded into the novel towards the end may save The White Rose from becoming, at least in its description of Yañez's utopia, an all too familiar repetition of the nineteenth-century Romantic's dream. But just as happy, even if illiterate, Mexican Indians will not become greedy American oil tycoons overnight, so American oil tycoons cannot be expected to understand the Indians' concept of "Heimat," which is to say "home," or to sympathize with such a concept and not to smash a man's home when they need to in order to extract its underground wealth.

Whether an awareness of a worldwide brotherhood of man on the part of the Indians of the White Rose outweighs the destruction of its age-old culture as well as of its physical features and appearance--or its transformation from a verdant, food-producing hacienda into a series of stinking, noisy, and ugly oil fields--is difficult to say. Traven is a realist as well as a romantic, and he no doubt meant to show how meaningless "home"--when compared to a Mexican Indian's rootedness--is to Americans generally and how little Americans are able to understand another culture or give a damn about anything except their own immediate material interests.

If the 1929 Büchergilde Gutenberg edition of The White Rose is an effective novel, and if Marut-Torsvan deals in it with what we today call Third World problems in a way most liberal-minded people would deal with those problems, or think about them, today, then the 1965 Robert Hale edition is strangely ineffective and weak. It appears to be written down to the reader; it tries to be a conventional novel and furnish conventional motives for the actions of its characters; it even changes the background of important people in exaggerated ways whose purpose is unclear. Take Betty Cuttens, Mr. Collins's mistress, for instance, who, in this British version, is called Basileen Longville. Torsvan-Croves writes about her:

> For a few weeks she mixed with the Greenwich Village crowd, hoping to meet some creative giants; but she met only gnomes, male, female, or not quite either, who thought themselves so important and so interesting that they put on a perpetual three-ring circus, performing but mostly talking day and night, about the phenomena of themselves in this age. Few of them made any real effort at anything, and too many of them lived off crumbs or bequests from relatives, especially off Mama. Some of them pimped, oh, just a little bit, some peddled junk, and quite a few milked old society cows in a mockery of love or on the claim of future accomplishments.
>   Basileen soon wearied of these supermen who claimed to be the core of our culture, these makers and unmakers of civilization, who succeeded only in nauseating her. (64)

This passage, _not_ found in the 1929 German version, with its heavy-handed irony, hectors the reader in a curious, un-Travenish way. It continues:

> But she did find her own America in two New York places, [sic] one was at the Yankee Stadium baseball game, with its customary side attractions; and the other was Coney Island on Sunday.
>   Later she said, "Yes, there are enough Americans living like themselves in New York, so that one can say that that City is still part of the U.S.A."

It is most unusual for Traven to be condemning petty bourgeois bohemianism or, indeed, to be bothering with it at all, whether real or phony; for him to be expressing American patriotic sentiments in which baseball, Yankee Stadium, or "Coney Island on Sunday" are extolled is practically unthinkable. Nor would the girl we meet in the 1929 version of _The White Rose_ express such sentiments, if only because we are meant to sympathize with her unconventional approach to life, which makes her fall in love with a very uncommon

American and--to our delight--take him for a ride.

The 1965 edition omits the three-page passage containing the novel's countertheme about a worldwide brotherhood of man that the Indians learn about after they become oil workers on what used to be their own agricultural land. In the context of an almost simplistic story, told without many of the ironies of the 1929 edition or with attempts at irony as clumsy as those in the passage cited above, it appears as if the omission of the countertheme were the result of the writer's wish not to make the reader think!

On the other hand, the 1965 edition contains one episode not included in that of 1929. Thematically speaking, this episode may be regarded as completing a statement the novel makes about capitalism. It begins at the time Collins manipulates the stock market in order to make the million and a half dollars he needs to pay for a party Basileen has just thrown in her new house--which must also still be paid for. It ends with an interview Collins is granted by the aging Rockefeller. Rockefeller is not named; he is merely described and called one of the two kings in America: the men who really run the country. (The banker Morgan, who is referred to elsewhere in this edition, is no doubt meant to be the second king.) Rockefeller, who has come out West to speak to Collins, proceeds to give him hell for his recent maneuver on Wall Street. He succeeds in scaring Collins, at least temporarily, for Collins recognizes with a start that there are men in the world more powerful than he. (Even the wheels of the system experience moments of consciousness!) It is an episode that had already been included in a number of German editions of the novel during the 1950s, and it is, of course, contained in the 1962 rororo paperback edition of The White Rose and has been retained in all subsequent rororo reissues.

John D. Rockefeller (1839-1937) and John Pierpont Morgan (1837-1913) give The White Rose a historical focus. Yet as soon as we try to locate the action in history, we realize that we are being led about by the nose. The events of the novel could have taken place almost any time between the turn of the century and a decade and a half after the beginning of the Mexican Revolution. Under Porfirio Díaz, foreign oil companies were invited to come to Mexico, appropriate land, and turn it into oil fields; but even after 1910, it is conceivable that a Jacinto Yañez would lose his hacienda to American oil interests under similar circumstances--first, through attempts to buy him out, then, through betrayal, and, finally, through his being murdered. For it was not until 1938 that foreign oil companies were expropriated.

30

In the 1929 German version of the novel, the few references to a precise time, such as hints about Collins's age, would appear to point to the year 1923. But why the story should take place in that year is not at all clear, unless Marut-Torsvan wanted to call attention to the Bucareli Agreements of 1923, which defined subsoil rights in Mexico but did not regulate the behavior of American oil companies vis-à-vis powerless hacienda owners like Jacinto Yañez.

The 1965 British version of the novel compounds the difficulties we have in identifying the time of the action. The chronology of Collins's life is no longer clear, and the historical references to events in Mexico and the United States make it impossible to pinpoint the year. It would be tedious for me to list all the deliberate historical inconsistencies by means of which Torsvan-Croves moves us back and forth in time, from the first to the third and back to the second decade of the twentieth century. Instead, I shall cite one odd example of the game being played here. Torsvan-Croves writes, at one point:

This was a period of world confusion and change. One of the great powers had been snatched up by a gang of long-haired radicals spouting a bunch of half-baked ideas, converting royal capitalism into a vast land of experimentation on ancient communal lands, ideas which any businessman knew were basically wrong, disproven, unprofitable to certain individuals and relying on prophesies which hadn't yet been realized on earth, except in some limited ways, perhaps by the Incas. (79)

Once again we must put a heavy-handed irony aside in order to study this ambiguous allusion. The phrases "one of the great powers" and "royal capitalism" are probably meant to refer us to the Russian Revolution, whereas "ancient communal lands" would refer us to the Mexican Revolution. How confusing the comment is in the context in which it is made becomes clear when we realize that the "period" commented upon is that of Collins's first brilliant coup in the financial world, his engineering of the anthracite coal miners' strike. Yet how can either revolution, that of 1917 or that of 1910-20, add to our understanding of something that happened in the United States in 1902?

After the difficulties we experience in attempting to pinpoint the time of the action of the 1965 version of the novel, it almost comes as a relief to be able to establish when certain passages must have been added to it. One such passage is found in the scene in which Collins asks the members of the board of the anthracite coal company--in whose interests he is in the processs of fomenting the above-mentioned strike, which will make the company rich by ruining competing companies (because it has hoarded coal that it will later sell at inflated prices)--to keep calm while he continues to manipulate the newspapers, the market, and the workers; Collins says: "'Don't get jittery, no sir, and don't call off your bets. If our horse doesn't win and win big, I'll shoot, hang, poison, drown myself, or jump from the top mark'" (79). Jump from the top mark? Surely, this is an error made in copying from a manuscript that had said "off the top of the Mark," that is, off the Mark Hopkins Hotel in San Francisco. In the 1929 German version Collins also threatens to kill himself in the event that his maneuver fails, though he does not specify how he will do it; he merely offers to execute himself once the members of the board have condemned him to death, which he has given them his permission to do (83). Since the Mark Hopkins Hotel was not built until 1926 and the top floor was not converted into the bar-restaurant with its view of San Francisco and the Bay--and known thereafter as "the top of the Mark"--until 1939, this passage had to be written <u>after</u> 1939. What confirms my reading--that "top mark" was meant to be "the top of the Mark"--is the 1951 Spanish edition of the novel, which has Collins threaten to be "saltando del edificio mas alto" (157).

In this Spanish edition of <u>The White Rose</u> we discover yet another complication. Esperanza López Matéos, Traven's Spanish translator in Mexico, used the English, not the German, versions of Traven's books to do her work, for she is not supposed to have known enough German to translate directly from that language into Spanish. Quite surprisingly, the 1951 Spanish edition is considerably longer than the 1965 British edition; it contains the 1929 countertheme <u>as well as</u> the 1965 Rockefeller interview, in addition to material found neither in the 1929 German nor in the 1965 British edition. All this points to the existence of a version of <u>The White Rose</u> that must have served as the master manuscript for both the 1929 German and the 1965 British editions; it would have to have been a manuscript written before 1929, and it would have to have been written in English--but by whom?

That Torsvan-Croves's own English was extremely poor the several passages quoted earlier amply illustrate. His was a Germanic English of embarrassing crudeness. The same thing must be said about Marut-Torsvan's English. The three novels he sent to Alfred A. Knopf during the 1930s--<u>The Death Ship</u>, <u>Treasure</u>, and <u>Bridge</u>--remained language cripples even after editor Bernard Smith doctored them up in a desperate effort to Anglicize and Americanize their English. Traven scholar Hubert Jannach recognized these American editions as translation as early as 1963;[3] no headnote saying "Written by the author in English"[4] can obscure that fact. Indeed, it is safe to propose--alone on the basis of the deplorable but strikingly similar English prose found in those three 1930s novels and the 1965 White Rose--that Marut-Torsvan and Torsvan-Croves were one and the same man. This, in turn, would mean that if a master manuscript of The White Rose, written in English, did exist prior to 1929, it would have to have been written in an atrociously Germanic English, or Torsvan (Marut- and/or -Croves) did not write it. I shall return to this question later. For the moment, let me cite a few of the most glaring examples of the peculiar, Teutonic English found in the 1965 edition of the novel.

"'Oh, that Loro,'" Torsvan-Croves has Conchita, Yañez's wife, reflect at one point, "'he [the Loro--or parrot] is badder than anybody'" (29). (Emphasis here and following is mine.) Unless Torsvan-Croves wanted to make fun of Conchita by having her talk illiterate English--that is, illiterate Spanish rendered into illiterate English--"badder" is a literal translation of the German word "schlechter" made by someone ignorant of, or indifferent to, the fact that the comparative form of bad is worse. Fairly early in the novel, Torsvan-Croves has Collins phrase the thought, "If I need land on the Jupiter, I swear I'll get it" (40). Here the reader who knows German knows that in the phrase auf dem Jupiter, of which the English phrase is a literal translation, the definite article is needed. There is a Mr. Scheller in the novel, a contractor, who "perceived the bright idea of how to crush his rival..." (70). The author writes that "no one knows who is pulling the strings and to which object" (zu welchem Zweck), that much money is "about the nation," and that "the woodlots and forests and parks stood implanted where the maps said they stood" (98). Once "rain fell as it had [not?] fallen since man had memory" (seit Menschengedenken) (99). Or he says, "It proved out that Mr. Collins couldn't and never had satisfied his wild hunger for women nor his aching for sexual expressions..." (111). And, "Now they all knew that this week-end party would be hot and heavy, far out of bounds from any other week-end parties they might be privileged or obliged to attend...to miss it would be to commit a crime against one's own flesh and spirit" (114). We find the phrase "due to fear of saying something out of social form" (114). Basileen "hired two bands, a jazz and a string" (115). Collins thinks "...then I'll give him a whack that'll send him into the middle of the next week!" (125). Rockefeller says to Collins: "'I had

believed you <u>not</u> <u>so</u> <u>dumb</u> <u>as</u> <u>to</u> <u>go</u> <u>that</u> <u>way</u>'" (133). There
is talk of "ambition-ridden party members fighting each
other for a <u>guzzling</u> <u>spot</u> at the national <u>swill</u> <u>trough</u>"
(148) and of notary publics "and tough guys, and whoever
else was sniffing around with an eye on the <u>jam-pile</u>" (159).
Collins says, "'Here we can negotiate with him <u>in</u> <u>leisure</u>'"
(<u>in</u> <u>Ruhe</u>), instead of <u>at</u> <u>leisure</u> (168). The governor of
Veracruz, in talking about the legal papers for transferring
the White Rose to Condor Oil, comments, "'I'd say they're
just too perfect to <u>avoid</u> suspicion'" (194). Towards the
end of the novel, Collins crumples a piece of paper so "that
he could thus <u>throw</u> <u>off</u> <u>from</u> <u>his</u> <u>mind</u> the haunting name of
Abner that had been <u>thrust</u> <u>onto</u> <u>him</u>" (205). And so on and
so forth. The list can be extended at random.

What becomes clear when we study even this partial list is
that, though we may not be able to alight on an exact German
equivalent for every awkward English phrase, the translating
mind is thinking in German and fishing for literal word
facsimiles. English or American idioms are unknown to that
mind.

There are a few genuine English or American expressions in
the 1965 edition of <u>The</u> <u>White</u> <u>Rose</u>, such as "causing him to
wipe off his smile" (58), "in the know" (59), "the run of
North American businessmen" (60), "and then some" (81),
"four-bit cigars" (82), "to beard the president in his den"
(82), "another bone to pick" (106), "close to chucking the
oil business" (107), and "that's about the size of it"
(120). "Illegal <u>junk</u>" (64) and "how <u>to</u> <u>lay</u> <u>on</u> a sales talk"
(114) appear to be phrases of mid-century vintage. But all
these expressions are so strikingly different from the prevailing prose that we are forced to ascribe them to someone
other than Torsvan-Croves, if only because the hopelessly
Germanic English he was producing during the forties, fif-
ties, and sixties (in <u>The</u> <u>White</u> <u>Rose</u> and in several unsuccessful film scripts[5]) shows, in its total absence of such
expressions, that he had never learned to use idiomatic
English. That leaves only a British editor working for
Robert Hale as the inventor of those phrases, following in
the footsteps of Bernard Smith, or--and this seems more
likely--one of the Americans Torsvan-Croves employed during
the fifties and sixties to polish his English prose.[6]

Marut-Torsvan's ignorance of American idioms becomes an
even more serious problem where we would least expect to
encounter it, namely, in the 1929 German version of <u>The</u>
<u>White</u> <u>Rose</u>. Not only do we find innumerable American words
and phrases left intact--that is, untranslated into German--
in the German text, but we also come across many awkward
expressions that, upon closer inspection, turn out to be

either badly translated American or English idioms or such idioms misunderstood and therefore totally distorted in their meaning when they appear in German. Finally, we find American syntax in German sentences.

A systematic study of these Americanisms strongly suggests that Marut-Torsvan was working from an earlier English text when he composed The White Rose in German. This, in turn, means that we are forced once again to contemplate the existence of a master manuscript of The White Rose written in English before 1929. In 1925 Traven himself makes a case for the existence of original English manuscripts. In a letter to his German editor he declares that he had translated the manuscripts he was sending from English into German and added that he himself had first written most of those manuscripts in English. Viewed superficially, this declaration—and the use of English words and phrases in the German texts—might appear to be an ingenious ruse Ret Marut used to cover his tracks and build up an American persona. A careful look at the texts, however, makes a contradiction in terms of a writer of German prose filled with Americanisms that are misunderstood and falsely translated—so long as we equate Marut-Torsvan (and, later, Torsvan-Croves) with B. Traven. Whoever first composed the manuscript of The White Rose (and of nearly all the other B. Traven manuscripts, since what is true of The White Rose is equally true of all of Traven's works published in Germany—and, in German, in Holland—between 1925 and 1940) knew exactly what his idioms meant and how they fitted into what he was saying. He was thoroughly familiar with English "as she was—and is—spoke." Marut-Torsvan-Croves was not. "B. Traven" thus becomes a composite. We do not know who the component was who was not Marut-Torsvan-Croves, and we may never find out. If frequently repeated rumors that Torsvan-Croves burnt a pile of papers before his death are true, we may have to relinquish the hope of clarifying the question by means of written documents, since holograph scripts that have turned up—and may still turn up—need not be original manuscripts at all but may be copies, translations, or revisions of earlier manuscripts. For the time being, the most compelling evidence we have for the existence of an American component of the "B. Traven" entity is Traven's German prose. Let me present some of that evidence now, taken from the 1929 German edition of The White Rose.

After thinking about Yañez as "dieser Chunk von einem dreckigen Indianer," Collins makes a statement we are already familiar with, but he ends it with the imprecation—in English: "'Wenn ich Land haben will und es ist auf dem Jupiter, ich bekomme es, sure as death" (36). On the same

page we find that "nur der jüngste Officeboy...lachte nicht
darüber, sondern sagte zu der jüngsten Officegirl...: 'So
ein Cabbage, und er nennt sich Präs, wie will er denn rauf
auf den Jupiter!'" Since it is the German word "Kohl" and
not the English word "cabbage" which is often used to stand
for "nonsense," one wonders, of course, why Marut-Torsvan
used the English word instead. Was he practicing being
ignorant with a vengeance? At one point, Collins's girlfriend Betty Cuttens says to him: "'What's the bloomin'
idea, you little shrimp! Was denkst du dir denn eigentlich,
du kleines, armseliges mickerndes, winselndes Jammerwürm-
chen, das Du bist!'" (64). "Bloomin'" is, I think, the only
Britishism found in the novel, and Marut-Torsvan may well
have picked it up in Brixton Prison. Considered as his own
contribution, it is an expression peculiarly out of place
among its American cousins. However, we hear that Betty
"sprach Slang mit voller Absicht," and so did "ein tüchtiger
Businessman, obgleich er College und Universität besucht
hat..." (65). Few Germans could have known what an American
college was in 1929--few Europeans, for that matter, know
what it is today; one wonders whether the writer himself
knew, for Collins, the businessman being talked about, has
no graduate degree--from a university.

We also find out that "den Reportern wurde erzählt, dass
die Company übermässig overstocked sei" (86); that Mr. Collins worked "in seinem Office" (86) ("Office" sometimes
appears as a feminine word: "die Office"); and that, if
someone maintained that "ein materielles oder ein seelisches
Ding mehr wert sei als money, als selbst die höchste Summe
von money" (148), he would be using a "Trick" in order to
get still more money. We also hear about "kidnappen" (148),
"fettgedruckten Lettern der Headlines" (204), "eine twist-
ende Schleife des Stahltaues" (205), and "ein Raid von den
Agenten der Prohibition" (71). The author says, furthermore, "Sollte wirklich von den Agenten der Prohibition ge-
raidet werden..." (72). He talks about "dem snickernden
Stile einer Gloria Swanson" (73); about "Broker" (84), a
plural word in German; about "Eiscreams" (40); about "Oil-
Companien" (43), as well as about "Öl-Companien" (66); about
a person's "hundert tausend Dollar missen können" (47),
instead of "vermissen"; about "Brats" (52); about a "House-
Warming Party"; about "tipsy-topsy" (72); about "Real Estate" (79); and about starving "Miners" (101). Traven continually writes "Union" (or "Arbeiterunion" or
"Unionführer") instead of "Gewerkschaft," and we find the
typical Traven confusion between the verbs wissen and können
whenever they are translated from the English verb to know:
"Mr. Collins arbeitete, wie nur ein wahrhaft grosses Genie

zu arbeiten weiss" (193), instead of "...wie nur ein wahrhaft grosses Genie arbeiten kann."

Sometimes Marut-Torsvan even transfers the sound of an
English word. For example, after Mr. Abner, Collins's minion, had botched the job of killing Yañez by forgetting to
dispose of the body, Collins suggests that he buy a revolver, and he adds sarcastically, "'Und kaufen Sie einen
guten, der nicht fehlt im rechten Augenblick'" (193). Collins here implies that Mr. Abner should shoot himself with a
gun that won't "fail" at the right moment. "Fehlen" and "to
fail" have the same sound, but according to the way the
sentence reads in German, the gun will be absent when Mr.
Abner is supposed to be using it on himself. People in The
White Rose say "Come in" (122) and "So long" and "Good bye"
(123), and they give "Orders" and know about the "Trust-
gesetz" (anti-trust law) (103); they are "smart" (105), wear
"Overalls" (126), and state, "'Wir werden besser tun, uns
nebenbei einen Curbstone Polisher, einen Eckensteher, zu
halten..." (138). The appositive "Eckensteher" hardly helps
the German reader understand the meaning of "curbstone polisher." If "Poolrooms" is used because there were none in
Germany, what about "Cookies mit Sodageschmack" (162), meaning crackers? And does an appositional "Portier" help a
German reader understand what a "Janitor" (198) is? A
European portier is, surely, something very different from
an American janitor.

The list of American words and phrases left untranslated
in the German text seems endless. I shall now turn to three
English idioms that are clearly misunderstood--or too sim-
plistically transliterated into German. We read, for example, that "Betty war good sport" (72). Then the author
explains what a good sport is without apparently realizing
that the indefinite article is an essential part of the
English idiom and that without it Betty would immediately
become the plaything of the men she is supposed to be superior to. Near the end of the novel, Marut-Torsvan writes,
"Dann endlich kam der erste Brunnen ein" (203). He means,
of course, that the first oil well began producing oil, that
it "came in." The translator forgets that there is really
no such verb in German; "einkommen," if it existed as a
verb, would mean something very different. Finally, we find
out that Collins, in his youth, had difficulties "beide
Enden zusammenzuhalten" (39). For German readers, this
might as well be Etruscan for all they can tell that Collins
had a hard time "making both ends meet," even if English
readers will immediately recognize the idiom in the German
sentence. And there are numerous other idiomatic miscar-
riages like these in the novel that German readers will

continue to have to stare at uncomprehendingly. True, the 1962 _rororo_ edition of _The White Rose_ at last transformed "_Union_" into "Gewerkschaft" (79), "_Raid_" into "Razzia" (62), "_geraidet_" into "nachgeforscht" (62) and "_Miners_" or "_Minen_arbeiter" into "Bergarbeiter" (79). But it also introduced such fresh nuggets as "Weisheit in einer _Nuss-schale_" ("in a nutshell") (113) embedded in new material (old material taken from the English master manuscript?). No German equivalents will ever exist for "oil driller," "tool dresser," "time-keeper," and a dozen other terms having to do with the production of oil, so I shall not find fault with the 1929 edition of _The White Rose_ for carrying them.

Perhaps the most disturbing example of American syntax found in a German sentence in _The White Rose_ is the one Tucholsky already bemoaned in 1930.[7] It illustrates our American proclivity for using the present participle. Marut-Torsvan writes, "In solcher Umgebung lebend, nur solche Farmer kennend, wie konnte man erwarten, dass Mr. Collins die weisse Rose verstand!" (150). No native speaker of German, not even an uneducated one, would attempt such a construction. Yet a self-educated American might easily say, without worrying too much about the dangling modifier he was concocting, "Living among such surroundings and knowing only such farmers, how could one expect Mr. Collins to understand the White Rose!" And Marut-Torsvan obviously translated this little monster literally into German.

In his early letters, B. Traven gave his German editors to understand that he was knowingly writing for German working-class readers. Yet such readers in the 1920s and 1930s could not have been expected even to begin to grasp the meaning of the English and American words and phrases Marut-Trosvan tossed at them in his German texts, let alone his transliterations of American and English idioms he himself didn't always understand. Traven's becoming a best-selling author in spite of these language excesses has, of course, nothing to do with his pretense of writing simply for uneducated readers. He was in a hurry to get his translations done and his manuscripts sent overseas, where a market awaited them. This is shown by the fact that the reflective passages of _The White Rose_ (and of all the other novels and stories published in Germany--and Holland--until 1940) were written in absolutely correct German--the German, in fact, that Ret Marut had learned to use _in_ Germany as a contributor of essays and stories to German newspapers and as editor and writer of his own magazine, _Der Ziegelbrenner,_ which he had brought out irregularly between 1917 and 1922. It is the German in which he had expressed his ideas in Germany until 1922 and in which he continued to express them in Mexico after 1924. He knew what he wanted to say--and he said it correctly, using German idioms and expressions. The incorrect German I have been analyzing is found in the narrative and dialogue portions of The White Rose (and of all the other novels and stories). We can assume, therefore, that Marut-Torsvan took over the story part of The White Rose (and of all the other novels and stories) from manuscripts written by the person who formed the other component of the writer we have come to know as B. Traven. That is why I have called the composer of Die Weisse Rose (and of the other B. Traven books published during the 1920s and 1930s) Marut-Torsvan and the writer of film scripts and translator of Die Weisse Rose into English Torsvan-Croves (he had started calling himself Croves by 1946), in order to underscore the proposition that either person was only a part of the entity "B. Traven." I have called him B. Traven or Traven whenever I wanted to refer to both men--that is, to the author of all the works, including the letters--and to what the name "B. Traven" has come to stand for.

If there is truth in what B. Traven wrote to his American admirer Arthur H. Klein in 1935, namely, that no American market awaited his writings, because, as he explained, he had unsuccessfully submitted his manuscripts to American editors year after year for five years (before 1920!),[8] then he must have been referring to the writings--the manuscripts --of the American component of the B. Traven entity. In that case, Marut-Torsvan's hurry, after the smashing success in Germany of Das Totenschiff in 1926, becomes even more understandable. Hurry may thus explain why the translator and transcriber Marut-Torsvan did not wait to find help in order to raise the poor quality of the translated passages of The White Rose (and of all the other novels and stories). And pride--in what we must characterize as a woefully inadequate knowledge of English, particularly of English and American idioms--coupled with the fear of the exposure of his identity may explain why that translator and transcriber did not even seek help. But whatever the final explanation may be, the one thing we as critics and scholars cannot afford to do is to dismiss or trivialize this language problem. It is real; it exists. And we must face it head-on.

III

Which edition of The White Rose is more--is most--authentic? Which contains the "essential" B. Traven? I hope to have made clear why I cannot consider the 1965 British edition as the one I would use in order to discover Traven's intention, even though it contains the Rockefeller interview. At best, that edition strikes me as stale B. Taven.

Fresh B. Traven--in both senses of the word, for we want the audacious, challenging author at the height of his indignation--we find in the 1929 German edition of The White Rose (and all the other Büchergilde novels and stories) in spite of the language problem. That edition represents the best possible combination we shall ever have of the American's story and of Ret Marut's philosophy. For even if we were to find a copy of the original English master manuscript of The White Rose, it would probably be, except for its healthy English and American idioms, a far cry from the work created by both components of the "B. Traven" entity. In order to have the complete novel, we need Ret Marut's own reflective passages--written in German--and his shaping hand. For readers who wish to understand and enjoy the Americanisms embedded in the German text, a knowledge of both German and American English becomes useful. For B. Traven scholars and critics, such a knowledge becomes imperative, even if it diminishes their ranks, as it has already done in the United States. It is part of the hell Traven created for us.

IV

I have spent more than twenty years in that hell. Yet I have always had a feeling that somewhere inside its creator there resided, perhaps quite contre lui, a sense of honor which kept him from always telling lies about who he was or what he had or had not written. Most readers of his works will second that feeling, for it is, after all, the sense of honor expressed in Traven's rebellion against the injustices of this world that draws us to him as a writer. This sense of honor may also be felt in some of his letters; it may show up in his very spontaneous answers to reporters, beginning in 1948. "I did not write the works," he would say, "I helped in the writing of only some of them." If we could bring ourselves to accept Traven's sense of honor in fundamental matters as a genuine possibility, it might help us along in our understanding of the B. Traven phenomenon. Could it have been not only Torsvan-Croves's desperate attempt to preserve his anonymity but also his honor which made him deny being the author of all the works of B. Traven? And could he have meant that he had contributed some element to all of them? If my perception of this sense of honor is correct, then it may also help to explain why Marut-Torsvan-Croves did not use more material from the original English manuscripts when he translated The Death Ship, Treasure, Bridge, and The White Rose from German into English in preparing these novels for publication in the United States and in England, although the master manuscripts might still have been available to him. At least that of The White Rose appears to have been, as its use in the creation of the Spanish version--and the addition Torsvan-Croves made to the 1962 rororo edition, taken, as it is, from material written in English--indicate.

By the same token--and without having to stray any further into the realm of speculation--we would not be able to take seriously Traven's claim that he was an American, applying it, however, to the writer of the original English manuscripts only, not to Marut-Torsvan-Croves. It would help us to understand the "American" factor in Traven's writing, otherwise irreconcilable to the data we have about Marut-Torsvan-Croves. It would explain why we find an American narrator's authentic-sounding American voice, particularly--and ironically--in the German editions; and it would explain his acquaintance with the midwestern and southern states (to whose flora and fauna he refers) and his knowledge of U.S. history, politics, literature, and native speech. It would account for the oeuvre's ties to works by American writers and their echoes in individual Traven novels and stories. It might, in fact, explain why the plot of The White Rose is essentially the plot of Frank Norris's The Octopus, with the San Joaquin Valley wheat farmers having become the Veracruz Indians of the White Rose, and the Pacific and Southwestern Railroad, Condor Oil. Even the inability of Americans to love and value their homes is already illustrated in Norris's novel. As for the Rockefeller interview in The White Rose, a similar interview between the president of the Pacific and Southwestern Railroad and the observer-protagonist of The Octopus prefigures it and perhaps inspired Traven to invent it.

If Marut-Torsvan-Croves translated and transcribed rather than originally wrote The White Rose (and all the other novels and stories), he was obviously not the creative genius some critics have made him out to be. This does not mean that he was not an extraordinarily talented writer. But it does mean that we can stop imputing to him a creative outburst within the limits of a most improbable time schedule, during which he was supposed to have collected the material for all those novels and stories that made him famous--and written them too. We now know that Ret Marut could not have gotten to Mexico before the early summer of

1924. Yet in the fall of that year, he had ready for publication the first part of The Cotton Pickers,[9] after having lived its adventures, those of an American in Mexico who works as a cotton picker, oil driller, and baker over a period of months. A year later, he had ready for publication the second part of The Cotton Pickers, containing new adventures and work experiences; the complete Death Ship; an early form of Bridge; and two short stories dealing with Mexican Indians. And so on and so forth. By 1929 Traven had published five novels, three of which recreated adventures in Mexico he had himself had, according to those critics; a book of short stories, the most significant of which recount at novella length his further adventures in various parts of Mexico; and a long nonfiction work about Chiapas--and Mexico itself--that likewise grew out of his own experiences. And all of these books Ret Marut was supposed to have written while working at a hundred different odd jobs; farming on his own; studying Spanish, anthropology, and photography in Mexico City; and constantly traveling around the country as an American lumpen proletarian. Seven substantial books, filled with personal adventures, Mexican history, the conflict between Mexico and the United States, political philosophy, and a whole Weltanschauung in five years! This is obviously a myth which Traven himself, in a less than honorable mood, did his utmost to foster by saying, in letters to Germany, that he was always writing about his own experiences (or implying he was by stating that he found himself unable to write about anything he had not himself experienced). The White Rose perfectly illustrates that he was able to do so--and what about the six Caoba novels of the 1930s?

We must use the language problem to explode the myth. We are not dishonoring a great writer by being honest with our findings. No other key to the B. Traven mystery appears to fit the facts so well. With it, we may be opening the only portal we shall ever find leading out of the hell Traven created for us.

Notes

1. Die Büchergilde, Feb. 1928, quoted by Werner Sellhorn, B. Traven: Erzählungen, Vol. 2 (Zurich: Limmat Verlag, 1968), 342.

2. "Das Prinzip der namenlosen Differenz. Gesellschafts- und Kulturkritik bei B. Traven," Das B. Traven Buch (Hamburg: Rowohlt Verlag, 1976), 362-403.

3. "B. Traven--an American or German Author?" German Quarterly 36 (1963): 359-468.

4. Note found on verso of title page of Death Ship (New York: Collier Books, 1962). A similar note is found in March to the Montería (New York: Dell, 1964).

5. Cf. film scripts in B.T. Archive of Büchergilde Gutenberg, Frankfurt, and B.T. Archive of Theo Pinkus's Arbeiterbibliothek, Zurich.

6. That Croves hired Americans for this purpose was told me by Traven's widow, Rosa Elena Luján, in 1977; it was confirmed by Charles Miller at the Conference in 1982 (he had been one of those hired).

7. Kurt Tucholsky, Gesammelte Werke, Vol. 3 (Hamburg: Rowohlt Verlag, 1967), 614.

8. Letter to Klein quoted by E. R.Hagemann in "¡Huye! A Conjectural Biography of B. Traven," Inter-American Review of Bibliography 12 (Dec. 1960): 377.

9. Cf. B.T.'s diary, quoted by Rolf Recknagel, Beiträge zur Biographie des B. Traven (Berlin: Klaus Guhl, 1977), 13.

Editions Used

Die weisse Rose. Büchergilde Gutenberg, 1929.
The White Rose. Robert Hale, 1965.
Die weisse Rose. rororo (Rowohlt Paperback), 1962.
La Rosa Blanca. Cia. General de Ediciones, S.A. Mexico, 1951, 1975.

FROM RET MARUT TO B. TRAVEN
More Than a Change In Disguise

Robert T. Goss

It has been claimed that the B. Traven mystery is now solved. Marut, Traven, and Croves--we are told--were all a single author. If this is so, however, much work remains to be done to explain the single identity that lies behind the writing published under their names.

The problem can be illustrated if we consider recent studies of the work of Marut and Traven. Both have been discussed in some detail, although the writing published as B. Traven's after "Hal Croves" appeared on the scene has been mostly ignored. There is virtually nothing on the change of B. Traven into Ret Marut, or on how Traven evolved into Hal Croves. In both cases, there must have been development in the essential characteristics of a writer--his ideas, attitudes, purpose, methods, goals, likes and dislikes, implied experience as well as the way he put words to paper, style in the widest sense, the style that "is the man." That this development took place has been mainly taken for granted or merely asserted. Even when approached by scholars of literature who had the tools to deal with it adequately, the problem has remained a minor issue. It has not engaged their best energies.[1] Just to enumerate a few prominent examples:

When Erich Mühsam lectured in Vienna in 1931, he explained to his friend Leopold Spitzegger that he had detected stylistic similarities between Ziegelbrenner and the first B. Traven works. Unfortunately, we do not know what these similarities amounted to.[2]

In the late fifties, Rolf Rechnagel appropriated the thesis that Marut wrote the Traven fiction, and he began the years of determined and admirable literary detective work into Marut's life that culminated in his book B. Traven. Beiträge zur Biografie. Early steps he took along the way included articles subtitled "a literary inquiry"[3] and "a stylistic comparison."[4] In their day they may have been revelations, but they now seem very superficial. The pages in Recknagel's biography which attempt stylistic comparison between Marut and Traven[5] would have to be attacked point by point, at greater length than we have here. It would be easy to show that Rechnagel places much weight on characteristics (a tendency to alliterate, for instance, or repeated use of hin and her) which are trivial or are shared by any number of other authors or by folk speech. Rechnagel also makes much of things which occur only once in the Marut and once in the Traven oeuvre (for instance, an ecstatic onomatopoetic passage that climaxes a love scene). This is not the systematic demonstration of shared, unmistakable, principal characteristics that is needed.

Michael Baumann's well-known book, B. Traven, An Introduction, presents some of the most interesting problems so far raised concerning Marut and Traven: Marut's peculiar German, the very peculiar American English of the 1934 Death Ship, Marut's Stirnerite anarchism, and the evidence for an American background or American experience in the Traven works. But it becomes harder to agree with Baumann when he tries to show how strong characteristics of Marut's writing might be supposed to survive in Traven's books, or how elements of Traven's writing seem to be anticipated by Marut's works.[6]

Until recently, the basic reflex of a large group of Traven scholars has been to demonstrate the unity of Marut and Traven by twisting even tenuous connections into proofs of resemblance. Many of these reeds have been too weak to bear the weight of emphasis put on them. If the identity question is indeed settled, then we need to explain a very different problem. We must admit that there are striking-- in fact, amazing, dumbfounding--differences between the writing and self-images identified with Marut, Traven, and Croves. These differences may all be resolvable within the imagination and personality of a single man--it cannot be denied absolutely. In fact, I will point out some resemblances in this paper. But a great deal remains to be done to make the identification of Marut, Traven, and Croves as writers plausible, much less convincing. These three personae were distinct. All three had quite different goals in writing; all three tried for--and achieved--very different effects on their readers; all three expressed social concerns which were strikingly different in important ways.

Marut's life is, historically, extremely interesting. He would remain a forgotten minor writer, however, if the connection to B. Traven had never been made. Of the fiction published as B. Traven's since World War II--that is, by "Hal Croves"--only the novella Macario is of much literary interest. The important accomplishment is "B. Traven's," and it can be dated to between 1925 and 1940. This is an obvious fact that has been consistently ignored in the excitement over the discovery of Ret Marut.

Ret Marut was a lumpen intellectual who tried to soar to hopelessly passé stylistic heights on the wings of Max Stirner's individualist anarchism. In Khundar, for instance, his style, alas, resembles Carl Spitteler much more than it resembles either his Expressionist contemporaries or B. Traven. Only among his straightforward, simply told, and ironical observations of his contemporaries in the last years of the Prussian Empire are there hints of the sardonic view from the depths always found in the B. Traven of 1925–40. See, for example, the short grotesques collected in Der BLaugetupfte SPerlinG. The Marut of Ziegelbrenner is not very prepossessing at first: precious, pretentious, striking poses, affecting to despise the gallery he was playing to. World War I changed him from a disappointed actor into the publisher and editor and (apparently) only writer of an inflammatory subversive magazine. The Räterepublik period made him a practicing revolutionary and, ultimately, a fugitive for several years afterwards. If the seeds of B. Traven were planted in Ret Marut, it was not by reading Max Stirner, but by the November 1918 uprising and its results, and by the thinking and example of Gustav Landauer--a very different kind of anarchist (though we should note Stirner's temporary influence on the early Landauer).

B. Traven wrote about work. This turned out to involve adventurous doings in exotic countries, but his adventurers were almost all working men and (among the few women in his stories) almost all working women. And he is the foremost white writer of exotic adventure to want to find out what the real feelings and experiences of "the natives" were. One only has to compare him with Joseph Conrad to see how remarkable this quality in Traven is. If Traven never attained the symphonic orchestration of a virtuoso display piece like Heart of Darkness, he was also--when writing about Indians--innocent of the white superiority that taints that story from beginning to end. (It should be noted that he was capable of expressing racist sentiments towards the Chinese and the American Blacks. But the longer he studied the Indians, the stronger his admiration for them became.)

Traven did not often allow conventional considerations of narrative structure or syntactical polish to hold him back from using his fiction to make points to his readers, explicitly and sometimes tediously. His few attempts at carefully organized and balanced architecture, Bridge and "Night Visitor" in particular, succeeded well enough, however. If the great mass of Traven's work has a characteristic style in the usual sense, it is in a way that resembles Van Gogh. He used rough blocks of brilliant color with an immediate appeal that captivates in an obvious, unsubtle fashion and puts across subject matter which is everyday and down-to-earth in its own land, but which is made appealing by its foreignness and distance.

What is so unusual--indeed, unique--about Traven is the
gripping interest he gives to the crudest, most exploitative
kind of work: keeping a dangerously decrepit steamship
operating, maneuvering a column of oxcarts, finding and
concentrating gold dust, clear-cutting the mahogany jungle,
picking cotton and baking and whoring and driving cattle.
And so on through the eleven novels and twenty stories
published by 1940. There is nothing like this in either
Marut or Croves.

Traven also wrote about other people, where Marut wrote
about himself. Marut's fiction tends to be populated by
puppets acting out his inner struggles, surrounded by named
or anonymous shadows. Even Traven's sketchier characters,
such as the cotton pickers, are at least lively types. At
his best--in Gerard Gales, Andres Ugaldo, Celso, and many
others--he shows in telling detail how intimately experience
(especially the way a person gets a living) shapes human
life. Traven is even capable of sharply observed miniature
portraits like Perez, the money-hungry lawyer at the beginning of The White Rose. The Traven fiction gives its readers the conviction that it is authentic, in contrast to the
work of Marut or Croves. There is a feeling that the author
has been there and done the work himself, or seen it and
understood it as a mechanic's hand understands a wrench. It
is even easy to point out the places where Traven has not
been, from the inauthentic, tall-tale flavor of the details
of the supposed experience: the cattle drive section of Der
Wobby, for example, or the world of North American high
finance in The White Rose, which seems to have been pieced
together from newspaper scandal, radical theory, muckraking
novels, and shrewd conjecture--anything but firsthand observation.

B. Traven hated newspapers, publicity, advertising, publishers' blurbs on his books, celebrities, film adaptations,
movie producers, and the making and breaking of star attrac-
tions, as he reiterated through the twenties and thirties in
published letters and the novel The White Rose. He refused
all offers to film his books in Germany. He thoroughly tied
Alfred Knopf's hands, assuring that his first books published in the United States--his greatest successes in
several other countries--would fail even though they had
received critical acclaim in all the leading reviews.[7]

Of course this was very like Ret Marut, who hated the
corrupt German war press with a deep and bitter passion.
But it was only apparently like Hal Croves. In spite of all
his desperate flight from reporters and cameras, Croves was
a media manipulator. Media manipulation was the obvious
purpose of his mimeographed scandal sheet BT-Mitteilungen.

And that was just one of the ways he turned Traven's reclusiveness into a coy means of generating publicity, a public relations trick for attracting the attention of publishers and film producers and for reviving interest in the Traven books after World War II had ended. The Treasure of the Sierra Madre was the first film made from Traven material, in 1947. But Croves's agent, Esperanza López Matéos, had written Knopf inquiring about obtaining the film rights to Traven works as early as 1939.[8] Croves wrote many film and stage adaptations of the important Traven works and contributed to the Mexican screenplay of La Rebelion de los Colgados.

The novel he sent off to German publishers, Aslan Norval, was so radically unlike the earlier Traven novels that it had to wait two years before a publisher believed it could be authentic and accepted it.[9] Where Traven's novels in the twenties and thirties told the stories of underdogs with an urgent feeling of authenticity, Aslan Norval tells how a beautiful millionairess uses people's gullibility and greed to engage the entire United States in a great media hype. In style, this novel has long passages of a scriptwriter's pure dialogue, not to be found in earlier Traven works. Where earlier Traven fiction treated sex matter-of-factly or sociologically if at all--those novels were about the struggle for existence--this novel is full of soft-core pornography.

The fiction not offered for publication until after the last of the jungle novels deals sympathetically with American businessmen and priests and millionaires and the manipulation of public opinion, all of which had been execrated by the pre-1945 "Traven." And the Croves fiction is marred alternately by sentimentality and shock sensationalism, two ways of committing the same artistic sin, demanding that the reader feel more than the writer gives him reason to.

Rolf Recknagel considered Croves the cynical exploiter of the works of another man until the second (1971) edition of his biography, and he was far from the only one who did not believe that Croves could have been either B. Traven or Ret Marut. It is easy to understand why. Marut had claimed to write for himself alone and not for money, recognition, or to please his readers; Traven had broken off with the magazine Das Buch für Alle when the editors added one sentence to the beginning of his story "Ein Hundegeschäft" in 1927. But Croves was working the Traven books for profit without much regard for the details of what they had once said or how they had once said it. Aslan Norval, written in awkward German, was given to former Büchergilde Gutenberg editor Johannes Schönherr for a rewrite, during which Schönherr reportedly took it on himself to tone down the novel's eroticism.[10] Where Marut had wished that his name and memory be blotted out after his death, where B. Traven had insisted on preserving his anonymity at all costs, Croves spent his last years posing for a larger-than-life-size bust and playing several reporters and agents and inquirers off against each other. They were given biographical details which he partly revealed, partly hinted at, partly left to their imaginations, and partly made up out of whole cloth. Since his death, a Mexican town has been renamed in Traven's (which, of course, means Croves's) honor.

If, as we have been told, there can now be no doubt that Marut, Traven, and Croves were the same man, it seems imperative to me that these and other differences now be acknowledged and accounted for. Here is a problem worthy of the sharpest tools of the most ingenious literary analyst!

To give an example of one area where I think the currently prevailing consensus on the continuity of Marut to Traven to Croves is demonstrably incorrect: their anarchism. Croves in the 1950s is said to have recommended strongly to Mexican president Adolfo López Mateos that the ejido system be implemented and once-communal land be redistributed to the Indians.[11] This harks back to Zapata's Plan of Ayala. But beyond this, what is publicly known of Croves—the ideas in the B. Traven books from his time, his public statements, his choice of friends, his umbrage at John Huston's recollection that his clothes had been shabby at their first meeting[12]—all point anywhere but toward anarchism. I would suggest that Croves can be excused on this point.

Ret Marut was a disciple of Max Stirner. Among the few advertisements in Marut's Ziegelbrenner was an announcement that Stirner's Kleinere Schriften, edited by John Henry Mackay, could be ordered—if necessary through Ziegelbrenner. It is clear to readers of this journal that Marut has reflected long on Stirner's ideas and is trying to apply them in his own day and to his own situation. This point has been ably made, for instance in Baumann's book[13] or Wolfgang Essbach's excellent essay in Das B. Traven-Buch.[14] There are few difficulties with the parts of their arguments dealing with Marut and Stirner.

It is more troubling when the B. Traven works are mined for specific instances of the influence of Max Stirner in order to make Traven into Marut by ignoring what Traven is in his own right, by sweeping it under the rug of the Marut-to-Traven argument. One example of many that could be taken is the majestic motto over the entrance to the crew's quarters on the Yorikke:

```
He
Who enters here
Will no longer have existence;
His name and soul have vanished
And are gone for ever.
Of him there is not left a breath
In all the vast world.
He can never return,
Nor can he ever go onward;
For where he stands there he must stay.
No God knows him;
And unknown will he be in hell.
He is not day; he is not night.
He is Nothing and Never.
He is too great for infinity.
Too small for a grain of sand,
Which, however small,
Has its place in the universe.
He is what has never been
And never thought.[15]
```

This passage has been interpreted as a reference to a
higher stage of Stirner's egoism, the _Einziger_,[16] while,
amazingly, only one commentator I know of ever tried to make
anything meaningful of the more obvious and compelling
parallel to Dante.[17] To me the question seems to be: Are
the crew of the death ship exalted or are they damned? The
life that Gerard Gales is introduced to in his initial
evening of work is so exhausting, degrading, and miserable
that he is moved to jump in the ocean and kill himself. Why
doesn't he? Because the only friend he has found on the
ship, or in the novel for that matter, begs him not to leave
all the work to him alone. Then his friend, Stanislav,
would have to go over the railing too. Gales stays alive--a
harder thing for him to do than end his life at that point--
because of friendship. (I have been tempted to surround the
words "friend" and "friendship" in the last sentences with
quotation marks.) Surely, this has little to do with the
egoistic philosophy encountered in the works of Max Stirner.
Traven usually tells his reader, loud and long, what his
thinking is. Several passages in The Death Ship indicate
that Traven (in the person of his mouthpiece Gales) considers death preferable to living in slavery or insufferable
servitude, and he rails against human beings who choose to
live under such conditions. Yet they do. Gales does. And
Gales's reason, the reason that provides the fulcrum on
which The Death Ship turns, is friendship. If this is
Traven's further development of Stirner's philosophy, it

looks strongly to me like a development that has become a direct contradiction.

B. Traven's thinking is complex, comes from more than one source, and is sometimes contradictory. It cannot be dealt with as if he were a philosopher. His use of vocabulary is neither scientifically precise nor thoroughly consistent. He is a novelist (a good one). It is not enough to find discussions or events in his books that may have been suggested by reading Stirner, when the Traven books do not thereby proceed to make Stirner's sense of the world they depict.

The sense Traven does make of the world has been written out specifically in at least one place, in his one nonfiction book so far published, Land des Frühlings.[18] For Traven in this book (the central argument is in chapters 16 and 17), the heirs of Old World civilizations, Europeans and Asians, are Individualisten, sozial ohne Solidarität, and Spezialisten. American Indians relatively unaffected by Westernizing are gesellschaftlich, they depend on each other, and they know only the beginnings of the division of labor. Each can make everything he needs, except perhaps a machete. Therefore, they do not habitually covet and steal property. Because property needs so little protection, primitive Indians do not have Regierung, they have Verwaltung. This echoes Engels's cry, "Not the ruling of men but the administration of things!" But of course that is a sentiment shared by the classic thinkers of nineteenth-century anarchism. For Traven, the Indians are already at that enviable stage of social and economic development; they have never been anywhere else.[19]

Traven is far from being a collectivist:

...nothing is more deadly to man and his development than regimentation....Bees and ants can construct and tolerate a perfect state but not man because he procreates individually, gives birth individually, thinks individually, and finds his fulfillment only in individual activity. His individual activity always serves the common good because he needs the community for the preservation of his individual existence....This instinct to serve the community through individual activity, developed strongly in the human race and found only rarely or in atrophied forms in animals, is taken advantage of again and again to create a regimented state....For millenia, since the first day on which a political body [state] was created, the political struggle of men has revolved around the form of this body....In whatever form the state may emerge...man is not going to cease to struggle until he has recognized that he is fighting and has always been fighting against regimentation, against enslaving organizational force.[20]

Although he upholds the individual this way, Individualismus is a word with bad connotations here for Traven. The individualism of Europeans and Asians is equally pernicious, though different, in his opinion. Europeans organize states that allow individual wills room to expand and oppress other individuals. Asian individualism tends to form despotic autocracies, families, and clans. Traven is pointing out that the institutions in both parts of the world are created to chananel the thrust to self-assertion. They are the means of persuading the great number of people in society that, if they will wait their normal turn peaceably, they may expect to advance eventually to a position within their reach where everything in the society supports them in unfolding their individuality to the customary extent at the expense of the autonomy of others.[21] As for the Indians, "One must emphasize again and again that the Indian is absolutely unique, absolutely original, that in his inner being he has never been influenced by the European."[22]

Traven states that "the" Indian never wants to become someone else's master or to force his beliefs on another or to increase his possessions at another's cost. In fact, the entire European and North American concept of ownership is foreign to Indians. When an Indian needs land nobody is using, he indicates the boundaries and calls it "his" land. But he only takes what he needs and only considers it his because he needs it to survive. Above all, he has no drive to self-aggrandizement through seizing more than he can use for himself. Traven emphasizes that the Indian has only cooperative (gesellschaftliche), not individual, ambition. He places the Indian's inability to understand Christianity here because, for Traven, a significant part of Christianity is the Old Testament setting of man as master over everything that creeps and grows, and setting a chosen people over rejected peoples. The Indian "...can simply not comprehend that a man or nation should rule over and command others; with his concept of society he does not understand that one nation (should be) is better than another one..."[23] That the Indians also waged war and took slaves is dismissed by Traven as the result of population pressures. In any case, he says, it was more humane than what Europeans understand under those words.

Traven's conclusion to his central argument is: "We are...inclined to insist that the Indian will probably die out, according to the law of survival of the strongest, if he possesses no individual ambition and no greed and thirst for power, even to a limited degree. But who will finally be the stronger, the individualistic European or the community-minded Indian, that will certainly be decided according to different rules than the ones which have guided the policies of the European race so far."[24]

It has been seriously maintained that Traven applies Stirner's ideas to whites but not to Indians. That is, since the Indians have a totally different culture, he does not try to impute egoistic motives to them. This argument does not explain why Traven, if he was an admirer of Stirner's ideas and accepted their influence and if his writing was formed around an egoistic ethos, would praise the Indians for <u>not</u> being egoistically individualistic and then enthusiastically devote the major part of his writing to them. Nor does it explain why Traven tells his readers in <u>Land des Frühlings</u> in simple, straightforward, unmistakable language that Indians will take mastery of the world from Europeans precisely because Indians have a superior social sense, and that the Indians' world, when it comes, will be a great improvement.

Ret Marut plainly was a disciple of Max Stirner. B. Traven plainly was not. Traven's writings are from the beginning guided by a quite different kind of "anarchism," the communal or communist (Communist with a small "c") anarchism that we associate with Kropotkin, or (in America) with Alexander Berkman's book, <u>The ABC of Anarchism</u>. Communitarian anarchism could have come to B. Traven as Ret Marut, but from Gustav Landauer. There are parallels between Traven's thinking in <u>Land des Frühlings</u>, the jungle novels, <u>The White Rose</u>, and elsewhere, and Landauer's thinking in works like <u>Aufruf zum Sozialismus</u>, <u>Die Revolution</u>, and "Dreissig sozialistische Thesen." Traven's peculiar notion in <u>Land des Frühlings</u>--that a union of North and South America was possible and desirable, but only as a union of unions (first all North America unifies while all South America unifies, then they can unify on an equal basis...)--is close to being a reprise of Landauer's predictions for the exploded pieces of post-World War I Germany in "Die vereinigten Republiken Deutschlands und ihre Verfassung," for instance. But to demonstrate Landauer's influence on Traven goes beyond the scope of this paper.[25]

Notes

1. Though now, see Küpfer, 1981.
2. Spitzegger, 1946, 670.
3. Recknagel, 1959, 4-5.

4. Recknagel, 1962, 13.

5. Recknagel, 1982, 250-66.

6. Baumann, 1976, 20-27.

7. Traven's conditions are described in Knopf, 1935, 4. Total sales at Knopf's for both The Death Ship (1934) and Treasure (1935) were less than 6,000 by September 1938, according to Hagemann, 1959, 43, 45.

8. Suarez, 1966, 8, includes as illustration at the top of the page a letter from Esperanza López Matéos to Knopf inquiring about film rights to Bridge and Rebellion for Mexican production. The letter is dated August 9, 1939, if it is authentic.

9. Aslan Norval was offered in BT-Mitteilungen No. 29, Late March 1958. No doubt the legal proceedings by Croves's agent, Josef Wieder, against two men (Kurt Adler and Heinz W. Schilling) who had tried to have books published under the Traven name had also made publishers wary, as Recknagel indicates (Beiträge zur Biografie, 304). The novel was published early in 1960 by Kurt Desch Verlag, Munich.

10. Recknagel, 1982, 304, 308, and 866n.

11. Humphrey, 1965, 105.

12. Croves, 1948, 13; Blum, 1970, 21.

13. Baumann, 62-67.

14. Essbach, in Beck et al., Das B. Traven-Buch, 1976, especially 376-383.

15. B. Traven, Death Ship (New York: Collier Books, 1977), 95. This is a reprint of the Knopf, 1934 edition.

16. Baumann, 96-99; Recknagel, 179.

17. University of California, Los Angeles, Special Collections, box 870, folder 12, contains notes by E. R. Hagemann for a comparison of various stages in Gales's descent into the hell of the Yorikke with Dante's descent into the inferno. Baumann goes extensively into the possibility that Traven had Dante in mind in this passage, but the meaning he finds in it is Stirner's.

18. The first edition of 1928 is quoted from here because it is the original and is partly falsified by subsequent editions, especially the extensively cut, edited, and bowdlerized third edition of 1951. The 1982 Büchergilde Gutenberg Werkausgabe edition is based on that of 1951 but comes with a separate volume of variants which makes it relatively easy to reconstruct the 1928 edition in reading. The passages quoted in this paper are not among those extensively changed in 1951.

19. B. Traven, Land des Frühlings, 1928, 214.

20. Ibid., 201.

21. This Old World Individualismus is also called Egoismus by Traven. Can that mean Stirner's egoism? Is that what

Traven is disavowing--or part of what he is disavowing--so
strongly here?
22. <u>Land</u>, 202.
23. Ibid., 206.
24. Ibid., 207.
25. Landauer, 1976, 79-87.

UNKNOWN LETTERS OF RET MARUT FROM 1914

H. D. Tschörtner

Several years ago, a note appeared in the GDR-literary journal <u>Sinn</u> <u>und</u> <u>Form</u> in which the Berlin publisher, Volk und Welt asked the owners of Traven letters to make them available for a planned supplementary volume to the edition of the works of this world-famous author. The city archive of Schwerin responded to this notice with the information that its branch in Frankenhorst, the Hans-Franck-Archiv, had letters written by Ret Marut to Hans Franck in 1914. The publisher ordered copies and received a collection of thirty-nine pages, including fourteen typed letters with handwritten additions, on paper with the letterhead Hochschule für Bühnenkunst Düsseldorf, as well as a handwritten postcard. It is exclusively business correspondence from between March 19 and June 28 of 1914, and it reflects an important stage in the development of actor and journalist Ret Marut.

As can be noted from Rolf Rechnagel's study, at the end of 1911 while in Danzig, Ret Marut had applied for a job at the theatre of Düsseldorf, which was under the direction of Louise Dumont and Gustav Lindemann. Dumont and Lindemann had founded the Düsseldorf Schauspielhaus in 1905 and helped it establish a solid reputation. In his application, Marut calls it the leading theatre of Germany. He explains that in spite of his youth, he is determined to play character roles and that he does not feel satisfied in Danzig, especially since serious theatre is almost completely overshadowed by opera, operetta, and farce. Of particular interest is the sentence, "My personal situation allows me to regard a so-called good salary as a by-product."

Thus, from May 1912 on, Marut lived in Düsseldorf. He received 170 marks per month and played only small roles, which he very often had to relinquish. Ephemeral activities included his work as a kind of secretary in the newly founded Hochschule für Bühnenkunst (Academy for Theatre Arts), as well as his journalistic work on the editorial staff of the magazine <u>Masken</u> (a predecessor of our program notes), which was published by the principals of the theatre. From July 1914 Marut was engaged at special performances of the Munich Künstlertheater, and he therefore moved to Munich. Later he also took part in productions in Solingen and Cologne, and, after the war broke out, at the front. In mid-1915, he was notified that due to economic reasons his contract could not be prolonged. On September 1, he was released from the ensemble of the Düsseldorf Schauspielhaus and thereafter never again worked in the theatre. Journalism and writing became the center of his life from then on.

The writer Hans Franck (1879-1964) was employed as director of the Hochschule für Bühnenkunst and as assistant to the director at the Düsseldorf theatre from 1914 to 1921. At the same time, he jointly edited the magazine Masken with Louise Dumont and Gustav Lindemann, who were also the publishers; it was now called Zeitschrift für Politik, Kunst und Kultur (Journal for Politics, Art and Culture). (It was continued by Gustav Landauer from 1918 to April of 1919.) The journal contains, however, no articles by Ret Marut, who had been writing articles and stories since 1910. During this time, Hans Franck published two historical dramas and his first novel. In 1921 he moved to a farm in Frankenhorst in Mecklenburg, where he died. His numerous novels and stories mostly deal with people in the history of civilization and are based on cultural-historical material. Examples include the novels Reise in die Ewigkeit ("Journey into Eternity," 1934, Hamann), Annette (1939, Annette von Droste-Hülshoff), Sebastian (1949, Sebastian Frank), and Marianne (1953, Goethe).

The object of the correspondence between Ret Marut and Hans Franck, who at the time lived in Dockenhude near Hamburg, was the compilation and printing of a prospectus for the Hochschule für Bühnenkunst. In the beginning, it dealt in great detail with teachers, their appointments, and their duties. The first two short letters of March 19 and March 24 are typewritten and signed "Mit vorzüglicher Hochachtung" (with best regards), but the third one, on April 24, concludes with a handwritten "Mit herzlichen Grüssen für Sie und Ihre werte Gemahlin" (with fond regards to you and your dear wife). Therefore, there must have been a personal contact in the meantime. Indeed, Marut was recognized by Hans Franck with ninety percent certainty on a 1939 passport photo which was sent to him by Rolf Recknagel.

The first letter, which contains only two formal sentences, accompanied contracts which were to be sent back immediately because they still needed to be sealed. Hans Franck had outlined his reply under Marut's text. It can be deduced from this text that the contracts concerned him: "I do not want to miss this chance to thank you sincerely for the extraordinary confidence placed in me with this contract." At the same time he must have made several requests since, under the instruction of director Lindemann, Marut informs him in his second letter "that it would be difficult to reach a mutually acceptable agreement through correspondence on the questions that have been raised." He mentions

that this should be discussed at a joint session of the
board of directors: "As soon as a date has been set, we
will notify you. However, Director Lindemann would like to
ask you today to participate in this meeting." Hans
Franck's reply was also noted in handwriting on this letter.
He wrote that he obviously would like to participate and
that he would reserve all his questions until that date.

The next letters are more detailed. The letter of April
24 begins with Ret Marut's apology: "Of course, I regret
that I was not able to talk to you on the Sunday in question, but I could hardly have been expected to be at home at
that time on such a beautiful day. Think of the few rehear-
sal-free days one has!" According to this note, Marut was
not free of theatrical duties even at the time of his secre-
tarial employment. He reports on the "pending employment
prospectus that would be available in a few days. I have
read the first correction. An apprentice had obviously been
involved since it needed much time-consuming work. After
consulting the board of directors, I made stylistic changes
in some sentences and hope to receive your absolution for
taking this liberty. As soon as the new proof is in my
hands, I will send it to you. I discussed the question of
the cover with Herr Ström on the day of your departure.
Herr Ström will use the stylized lion which is located on
the theatre as a heraldic figure."

Difficulties with a fencing teacher are described in detail. The retired captain under consideration had not yet
accepted the position. He also lived in Cologne rather than
in Düsseldorf, and rumor had it that he could not teach
fencing with a rapier. Therefore, Marut had turned to a
senior gymnastics teacher "who up till now has led the
fencing classes at the dramatic academy," in order to get
from him the official acceptance for the Hochschule job: "I
have written to him that the number of lessons will probably
be increased (so far he teaches one hour per week) and that
you personally will talk with him this summer regarding the
conditions of payment." One can see what type of details
Hans Franck had to deal with as the head of the Hochschule,
but it is also clear how much of this work Marut could do
for him. We will find yet another example of such negotiations described in detail in his letters.

Good news follows: "The secretary, Fräulein Maria Wilke,
has confirmed the contract which was settled with you and
will start work on May 1. (Thank God!) In any case, I will
inform you regularly about all negotiations with the full-
time professors so that you will stay informed. I have
already handed the list of the adjunct members to the print-

ing office; they have reached the number of forty-six so far."

It is safe to assume that the full-time professors were the permanently employed teachers, while the adjunct members gave lectures only occasionally. The surprisingly high number of adjunct members can be explained in this way. The founder of the Hochschule developed high ambitions in this respect, as can be seen by the individuals who were contacted. To illustrate this point, some of them are listed here. It was reported on April 29 that the contract of Julius Bab, whose visit was already mentioned in the second letter, had not yet been finalized, "because the session in which the confirmation was to take place has not yet occurred." Not until May 9 could Marut report that "the contract with Herr Bab has been confirmed and signed during the last session of the board of directors." On April 29, he wrote, "agreement has not yet been reached with Dr. von Lukácz"; on May 9, he reported, "Dr. Georg von Lukácz is no longer under consideration because he raised conditions which could not be accepted by the board of directors under any circumstances." On May 29, Marut wrote, "A good number of the adjunct teachers have again accepted. You will find a list of earlier acceptances on the proof. From the new members I would mention Eugen Wolf of Kiel, Richard Strauss and Professor Julius Dietz of Munich. Some of them have not agreed, some only under certain conditions. We are greatly interested in engaging these three gentlemen, as well as the brothers Thomas and Heinrich Mann. Therefore, I enclose responses of these gentlemen and ask you to use all the persuasive powers of your name to obtain their agreement." The letters also note that, on May 16, acceptances for the adjunct teachers included Oscar Sauer ("Paul Schlenther refused"); and, on May 26, new acceptances included Professor Dr. Hans Pfitzner (refusal: Knut Hamsun).

The extensive letter of April 29 contains many details about a large number of contracts. "I am asking you to write these contracts," Marut explains, "because I would like you to be informed about every detail of the rights and duties of faculty members in order that the contracts will be written as uniformly as possible." A Fräulein P. agrees to a salary of 2,000 marks but expresses special wishes with regard to meeting times for classes. Marut explains, "I am of the opinion that we cannot agree to her specific wishes concerning the scheduling of lessons at most convenient times for her. She must absolutely adjust herself in favor of the main subjects. If it seems possible at the time the schedule is set up, we can still take her wishes into ac-

count. We should, however, not bind our hands by writing
this into the contract."

Special problems occurred with a Herr Blensdorf. He generally agreed to the suggested contract; he "wants, however
to extend the part about private lessons in such a way that
he would be allowed to give private lessons to persons who
want to obtain a teaching certificate." Marut recommends
acceptance of this revision under the explicit condition
"that the number of private students should not be higher
than four persons per year." A financial problem is more
difficult. Herr Blensdorf teaches at a city school in
Düsseldorf, where he can expect a cut in salary if he gives
fewer lessons because of his duties at the Hochschule: "A
possible consequence might be that his income will be
lower....We should be responsible for the difference, because he does not want to be worse off. Maybe we can put
down in the contract a fixed amount which the difference
should not exceed. I leave it to you to decide how high
this amount should be." The negotiations on this point were
not finished on May 1: "Therefore, please leave a space in
the contract where we can fill in, in numbers and spelled
out, the amount we agree to pay." Not before May 16 did
Marut report that the clause regarding additional compensation "was taken care of in a way that our responsibilities
regarding special compensation should not exceed the amount
of 500 marks."

The fencing teacher was again the topic of a letter. One
of them cannot yet make up his mind, since he expects other
offers, while the present teacher is angry that a professional colleague will be hired to supervise him. He therefore threatens to quit the faculty at the end of the
semester. Marut expressed the opinion that fencing was not
in fact such an important subject for future actors that one
should make unnecessary and controversial changes. He
pleads that "the instruction in this subject be left" to the
old-established colleague--especially since one cannot know
whether the other man would finally agree, and "then the
whole issue would have to be raised all over again."

The end of the letter is especially interesting in view of
Marut's future literary production and the still controversial question of his national origin and education. Hans
Franck is informed about changes in the text of the prospectus; the proof is included. "The changes in the proof are
only of a stylistic nature," Marut writes, "but in order to
effect some formal changes to make it more beautiful, the
sentences have also been changed in substance. However, big
changes were not made. Rather, I altered only one sentence...without changing the meaning; I made the change only

because three equal sounding pronouns ('der') followed one another in close sequence which did not sound right according to my sensibilities." Ret Marut, therefore, did not lack self-confidence and candor in facing the author Hans Franck. On May 1, Franck already receives a reminder, "I would like to urge you to read the proof at once and to send it back to me at your earliest convenience." On Saturday or Monday another meeting was to take place during which the final proofs of the prospectus would be presented.

In the following letters more contract negotiations are mentioned. On May 9, for example, "Herr Emil Lind will receive a contract according to which [dergestalt] he will be paid a certain salary by the <u>Hochschule</u>, while the <u>Schauspielhaus</u> will pay him an honorarium for his work as an actor and director." The expression "dergestalt" (in such a way), which was often used by Heinrich von Kleist, is noteworthy; it also appears in another context. On May 16 it is mentioned that after talking personally with Director Lindemann, Dr. Paul Mahlberg agreed to join the full-time faculty and teach art history. "In place of Herr Dr. Georg von Lukácz," Marut reported, "we have managed to engage the lecturer in philosophy at the University of Bonn, Dr. Ohmann. I would like to ask you to negotiate with Dr. Ohmann by letter, that is, about salary, number of lessons, and about the subject matter of his lectures." Some personal suggestions follow which shed light on Marut's long experience in the theatre: "I would also like to suggest that we engage for our subject faculty Dr. Ludwig Seelig of Mannheim, who is general secretary of the <u>Cartell deutscher Bühnenangehöriger</u> (Union of German Theatre Personnel). Dr. Ludwig Seelig, well-known through his lectures and numerous articles, is to my knowledge the best expert on theatre law....Should one also ask the presidents of the <u>Schutzverband Deutscher Bühnenschriftsteller</u> (Society for German Script Writers) and the <u>Schutzverband Deutscher Schriftsteller</u> (Society of German Writers) to have these two associations as patrons so to speak--or do you think that wouldn't be necessary?...I would also like to suggest recruiting a special physician for throat and larynx diseases...in order to demonstrate with anatomical posters, or--since that is now possible--with a living subject, the anatomy and movements of the speech organs."

Marut regrets having to repeatedly bother Hans Franck during his vacation, but he states that it is unavoidable. In conclusion, he again talks about the prospectus: "As far as I have heard, the prospectus will have radical changes in respect to the execution of the print, and therefore, the completion will be delayed." Hans Franck must have reacted with concern, since Marut sent him a handwritten postcard on May 23 to the vacation village, Plau/Mecklenburg: "To put you at ease, I would like to inform you: The radical changes of the prospectus obviously do not concern your work--that is, the text--but refer to the print. We gave the prospectus to an art print shop which will give us the assurance that the type and the layout of the prospectus will be less boring than if done by the Düsseldorfer Zeitung. It will now be a little work of art."

The most important point in the letter of May 26 concerns a phrasing in the school regulations. Until that time the rule read, "The student has to attend classes for two years." The rationale for revising the rule makes sense: "We want to give those students who for certain reasons cannot obtain a diploma within two years because they develop slower than expected, and those students who want to achieve something special above and beyond the average, the opportunity to stay in school longer." A passage prohibiting students from taking lessons in other places was also deleted because it "could not be enforced by law and was practically worthless."

The next letter, of June 2, contains alarming news. A letter from the Department of Culture (Kultur-Ministerium) had arrived three weeks late due to delays in handling by the royal government in Düsseldorf (Düsseldorf was a Prussian center of administration). A copy of this letter was included with Marut's. Hans Franck is urged to react and outline a report which could be sent to the Department: "For your orientation, I'm sending you copies of all the material which we had sent at that time, (I myself was in charge) to the Department of Culture. They contain an extensive report about the necessary funds and their sources, and thus, I do not quite understand why the Department of Culture is asking for another report of the same nature." The officials inquired especially about the economic backing of the Hochschule; in addition, they asked for information about the general and technical educational background of students and about the course of studies for full-time students, including information about the distribution of subject matter over the years or semesters and weekly lessons, information about possible exams and certifications as well as about teachers. Apparently, they had only now learned about the project--maybe some concerns had been voiced about the reliability of the enterprise. Marut suggests including a galley proof of the prospectus and referring to it in the answer. "Concerning the educational background and teaching ability of the faculty," he notes, "you will have to write a report, since I am not informed

well enough about it....Maybe it will also be possible for
you to defuse the Department's concern about the designation
'Hochschule.'" It is obvious how important this official
government letter was, since it calls all preparations for
the Hochschule into question. Nevertheless, Marut was of
the opinion that the publication of the prospectus should
not be halted because of the official query, "because we
have to publish this prospectus by all means, since too much
time has passed already." Apparently it was possible to
clear up all of the Department's doubts with the answers
Franck provided. On June 9, Hans Franck was asked to "write
a resumé of himself which pays special attention to the
wishes of the department" and to "send this text immediately
to Herr Regierungsrat Kamlich, Düsseldorf, royal government." The author did this at once, producing the beginning
of a handwritten biography, which was probably jotted down
on the back of the page; it makes up page thirty-one of the
collection of letters.

On the same day, June 9, the Hochschule received the
important prospectus from the print shop. "Dear Herr
Franck," Marut writes, "I am very pleased to send you
finally! finally! the finished prospectus." Naturally, the
recipient inspected the prospectus very carefully. He
noticed a serious mistake which concerned him. Ret Marut's
last two personal letters, which refer to this mistake,
follow in their entirety:

Düsseldorf, June 24, 1914
Dear Herr Franck!

Today I received your letter which you had directed to
the board of directors. You object to not having been
named in the prospectus as the Director of the Hochschule.
In some respects, this complaint directly concerns me,
since the corrections, with a few exceptions, were done by
me. It goes without saying that this is not a case of
intent on our side or even more, on my side, since we have
no interest in not stating your position in the program;
on the contrary, we have a special interest in publishing
it for everyone's notice, for that can only be in the best
interest of the Hochschule. Yet, I must point out that
you really are to blame for not being mentioned as the
director. You read all the proofs, and therefore had the
opportunity to change anything and especially to mark
whatever you considered important or at least indispensable in regard to yourself. I really do not feel entitled
to write something about you personally which you might
not have liked. I have always been of the opinion that
your position as director of the Hochschule is expressed

in the signature of the prospectus, where you signed
first, followed by Herr Bab, for the faculty as a whole.
I thought that you wanted to express your leading position
through this signature and that you, for some reason,
avoided on purpose noting your position in another place.
In none of the proofs of the Düsseldorfer Zeitung, which
we have all here, can I find the remark you have mentioned. Naturally, it would have been included in the
prospectus. But on one of the individual pages which you
have sent us, I do, however, find the notation: "Direction, Hans Franck." You have sent these pages directly to
the print shop and I assume the printers disregarded the
note because the page was written on both sides. At that
time you also sent those pages without indicating where
the individual headlines should be placed. We had to
figure out ourselves where they would fit best.
    You also accuse us unjustly with regard to the inside
title page. The inside title page caused the delay of the
prospectus. We had asked for drawings from the gentleman
Ström, v. Putlitz and Paetz, as well as the emblem-plate
of the Schauspielhaus. But one design looked more common
and inartistic than the next--and we, therefore, became
convinced that the title page would look more distinguished if there were only writing on it. It is, as I
would like to add, rather difficult to meet someone's
expectations who is not present himself and who envisions
things differently and has envisioned them differently,
than can be described correctly in a letter.
    Since the prospectus will without a doubt soon be sold
out, you will have the opportunity to take all the new
concerns into consideration in a new edition.
    We have verbal and written evidence from, among others,
both our patrons, Excellence von Schorlemer-Lieser and
Excellence von Rheinbaben, that the prospectus, as it
looks today, pleases everybody who has gotten hold of it.
    The construction progresses steadily.
    With friendly regards,
                            Ret Marut

The last letter is dated Düsseldorf, June 28, 1914:

Dear Herr Franck,
    Thank you for your friendly letter which clarified the
misunderstandings--if they can be regarded as such. Unfortunately, I am not able to be present when you arrive,
since I have to move to Munich tomorrow; Herr Holl will
also depart tomorrow. I am very sorry that we have not
been able to talk to you, and we have asked Herrn Dr.

Bertholdt to take over our official duties. As far as
business matters are concerned, our secretary, Frau Wilke,
whom I have informed thoroughly, will explain all necessary details.

I understand that we will not see each other before
Fall. Until then, all instances of mutual misunderstand-
ings--which are nearly always part of a common endeavor--
will hopefully be resolved.

With best regards,

Ret Marut

The beginning of World War I prevented the realization of
the ambitious plan to establish a Hochschule für Bühnenkunst
in Düsseldorf. The name was used until 1932, however, for
the Theaterakademie, founded in 1904. Louise Dumont suddenly died in that year, while the Jewish director, Gustav
Lindemann, was removed from his position by the Nazis. The
theatre then came under the direction of their student,
Gustaf Gründgens. It is not known whether Hans Franck and
Ret Marut ever met again. In 1917 the first issue of
Marut's journal, Der Ziegelbrenner, appeared. He had undoubtedly gained much experience while working for the
Masken and through the work reflected in this correspondence. In it Marut is pictured as an ambitious and compe-
tent, energetic and self-confident editor. The letters are
factually oriented, sometimes wordy, and not always exactly
formulated. Stylistically, they range from bureaucratic
jargon to informal, lively, and even casual expressions. It
resembles Traven's correspondence with the Büchergilde
Gutenberg only in the repetitious use of substantives and
factual concepts. In any event these letters reflect a
short stage of Ret Marut's life and a little-known aspect of
the historical development of German theatre.

SECOND THOUGHTS ABOUT THE MYSTERY OF B. TRAVEN

Judy Stone

When I interviewed "Hal Croves" in the 1960s, he gave clear indications that he and Traven were distinct people. He told me, "Personally, I cannot accept to be called Mr. Traven. I have no right to accept that name." On the other hand, he said, "It is impossible for me to separate from B.T. I am part of it. Even to copyright and translation. I took the responsibility." Once, looking lovingly at his wife, he told me how she had saved him from death. He carefully added, "I am talking about myself, not B.T." He was even more forceful when he was tracked down by Luis Spota in 1948. Spota reported in <u>Mañana</u> that Croves declared, "You are a son of a bitch. I am not B. Traven."

The problem seemed to be solved by the Wyatt documentary, but in 1980 there began a series of events that has led me to suspect that Croves may indeed have been telling the truth. We know that "Traven" left a widow--Rosa Elena Luján--but is the shade of "Traven" inhabiting the house of another woman? To be exact, was there another Traven persona who can now be identified? The "other widow" in question is Mrs. Ursula Beckmann de Bourba of Cologne, married to Wladislav de Bourba on October 30, 1941, and widowed on August 12, 1942, when the German ship (Hamburg Freight Line Bolton) on which her husband was working as a second machinist sank off the coast of Norway. Mrs. Beckmann's story is as complex as anything else in the Traven conundrum. She has almost no evidence to back up her claim and yet when I met her in Cologne, I felt that she had a directness and honesty that merited further research into her story--insofar as it is possible. Investigating her theory is a horrendous, if not hopeless, task. What I am presenting are not answers but another variant of the question that has been asked over and over again: Were the novels the work of more than one man? Were Ret Marut and de Bourba collaborators?

On January 1, 1980, I received a letter from Ursula Beckmann de Bourba, the first of many convoluted and confusing accounts about her husband. In summary, she wrote that Vladislav Bourba (the spellings were sometimes slightly different) was a Russian and the son of Irena Bogdanov (or Bogdanoff), an artist and a lady-in-waiting to the last czarina. Irena Bogdanov was married to Dr. Simon de Bourba of St. Petersburg. My correspondent had met Bourba in Stettin in 1940, when she was twenty-three and the unmarried

66

mother of a one-year-old boy. Although Bourba had the
papers of a stateless person, issued in Sweden, he was
working on a German ship and kept an apartment in Norrkö-
ping, Sweden—a fact confirmed by the Swedish Information
Service. He told her he had lived in Mexico for ten years
from 1921 to 1931, when he became involved in a Calles-
Cárdenas uprising and had to leave for political reasons.
He returned to the Soviet Union and then lived in Sweden for
several years while going to sea. He said he had written
eight books which were famous and that he was listed in the
Brockhaus Encyclopedia under his pen name. He wouldn't tell
her the titles or his nom de plume, since (in 1940-42) he
could be endangering her. She didn't really believe him and
was disturbed that a husband would have secrets from his
wife. He told her that his "best friend" in Mexico took
care of his business arrangements, kept meticulous accounts,
and was also safeguarding his violin, piano, and Remington
typewriter. During the Munich revolution, this friend had
saved his life, and they met in Mexico years later. He
described the friend as a "self-taught genius."

De Bourba had gone to Munich by a very circuitous route.
He had been a student at a boarding school in Dorpat, Lat-
via, which was attended by children of Baltic nobility.
While there, he started to study English at the age of six
and eventually spoke English, French, Russian, Latvian,
German, Swedish, and Danish. After his graduation, he returned to St. Petersburg, but he was arrested in 1917 and
imprisoned by the Bolsheviks. When the warden found out he
was multilingual, he sent him to Schlüsselburg on the Baltic, where he met many people from the "high nobility." It
gave him an insight into what that society had been like,
and he was shocked at the evidences of their corruption.
One morning, he was summoned by the commissars and told he
would be pardoned and sent back to Petersburg. Because of
his knowledge of languages, he was given a special assignment training with some other people and then received an
order to leave. He was told to take the route via Siberia
to Vladivostok and was given papers sewn into his coat. His
photograph was affixed to a passport with the false name of
Bogdanov, and the age listed was ten years older than de
Bourba's. When he protested the falsity of the name and
age, he was told not to worry because Bogdanov was dead. De
Bourba was "terrified." He fled with other banished people
—peasants, soldiers, and civilians—further and further to
the east and finally arrived in Vladivostok.

There he managed to get on a ship as a coal shoveler. The
ship sailed to India, and from there a Swedish ship took him
to Europe. When he arrived in Berlin, there was chaos and

67

he was ordered (by whom, she doesn't say) to Munich. He told his wife he worked as a journalist for Ziegelbrenner, but he never mentioned the name of Ret Marut. He was known to friends in Munich as Wollek. During the fighting and occupation of Munich by the Freikorps following the Räterepublik in April/May 1919, he was slashed in front of a restaurant. The scar from the bayonet wound could still be seen in 1940 on his neck, and there was a scar on his thigh.

When Ursula asked the name of the friend in Mexico, he said he was bound by a promise not to reveal it. For this reason, she said, "I never heard the name of the friend in Mexico," although a manuscript she wrote refers to him as Feige. De Bourba stayed in the Russian embassy in Berlin for a long time while writing for socialist papers such as Vorwärts. His only real friend then was an artist from Cologne, Wilhelm Seiwert, for whom he helped to arrange an exhibit. Their political opinions coincided completely.

De Bourba obtained another passport in Berlin and disappeared one day. He had lived for twenty years with that passport and traveled around the world. For three years he was on an expedition in Mexico, but most of the time he spent aboard ships. The sea had a great fascination for him--he felt "free as a bird." On that first trip to Mexico in 1921, he was shipwrecked in the Bay of Biscay and was eventually rescued by Spanish fishermen. He took a Spanish ship to Mexico. When Ursula asked him the most important event in his life, he described the loss of his friend, a Polish shipmate, when their ship sank. The two men were on a raft, but his friend was swamped by waves and de Bourba couldn't save him. He told his wife that another man who had shipped out with him was a "man of the world" who also lived in Mexico from 1921 to 1925, and he had used some of that man's stories in his books. She said he told her that he had sent his last manuscript overseas via Sweden in 1941.

De Bourba didn't see the artist Seiwert again until 1931, the year Seiwert died. Later he told Ursula that he had sent Seiwert's drawings to Sweden and Mexico for safety in 1940. He said if she ever saw Seiwert's paintings again in connection with the word Traven, she should reveal de Bourba's true biography to the world. When she asked what Traven was, however, he said only that it was a word for a trade union organization with many Poles. He refused to write the name down for her. When she asked if it was his pseudonym, he replied, "It's a secret. I can't tell you." He told her he had gone to Spain as a reporter during the Civil War and had lost the three middle fingers of his left hand in a battle at Santander, Spain. He was fitted with false fingers in Paris. He said that he had broken with the

68

Mexican woman he lived with off and on for ten years when she laughed at his wound. After Spain, he went back to the Soviet Union to get his correct papers and documents because he had used false ones for twenty years. Then he returned to Sweden in 1939. The second time Ursula met him, he accidentally pulled two passports out of his trousers. She picked up one with the name Torsvan and saw the birthdate of May 3, which struck her as funny because her own birthday was May 3, 1917. De Bourba said it wasn't his passport; it belonged to his friend in Mexico. She thought she saw a resemblance between de Bourba and the photograph and asked if it was a photograph of him when he was younger. When they were married, he said he had traveled around the world with that passport for twenty years and that he was going to send it to his friend in Mexico to care for it. When she visited his quarters aboard ship, she saw a diary-like book written in English which seemed to be about a general from the jungle. He quickly put it away when he saw her looking at it. He told her he wrote all his manuscripts in English and later translated them into German.

Ursula said she was skeptical about all these stories and didn't really believe he was a world-famous author.

One day, he took her with him to the former Russian embassy, then occupied by Goebbel's ministry of propaganda, saying he wanted to apply for a job as a translator. After leaving her alone for a long time, he appeared to say it had gone well. He had to write a page in Russian, translate it into English and then into German. Later he was told to reverse the procedure. He said there were very few people in the world who could do that and he had the impression that he passed the examination. She was very glad when they finally left that "eerie" building which he seemed to know very well. On that last holiday in Berlin, he told her that when he wrote, he thought in Russian, wrote in English, and then translated it into German. He was worried about her and thought they should visit a lawyer in case something happened to him and she would be without support, but he didn't trust the German lawyers because they were all Nazis. They decided to go on their next holiday to Breslau, where an uncle of his had a law office. "Volodya" gave her a photograph of himself and said: "Treat this well and never lose it. It is extremely important for you and for the child because there is nobody in the world who has a photo of me that size. I have always tried to avoid being photographed." The photograph, taken in 1941, showed him in Bergen in front of the monument of Wilhelm II. She asked why he had chosen that site since he didn't think much of the Kaiser, but he said there were particular reasons for this. He had made a number of copies and wanted to send one to a friend in the Büchergilde Gutenberg and one to his bank, because nobody there had seen him for years. He put the date of March 26 on the photo so she would remember it as the date he sent his papers to Mexico. He said it would be historic one day.

He told Ursula he had written to his friend in Mexico about their marriage. He didn't want to accept her suggestion that he become a German and told her, "You have no idea how hated the Germans are all over the world." She gave up her German citizenship so they could go abroad together, and she didn't get it back until she married Beckmann. De Bourba adopted her son and wanted to make sure that she would never tell him that de Bourba was not his real father. When she protested that she would have to tell the boy when he was older, de Bourba was against it because he said he had seen too much unhappiness arising from situations like that. He talked about traveling to Sweden when the war was over and going on to Mexico. When she asked if that wouldn't cost too much money, he said he kept a bank account abroad. He told her he wanted to collect his paintings, his manuscripts, and his Remington typewriter in Mexico and that he would like them to live in Yucatan. He had burned things with the name Bogdanov, the name on his false passport from Russia to Munich.

Once, when she was packing his things, she found a picture card written in Spanish and signed "Esperanza." The photograph showed many fountains. She asked if it was important to him; he said that it was. When she questioned him further, he said it showed Geneva and Esperanza was a "very good comrade of mine."

She had the feeling that he was a man who acted as if he were being watched. She knew he was a follower of Trotsky and had allegedly helped him at one point, although no one connected with the Trotsky archives had ever heard of anyone named de Bourba or Bogdanov as being involved in helping Trotsky leave Europe or go to Mexico.

After her husband's ship sank, Ursula was visited two or three times by Gestapo agents who asked questions about de Bourba and Ret Marut. The first visit took place before she knew her husband had died. She had never heard the name Marut before that time. Eventually, she, her mother, and child left Stettin and moved to the Polish countryside because they were afraid of more visits from the Gestapo. While her mother cared for the child Ursula worked as a secretary at a pig farm where seventy-five prisoners of war were detained. On March 3, 1945, she left because the Russians were advancing and she was afraid of them. Helping

three hundred people to escape in twenty-five wagons driven
by Russian and Polish prisons, she rode six hundred miles on
horseback until they got to Schleswig-Holstein.

In September 1945, Ursula met a sailor, Marcus Beckmann,
and they were married one year later. In 1956 Beckmann's
brother read The Death Ship, a title she didn't know. He
passed it on to her son, Peter de Bourba, who thought it
sounded like the story his mother had told him about de
Bourba. Finally, she read it and believed that her husband
had written the book. A relative disagreed, saying that the
author was living in Mexico. Thinking that perhaps the news
of de Bourba's death was inaccurate, she sent a letter to B.
Traven in Tamaulipas. She wrote, "My husband is dead," and
informed Traven that de Bourba had sent paintings by Seiwert
to his friend in Mexico. She gave him the date of her
husband's death and asked, since de Bourba had told her not
to forget the word Traven, if he knew her husband. Not
receiving a reply, she thought for a while that perhaps it
was de Bourba who was in Mexico, afraid to return to Germany
because he was Russian and had worked in the underground.
In 1978 she saw an article on Seiwert's paintings and Rosa
Elena Luján's trip to Cologne. She went to a lawyer who was
apparently also Luján's attorney in Cologne. Another attorney suggested she contact all Traven researchers with her
story.

When she read stories about Traven being the illegitimate
son of the Kaiser, she wrote to the Hohenzollern archive to
find out if the Kaiser had visited the czar and czarina in
Russia in 1899, about the time her husband may have been
conceived. The archivist replied that the Kaiser had not
visited Russia, but he had been on a brief vacation with the
czar and czarina in Potsdam on November 8 or 9, 1899. Another member of the Russian party was the foreign minister,
Mikhail Nikolaievich Count Murav'ev.

All of the above information came from Mrs. Beckmann,
either in correspondence or during my interview with her.
My attempts to obtain independent verification of some of
the facts about her husband have so far been unsuccessful,
but I am left with the feeling that her story should be
researched. The only thing that seems incontrovertible to
me now in the assumptions I made in my book, The Mystery of
B. Traven, is this sentence: "It is a story so complicated
by life and so obscured by design that it would take an
international team of detectives to unravel all the
threads..." And I'm not sure such a team would be able to
come up with a definitive solution to the mystery. If Mrs.
Beckmann's story is true, did Croves know that de Bourba was
dead? Did he suddenly want to protect his own vested inter-

ests in his old age? Did he feel a sense of shame about a
guilty secret? Is that why he repeatedly denied he was
B.T.? All the "Traven hunters" have wondered why the man in
Mexico persisted in denying that he was Traven. Is it
possible that he was telling the truth all along?

B. TRAVEN'S ANARCHISTIC TREASURES
Reflections on The Treasure of the Sierra Madre

Charles H. Miller

I

Along with millions of readers scattered over several nations, I regard B. Traven as a master storyteller apart from his German, Mexican, and American ties, for he belongs to international literature as surely as his books were saluted by such figures as Albert Einstein, Winston Churchill, and Halldor Laxness. Yet, such luminaries had little or no influence on Traven's legions of readers in the recent past, and Traven still lacks critical recognition because he lacks a ranking critical biographer--a Richard Ellman, a Leon Edel, a Hugh Kenner, or even a Swanburg. He also lacks uniform and authoritative translations from his original German texts.

In the 1930s Traven rendered some of his novels into English, producing powerful but amateurish versions such as the Treasure published by Knopf in 1934, a trove of linguistic anarchy despite the earnest editing of Bernard Smith. Before we examine its linguistic nuggets, let us look at the starting point of the Treasure hunt, Mexico's Tampico port, Traven's first New World address. He arrived in vibrant Tampico as a survivor of the fallen Bavarian Council Republic in which he figured, and he found old Tampico refreshingly exotic, its tropical hinterland visible from downtown. But his man-eating lions and tigers, hitherto harmless in Latin American literature, were projections of his Old World political fears. Yet immigrant Traven, an Old World pawn, went fearlessly into the Mexican socialist republic which had defeated a repressive government, just after Traven's short-lived Bavarian Republic had been routed by elitist repressors.

We can imagine the exuberance of a veteran immigrant, an underground writer, finding himself above ground in a vibrant open society, on his own at last, far from his petty enemies, the police and bureaucrats of weary old nations. Writers should write. And Traven did. Within months he had workable drafts of The Death Ship, Der Wobbly, and many stories, essays, and sketches. Most writers have periods of extraordinary creativity, and Traven was primed for such a period. He expended immeasurable ergs of creative energy in a dozen years.

Hal Croves-Traven told me, early in the 1960s--I didn't ask but he told me, as we stood among the piles of Traven titles I was cataloguing in his library at Rio Mississippi-- "Ya-aas, Trr-aav-an r-wrote his bouwks in a grr-r-ade hur-rry, andt it's too ba-aa-ad thadt he did!" I'm not con-vinced that it is "too ba-aa-ad," for in his exuberant haste, Traven left inadvertent clues to his own life, his own creative raw materials.

Slang is an attractive clue. Early in Treasure, the narrator sights the masts of ships in Tampico port, and to him a ship is a "bucket" as it was to Gales in The Death Ship; workers "spit on their hands" as they take up tools, as workers of my Midwest boyhood did. To Dobbs, Curtin, and Howard, a man may be, variously, a "mug," a "sap," a "bone-head," a "hick," and in Howard's words, too often a "baby." Traven uses "sob-sisters" in the 1920s sense but when he attempts "jail bird" it flips off into "pen-bird," (a pun perhaps?). The semantically besieged author refers to a man who has "broken Leavenworth," a feat that must astonish convicts who merely try to "break out" of Leavenworth. He uses the Mexican "cabo" correctly in Treasure, long before "cabos" or bosses became familiar figures in his Jungle novels. But he uses "chingando," whereas I hear "chin-gado"--an epithet extolled by Octavio Paz--in all parts of Mexico. Traven uses "smackers" for dollars, as another international author, W. H. Auden, did. At one point, Traven uses "bump off" a man in correct gangsterese, but later it is "bump him," as in a third-class bus. Traven uses the venerable "squabash" correctly, asking not to be "squashed and bashed" with picky criticism, so we won't.

A semantic sleuth will not be tempted to attribute such lapses to a "style editor" of Bernard Smith's ability; they are the lapses of a linguistic anarchist who stormed low points of English language from international sailors and workers whose own usage was often erroneous.

In the 1960s, I heard Hal Croves use slang which I'd heard in the 1920s in my native Midwest; this strengthened my belief that Traven had lived in the Midwest, but I'd forgot-ten what a young Herman Melville noted: that our nation was but a nursery for sailors. In Melville's experience, and certainly in Traven's, Midwest slang and half-illiterate terms were uttered in the fo'c'sle of tramp steamers and on the greasy docks of world ports. Some of Hal Croves's slang of the 1960s appears in Treasure, but some of it could have been inserted into the ever-revised English text after the

1920s publication of the German text and before the 1930s Knopf "American" edition. In any case, I'm glad to bequeath this and similar details to literary sleuths who should have a mastery of German, English, and Spanish--at least--to do justice to a job on which I merely reflect.

Certainly slang and humor have a place in serious anarchist writing; slang and humor appear too infrequently in anarchist and philosophical writing. They are semantic weapons, civilizing weapons, bare-handed weapons, which Traven uses to good advantage in Treasure and elsewhere, just as Shakespeare used puns and pit humor to hook his live audience. Some of Traven's humor is heavy-handed workers' humor, but some of his jokes are grand and terrible; for instance doña Catalina achieves her goal over terrible odds, but disappears, dissolves, beyond the portals of authority, a "foolish woman who thought that nobility stands for honesty." The grandest joke of all is down-to-earth and so cruel that young Curtin is too innocent to recognize it as a joke, even while Howard is bellowing in anarchic glee because the invisible wind (with some poetic license) carries the "guilty" treasure back into its natural habitat in the high Sierras.

There is anarchic exaggeration in Treasure, if less apparent in later novels and stories, evidence of Traven's early efforts at literary organization. For instance, when the three prospectors have been together only a month or so, "Each had heard the same jokes and stories 300 times." Now, any survivor of a family or other social group will know that 300 times is about 290 times too many to repeat a joke or even a juicy story. But the speed-writing Traven is already loading it on: "Each, after a few weeks, knew the whole life-story" of the others. Later Traven contradicts this, with conjectures about Dobbs's possible prison record.

Traven exaggerates seriously when he writes, "Any decent woman would have preferred to drown herself or cut her veins rather than keep company with these men." What would liberated women, or Latin American women guerrillas, say to that exaggeration--which he uses to convey the toughness of the three partners? In praise of the Indians as a "healthy lot," Traven opines that they will "reach ages which would make old man Methuselah a poor runner-up." This crowns the exuberant exaggeration of Baron Münchhausen-Traven--pot-shot exaggerations which contribute to the anarchistic aspects of Treasure as conceived by an author who was so completely outside of government, society, family, and literary organization.

Women have little part in Treasure, except to wait for their men, as prospector Tilton's woman does, and as Curt intimates that his woman may be waiting; or they are victims of a train robbery and massacre, and martyrs to mammon, as doña Catalina is. Traven pays tribute to women in other books, especially in Bridge, in The White Rose, and in the Jungle novels; but women have little part in Treasure because gold prospecting was not women's work at that point in history, nor did women have much part in the construction of the Panama Canal, or in the Alaskan gold rush.

Traven notes women's place in that ordinary depot of anarchism, the Oso Negro Hotel. No antirape, no antidiscrimination law was in effect there, but a higher law: The women were safe under "the unwritten law of the hotel," its benevolent anarchism. The Oso Negro is Traven's New World home-office of anarchism, and there he scatters clues to his Old World, to death ships, lost souls, adventurers, wanderers, and fugitives like himself. Its murky baggage room was "glutted" with items left by men who "were at the other end of the world," men who "might be dead or working deep in the jungles." Letters might moulder away in the Oso Negro, waiting for men who "had no time to think that the letter-writers back home might be crying their eyes out over a lost sheep." We recognize this lost sheep, this "gob" Traven on the lam, this partial Pip-pip, we who have been lost sheep in a foreign land, hiding from home, from indifferent family, friends, and the past. And hiding from a homeland of which we might be, in some respects, ashamed.

Among hundreds of unclaimed or forgotten items on Oso Negro shelves is a theodolite, a surveying instrument of the type used by a young Thoreau in Massachusetts. Traven mentions the theodolite, for perhaps he used one on his expeditions in the southeast Mexican jungles; certainly he had seen such space-factoring instruments used in his travels and voyages, and perhaps he had sprung a theodolite from a Tampico pawn shop like the Oso Negro. The theodolite is a real artifact from his past, as is the wheezing boiler he describes in Bridge, a boiler which he notes might well have been used in a death ship.

Metal artifacts aside, there are more elusive artifacts of word usage; a great issue for the reborn Traven of Tampico. From there he wrote to Alfred Knopf, almost half a century ago, about his own ungrammatical Death Ship language:

...[the bad language] is at the same moment the greatest virtue of the book...the American sailor peeps out of every page....No other sailor in the whole world would have written this book in the way it is here presented.

Continuing his pitch for individuality, he confesses:

So there are 100,000 phrases, sentences and lines wrong or misplaced or ready to kill the book... [but] in no other edition or version of the Deathship [sic] you will find so distinctly visible the embryo and protoplasm of all my works as in [this] version which I recommend. Take it. Take it with all its faults and shortcomings...because this is the book, there is no other like this.

Very truly yours
B. Traven

All typed. Name, too. Knopf did take it. Luckily for literary history, Knopf took the letter and spirit of a philosophical anarchist; now literary detectives can benefit from the "American version" of The Death Ship, which with its "100,000" errors is a splendidly disorganized document, an ungoverned handbook of anarchy, a cargo of real and imagined life.

Master storytellers are masters of digression, and Traven's digressions are satisfyingly anarchic, outside the loose organization of his narrative thread; but like a great weaver of tales, Traven loops his digressions into the warp and woof of his powerful Treasure story. The great train robbery and massacre may seem to be a wild digression, but it is a weapon Traven uses against the Roman Catholic Church, which he opposes as did his metamorphic Ret Marut. The Cristeros who rob and murder a trainload of Mexican Catholic citizens are themselves Christian crazies related to such fringe groups as Jim Jones's branch of the People's Church. In his New World, Traven was shocked to learn the record of the Catholic Church in colonial Mexico. The Cristeros are a good example of the complexity of the 1920s; they were as devoutly murderous as any religious sect at any time in history, be it in Iran or in imperial Rome. The Cristeros murdered Catholics who were supportive of Mexico's new socialist government, which restricted the rampant Catholic Church. By depicting the terrorist Cristeros so casually but powerfully, Traven was getting back at the Catholic Church that enslaved millions of native human beings while it prevented social progress and enriched its own "Roman" organization. The thousands of churches and hundreds of cathedrals still standing in Mexico are monuments to the power of the Church.

Traven's Mexican Indians make their fictional debut in Treasure, and the Indian who accompanies Dobbs and Curtin through the Tampico hinterland is a Traven version of Melville's Queequeg--a solitary Indian worker who forces himself onto the two Americans, squeezing himself between their sleeping forms for protection from nonexistent lions and

tigers. This nameless Indian testifies to Traven's Tamaulipas inexperience, but soon he comes to know the Indians, to
honor and love them. Anarchists themselves, they become his
true treasure. No other Latin American writer has done for
Indians what Traven did in a dozen years of passionate
writing.

Traven glorifies his Indians; some of my Mexican colleagues have growled, "Para Traaaaaven, todos Indios son
angelos!" (All Traven's Indians are angels!). There is some
truth to this statement, but Traven saw the Indians as more
sinned against than sinning. He longed for their disappear-
ing utopias, one of which is glimpsed in the closing pages
of Treasure, and within months he was obsessed with the
Totonacan utopia Rosa Blanca. Within another decade he
completed his Mexican epic of the Jungle novels, and of
course he was historically correct in his championing of the
Indian cause--basically correct in his praise of Totonacan
benevolent anarchism as opposed to the toxic social disorder
of Pozo Rico, to the political oppression of Mexican Indians, whose will-o'-the-wisp freedom is akin to that of the
freed Blacks in the post-Civil War United States.

Traven admires one Indian anarchist, chieftain Aguila
Bravo, who turns over his gold mine to the avaricious
Spanish-American don Manuel, a healer who is at the opposite
pole from Howard the healer. In Treasure Aguila Bravo tells
the gold-greedy don Manuel:

> I do not need gold nor do I want silver. I have plenty
> to eat always. I have a young and beautiful wife, whom I
> love dearly and who loves and honors me. I also have a
> strong and healthy boy, who now, thanks to your skill, can
> see and so is perfect in every way. I have my acres and
> fields, and I have my fine cattle. I am chief and judge,
> and I may say I am a true and honest friend of my tribe,
> which respects me and obeys my orders, which they know are
> for their own good. The soil bears rich fruit every year.
> The cattle bring forth year in, year out. I have a golden
> sun above me, at night a silver moon, and there is peace
> in the land. So what could gold mean to me?...You whites
> spoil the beauty of life for the possession of gold. Gold
> is pretty and it stays pretty, and therefore we use it to
> adorn our gods and our women...it is a feast for our
> eyes...but we were always masters of gold, never its
> slaves.

This biblical speech, like all Traven's early digressions,
is superior in grammar and rhetoric to the langauge of the
main story, and like the other digressions, it can stand

alone. Perhaps it and other digressions did stand alone.
All of them could have been written earlier, as essays, in
less hurried days than those in which the young Traven was
fictionalizing at top speed; they may well have been written
with separate publication in mind. But they shine, prime
gems for reader and literary sleuth alike.

Aguila Bravo's biblical speech is a long, idealized leap
forward from Gales's' soliloquy in The Death Ship, which
concludes:

> Where is the true country of men? There where nobody
> molests me, where nobody wants to know who I am, where I
> came from, where I wish to go, what my opinion is about
> war, about the Episcopalians, and about the communists,
> where I am free to do and to believe what I damn please as
> long as I do not harm the life, the health, and honestly
> earned property of anybody else. There and there alone is
> the country of men that is worth living for, and sweet to
> die for.

This, from the lonely hold of a death ship, to the utopian
pronouncements of Aguila Bravo, is full-circle benevolent
anarchism, akin to Thoreau. In the New World, Traven refined his Old World anarchism and found his ideal, however
remote and removed, in the tribal anarchism of Aguila Bravo,
that "brave eagle" south of the huge northern "bald eagle."

II

Here I wish to relate some of my experiences with the Hal-
Croves-B. Traven I knew from 1961 to 1969, in the hope of
illuminating Traven's anarchic attitude toward critics and
reporters.

It happened that I met Hal Croves-Traven because I wasn't
a reporter, because I wrote about his books rather than his
person. In 1951 I rested on a cot in front of the large
fireplace I'd built with my own hands in my house in the
Green Mountain National Forest. A blizzard raged beyond my
solar windows. But I had in hand a recent paperback edition
of Treasure. By 3 a.m. I read the last words; I put the
book down and thought, "What a wonderful story!" It didn't
occur to me to think about the author, or Mexican history,
or anarchism: I came to Traven as a reader.

A few years later in Mexico, I read many novels in Spanish
and asked my Mexican friends, "But where are the real novels
of Mexico--those dealing with campesinos, workers, mountain
people, natives, Indians?" And they said, "Pues, there is
only one person writing that kind of novel--a gringo named

B. Traven." They handed me <u>Bridge</u> in Spanish. I knew I was
with a great storyteller. Rapidly I read all the other
books available in Spanish. Months later in other countries
I reread them in English and was seized with the desire to
"bring B. Traven home" to the United States, for his books
were out of print.

I wrote apprentice essays on his books, and some of them
were published. In the fall of 1961 I was in Mexico City
again and took some of my essays to Traven's publisher, then
on Schiller not far from Fuente Diana. He was friendly and
polite and suggested that I take the essays to Luján and
Traven's home nearby. You can imagine what this did to me!
But, anarchist that I was, and prepared to jump into any
joke connected with B. Traven, I walked over to Avenida
Durango, where I rang R. E. Luján's doorbell and was admitted by her teenaged daughters--and given refreshment by
Señora Luján, who said, "We are always ready to talk about
the books of B. Traven." Some days later after several
return visits, I was sitting alone in Luján's dining alcove
drinking Dos Equis when a short, ruddy, spare, and spry man
with thick glasses and a hearing aid came and sat opposite
me, addressed his Dos Equis and me, and began to talk about
my essays, which I had given to Rosa Elena Luján. Soon, Hal
and I began to talk about anything--horses, schools, mountain climate, Danish speech therapy (concerning my own spor-
adic speech difficulty). There was no difficulty in talking
with Hal; he was vital, he had presence and dignity, and he
was oddly positive, even while talking about troublesome
subjects. For instance, he asked me if I'd seen the film
<u>Rosa Blanca</u>. No? <u>Pues</u>, he'd arrange for me to see it. I
was then engaged in stylizing the English text of <u>Rosa
Blanca</u> for United Kingdom publishers. But the film--
"Chaaarles, I dondt blame the Mexican government for banning
the film! Anyone who sees it will be angry!" This in
brief--for he talked about many aspects of that film.

Horses. I'd ridden my first horse alone in my sixth
year. I'd trained them. We spoke of the American way of
"breaking" horses, and Hal spoke of the better way, the
Mexican way of "gentling" them, a significant difference.
We talked about Mexican agriculture, and whether or not
Mexican industrial workers would ever get organized. These
were the proletarian topics we addressed.

At that time I wore ankle-high work shoes, carefully
polished for preservation as well as appearance, and Hal
asked me, casually, "How much did those brogues set you
back?" I hadn't heard the noun "brogues" used for a few
decades; I had heard brogans, but my dictionary later confirmed the fact that "brogues" was correct Scottish. "They

set me back two hundred pesitos," I said, and Hal intimated
that I might bring him "brogues" like mine the next time I
crossed the border. But I didn't because I never had two
hundred extra "pesitos," about sixteen dollars at that time.
When I crossed the border I felt lucky to get back into
Mexico in my own anarchist "brogans."

In the 1960s I gladly resisted pressures from editors and
advisors to write about the author. I gave all that I wrote
to Señora Rosa Elena to read to Hal. She often quoted his
reactions. I knew without asking that I shouldn't question
Hal, but having done research on the Wobblies, and having
copyedited the "Wobbly" Cotton Pickers, I wrote an essay on
Traven's "Wobbly" principles and gave it to Rosa Elena.
Soon I said to Hal, "The Wobblies must have been an interesting force in old Tampico!" He looked at me, but said
nothing. As soon as my article on Traven's Wobbly principles appeared in the Michigan Quarterly Review and rested
in the library at Rio Mississippi #61, Hal said to me,
"Traaa-ven was never a Woobbbly, but some of his friends
were, and he visited them; he admired them." So I said in
my mild, benevolent way, "Why didn't you tell me this when I
gave you my manuscript? The essay would have benefited!"
And he shrugged, "Any writer may write what he pleases about
Traaaaven and his books--I won't interfere." This was puck-
ish enough to inform me of the fun Traven had with his
followers.

My personal journals of the 1960s contain many golden
anecdotes on the Hal Croves-Traven I knew and admired; there
are a few glum anecdotes, and not a few of my own shortcomings, my own anarchic nature. But there was a final
golden one: I went from my adopted Mexico in 1967 to a
grant-residence at The Newberry Library in Chicago, where I
wrote to Hal and Rosa Elena about Lynn Perry, an exchange
student with whom I shared my life. In early August 1967, I
was back in Mexico and received a wire from Lynn that she
was flying to San Antonio and would I go to meet her there?
The wire was a day or so late. I just had time to get to
Rio Mississippi #61, where my friend Rosa Elena ordered me
to use her telephone to page Lynn at the San Antonio air-
port. I did this, and to make a long story short, Lynn
arrived in Mexico, where Rosa Elena and Hal made her feel at
home.

At that time, in the 1960s, I was devoted to proletarian
literature as an antidote to academic literature, and I
wrote a blue-collar novel about bricklayers, of whom I was
one for twelve years; but I soon began to write about
"brickburner" B. Traven, the impassioned outsider who write
from deep inside Mexico. Readers worldwide have embraced

his Mexican books, and it is now past time for a qualified critical biographer to pinpoint Traven's novels and stories on the international shelf, south of Jack London and Dreiser, to the left of Hamsun, but level with Laxness, where they belong.

BEING AS ADVENTURE
The Death Ship and The Treasure of the Sierra Madre
as Novels of Adventure

Manfred Keune

B. Traven's Death Ship and Treasure of the Sierra Madre are
generally understood and classsified as adventure novels.
Their adaptation into films, their popularity as novels and
the recognizable criteria of the traditional adventure novel
can easily qualify them for this category. Yet, for some
readers, these two novels leave an ambivalent aftertaste
because of our preconceived notions of what an adventure
novel should be, and Traven's unique depiction of adventure
as a situation of dilemma and even paradox, which portrays
his heroes in a closed circle of existence. Despair, longing, and resignation seem to overpower the spirit of resistance or revolution in his heroes of adventure and project
them beyond traditional definitions and criteria into a kind
of modernity which can be considered Traven's contribution
to the gehre. In order to clarify these statements, the
following investigation is offered. It is my contention
throughout that genre and thematic assignment of these
novels was intentional, that Traven consciously set out to
structure his "material" as a new novel of adventure, and
that he succeeded in writing a serious literature of adventure.

                              I

Certainly, Traven's early novels fulfill the traditional
criteria for the adventure novel. These early stories remain popular because they satisfy the less demanding literary appetites of the ordinary reader. The hero encounters
unforeseen events and performs exploits remote from a tran-
quil domestic setting. In meeting his fate he exhibits
virtues, such as cunning, courage, and strength with which
he faces a formidable opponent. Danger and the struggle for
survival are always present--and, yet, all these elements
are given a unique coloring in Traven's novels. Even his
use of the traditionally proven and most successful thematic
structures of the novel of adventure--the seafaring tale and
the search for treasure--cannot reduce plot and protagonist
into simplistic literary concepts. On the contrary, the per-
spicacious reader senses a conscious attempt on the part of
the author to give these concepts new structural life in the
face of the new realities of his time and his experience.

Traven's notion of adventure and the modern hero has attracted some attention in the growing body of secondary literature. Even Merker and Stammler, in their dictionary of literary terms, have incorporated Traven into the canon of the _Abenteuerroman_, with due emphasis on the social question, seen here combined with the motif of adventure and a clearly anticapitalistic tendency in The Death Ship.[1] More detailed treatments of the theme of adventure were undertaken by Erik Ertl and Helmut Reinecke, who made valuable contributions by explicating Traven's concept of adventure, particularly in relation to the idea of revolution and socialist themes in his work in general.[2] Certainly, the spirit of revolution, as it speaks to the reader in Ret Marut's _Ziegelbrenner_, had not faded in the early novels, but that spirit was more of a general humanitarian attitude against the oppression of the downtrodden, now in search of a new literary form.[3] In the specific case of Germany, Traven's revolution was directed against the imbecility of German militarism, dynastic-monarchical profusion, war, aggressive foreign policy, unjust electoral laws, social injustice, and the stupidity of the German people, which Traven thought to be beyond comparison.[4]

Since The Death Ship and Treasure occupy a particular position in relation to the problem of revolution and the novel of adventure, it is necessary to view them accordingly and stress some of the mythological dimensions underlying the structures of Traven's heroes and their adventures. The juncture of the traditional elements of the mythological hero and the dilemma of modern adventure presents a key to the popularity of these novels which may not have been totally by design of the author himself.

Helmut Reinecke emphasizes the revolutionary, socialist formula and alludes to some common ground between B. Traven and Karl May (1842-1912). May's numerous and popular adventure novels Reinecke considers unsuitable to be "materialized" in socialistic processes, since the spiritual (Christian) values of May's heroes and superheroes are of an individualistic nature. In contrast, Reinecke sees the modernity of Traven in his alignment of the notion of adventure with work and revolution. But the hero who performs deeds could essentially tread the standard path of the mythological adventure. Joseph Campbell states that the hero ventures forth from the world to encounter fabulous forces and win a decisive victory and then returns "with the power to bestow boons on his fellow man."[5] We need only to update the ancient formula for the sake of ideological relevance. Martin Green points to the possibility that the modernist adventure features a hero who meets his challenges "by means of the tools and techniques of the modern world system."[6] But this definition of modernist adventure is not that easily applied either. Karl May's hero Old Shatterhand, for example, uses the most up-to-date semiautomatic miracle weapons in order to enforce and promote a code of conduct reminiscent of King Arthur's court. Maybe the spirit of irony is alive here and, as Green puts it, "the spirit of adventure had died,"[7] but Traven's effort was much too earnest and his disillusionment much too complete. Whatever Karl May's ambivalent methods were for the establishment of a noble race of men, Traven's heroes of The Death Ship and Treasure do not actively cultivate a doctrine of salvation. What can be said of them, however, is that within the realm of adventure that they must live in, they give a voice to the energizing myths of our age. The hero may even de-energize one of the predominant myths, the myth of capitalism, but he does not do so in favor of a dialectical materialist counterpart. And there may be almost archetypal necessity for this. The modern ideal of the democratic, self-determining individual has transformed human life and caused the collapse of our universe of symbols. Campbell maintains, "The social unit is not a carrier of religious content, but of an economic-political organization. And the ideals of this organization are the secular state, in hard and unremitting competition for material supremacy and resources."[8] This is the situation that Traven's heroes face, and this myth without a myth spins off the individual as a hero into the realm of so-called adventure, a giant holding-tank of discontent and alienation on the periphery of civilization. Here, adventure becomes an end in itself, a form of being and not becoming.

Conscious of the entertaining ersatz-myths of his time, which were celebrated in popular fiction, Traven used the literary structure of the adventure novel to cast his protagonists in their roles. Throughout The Death Ship and Treasure the author points to the lost energy of the contemporary adventure story and the diminished function it should have in the face of his own efforts. Although we do not have a ready-made theory of the modern adventure novel in Traven's writings, the remarks on this subject, strewn about in these two novels, and the structural use of traditional adventure stories as epic stratagems allow some reflections. Traven's letter to Raymond Everitt (1939) offers a critically more important perspective on the problem of the hero and epic unity in the novel of adventure.[9] The publisher had criticized the collection ("Swallowed by the Bush, Bone and Soul") as lacking unity. Traven, on the other hand, argued that there was a unity, one which would make the book popular. He shifts the appeal from the heroes and heroines to the "unity of one or more problems" and cites The Death Ship as an example in which it is not the hero Gerard Gales who is of importance, but "the restriction of man's natural right to move freely about the world into which he was born." The idea that the hero or heroine is the manifestation of a more abstract principle is interesting and might help to sell a publisher on a marketable continuity that holds together a seemingly disconnected array of stories, but whether it affects the reader that way is another matter. In his remarks on the reception of The Death Ship Peter Küpfer points to the exceptional position occupied by German literature when Traven's "aufklärerischer Arbeiterroman"' encountered the vacuum, which in other countries was occupied by the realistic social novel.[10] We are not surprised therefore that the novel was hailed by German critics in particular as the first real seafaring tale of adventure by a German writer. Although German critics may have had reason to celebrate the partial demise of the popular operatic myth of the seafarer in German film and fiction, Traven attacked that popular myth on a much broader scale. As in the case of Jack London, Joseph Conrad, and, later Ernest Hemingway, experience preceded Traven's fiction, and the gap he observed between reality and fiction prompted his plea for a more honest realism in the tale of adventure. Thus he criticizes the characteristics of popular adventure stories, in particular the false claims they seem to make in their invitation to vicarious adventurous experience within the comfort of the domestic sphere. He remarks in The Death Ship:

> There are sea-stories and sea-stories, millions of them. Every week an output of at least seven hundred and fifty. If you look closely, however, at those interesting sea-stories, you notice that they tell of sailors who are opera-singers in disguise, who manicure their fingernails, and who have no other worries than their goddamned silly love-affairs.[11]

Rolf Recknagel correctly maintains that B. Traven set out to destroy this false seafaring romanticism in The Death Ship.[12] Recknagel goes even further and considers the above description as being directed against Joseph Conrad, who had a way of writing seafaring novels from the perspective of the bridge and not the quarters of the crew. In reality, common sailors had nothing to gain by showing ambitions or high ideals as they were portrayed in popular fiction. The romantic frills and distortions of the adventure tale con-

tributed to the dilemma of the adventurous outcast of civilization, according to Traven. He saw the virtues of popular
adventure tales, as depicted in pulps, as lures which contribute to the downfall of many a susceptible soul. For
example, when Stanislav, the friend of the American sailor
on the Yorikke, tells his story, the narrator comments that
the American's departure from his homeland was prompted by
"a couple of hundred stories in imitation of Cooper's Last
of the Mohicans, sold at a dime a piece, and another couple
of hundred sea-stories and private yarns."[13] A "spiritual
ambush" then, a seducer of whole segments of the population,
the industry of popular fiction is yet another link in a
chain of exploitation.

Within the narrative structure of Traven's novels, the
reading of adventure tales precedes or accompanies deeds and
decisions on the part of the protagonist. When in Treasure
Dobbs and Curtin come to the hotel "Oso Negro," they find
Howard lying about "reading about bandits in a pulp." "He
was right afire," says the narrator, and after the plans to
go prospecting for gold have been discussed and Howard is
asked if he wants to go, he speaks as if under the influence
of popular adventure fiction: "Me? What a question. Of
course I'm going. Any time, any day. I was only waiting
for one or two guys to go with me. Out for gold? Always at
your service, I take the risk and make the investment."[14]
It seems amazing that the experienced and older Howard, who
considers the others "puppies," is such a sap for the tale
of adventure. The irony of reading about bandits need not
be stressed in light of the final phases of this expedition-
adventure. It also points to the contradictory nature of
Howard himself, since, at another juncture during their
journey, he preaches: "Gold means work, and very hard
work at that. Just discard everything you have ever read in
stories in the magazines. Forget it. It's all lies. Bunk,
that's what it is."[15] Although his temper is easily inflamed by pulps, Howard also uses adventure tales as a
teaching tool. He tells the story of the unfortunate Doña
Maria to make a point: "I wanted to tell you this tale to
show you that to find gold and lift it out of the earth is
not the whole thing. The gold has to be shipped. And
shipping is more precarious than digging and washing it."[16]
It seems clear that exponents of the oral tradition like
Howard and Stanislav are important epic elements in Traven's
novel of adventure. Not only can they profess the author's
polemic intention with regard to structure, but by presenting traditional adventure stories within the modern novel of
adventure, the epic sense of adventure thus created ties
Traven to a literary tradition far more important than the

mere contrast of his endeavor to that of the contemporary pulp industry.

The most serious accusation Traven brings is directed against the false representation of heroics in the contemporary tale of adventure. Here conflicts are usually romanticized and misrepresented. "Sailors," the narrator informs us in The Death Ship, "do not fight one-tenth as much as sea-stories and pictures try to make the paying public believe. Sailors have more sense than the movie producers."[17] In the final moments of Dobbs's life, Traven makes his strongest point against the hero of the popular adventure story by emphasizing the tragic consequences. Dobbs has walked into a trap with all the gold he believes to be now his, and it is in the trap of the bandits that his final realization is accompanied by reflections on that which is real and that which is the illusion of adventure:

> It flashed through his mind that he had seen many a movie in which the hero was trapped in a situation like this. But he realized at the same time that he could not remember one single picture in which the producer had not done his utmost to help the trapped hero out again to save the girl from the clutches of a bunch of villains. Before he could think of any of the tricks he had seen in the pictures by which the hero finally escaped, he felt, with a strange bitterness in his mouth, that this situation was real. And whatever is real is different. No smart film-producer was on hand to open the trap with a good trick.[18]

Shortly thereafter, Dobbs's head is severed by the bandits. "And whatever is real is different." The sentence has a haunting quality and ought to be taken seriously. In the last moments of his life, Dobbs, the modern adventure hero, understands that he is caught within reality and illusion, and it is within this dilemma that he finally realizes that adventure, once an illusion, is life itself--his life.

II

In his efforts to decipher Kafka's essential literary energy, Jorge Luis Borges elucidates Zeno's paradox against movement as Kafka's precursor.[19] Although B. Traven is not Kafka, some of the labyrinthine qualities of Kafka's protagonists could have parallels in the heroes of Traven's Death Ship and Treasure. Traven's design of a new hero for a new adventure novel gives his characters a quality of what might be called Auswegslosigkeit ("no way out-ness") in German. They move, like Kafka's characters, but they also move increasingly away from where they want to go. Thus Traven's hero faces a dilemma of two worlds: the civilization which denies him his identity and which he views with great distrust; and the world of adventure, a circle of confinement, where he is the victim of his own longing for home and where he hopes to establish his legitimacy to return. Being caught in this labyrinth without Daedalus's skein of linen thread, i.e., alone without a supporting myth of belonging, he is eventually deprived of his identity, both extrinsically and intrinsically. Having lost the ability to participate in the myth of his civilization and having no recourse to affirm its sociological function in order to validate and enforce the contemporary social and moral order, Traven's modern adventure hero embarks on his venture.[20] This is the essential meaning of the journey of Traven's hero, and its depiction in Traven's novels of adventure unites elements of the ancient as well as the modern hero.

The dilemma of the two worlds which Traven's hero faces first introduces the reader to the obvious denial of identity from without. It is interesting to note that Volker Klotz considers one of the characteristics of the new adventure novel to be what he calls the "bedenkliche Entwicklung des kapitalistischen Prinzips."[21] This questionable development of the capitalistic principle is amply expressed in Traven's novels and has been frequently dealt with by critics. In general, according to Traven, capitalism enslaves and corrupts civilization, and all the institutions of state, politics, and the economy are at its disposal. Traven's heroes are victims of the "myth" of capitalism; they are pushed out to the periphery of modern industrial civilization by fate, or even of their own volition, and there they drift with or without hope of reentering.

The often cited search for the sailor's card and a passport in The Death Ship is one of these hopes that would enable Gales and Stanislav to reenter a more civilized variety of the sailor's life. The appeal to appropriate officials, in particular Gales's dialogue with "His Holiness the American Consul," is a veritable study in paradox. Appointed to help Americans abroad, the consul belies his function by refusing to accept Gales as an American, since he is a sailor. And every authority always wants that which Gales does not have and which would officially certify him to be that which he already is. "It seems to me," says Gales, "the sailor's card, and not the sun, is the center of the universe."[22] It is the card that makes the man, not his humanity, and all the upheavals in the world to establish a self-evident human identity come to naught. "Every age has

its inquisition. Our age has the passport..."[23] Gales even
denies his "decent American name" during the interrogation
after he is caught on a French train without a ticket. But
he vows, "Some day I might belong to society, it is only a
question of making money."[24] Having is indeed being, and
Gales, having to survive without papers in a bureaucratic
world, loses himself ship by ship, more and more onto the
periphery of the legitimate world of which he was once a
part. Caught in the labyrinth of modern bureaucracy, the
hero faces the dilemma of his identity. As Stanislav puts
it, "I have it from a first-class Polish authority that I am
not a Pole, while the Germs, on the other hand, take me only
as a Polish swine. There you are."[25]

In a world where prejudice and rejection mercilessly abuse
the man without a country on all levels of society, the
Yorikke seems an odd haven. The often quoted inscription
over the crew's quarters of this death ship takes on symbolic significance in view of the problem of identity.

He
Who enters here
Will no longer have existence;
His name and soul have vanished
And are gone for ever.
Of him there is not left a breath
In all the vast world.
He can never return,
Nor can he ever go onward;
For where he stands there he must stay.
No God knows him;
And unknown will he be in hell.
He is not day; he is not night.
He is Nothing and Never.
He is too great for infinity,
Too small for a grain of sand,
Which, however small,
Has its place in the universe.
He is what has never been
And never thought.[26]

And this is the final station on the path of adventure for
the modern hero, where pathos and banality join to fix
destiny within the myth of capitalism: "Morituri te saluta-
mus! The moribund are greeting you, O Caesar, great Imperator Caesar Augustus. We are ready to die for you; for you
and for the glorious and most holy insurance."[27] Thus the
ship must turn its final profit and go down, and the effec-

tive vignette of all seafaring tales--the shipwreck--will become the insurance claim.

As mentioned before, the civilization that spins off Traven's hero into the realm of adventure cannot kill within him the dream of returning. This curse of hope belongs to the paradox of adventure. In fact, in Treasure Traven makes the point that all the hardships of the search for gold will be in vain if the hope for the triumphant return cannot materialize. It is no wonder that the return to civilization with the gold seems like one of the trials of the ancient hero. After Dobbs thinks he has killed his partner Curtin, and Howard is detained by the Indians, he heads toward civilization with the gold all to himself. He hears the rumbling of the trains and is already within sight of the railroad tracks when the narrator gives an objectified appraisal of his thoughts: "He longs for civilization, for law, for justice, which would protect his property and his person with a police force."[28] Dobbs is certain that once he is rich, civilization will be on his side and he can even face the accusing Howard, whom he plans to cheat out of his share of the gold by legal means. With gold, his identity will be secure within society and cannot be assailed by bums.

But Traven's tale of adventure does not provide such an ending, and there is no easy escape out of the circle of confinement that is the realm of adventure. The shacks of the town are hardly five miles away, and as the hero braces himself to enter the threshold to his identity, fate strikes in the guise of the simple question "Tiene un cigarro, hombre? Have you got a cigarette?" The sense of irony that speaks through the voices of the bandits is heightened by the realization that having is not being after all. Of course, the reader has been prepared for and warned about the dangers of reentry to this kind of civilization, and when the bandits kill Dobbs and scatter the gold out of ignorance, the reader becomes aware of the absurd joke at the expense of the modern hero.

Traven's concept of the modern hero is worthy of consideration and has proven problematic, if not contradictory, for critics who viewed the author as a communist or anarchist. As mentioned in the beginning, the idea of the revolutionary hero by design, the carrier of an ideology or a political doctrine of salvation, does not totally exhaust Traven's protagonist. Recknagel correctly observes that Traven's heroism departs from the common variety of the war hero, worshipped during and shortly after World War I.[29] Renewing the concept of the hero meant renewing the human being itself, creating a new man in the same way as Traven understood his world revolution. Reinecke suggests a more specific framework when he maintains that the adventures of the hero must have social implications and become an element of revolution: "Die Armen und Unterdrückten sind für Traven das werdende Subjekt der Revolution."[30] Perhaps Traven's heroes are those of revolution, particularly in works other than those discussed here, but in The Death Ship and Treasure adventures represent a deeper dimension of the protagonist than mere literary figments of the workers' movement. Traven's depiction of the hero as a member of the working class evokes understanding, enlightenment, and compassion, but the novels and their working protagonists also have lives of their own. Their failure to provide a clear-cut blueprint for the revolution or to provoke a rational or irrational political activity to break the existential dilemma seems to have deeper causes, which are founded in Traven's realistic portrayal of the hero as a human being. That limitation is crucial for the understanding of Traven's adventures since it also contributes to the circle of confinement from which it is so hard to escape.

The perpetuation of confinement and dilemma as a direct cause and effect of the limitations of human nature makes it difficult at times to like Traven's heroes. Their coarseness, base behavior, linguistic poverty, and a sizeable array of vices border on tragic flaws. Admiration for this modern hero is particularly hampered by his apparent lack of an inner, spiritual life. Religion, in particular Christianity, is portrayed in a highly suspect manner as a servant of the capitalist myth and its aberrations, such as war. To explain the baser side of human nature, for example, Lacauld tells the story of the bandits and explains that they had Jesus as their king, fighting on behalf of the Roman Catholic church for religious liberty. Traven even introduces revolutionary priests who are actively involved in a train robbery, thus "besmirking the name of a civilized nation."[31] The power struggle between church and state notwithstanding, Traven maintains through his characters that bandits were still less to be feared than high officials and high dignitaries of the church. After all, the narrator explains, Latin America, where the Inquisition lasted much longer than in Spain, suffered much at the hands of the church.[32]

The church as an established ecclesiastical power and an oppressive force can be easily understood in Traven's novels, but the attitude of the heroes toward women is a different matter. Generally, women are referred to as "Janes," peripheral in function and far removed from any notion of the eternal feminine that purifies and saves the hero.

Reinecke explains that sensuality, destroyed by the bourgeoisie, should be recaptured by the revolution.[33] The proletarian hero takes in stride women who express their working potential in bed. A decent woman is, therefore, beyond the reach of Traven's heroes—and why pretend a false morality? Life on the Yorikke was hard, but Gales finds he gets used to it; he can even live and laugh on the ship. Occasionally they make port, and the skipper is even generous enough to provide an advance so that the crew "can go and lift a skirt or two." No wonder that Gales concludes in the same breath that "all civilization is only a thin layer of varnish on the human animal."[34] What it all amounts to is that those men and heroes without a spiritual life, religion, and real women to love have no basis for an idealistic ethic. It seems quite consistent also that they are incapable of being revolutionary because of those very shortcomings. But the ethical dilemma in Traven's heroes is basic and hinders the development of the characters. It confines the individual; and efforts at creating a community with self-evident virtues beyond the level of theft, murder, greed, distrust, and so on seem impossible on a death ship, as well as in the camp of the gold diggers. Whether we talk about the prospectors' daily division and hiding of the gold from one another or the unsuccessful attempt to create an honor system for the distribution of the much-coveted sugar on the Yorikke, the limitations of the human character are insurmountable and leave no room for noble alternatives. Traven could not see anything but hypocrisy in the way values were taught and practiced in the civilization of his time, and thus the circle of adventure becomes a world in itself, where those values are suspended. While this world is held together by a peculiar pragmatism that only rarely approaches friendship, there remains only the hope that the inborn ethical impulse of the individual might again find a home, a community.

The inborn ethical impulse does not overcome the limitations of the human condition on a communal basis and manifests itself in a revolutionary kind of solidarity. In fact, it causes inner contradictions even on the part of the heroes. These men without an identity, homeless and on the road to gain the world, as Ertl puts it, are, therefore, caught in a perpetual state of having nothing and being nobody. Their love for a homeland, however, breaks through in spite of the irony and cynicism which equates home with citizenship: "If you don't belong to a country in these times, you had better jump into the sea. No other way out."[35] The death of Kurt, one of the drags on the Yorikke, bring reflections on homeland and homesickness, which had once been described as "only a bum's comedy." But homesickness is not a refined emotion confined to the upper classes. In fact, adventure itself is the hero's paradoxical attempt to kill his longing for his true home, as the narrator explains: "I was homesick. I am homesick. All my struggling and roaming is but a dope to put to sleep my homesickness."[36] "Where is the true country of man?" he concludes. Indeed, the question has mythological dimensions and has been posed by many an adventure hero in the history of the tale of adventure. But as far as Traven's adventure hero is concerned, it emphasizes again the dilemma in which he finds himself. Cast off without an identity, he drifts onto the periphery of civilization in the realm of adventure, from whence a return is denied. The images of the literally drifting Gales at the end of The Death Ship, and the decapitated Dobbs within earshot of a return to civilization at the end of Treasure, bear witness to the paradox of the modern hero. Adventure itself has become a way of life: Being is adventure.

III

Conscious of the external and internal limitations which bring about the dilemma of adventure for Traven's hero, we might ask whether there are any clues in The Death Ship and Treasure to reach beyond the circle of confinement to find meaning and purpose in being. If there is one theme that dominates Traven's work throughout, it is the problem of work. Workers and work as human activity belong to Traven's most essential concerns. He sees the worker as a member of a working class that is exploited and abused within the capitalist system; he sees members of this class as genuine people, although he does not idealize them as such. The socialist-revolutionary angle has often been applied to Traven's working hero, and there is ample justification for this, but his working hero also reaches beyond the socialist cause. Traven wrote in a letter to Ernst Preczang (1925) that the human subjects he sees are workers by accident and that his own contacts and experience have taught him that the proletarian is the most interesting part of mankind.[37] In general, it is fair to say that if the downtrodden and exploited in Traven's novels experience a sense of being, it is in the experience of work, even though they may curse it. In fact, the hero in his desolated state yearns to be through work, and even the basic activity of keeping a fire going in the ship's boiler is an art that not everybody can do. In one passage, for example, Stanislav spreads "out the inner part of his soul" by explaining what it means to be without work: "You do your best to land a job but you cannot get one--You see, you want to do something. You wish to be useful. I do not mean that stuff about a man's duty. That's bunk. There is in yourself that which is driving you on to do something worth while.--Hell, I can't explain what I mean, it is that you want to create something, to help things going."[38] Apart from all idealistic values and other external motivation, work is deeply ingrained into the metaphysical structures of man; it is his very creativity that allows him to see art in physical labor. In whatever simplistic language Stanislav puts his ideas, this goes beyond any romantic notion of the working classes versus the exploiting capitalist system. What religious doctrines and love do not seem to accomplish, work does; it becomes one of the most intrinsic qualities of Traven's hero.

Of course, the hero participates in the insanity of the industrial age, where the obsession for work and production becomes the devouring Moloch, but Traven adds the dimension of myth to work. Who can forget the passages in The Death Ship in which the fireman is faced with the problem of six dropping grate-bars?

I soon learned that to put them back into their berth not only cost blood, not alone flesh torn off, large pieces of skin scorched, but cost bleeding sperm, shredded tendons, and painfully twisted entrails. The joints of all limbs cracked like broken wood. The marrow in one's bones asppeared to flow out like hot lava. While we worked like Egyptian slaves to bring the bars in again, the steam was falling and falling. Ahead of this hard work we saw already, crawling upon us, the hard work that was to follow to bring the steam up again to its full pressure. The longer we had to work with the bars, the lower fell the steam. I may justly say, though that since that night, my first night with grate-bars in the ash-pit, I feel myself standing above the gods. I am free. Unbound. I may do now whatever I wish. I may curse the gods. They cannot punish me any more. No human law, no divine commandments, can any longer influence my doings, because no longer can I be damned. Hell is now paradise. However horrible hell may be, it cannot frighten me any more. There is nothing under heaven and hell that can be compared with putting back fallen-out grate-bars on the "Yorikke."[39]

The myth of Sisyphus seems to come alive in the hero as the working slave. All speculations about wages, working conditions, exploitation, and class struggles cease in the abso-

lute adventure that is work itself. "No language," says the
narrator, "could possibly express in words the feeling any
sane person simply had to have when confronted with a problem like setting in dropped grate-bars in the stokehold of
the 'Yorikke'."

The realm of this kind of work also provides isolation
from any kind of supervision. The fireman and the drag face
imminent danger of death, and the hell which is their assigned workplace makes them immune to any reproach this side
of death. This work-heroism has often been led to its
socialist conclusion in the communist state, but in Traven's
works it confirms the irony of the adventure as "being"
without identity. Work in adventure is the energy of the
hero expressed in the dilemma of his confinement: With all
his soul he tends the fires of the ship that goes nowhere.

The willingness of the protagonist to accept the confinement of adventure, even if it means excruciating labor,
could be viewed as a kind of negative socialization process.
The Yorikke is in the end a peculiar object of affection for
the sailors who serve on her, and any notion of rebellion,
revolution, or mutiny seems out of the question. Is this
kind of work, which destroys all semblance of the civilized
life, the only way for our heroes to momentarily overcome
the dilemma of their situation? Can the adventure hero of
our century return with the boon for mankind that is so
characteristic for the ancient hero? Traven's hero seemingly lacks ethical preconditions, such as the virtue of
self-control, as part of the nobility of his character. The
Death Ship ends on a somewhat ambiguous note in this regard,
but Treasure leaves some possibilities for speculating
otherwise. Of course, the idea of work is similarly portrayed in both novels. Traven even intensifies the work
equation in Treasure by introducing gold as reward and
remuneration. But here, too, the work that has to be done
is excruciating and exhausting physical labor. "Convicts in
a gang," says the narrator, "would have gone on a hunger-
strike, and not have minded the whipping either, had they
had to work as these three men were doing to fill their own
pockets."[40] Greed for the means for the return to civilization fills the hearts and minds of these men, in contrast to
the tone of resignation that predominates on the Yorikke.
Yet, Traven does not provide for a meaningful and effective
reentry into the defective civilization whence these heroes
came. There is something seriously wrong with a civilization that forces these men out from its borders, deprives
them of their identities, and demands such a heavy price for
a return. Reentry into civilization or finding a home must
be under more genuine and humane conditions. What does not

seem possible in The Death Ship seems to be approached in Treasure in the character of Howard, who, with his natural talent and interaction with a natural people, comes closest to the ancient returning hero who bestows boons on mankind, thus ending the circle of the confinement of adventure.

The idea of fleeing European civilization in order to hide out in primitive surroundings is mentioned early in Traven's writings.[41] A civilization whose idea of heroism is war and which lives on the exploitation of those who work is certainly not a home for Traven. And so Traven's vision of a true society grew out of the sympathy he felt "for the small Indian communes he encountered on his travels"[42] through Mexico, and for the character of Howard, the oldest and wisest of the group of adventure-heroes. Howard, as Ertle maintains, comes closest to the real treasure in the novel, the "return" to a home where his work is respected, fulfilling, and a boon to mankind.[43] He becomes a healer among the Indians, but he does not do so with the superior skills of the medical technology of the white man. He does it with a natural talent, common sense, compassion, and a true understanding of the human condition. Howard had the potential for being wise all along, but the decision to go home to the Indians is not an easy one. He leaves the realm of adventure reluctantly, and for a while he is what we might call the master of two worlds.[44] Unlike Lacauld, who insists on joining the three partners at a considerable risk because he can't stand living among Indians any longer, Howard understands the Indians. But that understanding comes by experience. At first, when he encounters the uncompromising gratitude of the Indians after treating one of their drowned members, he is at a loss to explain "to these simple men that business is the only real thing in life, that it is heaven and paradise and all the happiness of a good Rotarian."[45] In his mind, the semicivilized state of the Indians shows little hope for improvement for the next hundred years, but his self-ironic assessment of the whole situation points to a budding and deepening understanding. Thus, he separates from his partners, leaving the treasure in their hands. While still among the Indians he receives word of the disaster that has befallen the whole undertaking. An innocent Indian tells him the story in true epic fashion, and as Curtin joins in and the story unfolds, Howard begins to comprehend the absurdity and the paradoxical nature of their adventure. He lets out a roar of "Homeric laughter," as if to allay the fate of Sisyphus, and realizes that they have worked like slaves just for the pleasure of it. "Anyway," he says, "I think it is a very good joke--a good one played on us and on the bandits by the Lord or by fate or by nature, whichever you prefer."[46]

Howard explains his philosophy to Curtin, who does not yet see the humor in the situation. There is a brief retarding moment of indecision when two bags of gold are found among the packs after all, but Howard decides to go home to the Indians. His patients are waiting and, like the ancient deus ex machina, the Indians lift him onto his horse and hurry back home. If Howard follows the path of the mythological hero, he will, after wavering, find the freedom to live. "The hero is the champion of things becoming," Campbell says, "not of things become, because he _is_."[47] And so the reader is left with the hope that Curtin too will follow after his health is restored. Howard becomes a man with a real identity; he overcomes being the adventurer in a circle of confinement and, as a healer, he bestows his boons on his fellow man.

In conclusion, let us again relate the themes of adventure and hero in Traven's _Death_ _Ship_ and _Treasure_ to his call for world revolution, which he formulated so polemically in other writings during that time. In spite of his expressed hope that a civilization under the auspices of a primitive, natural communion might be possible, it is difficult to assign optimism to Traven. However real the portrayal of the oppression of the downtrodden is in the novels under discussion here, the limitations of human nature prevent a spontaneous and successful revolution for the establishment of a more human civilization, one without war and capitalist control and exploitation. Traven's heroes suffer from these limitations, and as they are caught in the confining circle of adventure, we become aware of the new hero as an outcast and representative of his civilization. These protagonists are anti-heroes and rather tainted, but their struggles seem sincere and lend themselves still to a comparison with the ancient hero. As the twentieth century has progressed, the hero may have become even more tainted, and worse, his struggles have dwindled to insignificance under the onslaught of the leisure society. He may even have given up to look for pure islands where regeneration and genuine being are still possible. At any rate, Traven's early novels of adventure follow patterns of the new _and_ the traditional adventure novel, where the dis-ease we might feel in understanding the sufferings of his heroes is by far outweighed by the affirmation of life exemplified by their struggle. This struggle may not have a divine plan to get painlessly through the labyrinth of being, but such occasional luxuries were not always available for the ancient hero either. The opposition was always formidable, be it the Gods or the anonymity of the industrial state. And when we read Traven's adventure novels we realize that all is a question of being and that life itself has always had its mysteries and hardships. After all, what is the worth of man the adventurer in the modern plan of things? Is he more vulnerable because he is open to his own sense of insignificance, since he is unrelated to a higher purpose and armed only with a "philosophy" against his own civilization, which might reject him? And what is the true country of man, if it is not first and foremost the obligation of becoming through adventure? Here, the ancient and the modern hero are linked through the tale of adventure, and in the possibility of conveying this understanding through Traven's literary art, we delight in the Homeric laughter of the modern hero.

Notes

1. Merker and Stammler, 1958, 3-4.
2. Ertl in Beck et al., 1976, 201-13; Reinecke in Ibid., 403-421.
3. Marut, Ziegelbrenner.
4. Ziegelbrenner, January 15, 1919, Heft 9-14, 1.
5. Campbell, 1954, 30.
6. Green, 1979, 23.
7. Ibid., 324.
8. Campbell, 1964, 387.
9. Letter of B. Traven to Raymond Everitt, April 27, 1939, 1-4. TS. Rare Books and Special Collections, The Pennsylvania State University, University Park, PA.
10. Küpfer, 1981, 203-311.
11. B. Traven, The Death Ship (New York: Collier Books, 1962), 108.
12. Recknagel, 1982, 182.
13. Death Ship, 187.
14. B. Traven, The Treasure of the Sierra Madre (New York: Hill and Wang, 1967), 71.
15. Ibid., 77.
16. Ibid., 210.
17. Death Ship, 221.
18. Treasure, 267.
19. Borges, 1964, 199-201.
20. Campbell, 1964, 387-91.
21. Klotz, 19.
22. Death Ship, 35.
23. Ibid., 48.
24. Ibid., 63.

25. Ibid., 235.
26. Ibid., 95.
27. Ibid., 119.
28. Treasure, 260.
29. Recknagel, 1982, 161.
30. Reinecke, 1976, 405.
31. Treasure, 143.
32. Ibid., 197.
33. Reinecke, 1976, 415.
34. Death Ship, 236.
35. Ibid., 30.
36. Ibid., 216.
37. Recknagel, 1982, 358, see footnote 484.
38. Death Ship, 206.
39. Ibid., 153.
40. Treasure, 80.
41. Ziegelbrenner, 87.
42. Baumann, 1976, 56.
43. Ertl, 1976, 210.
44. Compare Campbell, 1964, 229-37.
45. Treasure, 228.
46. Ibid., 305.
47. Campbell, 1964, 243.

A LANGUAGE WITHOUT A MASTER
Max Stirner's Influence on B. Traven

Wolfgang Essbach

We have to make a choice. If we pursue an enlightened discourse, we will talk about our subject as clearly and transparently as possible. If we choose the alternative, we will be seduced by a strangely solipsistic intimacy and consequently endanger our scientific imperatives. Traven forces us to make this choice. In short, he wants readers, but not interpreters, and this distinguishes him from the many authors who have made things easier for scholarship. Traven's work, however, is antagonistic in this respect as well. And as we are, by profession, not simply readers but also interpreters, the Indian proverb proves true for our academic occupation with Traven: When the ethnologists arrive, the spirits leave the island.

I

The influence of Max Stirner on Traven—with this subject we have made our decision for the moment. As far as I know, no one disputes such an influence. But what does "influence" mean when Stirner is being discussed? Max Stirner was part of the opposition intelligentsia of the German Vormärz, the term designating the years which preceded the revolution of March 1848. He belonged to the "Young Hegelians," a small group of radical students of Hegel, and he was thus a colleague of Karl Marx and Friedrich Engels, of Bruno Bauer and Ludwig Feuerbach. In reaction to these compatriots Stirner wrote his book Der Einzige und sein Eigentum (The Unique Ego and His Own), published in 1844. He died penniless and almost forgotten in 1856—it seems that he literally starved to death.

His philosophy—if one can really call it that—evades generalizations. Whenever they are attempted, they immediately turn into libel: childish, chaotic, monstrous, and so on. This being the case, what actually characterizes the influence of Stirner?

For the sake of comparison, let us take another example. When we say that Brecht was influenced by Marx's ideas, then those who know Marx and Brecht understand what this means. Brecht assimilated Marxist theories in his works and gave them literary form. His works contain a Marxist critique of bourgeois conditions, and his aesthetic theory is based on Marx's teachings on the necessity of class conflict. Of

101

course, there are other sides to Brecht, but without acknowledging Marx's ideas in Brecht's work, we would not get very far in its interpretation. We also know from Brecht's biography that Marx's ideas were transmitted to the playwright mainly by the leftist radical Karl Korsch, and therefore we can readily place Brecht within the broad spectrum which characterizes Marxist movements in all of their social and political ramifications.[1] We can also begin to debate whether Brecht was loyal to the official party line and its canonization of Marx, whether he supported Leninist conceptions, or whether he was linked to the tradition of an undogmatic understanding of Marx. Once all of this is analyzed, the influence of Marx on Brecht can be described quite adequately.

The case is simple: Marx's theory of the bourgeois world and the proletarian revolution is constructed with the aim that it "becomes a material power as soon as it takes hold of the masses." This theory leads to the "categorical imperative of overthrowing all conditions in which man is a humiliated, enslaved, abandoned, and contemptible being."[2] Marx's theory is constructed so as to influence and take hold; it desires an echo, and Brecht the writer lets this echo reverberate in himself in the hope that it may spread even more widely in the field of action.

On the other hand, let us listen to Max Stirner:

I see how human beings are frightened into dark superstitions by a swarm of ghosts. Do I therefore, to the best of my ability, let daylight chase away the nocturnal spooks because of love for you? Do I write out of love for mankind? No, I write because I want to obtain an existence in the world for my thoughts. And if I foresaw that these thoughts would deprive you of your tranquility and peace, even if I foresaw the bloodiest wars and the destruction of many generations germinating from this seed of thought, I would sow it nevertheless. Do with it what you want and are able to, that is your business and does not concern me....But not for your sake, not even for truth's sake do I say what I think. No--

I sing like the bird sings,
Who dwells in the branches:
The song that comes from its throat,
Is abundant recompense.

I sing--because I am a singer. But you I use, because I-- need ears.[3]

Let us take Stirner at his word: no theory to take hold of the masses, no categorical imperative to eliminate the misery of human beings. Stirner does not want to influence at all—he is indifferent to the effects of his ideas. All interpersonal orientations, such as love for human beings, their welfare, the lamp of enlightenment, and finally truth itself, are bluntly rejected.

Again we face a choice. If we were consistent and took Stirner at his word, we would soon be finished with our task—namely, our search for those whom he influenced—since every claim that Stirner desired followers would be tantamount to calling him a liar. Again we make our decision for the moment and say: Stirner's position is, to say the least, untenable. One of the classic objections to his writings is, after all, the claim that whoever speaks necessarily wants to influence others, whereas whoever sincerely does not want to be influential must remain silent. And our modern theoreticians in the field of communications would go even further and say that a case for noncommunication does not exist, for even he who is silent is saying after all that he does not want to talk. There is no noncommunication message.[4]

In order to obtain acceptable results, we have to put some distance between ourselves and Stirner and reject his claim that his speech is an end in itself. Stirner did influence others—not only his contemporaries in the Vormärz movement, but also the literary-political intelligentsia which was active before and after World War I, and to which Traven belonged. And after all, we do discern Stirner's echo clearly and distinctly in the dance-song of The Death Ship: "What do you care what pleases me? / Why do you care what I like? I live my life, not yours, in this world." ("Was kümmert euch, was mir gefällt? Ich lebe mich, nicht euch, in dieser Welt").[5] We also hear Stirner's echo in Ziegelbrenner: "I am no 'author,' but I shout. I want to be nothing but word. I want to shout it...not for your sake, but for my sake. Only for my sake!...The word is given to you, do with it, what you want."[6] What we have here is doubtless an example of Stirner's influence on Traven. Traven follows Stirner in defining his own cause: the only purpose is obtaining "for my thoughts an existence in the world," and to be "nothing but word." Traven follows Stirner even to the point of saying, "do with it what you want." And we hear the echo of Stirner's "I sing like the bird sings..." in Khundar's words: "Ask the blackbird why it does not care if you want to hear it."[7] Stirner emerges even more radically in The Night Visitor. When Gales asks if he has published the many books he has written, the doctor answers: "Never. Every time I finished a book, I read it, found it good, and ripped it up. Why should I publish my books? I had my enjoyment and pleasure when I wrote them. For the people? I would like to know why." To deal with people is "a matter of complete indifference" to him. And he goes on: "I am also of the opinion that the best books ever written, either on paper or in the mind, are those that were never published. Behind every published book something is lurking that does not speak in favor of the work and that prevents man from creating the best that he is able to."[8]

As researchers, we find ourselves in an impossible situation. We are tracing the influence of a mode of thought that is indifferent to, perhaps even rejects, influence. We are continually forced to put a distance between ourselves and our author. Or could anybody seriously defend the position that Traven lets his Doctor Wilshed propose: writing books, enjoying them, and ripping them to pieces? Traven himself is, after all, a successful author, and even if he may have torn up some manuscripts, he cared greatly about the publication and distribution of his works.

As a prime example of Stirner's influence on Traven, I have chosen their respective positions on the question of influence itself, in order to make clear the difficulties in investigating Stirner's thoughts in Traven's texts. Of course, we can talk about Stirner's influence on Traven, just as we talk about Marx's influence on Brecht. We can contrast the different topics that Stirner develops--the critique of religion, the social question, and the relation between egoism and union--with a checklist of Traven's statements, and we can then examine wherein they agree or diverge.[9] But I believe that as fruitful as this procedure may be in the case of Brecht and Marx, if we used it here, we would be passing up a chance to get closer to what "lurks" behind both Stirner's and Traven's texts.

When one works with such extremely intractable attitudes, a direct thrust at interpretation usually comes up empty-handed. Therefore, I would like to propose a detour, which for the time being avoids the traps and pitfalls that surround Traven and Stirner, a detour that leads us into the secure terrain of history, in order to again attempt from this vantage point to understand the mysterious gestures of rejection.

II

Traven moved in that network of small groups and loosely linked lone fighters that formed the literary-political left

intelligentsia of the first decades of this century. Max
Stirner was a frequently read author in these circles, but
he was also a rediscovered one. The Stirner of the German
Vormärz, who had forced his Young Hegelian colleagues Marx
and Engels to abandon many idealistic premises, had sunk
almost completely into oblivion after the defeat of the
revolution of 1848.[10] My digression is intended to call to
mind the "Stirner-Renaissance" of which Traven was a part.
For Traven's assimilation of Stirner's motifs is in an
important way determined by what Traven's contemporaries had
made of Stirner.[11]

From 1873 until 1895, the capitalist world experienced a
major and lengthy depression. In Germany, the Marxist social democracy continually extended its position; its membership and its deputies in the Reichstag continued to grow.
As a defense against the development of a powerful workers'
movement, factory owners formed an alliance with landowners
and the Prussian military, which attempted to suppress the
Social Democratic party press and organization. During the
time of the Sozialistengesetz (Anti-Socialist Law, 1878-90),
a spectrum of attitudes took shape within the German Left,
which was influential until the time of Weimar. This is not
the place to discuss the complicated history of the political left of this time. What is important is to grasp what
Stirner meant for Traven and his contemporaries.

A large gap formed between those adherents of the German
Left who consistently held to a political, parliamentary-
democratic, and long-term perspective, and those who developed in a variety of ways a direct revolutionary thrust that
was not politically mediated. One side held to the belief
that, with the crisis-ridden development of the productive
forces and with the spreading proletarization of the masses,
the political potential and dreams of the left would win out
as certainly as by a law of nature and would replace the old
self-destructive order with its own new political state.
The other side also believed in a future order, which,
however, would be actively obtained by the revolutionary
activity of the individual or by the association of active
individuals. These two attitudes contrast so sharply with
each other that they can be defined by simple dualistic
oppositions: passive expectation of the revolution versus
active bringing about of the revolution; political representation by party versus organization outside of and
against bourgeois forms; primacy of centralism and the political leader versus primacy of localism and of the group and
the individual; unified orientation towards one worldview
(Weltanschauung) versus the search for different philosophical and religious models of interpretation.

The rediscovery of Stirner in Germany coincided almost exactly with the repeal of the Sozialistengesetze. It was instigated by John Henry Mackay, who was in close contact with Die Jungen (The Young), an opposition faction within the Social Democrats. Not only did the social-revolutionary undercurrent of workers, which had grown in the time of persecution and which the party leadership regarded with suspicion, find its expression here; at this time, Die Jungen absorbed a strong influx of what was called Gelehrtenproletariat (Proletariat of Scholars). Beyond that, Bohemian elements as well as many representatives of the naturalistic school were involved with Die Jungen. At the party convention in Erfurt in 1892, Die Jungen was defeated and the party broken up, basically along the lines of division stated above. What Stirner meant for the "Independent Socialists" proceeding from Die Jungen is made clear by their manifesto of 1891, which states: "We opposition socialists place great value on the individualization of the worker....We do not immediately want to force on him this or that as the sole road to salvation, above all we want to encourage him to form his own opinion from discussion....The more developed the individuality of the worker is, the more powerfully he confronts outside influences which harm him-- in short, the more revolutionary he is."[12]

Let us stay with the slogan "individualization of the worker" for a moment. It is not only a practical answer to the quietism of the social democracy interested only in counting votes. It also addresses the experience of the "masses," regarded as threatening at this time, in which the individual disappears, and it is a reaction to the discovery of the social environment in which the individual is caught and which suspends his individuality. The slogan is an answer to the triumph of statistics, and to the rational bureaucratic management of humans in gigantic political and economic organizations. These ideas were already definitively formulated by the naturalistic school: "We despise Krupp--the capitalism that crucifies all ethics--the capitalist collectivism--the police sergeant and the official tutelage!" Hermann Conradi lets his protagonist Heinrich Spaldung draw the conclusion: "I am an individualist--hence an egotist of the worst kind--and perhaps therefore--perhaps therefore--a socialist."[13] Egotist/socialist, individualization of the worker--these notions characterize the tensions which inform the contemporary political opposition.

The subject is no longer the closed world of social democracy; it is no longer "this or that as the sole road to salvation." With the secession from social democracy, a wide range of different oppositional orientations makes its appearance. As Bruno Wille outlines the forum of the opposition:

> A crisis is currently developing in all social parties; disintegration of old ideas and new crystallizations are taking place. Especially in socialism new tendencies are emerging; groups of "independent socialists" have attempted to break through the coercive centralism of the party government, and minds of _Die Jungen_ are seething; their strange life experiences are put into theory: here individualism, there communist anarchism evolves, here Marxism is overthrown...there a sizeable group of disciples gathers around Hertzka's "social liberalism" and the freeland-movement, here violence is propagated, while...an anarchism rejects any use of force.[14]

Wille's statement is perhaps paradigmatic for the spectrum of oppositional attitudes that were tried out at his time.[15] A Social Democrat and the founder of the Volksbühnenbewegung (Movement for a People's Theatre), by means of which the working class was to participate in cultural life, Wille was a spokesman for Die Jungen and a coauthor of the manifesto of the "Independent Socialists." He lived in the Friedenshagen commune east of Berlin, about whose objectives and motives he wrote: "Nature's loneliness in the roaring metropolis, literary Bohemianism and socialist as well as anarchist ideas, a daring striving for a non-prejudiced and selfless way of life, companionship between intellectuals _and_ gifted manual laborers, but also intelligent representatives of wealth; creative love for the arts was linked to sociology, natural sciences, philosophy and religion."[16] In addition, Wille was what could be called a "Stirnerian." What does that mean? "If I am called a naturalist, an atheist, a democrat, a socialist, or an anarchist, I will tolerate it," Wille writes, "but with the reservation that I in no way submit to being stretched on a Procrustean bed and raped by some kind of party concept, and with the understanding that not every deduction derived from those categories may apply to me."[17] Theoretical-political concepts are not decisive; they are not valid as a measure for the individual's activity. What is important is the exposure of that point of reversal at which--as Stirner writes--"a cause stops being _our_ cause and our _property_, with which we as proprietors can operate as we please; where it becomes a fixed cause, or a monomania, where it begins to inspire us, makes us enthusiastic, fanatic, in short where it turns into our obstinacy and becomes our--ruler."[18] The existing political and cultural program of the opposition is not simply negated in order to put a new one in its place; it is rather a medium of participation that can in the final analysis be negated as well. The idea is coexistence: Einsiedler und Genosse (Hermit and Comrade) is the title of Bruno Wille's collection of poems of 1890--a title that would also fit Traven well.[19]

But Traven was about eight years old at the time of Stirner's rediscovery. Approximately fifteen years later, when his first political and artistic activities became apparent--with his radical speeches before the workers (1907),[20] his acquisition of a reputation as an actor (1907),[21] or the efforts at agitation in his parents' home (1904),[22] (if we can believe the police confession discovered by Wyatt in which Ret Marut admits that he is Otto Feige)--leftist organizations in Germany were already widespread. The left radicalism into which Traven was drawn represented an unending organizational and schismatic debate of the various socialist, syndicalist, and anarchist groups and tendencies. Stirner had been given a fixed place here. He had been put on the market as an advocate of "individualistic anarchism"--a strange label, since Stirner was a theoretical point of reference neither for the Bakunists of the First International nor for the anarchists as defined by Kropotkin. Bakunin, who may even have known Stirner personally, regarded him as a "cynical logician," just as he later regarded the Russian nihilists.[23] Kropotkin found that Stirner lacked "the idea of a new society founded on justice," while his "aristocratic individualism" was all too familiar to the bourgeoisie.[24] In the context of the classic European anarchism of the nineteenth century, Stirner was not an anarchist.

"Individualistic anarchism" was coined by John Henry Mackay, who combined the theses of the American anarchist Benjamin R. Tucker with Stirnerian notions.[25] However, "individualistic anarchism" thus defined meant primarily opposition to "communistic anarchism," which Mackay attacked as vigorously as he did the ruling order. The subject matter of his widely read novel The Anarchists becomes the simple schematic oppositions mouthed by its individualist hero Auban and his antagonist Trupp.[26] Mackay's version of Stirner, which came to German anarchism by way of Die Jungen, contributed to the fragmentation of groups because it opposed even the smallest organizational associations with a loudly proclaimed subjectivism.

Stirner, reduced to the "individualist anarchist," was used by the one side as a welcome legitimization for undermining collective efforts toward emancipation. For the other side he became a welcome caricature of the counter-

revolutionary hostile to emancipation. Mackay's view of
Stirner has had fatal consequences up to the present time,
since he reduces the heretical, productive uproar of Stirner's argumentation to a simple, stagnant, antisocial, individualistic program susceptible to schematic stylization.
This reductionist concept of Stirner, also prevalent in
Traven research,[27] distorts Stirner. Programs calm people.
But Stirner disturbs, since he bases his cause on nothing,
and because he lets death's shadow grow, and there is no way
to make a proram with one's own death. Not only contemporary dissidents, but also those at the beginning of the
century, were hungry for programs. And Stirner became a
program in spite of himself.

But the reading of Stirner may lead to conclusions different from those drawn by Mackay. Gustav Landauer, who initially wrote under Stirner's officially registered name,
"Caspar Schmidt," describes in his novel Der Todesprediger
(The Preacher of Death) how the hero, Karl Starkblom, at
first becomes an enthusiastic socialist. He is a popular
speaker for the worker's cause until the day he faints in
the middle of a lecture on the future society. He is suddenly overcome by an "inner laughing, struggling and gnawing
doubt. 'Give up man! It's all wrong! It's all senseless!'
These thoughts kept spinning around in his head."[28]   Starkblom suddenly feels the impact of Stirner's words: "All the
things I'm supposed to be interested in! Above all, good
causes, God's cause, the cause of mankind, of truth, freedom, humanity, justice...everything except my own cause."[29]
When months later the Marxist agitator again turns to the
public, he has become a "preacher of death" who renounces
socialism, because it unquestioningly presupposes, "mesmer-
ized by old words," that "people are duty-bound to care for
their neighbors, that there exists a human community, and
further, that the individual has an interest in the future
of mankind and the world. He never supports this most
important of presuppositions with language...."[30]

The "preacher of death" shatters the "Judeo-Christian
moral law," as does Nietzsche, who had read Stirner.[31] Like
Stirner, Starkblom bases "his cause on nothing"; every truth
falls to pieces, and he advocates only suicide: "Let us put
an end as quickly as possible to this ridiculous comedy that
leads to nothing, literally to nothing."[32] And why is the
"preacher of death" himself still alive? "I have my pleasure, namely my pleasure in death....I have my fun with the
people who do not yet know death and the death wish. It
gives me satisfaction, superhuman satisfaction, to ridicule
and deride the human masses and nevertheless to bait them.
I am still alive because it gratifies me to play with my

anguish and to stretch my disgust as you might a tough dough. I love death, and therefore I live."[33]

The reading of Stirner opens here an alarmingly precipitous path, a suicidal plunge that, no matter where it ends, will never lead back to the positive attributes of a glorified individualism. We are interested neither in the fate of the "preacher of death" nor in Landauer's further development.[34] Rather, I am trying to show that Mackay and Landauer represent two different schools of interpreting Stirner. In the first school, Stirner's "unique ego" (Einziger) turns into a programmatic subjectivism rigidly antithetical to any collective dimension. In the second, Stirner's "unique ego" is understood as a symbol of death and transfiguration, with extremely anti-individualistic consequences.

Stirner becomes a brand name for individualism in the first school. Individualistic clubs are founded which enthusiastically proclaim the tenets of "individualistic anarchism." Stirnerian territories are marked off, from which everything resembling socialism or communist anarchism is banished.

The second school carefully avoids any positive reference to Stirner. One does not speak in the name of Stirner. The phrase "in the name of..." sticks in the throat. Instead, a deterritorializing unrest is spread, which continually destabilizes the various assurances of what is called subject, identity, and individual. This is diametrically opposed to so-called "individualism." The aim, rather, is the delimitation of the principle of individualization, the disintegration of the individual from within himself. To be sure, the second school can also be and has been termed "individual anarchism." But beyond the partisan labels authors give to themselves or to others, the distinction inherent in the subject matter itself is decisive.

III

And Traven? We took a detour in order to illuminate what was made of Stirner up to the point when Traven came in contact with him. We do not know who informed him of Stirner's "unique ego," but we can say that Stirner had for a long time ceased to be a secret of insiders.[35] And we can clearly define Traven's reception of Stirner by reference to the two divergent schools. In the narrative An das Fräulein von S... (To the Baroness of S...) of 1916, the first longer prose text, we are introduced to a war hero who greatly surpasses his companions in courage and valor. He is supposed to be honored with medals and decorations, but he declines: His deeds are neither patriotically motivated nor performed to increase his honor as a soldier; rather, he is an "...egoist. Nothing but an eogist. What do I care about the war? I am conscious of my reasons for being here."[36] He is so valiant because--as he says--"I wanted to commit suicide and therefore pressed my way through to all the places where I would have the best chance of reaching my goal."[37] In the dramatic battle scens, his eogism drifts ineluctably towards disintegration. "The worst mistake people can make," he says, "is to attempt time and again to paste together something that absolutely and under all circumstances want to tear apart. One should let it tear, even speed it up, and not glue it together."[38] At another point he declares: "I don't give a damn about my completely finished personallity. Therefore, why delay?"[39]

With Traven we are dealing with the second--namely, the Landauer--school of Stirner reception. This is indicated not only by the early story, in which an egoistic death wish dominates normative notions of securing identity.[40] Those who sail on the Death Ship (the crews' quarters of which display the epigram "Whoever enters here--your name and existence are effaced") are "completely finished personalities" as well.[41] Of course, there are boundaries that obstruct the delimitation of the "mortal creator" in Stirner's sense. This is the case with Curtin and Dobbs, who warily stalk each other in Treasure: "Curtin had the power, but he was afraid to use it. He was a politician, not a creator. Dobbs on the other hand could waste, but not squander; he could demolish, but not destroy. And therefore, he too was not a creator; for the creator can squander and destroy."[42] And those dimensions of behavior that Traven discovers in the Indians of Mexico have nothing in common with a glorified individualism; thus Sleighs says in Bridge: We have a higher-developed will than the primitive. For people around here believe that it does not pay to have a strong will. What for? they say to themselves. All you get are annoyances and additional work. Only we who want to exploit them, we want to develop their power of will and their energy, so we can enslave them more easily."[43] In European culture, individualism and the communal sense have not only fallen apart ominously, but both are cramped within themselves. Our individualism and our social relationships are filled with fears of loss. In Land Traven attempts to show his readers "how difficult it is to explain to a European an Indian's world of ideas." Further: "We have pity, the Indian has none. He does not share pain, he always suffers alone. It is this self-suffering, this continual confrontation with himself, that we do not understand."[44]

111

tinual confrontation with himself, that we do not understand."[44]

Examples from Traven's work could be added, but I would like to focus on something more important. In analyzing Stirner's influence on Traven, it is, in my view, not sufficient to rely only on easily identifiable passages, as for instance at the end of the text "Die Zerstörung unseres Weltsystems durch die Markurve," in which one "Ich bin einzig" (I am unique) follows the other.[45] We can see from such sentences that we are dealing with a problem of language. Stirner himself points out to his perplexed critics: "The unique ego is a statement which, in all candor and honesty, affirms nothing. The human, the intellect, the true individual, the personality and so on are statements or predicates replete with the fulness of thought."[46] In contrast, the "unique ego" is "a _thoughtless_ word, having no thought content."[47] Moreover: "What Stirner _says_, is a word, a thought, a term; what he _means_ is no word, no thought, no term. What he says is not _what_ he means, and what he means is impossible to express."[48] Is then Marx and Engels's dictum correct, that Stirner's "unspeakable language is the end of all language"?[49] Perhaps not of all language, but it is the end of "every philosophically articulated language," as the philosopher of language and friend of Landauer, Fritz Mauthner, remarks.[50] The hero of Traven's first story, who seeks an egoistic suicide, declares his profession to be that of "philosopher."[51]

But what does the death of the "philosopher" mean? And what consequences does it have for language? Let us suppose that one were successful in destroying the bond linking my statements to my person; let us suppose one were successful in making it impossible to trace those sentences that I speak back to my identity—how drastically would the nature of my speech change! It would be, in every sense of the phrase, a _language_ _without_ _a_ _master._

But who could take responsibility for such a thing? No one. This is Traven's great effort. By dying to society through his anonymity, he killed the "philosopher," the "prophet," and the "political ideologue," whose words are aimed at achieving acclaim and support. A close association exists between the social identity and the philosophical self, that in contrast to Stirner's "unique ego" always wishes to be more than a phrase. The philosophical self is the origin of societal norms: "If I am free as a 'reasonable self,' then reason in me or reason itself is free."[52] And what is reason? It is "a book full of laws against egoism."[53] The philosophical self is the self in the cage of societal values, the self that answers to authority and

112

state, as a self equipped with its certification of legitimacy and police identification card."[54] The death of identity, the end of this coercive societal institution, is at the same time the birth of a language without a master, that is, a language that is to be read without reference to the author. The Brickburner wants to be nothing but "word,"[55] and Traven monotonously insists that "the creative person should have no other biography than his works."[56]

But the "masterlessness" of language also refers to the process of writing itself. "I have to admit seriously that I cannot explain why I have chosen this end and not another,"[57] Traven writes to the readers of The Death Ship. And his comment on The Bridge is even more explicit: "I have to write, 'as it comes to me,' otherwise I am forced to lie to myself and others. The idea that I had originally was totally different. But once I got to know the people who appeared on the scene better and more exactly, ideas ceased. Logically, the action had to follow from the characters of the people."[58] One is reminded of the automatic writing of the Surrealists. The writer is not master of the language; rather, the text takes shape itself outside the identity of a consciously creative author. "I do not lead the pen, it is led by someone else who only uses my clumsy hand,"[59] he writes in Ziegelbrenner. Incidentally, one might also consider whether the well-known theses concerning the double figure of an experiencing individual and of an author of literary fiction found in Traven's works do not constitute a scholarly reflection of the theme of a language without a master.

Decisive is the fact that language, by becoming masterless, is transformed into a criticism of the ruling language. When, for instance, Stirner empties the phrase "unique ego" of all thought content, and on the other hand insists, "For me this pitiful language has not word,"[60] then this manner of speaking in effect means that the "coining of phrases becomes a dishonorable act."[61] It is not simply a criticism of langauge aimed at eliminating and creating new meanings, but an almost implosive procedure, so to speak. "Language or 'the word' tyrannizes us the most, because it opposes a whole army of fixed ideas against us. Observe yourself for a moment while you are thinking, and you will discover that you only make progress by becoming thought- and speechless in any given moment."[62] Stirner lets the words implode; language is not to be used for the expression of a coherent subject, but is to be "spent as property."[63] He declares, "To think and speak I use truths and words, just as I use food to eat."[64]

The specifically "Stirnerian" elements in Traven's texts cannot be defined in terms of any program. What we have instead is the appearance of a language without a master that exploits and consumes historically, politically, and philosophically transmitted meanings. Thus, we find in Traven's texts the traditional contents of socialist, anarcho-socialist, and anarchist thoughts; profound insights into the dynamics of capitalism, which suggest a knowledge of Marxist writings; and, as is only rarely pointed out, the traditional contents of theosophic speculation and mystic natural philosophy as well.[65] We find all these traditions, but fermented by a language without a master that allows traditional meanings to disintegrate and turn in on themselves, exposing a wealth of things and happenings.

What we value in Traven's aesthetic is the impact of a language without a master. "Art is always ahead of understanding and knowledge. Because it does not think,"[66] the Brickburner writes. Art which subjects itself to a thinking subject falls into the realm of identity, the most powerful censor that exists. Only an author who has abdicated, who is socially dead, can avoid it: "The greatest power of art [is] its total lack of premises."[67]

In discussing Traven's relation to Stirner, I believe one falls short in looking only for programmatic phrases, in order to classify them in the history of ideas. And Traven did not switch from a bad individualistic anarchist to a good anarcho-socialist either. This dragnet in the realm of politico-logical research does not lead far. Traven's narrative art is without "premises," because it consumes all programmatics; it is poetry in the sense of Georges Bataille: "Creation through loss."[68] Its great force lies in being able to lose and to exhaust itself totally. It does not simply shape some political theory in artistic forms, but it opposes all forms of homogeneous thinking whose aim is to "take, as much as possible, from the universe in which we live its sources of agitation, and to develop a servile human race only fit for the production, the rational consumption, and the preservation of products."[69] It has been pointed out with good reason, using Bataille as an example, that such an understanding of art as an uncensored effort constitutes a "threat to artistic existence"[70] Traven skirted this threat by steadfastly defending his anonymity.

Finally, whatever the masterless language has lost in authority is continuously added to the objects, events, humans, and animals which are the subjects of Traven's tales. To put it in a nutshell, the author subordinates himself to his narrated things and creatures. Their unmistakable and unique qualities are expressed in language, in an untrammeled positivism, so to speak. Alexander Kluge calls this an "antagonistic realism," because these texts are directed "against the rhetorical principal of reality." Traven "consistently violates the rules 'of the narrator' in the sense of traditional narrative art." He violates "all basic rules of a narrative art in which the narrator overshadows reality."[71] To be exact, the objects themselves speak in Traven's texts, especially those objects that usually are only decorative. The cart and the ox that pulls it chronicle the life of the Carretero; the death ship is the yardstick of the seaman; the objects of daily life--clothing, food, residence--all provide information. And this rebellion of the very material itself communicates with what we try to grasp by the words "author," "subject," "individual," "self"; but this rebellion is carried to such an extreme that it cannot maintain itself a moment longer and must exclaim, "Long live the world in which there are so many strange things!"[72]

Egoistic concentration on the self and glorification of the value of the things of the world, therefore, are not a contradiction when the self approaches its boiling point. The intensity that knows no boredom, the fury that makes one forget oneself, the grief that tears apart the body, the bad mood that makes one explode with anger, the joy that turns a straight path into reeling "Markurven"--are those moments really only qualities of the subject? Or, in this agitation, does not the general excitement of the universe--the excitement of every single thing and creature--communicate itself to us?

I am becoming uneasy. One cannot talk about this reasonably. Perhaps if the ethnologists capitulated, the spirits might return to the island. But I decided to join an enlightened discourse and to analyze Stirner's influence on Traven. To recapitulate, Stirner's influence on Traven is not found on the level of a positive political critique and program. It is not specifically Stirnerian to affirm that the bourgeois forms of states are instruments of ruling classes, that the capitalistic organization of economic life is inseparably connected to exploitation, that the Christian belief in a hereafter renders people passive towards the misery of this earth, and, finally, that a revolutionary overthrow of the whole manner of human life arises from the experience of misery and the will of self-determination. We also find these affirmations in Marxist, socialist, syndicalist, and anarchist authors whom Traven knew. They influenced Traven's works, as is known. Beyond this, however, Traven opened himself to Stirner's rigorous nominalism,

which enables language to become masterless, and thus prevents any transformation of texts into Holy Scripture.

Notes

1. For the Brecht-Marxism relation, see Heinz Brüggemann,
Literarische Technik und soziale Revolution, Versuche über
das Verhäalnis von Kunstproduktion, Marxismus und literari-
scher Tradition in den theoretischen Schriften Bertolt
Brechts, Reinbek, 1973, passim.
2. Karl Marx, "Zur Kritik der Hegelschen Rechtsphiloso-
phie," Einleitung (1844) in Marx-Engels-Werke (MEW), Vol. 1,
Berlin (East) 1974, 385.
3. Max Stirner, Der Einzige und sein Eigentum (1844,
edited by Ahlrich Meyer, Stuttgart 1972, 330f. This edition
is hereafter referred to by the abbreviation "EE."
4. P. Watzlawick, J. H. Beavin, and D. D. Jackson, Men-
schliche Kommunikation, Bern 1969.
5. B. Traven, Das Totenschiff, Berlin 1926, 230.
6. Der Ziegelbrenner, Heft 4 of 27 July 1918, 84.
7. Ibid., Heft 26/27 of 30 March 1920, 39.
8. B. Traven, "Nachtbesuch im Busch," in B. Traven,
Abenteuergeschichten, Zürich 1974, 209f.
9. Angelika Machinek has made an attempt in this direction with Die Verarbeitung Stirnerscher Gedanken im Werk von
Ret Marut/B. Traven, Germanistische Staatsexamensarbeit,
Göttingen 1981 (typewritten).
10. For Stirner's role in Germany before 1848 and for the
interpretation of Stirner, see Bernd Kast, Die Thematik des
'Eigners' in der Philosophie Max Stirners. Sein Beitrag zur
Radikalisierung der anthropologischen Fragestellung, Bonn
1979, passim; Wolfgang Essbach, Gegenzüge. Der Materialis-
mus des Selbst und seine Ausgrenzung aus dem Marxismus--eine
Studie über die Kontroverse zwischen Max Stirner und Karl
Marx, Frankfurt/M. 1982, passim.
11. With regard to the following elaborations, the following works should be especially mentioned among the mass of
secondary literature: Kurt Brandis, Der Anfang vom Ende der
Sozialdemokratie (1927), Berlin 1975, 36ff.; Hans Manfred
Bock, Geschichte des 'linken Radikalismus' in Deutschland.
Ein Versuch, Frankfurt/M. 1976, 38-78; Ulrich Linse, Organi-
sierter Anarchismus im Deutschen Kaiserreich von 1871, Berlin 1969, passim; Hans G. Helms, Die Ideologie der anonymen
Gesellschaft, Köln 1966, 295-426.
12. Manifest quoted according to Hans Müller, Der Klas-
senkampf in der deutschen Sozialdemokratie, Zürich 1892,
118.

13. Hermann Conradi, Phrasen, Leipzig 1887, 232f. and 314.
14. Bruno Wille, "Eine Dichtung Mackay's," in Freie Bühne für modernes Leben, 2. Jg. Berlin 1891, 1251.
15. See also Bruno Wille, Aus Traum und Kampf. Mein sechzigjähriges Leben, Berlin 1920, passim.
16. Ibid., l.c., 33.
17. Bruno Wille, Einsiedler und Genosse. Soziale Gedichte nebst einem Vorspiel, Berlin, (1890), 103.
18. EE, 65f.
19. See note 17 above.
20. Der Ziegelbrenner, Heft 18/19 of 3 December 1919, 10.
21. Recknagel, 1971, 50.
22. Wyatt, 1980, 293.
23. Michael Bakunin, Staatlichkeit und Anarchie (1873), Berlin 1972, 185.
24. Peter Kropotkin, Die Entwicklung der anarchistischen Ideen, Berlin (Fritz Kater) n.d., 15f.
25. For Tucker, see Paul Ghio, L'Anarchisme aux Etats-Unis, Paris 1903, 79ff.; Eunice Minette Schuster, Native American Anarchism: A Study of Left-Wing American Individualism (Smith College Studies in History), Worthampton, Mass. 1932, 138-43, 152-53; Corrine Jacker, The Black Flag of Anarchy: Antistatism in the United States, New York 1968, 117-27.
26. John Henry Mackay, Die Anarchisten. Kulturgemälde aus dem Ende des 19. Jahrhunderts (1891), Berlin 1893, 105-42.
27. For the reception of Stirner in the research of Traven, see Essbach in Beck u.a., 1976, 376ff.
28. Gustav Landauer, Der Todesprediger (1893), Köln [3]1923, 54.
29. EE, 3.
30. Landauer, Der Todesprediger, l.c., 56.
31. See Franz Overbeck, "Erinnerungen an Friedrich Nietzsche" in Die Neue Deutsche Rundschau, 17. Jg., 1 vol., Berlin 1906, 227f.
32. Landauer, Der Todesprediger, l.c., 56, 66f.
33. Ibid., 68.
34. For Landauer, see Wolf Kalz, Gustav Landauer, Kultursozialist und Anarchist, Meisenheim/Glan 1967; Eugene Lunn, Prophet of Community: The Romantic Socialism of Gustav Landauer, London 1973.
35. Recknagel believes that Traven was influenced by Anselm Ruest's interpretation of Stirner. (Recknagel, 1982, 102, 121-23, 165.) However, the proofs for this are not convincing.
36. Richard Maurhut (B. Traven), "An das Fräulein von S..." (1916), in B. Traven/Ret Marut, Das Frühwerk, with a preface by R. Recknagel, Berlin 1977, 89.

37. Ibid., 105.
38. Ibid., 100.
39. Ibid., 101.
40. Any open reference to Stirner is avoided in Der Ziegelbrenner; only an advertisement of Stirner's "Kleine Schriften" is included in the two editions.
41. B. Traven, Das Totenschiff, l.c., 109.
42. B. Traven, Der Schatz der Sierra Madre, Berlin 1927, 163.
43. B. Traven, Die Brücke im Dschungel, Frankiurt/M., Wien, Zürich 1978, 135.
44. B. Traven, Land des Frühlings, Berlin 1928, 205, 214.
45. Der Ziegelbrenner, Heft 20/22 of 6 January 1920, 44.
46. Max Stirner, Kleinere Schriften, edited by J. H. Mackay, Stuttgart, Bad Cannstatt 1976, 347.
47. Ibid., 348.
48. Ibid., 345.
49. Karl Marx and Friedrich Engels, Die Deutsche Ideologie, in Marx-Engels-Werke (MEW), Vol. 3, Berlin (East) 1969, 435.
50. Fritz Mauthner, Der Atheismus und seine Geschichte im Abendlande, Vol. 4, Stuttgart, Berlin 1923, 210.
51. R. Maurhut (B. Traven), "An das Fräulein von S...," l.c., 115.
52. EE, 388.
53. EE, 372.
54. EE, 283.
55. See note 6 above.
56. B. Traven, "Mein Roman 'Das Totenschiff,'" (1926) in Beck, 1976, 148.
57. Ibid., 150.
58. A letter from Traven to Preczang of 20 March 1927.
59. Der Ziegelbrenner, Heft 4 of 27 July 1918, 89.
60. EE, 201.
61. Stirner, Kleine Schriften, l.c., 347.
62. EE, 389.
63. Ibid.
64. EE, 391.
65. The "Ziegelbrenner companion," Götz Ohly, remembers Ret Marut's arrival in Munich in the spring of 1917: "From his suitcase he unpacked a stack of manuscripts and a folder of strange drawings that he pinned to the walls; they were astronomical sketches." Götz Ohly, Das Rätsel um den Dichter Traven, l.c., 3f.
66. Der Ziegelbrenner, Heft 20/22 of 6 January 1920, 27.
67. Ibid.
68. Georges Bataille, "Der Begriff der Verausgabung," in G. Bataille, Das theoretische Werk, Vol. 1, Die Aufhebung

der Ökonomie, München 1975, 15.

69. G. Bataille, "La valeur d'usage de D.A.F. de Sade," quoted according to G. Bergfleth, "Theorie der Verschwendung," in G. Bataille, Das theoretische Werk, Vol. 1, l.c., 308.

70. Christa Karpenstein-Essbach, "Ökonomie und Ästhetik bei Georges Bataille," in Konkursbuch. Zeitschrift für Vernunftkritik, No. 5, Tübingen 1980, 100.

71. Heiner Boehnke and Alexander Kluge, "Die Rebellion des Stoffs gegen die Form und der Form gegen den Stoff," in Beck, 1976, 340-42.

72. B. Traven, Die Brücke im Dschungel, 186.

A SANE PROTAGONIST IN EXTREMIS
B. Traven's Gay Imagings of Participation and Suffering in The Bridge in the Jungle and The Death Ship

Richard Flantz

Protagonist

The Gales novels and stories are Traven's only first-person narratives. Hardly ever named, sometimes changing his name, referring but rarely and then inconsistently to his past, Gales lives and narrates very much in the present of his stories. A persona of Traven himself? Perhaps, but that is not my concern here.[1]

In The Death Ship Gales is a protagonist in the conventional literary sense: The action he narrates focuses on his own agon. In The Night Visitor stories and in The Cotton Pickers this also seems true. But in The Bridge in the Jungle he seems rather the central consciousness witnessing the major sequence of events--the agon, primarily, of another person, the Garcia woman, in her loss of her son Carlosito. And yet, Gales is the protagonist of this novel, and the way he fulfills this role illuminates much about our topic.

"Stick'm up, stranger!" this novel dramatically begins, and in the immediate anticlimax Gales learns another lesson about surviving in the jungle. Subsequent episodes are linked only by their being successive accidental meetings with Sleigh, the man who robbed him. Yet this establishes what we technically call a plot: the episodic plot of Gales's meetings with Sleigh. Of this plot, Gales is, technically, the protagonist, and the main action of this novel is an extended episode in this plot. In effect, Gales is shown as the protagonist, not of a work of literature, but of his own life, as a person who lives protagonistically.[2] Unlike the "hero" of classical literature, who usually has a specific goal which defines his one climactic agon; unlike the picaro (to whom he is more akin), who is usually goalless and unconcerned about other people; unlike the modern anti-hero--Gales has a goal, always, though it is not circumscribed: to know life and to live it sanely and decently. And when his way brings him into intimate contact with another person's agon, his own agon can involve participation in it without fear that this will somehow take him out of his own life.

Traven could have represented the agon of the Garcia woman and of her friends' and neighbors' participation in it quite effectively in an anonymous third-person narration. As he did so movingly in other works, he could have written this hymn to all motherhood and fatherhood, this vivid picture of native life, and he could have commented on the events from his own perspective, all without Gales.[3] Gales's presence, after all, hardly affected what happened there by that bridge.

Presenting it through Gales, Traven brings us a vivid image of a person with a capacity for sensitive, intelligent, empathetic imagining of--and participating in--another human being's suffering. This capacity as well as the willingness to activate it, is, I suggest, an essential characteristic of the sane and decent protagonist in the world--not only of Gales, but of the kind of person Traven's writings affirm. This capacity is also an essential component of the vision that informs all the Traven narratives, from The Death Ship to the last of the Jungle novels. All are instinct with such empathetic imagining, and in them there are other sane protagonists, too. But Bridge is unique in literature, in giving us this detailed imaging of a protagonist primarily involved in empathetic witnessing and participating, all without undue focus on the protagonist himself; for Gales is less interested in himself, his own reactions or reflections, than in what he reacts to and reflects on. The narration, contemporaneous with his consciousness, although the past tense is used for the most part, makes the persons, their actions, and the locale vividly present to us.

Mikhail Bakhtin, in his famous Problems of Dostoevsky's Poetics,[4] saw Dostoevsky's uniqueness in his having created the "polyphonic novel." Many-voicedness as a principle of artistic construction allowed "characters" to be conceived as "full-fledged subjects, not objects," like persons in the real world. The "dialogical intuition" of another's subjecthood, the sense of every other as a whole "thou," underlay, Bakhtin wrote, the major inspiration of Dostoevsky's work, the "struggle against the materialization of man, of human relations, and of all human values under the conditions of capitalism." And Dostoevsky's polyphonic achievement, he believed, had "destroyed the established forms of the basically monological (homophonic) [let's say single-voiced] European novel."[5]

Traven's novels are all basically single-voiced, the Gales stories more evidently so. But this is a "monology" which presupposes a world of "full-fledged subjects," which proposes that each human subject can have a sense of the constant polyphony all around him, and that other persons can be related to as subjects not only by an author or an invis-

ible narrator, but also, or rather primarily, by a protagonist, an individual person. The "dialogical intuition,"
which Bakhatin thought required polyphonic form, is in
Bridge exquisitely expressed in monological form through the
consciousness of the empathetic protagonist, Gerard Gales.
More important, perhaps, this novel posits such "dialogical
intuition," i.e., empathetic imagining, as a sine qua non of
sanity and decency, and it posits it tacitly, by showing it
operating in the protagonist.[6]

In Extremis

In the two books under discussion, Gales is shown experiencing extremes of suffering, horror, and grief in the two ways
a human can experience them: through suffering oneself,
alone, and through suffering, empathetically, another person's suffering. In The Death Ship, where he is the central
though not the only sufferer, he undergoes terrible physical
--and not only physical--torment. In Bridge he experiences
an equally extreme anguish not his own, which yet becomes
his own as well.

We know that extremity tests--in life and in literature.
If we begin again by suspending our disbelief and relate to
Gales as if he were a real person, not a fictional character
(The Death Ship seems to require more suspension of disbelief than Bridge does), then we find that Gales is not
looking for extremity, is not seeking tests. Extremity
befalls him in the situations these books narrate, as it
befalls many.

In The Death Ship he suffers the prolonged and complex
agon of "unaccommodated man" (to borrow Lear's phrase) in
the context of modern civilization, with its nation-state
organization and its capitalist economy. To be minimally
accommodated here, one must have proper (national) identity
papers, and money.[7] The three stages of Gales's agon are
complete strandedness (in Europe), incarceration in a physical hell (the death ship Yorikke), and confrontation with
imminent death (on the sinking hull of the death ship Empress of Madagascar). All three stages are extreme. Hypo-
thetical-fictional and quasi-allegorical though they might
seem, we cannot but be struck by their similarities to real
situations which we know people in our times have undergone,
often not surviving them.[8] This knowledge and the vivid
imaging promote a belief that Gales does undergo all this
suffering, which cannot but be an extreme test not only of
his physical endurance, but of his very sanity.

In Bridge the death of Carlosito is an extreme event. All
who participate in the quest or the mourning sense this,

even people who hardly knew the boy, like Gales, or the drunken teacher who articulates simply and unsentimentally over the grave the absoluteness of the loss: "The little boy is dead. He is completely dead. I am sure of that. We'll never see him again. We shall never, as long as this world may exist, never more hear his innocent and happy laughter" (209). Most extreme is the mother's grief, which only other mothers can empathize with fully: "Only a mother knows how a mother feels. No one else, not even God in heaven with all His immaculate wisdom, with all His stern serenity, can feel as a mother feels when her baby has been taken away from her" (114). (In context, as contents of consciousness at specific moments of the action, these are not platitudes.) All this extremity, when experienced so intensely and protractedly as it is here, can also test one's sanity; we may recall Ivan Karamazov's tormented question: How can life be right, just, or worthwhile, if innocent children suffer and die? Extreme, too, is the way Gales can participate in the mourning of this community with customs so different from his own.

We can imagine the extreme situations imaged in both books--which means we can believe that a person might undergo them as Gales does.[9] And while this means that we're crediting Traven with having created a valid, meaningful fiction, it has primarily to do with--and can primarily affect--our understanding of and our attitude towards life, rather than our attitudes towards literature or our appreciation of Traven. And, paradoxically, it is precisely this that testifies to Traven's great literary achievement.

And if we now want to qualify that, Bakhtin can again be of assistance. The forerunners of the Dostoevskian polyphonic novel, he says, are the seriocomic genres of antiquity, especially the _menippea_ (Menippean satire). Characteristic of the seriocomic is a "carnivalization," a "jolly relativity," which rejects or questions all absolute dogmas. And "the most important characteristic of the _menippea_ lies in the fact that the most daring and unfettered fantasies and adventures are internally motivated, justified, and illuminated...by a purely ideological and philosophical end--to create extraordinary situations in which to test a philosophical idea--the word or the truth, embodied in the image of the wise man, the seeker after truth. This testing occurs in one of three regions: on earth, in the nether regions, or on Olympus."[10]

We can recognize much of this as applicable to our books,[11] but more important are the differences. Traven's extremes are ultimately not fantasy. And what is tested in them is not any _idea_ or _word_ (i.e., ideology or philosophy)

but an attitude, a way of living--specifically, the attitude
of the sane protagonist. To illuminate the distinction
between idea (which has to do primarily with intellect) and
attitude (which has to do with feeling and imagining as much
as with thinking), and at the same time to further qualify
Traven's achievement in the "monological" form: Bakhtin
says that in a monological novel, an idea which retains
significance as an idea ceases to be artistically combined
with the hero; it could equally be placed in any other
hero's mouth. Also, thoughts which are polemically negated
cannot be represented.[12] But most of Gales's articulated
ideas are consistent with his essential attitude and derive
from it; on the other hand, things he sometimes does negate
polemically, like the dynamics of capitalist and bureaucratic "materialization" of humans, are represented in vivid
detail--sometimes basically, as in The Cotton Pickers, or in
extreme form, as in The Death Ship.

Imaging

Imaging is the artistic presentation of images. An image,
as distinct from an idea or a concept, is a whole, or holis-
tic, thing: To "have an image" involves sensing (actually
or imaginatively seeing, hearing, smelling, and so on),
feeling, thinking, and valuing all at once. Active empathetic imagining includes thinking, but its source or motive
force is what Traven/Gales several times calls the "soul
spirit and heart":[13] It is the combined activity, as Cole-
ridge put it, of "the whole soul of man."[14] The essence of
artistic mimesis in any medium is the creation and transmis-
sion of images which are always particular, unique, and
contingent, but at the same time are not isolated; they can
be imagined as participating in larger processes--personal,
social, historic, cosmic, each with its own contingency, but
with a universal aspect as well. In the central tradition
of Western critical thought, great literature is that which
richly transmits moving images which, while distinctively
particular, have universal significance. In this tradition,
not a very fashionable one today, imaging is the essence of
literature, to which language, structure, and style are
subordinate means. Traven is a master of imaging, of creating images of events and of processes. He is as perceptive of minute detail as of complex causality, and not only
with psychological and physiological perspicuity and a keen
sense of socio-economic-historic dynamics, but also with
empathy.[15] Thus he conveys to us not any idea or philosophy, but his--and Gales's--fundamental informing attitude,
by arousing in us what Gales's perception of the Garcia

124

woman's suffering aroused in him: that imaginative, empathetic intuition which is a mysterious compound of identification with and difference from some other person, actual
or fictional. "Aesthetic distance," this is sometimes
called; the ancient Greeks called it _methexis_, "participation."

Traven's imaging technique is comprehensive, detailed, and
often consecutive in all his fiction. The matter-of-fact
descriptions translate easily into vivid images--of moments,
aspects of moments, persons, places, processes--even when
the English is awkward, with its Germanisms, mismanaged
Americanisms, and other flaws; for the language is a means,
not an end: Traven had something to say.[16] Or, rather,
Traven had something to show: in the spirit of Conrad's
statement, "My task which I am trying to achieve is, by the
power of the written word, to make you hear, to make you
feel--it is, before all else, to make you _see_"[17] Often
highly cinematic, imaging audible and visible exteriorities,
Traven's work remains highly literary by his recurring focus
on interiority, his references to related processes, and the
frequent centering of the images in a polyphonic and multi-
dimensional world.

The opening scenes of _Bridge_ are polyphonic images of how
others live--Sleigh, the pump-master, and others--as perceived by an outsider. A center of concern arises when the
Garcia woman starts looking for her child. Gales's empathetic consciousness follows her, and the others who get involved, from this early stage through her growing anxiety,
her deepening certainty, her anguished search in which
others join, her numbed discovery of the rightness of her
initial intuition, and then the many individual actions--
hers and others--through the night of mourning, the funeral
march, and the burial. The imaging power reaches a climax
as everybody ("that multi-headed body") watches the board
with the candle making its way toward the bridge. Here
Gales thinks--and his thoughts never appear as "authorial
intrusions," but as imagings of his thoughts at particular
moments--that he may "never again behold such a grandiose
picture," and he can also develop the reflection that
"against the simple and natural clothes of the men the
women's dresses from modern sweat-shops make a pitiful contrast." Then the body is found (miraculously?), and the
imaging is equal to what follows, too:

At this moment, many women uttered a shrill, plaintive
wail, full of reproach.
That wail, which pierced the blackness of the night as
if it meant to break through and rise to the sun in the

sky swelled until all the women fell in. Then it sank and became a low moan. The women wrapped a piece of cloth, be it a rebozo, a black veil, or a shawl around their heads. Their faces hidden, they wept bitterly.

It was no longer only the death of the Garcia woman's child that they bewailed. By his untimely death the little boy had become every mother's baby. Only a mother knows...(114)

From here the passage moves into the piece quoted earlier. How does Gales know what the women are bewailing? He imagines it, intuits it, as later, watching the Garcia woman shake off her despair, he reflects:

The many obligations she faced helped her to forget her grief. And it was surely a very good thing that she had to get busy around her household. It would save her from becoming morose perhaps for the rest of her life. It is the first twelve hours that count. If one can survive and keep one's reason under control during this time, one can find life worth-while again in a few weeks. (123-24)

This is not an author theorizing or repeating platitudes, but a man in a specific situation realizing anew an ancient wisdom, by imagining. This imagining motivates his further participation, including the minimal help he can give, in the communal activity. And his perceptions fill the rich imagings of all that follows, to the funeral march with all its incongruities deriving from Western influences, and the scene around the grave, where Gales weeps with all the others, because, he says, he has become "one of them, and it was my boy who was to be buried as he was the child of everyone present." And not present? Gales weeps as if over something "recalled to mind by a well-written narrative," for, though he'd hardly known him, Carlosito had become "my boy, my little brother, my fellow man, who could suffer as I can, who could laugh as I can, and who could die as I shall die some day." So the protagonist feels at this moment, and so, he hints, his readers can feel, for fellow-feeling depends on imagining, which imaging can evoke.

Equally vivid imaging of circumstances, events, thoughts, and feelings mark the Death Ship narrative. In Europe, Gales is harassed by police, smuggled across borders, imprisoned, and has a spate of the "good life" in Spain; he is a decent protagonist at the mercy of a rational, "materializing" bureaucracy. And these conditions become still more intensely detailed on the Yorikke, as he learns to survive in the hellish conditions. The imaging rises to an inten-

sity of horror, and just when we think there could be no
worse, when we have read of the "living" quarters and conditions, the "chamber of horrors," the unbelievable hours and
working conditions of the coal-drag--unloading ashes, the
snake-dance descent through scalding steam into the boiler-
room, the inferno itself, where one's skin is burned and
torn--then we learn of the ultimate torments, the work that
must be done when grate-bars drop.[18] And then there are the
imagings of people on board, "the deads," of the other coal-
drags, Lavski in particular, and his stories of others;
imagings of the social hierarchy, the language on board this
nationless, international mini-nation, its gun-running activities and ports of call, the way its crew are treated
ashore; and, finally, imagings of Lavski and Gales's brief
careers on the Empress of Madagascar, culminating in magnificent images of their surviving shipwreck and storm on the
hull, then on a spar, until Lavski's sanity gives way,
leaving Gales alone again, a sole, sane protagonist in a
hopeless sea, still hoping.

The imaging in both books is also symbolic, and this
symbolism joins with the content of the reflections and the
nature of the behavior of the protagonist to qualify the
sanity of the perspective and the gaiety of the presentation.

Sane, Gay

The jungle and the death ships are both ultimate symbols of
the place and condition of human life, especially in our
time. The symbolism of the jungle is valid because the real
jungle is a place teeming with organisms struggling for
existence, where the strongest survive longest and the
powerful rule, often mercilessly. Life outside the jungle
is an extension, if also a dilution, of what happens there.
Upton Sinclair and others who have spoken of capitalistic
metropolitan life as jungle have a point. Yet, as we see in
Bridge and in Traven's other Jungle books, peoples who have
lived for millenia in the jungle have developed sane, humane
ways of social intercourse which overcome even corruptive
"materializing" influences from the West (or, here, the
North). For there is a basic humanity in which decency and
fellow-feeling are primary. So if the principle of materialization or objectification originated in the jungle, the
jungle is also where the humane principle has evolved.[19]

The death ships, however, are the ultimate end-product,
the rational result, and the epitome of materialization, by
which the powerful rule, exploiting whom and whatever they
can--people's desires, needs, energies, and lives, no less

than material resources—to turn a profit which can extend their own power and pleasures. Materialization, as Bakhtin probably knew, neither began nor ends with modern capitalism. Traven certainly knew it. It began even before the _Yorikke_ sailed out of Ararat or Phoenicia, with the merchants-slavers-deforesters, to build and extend the reign of Imperator Augustus Capitalismus.[20] In modern times it has perhaps become more streamlined and efficient: The owners of the _Tuscaloosa_ know that better conditions for workers can mean better work and bigger profits.[21] But modern capitalism also has its death ships, which it can man as long as men can be found who have no alternative. These ships are run and constructed rationally, by the logic of maximal materialization. Conditions on the _Yorikke_ show in an extreme form how men can survive deprivation, malnutrition, inadequate shelter, hygiene, and clothing, while doing labor which maims or destroys body and soul and which profits other people, who are under the rule of oligarchs (who profit from them too, whether the capitalism be privately or corporately owned, as in the West, or state-owned and Bolshevik.[22]

While some of those who materialize humans may be cruel and vicious, even psychopaths who enjoy their power to hurt or kill their victims, most exploiters are not malicious. They are rational; they do what is most profitable. Men and children may suffer and die as a result, but these are by-products, not goals, of the profiteers' activities. Carlosito's death was such a by-product and no simple accident: Partly responsible for it were the absentee oil company which erected the bridge without a rail, in order to economize (like the _Yorikke_'s builders, skimping on living and working quarters to make room for cargo); and the fascination with the ways and products of modern capitalism (where, in this, could one focus blame?) which took Carlosito's brother Manuel to work in the Texas oil fields and caused him to bring back the smooth-soled shoes in which the boy, losing his native agility, fell to his death.

Of the exploited, some submit while wholly accepting the materializing principle. "Give a proletarian a peso and he'll immediately turn capitalist,"[23] and, Gales adds, he'll also justify his actions of greed and exploitation with concepts of capitalist rationality, the national good, or religiosity.[24] Not everyone, though. Gales, for example, doesn't turn capitalist when he gets money. And when he submits, he does so like many others—like Andrés and Celso in the Jungle books[25]—not in affirmation or acceptance of materialization, but out of love for someone or something, or hope for a more humane life.

128

In _The Death Ship_, Gales gives all his money to a whore:
Her tale of an ailing mother just might be true. Later he
boards the _Yorikke_ (knowing it's a death ship), leaving his
paradisial though unproductive life in Spain, so as not to
miss what might be his only chance to get a job and perhaps
to return to Honey in New Orleans. When it is so bad there
that he wants to commit suicide, he doesn't, out of empathy
again, because then "there would only be another poor,
overtired, ragged, starved, and tortured coal-drag [Lavski]
who would have to go on double shift on account of your
having kicked off" (130). Lavski, too, landed on the death
ship because of a similar sense of values, and not only
because similar geopolitical conditions have claimed many
victims. Also stranded without nationality, because, doing
something he loved (working as a seaman), he didn't read
newspapers or government bulletins to learn about new citizenship regulations, he finally chose the death ship because
living by the "honorable trade" (pilfering; all that remained when he couldn't get a job without papers) made him
feel dirty, like living off someone else. Later, both men
risk their lives to save the Negro coal-drag.[26]
The two material necessities for survival in the modern
legal-rational systems of nation-state capitalism, the two
main "tools" by which men are materialized in these systems,
are money and nationality. Men identify with one or both;
and some, with the power these endow, and often with the aid
of ideology, use them to exploit others. The exploiters may
identify with either or both, or neither; they can use the
readiness of the exploited to identify in one of these ways;
or they can find ways of exploiting or enslaving those who
lack either, whether they identify with one or the other, or
neither. Gales, in _The Death Ship_, doesn't identify with a
nationality. He claims he's a native-born citizen of the
United States, but his language often belies this.[27] Later
he says he's Egyptian and calls himself Pippip. One symbolic effect of all this is to suggest that nationality, and
even proper names, are superficial, material matters, essentially irrelevant to the true being of "soul spirit and
heart." On the _Yorikke_ these things serve as identifying
tags, no more, with the added irony that all these de-
nationalized men are here named by the nationality they have
lost, as people are often related to in terms of national or
racial origin in modern nation-states which have some heter-
ogeneity of population. For the _Yorikke_ is also a miniature
nation-state, and its "no-exit" situation is symbolic of
those restrictions on individuals' movements across borders
by which nation-states facilitate rational exploitation.
Gales and Lavski talk about these things. They are indig-

nant about "this trade in human souls and this kicking out and pushing about of people"; they see the link between exploitation and national bureaucracy and how the majority of people in the world "fall for worn-out slogans" and thus help to sustain the systems that exploit and repress them and others. Lavski says (pessimistically? optimistically?) to Gales, who, like him, finds the situation cruel and insane, "As long as there are not five hundred million sane and decent persons found on earth who admit the same you say and I say, there will be no change."

Gales and Lavski don't condemn those who exploit, or those who fall for and serve worn-out slogans; nor do they pity the victims, at least not in the sense in which condemnation and pity are self-indulgent sentimentalism, as Gales explicitly calls them in The Cotton Pickers.[28] In Bridge there was not pity for the Garcia woman, but a true sharing of her grief. The sane and decent are not self-righteous, though they get indignant. Mostly they are gay and exuberant. They know well what Yeats called "all the tragic scene," and they build life again and again. They not only learn to survive on the Yorikke, but also to find true satisfaction in the skills they develop, a gay delight in creative accomplishment.[29]

The source of this gaiety--which characterizes both the protagonist's attitude and the narrator's (and author's) technique and tone--is not any ideology, doctrine, or philosophy, but the original empathetic-imaginative movement of soul spirit and heart. It is as ancient as man, perhaps, finding expression in the cultures of all continents--in the ancient wisdom of the Mexican Indians, as in that of the Tao and the "jolly relativity of [classical] antiquity"[30] in the teachings of Hillel and of Jesus[31]--and it has been reaffirmed in more recent times, primarily by Romantic poets and philosophers (Blake, Shelley, Emerson, Whitman, Thoreau, and Yeats being among its foremost exponents in English). It is probably the most difficult of attitudes to represent in novel form, for what is sane and decent is a priori far less sensational or titillating than what is not,[32] and its essential fatalism would make it seem less poignant. For it is fatalistic (what will be will be), though never quietistic or apathetic, as we see in the fatalistic Indians at the bridge, active in their search and concerned and constructive in their mourning. And it is anarchic--in the present (deriving its values from soul, spirit, and heart, and not from teachings, rules, and laws, it denies any oligarchy, orthodoxy, or ultimate authority over it) and in its social ideal, about which it is neither optimistic nor pessimistic, though it hopes. And since it knows its empathetic-imaginative source, which it grasps as more important than reason or rationality,[33] it affirms the value of art, which transmits images which are gay or beautiful, or which shows sane and decent persons living, loving, surviving even the fires of hell, as sane, gay protagonists, even _in extremis_. Traven's literary-humanistic achievement in these two "monological" novels rests, I believe, on his gay imaging and affirming of such knowledge.

Notes

1. The biographic interest in Traven, fascinating as it is (as he himself so often reiterated) irrelevant to a critical evaluation of his written works, though not necessarily to an evaluation of his total artistic achievement, which surely includes the creation of the mysterious persona "B. Traven."

2. Here I adopt and adapt Yeats's theater metaphor, when he speaks of the gay as those "worthy of the prominent part in the play," the "play," of course, being their own lives. To know, not what the future holds, but that death will come, and that one _is_ until then the protagonist of one's own life, as all others can be, to live by this positive inner sense rather than by others' demands or commands or one's own antagonisms to them—this is to live protagonistically.

3. This "hymn to all motherhood (and fatherhood)"—these words about _Bridge_ are Herbert Klein's (spoken to me in conversation). The "vivid picture of native life" is an aspect of Traven's literary achievement stressed by Robert T. Goss in his chapter "From Ret Marut to B. Traven: More Than a Change in Disguise," p. 44.

4. An English translation, by R. W. Rotsel, was published in 1973 under the Ardis imprint. No place of publication appears, other than "Manufactured in the United States of America." ISBN 0-88233-040-3 and 041-1. Worth searching out for its fine presentation of relations between forms and essences in the poetics of narrative fiction, not only Dostoevsky's.

5. Ibid., 4-7, 51.

6. If one were not examining a literary work, one might not have invoked Bakhtin. For the essence of "dialogical intuition" is not found first in literature, but in life. It is one of the two basic ways of being-in-the-world which Martin Buber outlined so precisely in his _I and Thou_ (_Ich und Du_, 1923; English translations: Ronald Gregor Smith, 1937; Walter Kaufman, New York: Charles Schribner's, 1970):

"When I confront a human being [or a tree, or any being] as my du...then he [or it] is no thing among things nor does he consist of things" (Kaufmann adapted , 59). Philosophically Buber completes the characterization of the "I" begun by Max Stirner in Der Einzige und sein Eigentum (and see Michael L. Baumann's fine "Appendix B: Max Stirner's The Ego and His Own" Baumann, 1976, 131-53). Traven's profound sense of the "Thou" as an "I" is embodied in Gales, especially in Bridge, though it is really ubiquitous in his writings and even finds explicit expression sometimes, as in the story "The Cattle Drive," where Gales shows how he learned "how to tame and train a horse without losing your patience or breaking his pride," where it informs his looking after the calves born on the drive, and his delight in the sight of the "giant herd of healthy half-wild cattle...trampling and stamping, the heavy necks, the rounded bodies, the proud, mighty horns....a heaving sea of gigantic vitality, of brute nature herded by one single purpose. And each pair of horns represented a life in itself, a life with its own will, its own desires, its own thoughts and feelings."

7. Berman (1981) writes of Traven's "mordant obsession with bureaucracy, passports, the police, authority run amok, the state, and the hapless individual" as being cast in a particularly "German or at least Central European mold." Yet the statelessness and depatriation here symbolized speak of the condition not only of many groups of people in the world today but also of the potential condition of any individual who does not obey the regulations imposed by nation-state governments, implemented by their bureaucracies, and enforced by their police.

8. If, after World War II, and facing an uncertain future we say we know of extremes far worse than any Traven imagined or imaged, let us recognize that in the two books under discussion, Traven has imaged the essences of the worst anyone could experience under any circumstances: suffering oneself, and suffering the suffering of others. And if the greatest trauma of our time lies in the realization that so many human beings could actively contribute to the torturing and killing of so many other human beings, "materializing" them absolutely with the aid of ideologies and for personal gain, we might note that here and in his other books Traven gives us vivid images of how and why the perpetrators and the sufferers do what they do. His apparently hypothetical fiction thus becomes more than naturalistic, and the quasi-allegory prophetically symbolic.

9. As Gales does, i.e., with that kind of sane, gay, attitude with which he enters each situation, and which sustains him even in extremis.

10. Op. cit., 87, 94.

11. The "carnivalization" and "jolly relativity" extend to the work's references to itself, by innuendo or explicit comparisons with other works in related genres, especially in The Death Ship. (Especially interesting in this context is the story of Gales telling his story to Fibby and earning twenty dollars for the plot, out of which Fibby, who owns a paper, expects to make thousands; Chap. 6.) The adventures, too, may seem fantastical, exaggerated, or caricaturistic, though not more so than much of what actually happens, and they occur in at least two of the regions Bakhtin mentions, the inferno of the fire-room being one of the most realistic-symbolic evocations of "the nether regions" in literature.

12. Op. cit., 64.

13. For Gales, this is the essential "I," the source of courage (see The Death Ship, Chap. 27, p. 130), of empathy, and of vision.

14. Biographia Literaria, Chap. 14, penultimate paragraph.

15. The images of working processes and living conditions on the Yorikke are marvelously done, and absolutely convincing with their concentration of interrelated stages. So also in the Jungle books. Robert T. Goss has drawn attention to this in his chapter "From Ret Marut to B. Traven: More Than a Change in Disguise," p. 44.

16. As Karl S. Guthke notes in his chapter "Was There Another Man? B. Traven as Author of His Own Works," p. 12.

17. Preface to The Nigger of the "Narcissus."

18. The horror is intensified by the sequence of description Traven uses, the technique of representing an accumulation of torments and leaving the worst till last. Thus, while the narration has been mostly consecutive-chronological, in this section of the book Gales narrates many things he learns about later, summarizing many aspects of life on the death ship, before coming to the most terrible of the recurrent experiences in the inferno of the fire-room.

19. One may see a "de-humanizing primitivism" in the characterization of Indian mores and the likening of certain Indians to ancient deities--as does Cynthia Steele in her chapter "The Primitivist as Anarchist," p. 307. I tend rather to see this as a humanizing, antimaterializing move in the Romantic tradition, less of Rousseau's (and Lawrence's) "noble savage" than of Blake's "Human Form Divine."

20. The mythic dimension of the imaging of the Yorikke, developed by the descriptions of its appearance as well as by statements about its ancient origins, links it to legendary vessels like The Flying Dutchman and Noah's Ark, with the added symbolism of mercantilism, ancient capitalism

based on slave labor, thus making it the ultimate symbol for the capaitalistic drive that has dominated human societies since ancient times, empires like the Roman being but an external consolidation of capitalistic power. This makes Traven's imaging of the source and essence of capitalism a profounder vision than the Marxian analysis. The ship's name, recalling the image of Hamlet holding the late jester's skull in the dug-up grave, links the associations of death and "infinite jest" which characterize Gales-Traven's ambivalent attitude towards capitalism, which is, after all, the ship that keeps us alive, in whatever conditions, as it takes us to our deaths. Significantly, both Gales and Lavski develop a love for the Yorikke. Even more significant, the Yorikke does not sink during the course of this story; the shipwreck that does occur destroys one of the death ship's latest incarnations, the ironically named Empress of Madagascar.

21. Tuscaloosa is an American city name; it may also be a symbol for the American way in modern capitalism. A portmanteau word?--Tus, Cal, USA? Callous? Loose ya (lose ya)?

22. Gales's representation of Bolshevism as state capitalism, a more cruel and coercive system than that of "private" capaitalism, at least on the whole, bears the animus of his sense of a revolution inevitably betrayed. He notes the most moving and truly revolutionary moment in modern history, when the Tsar's soldiers refused to fire on the workers; and he notes also that soon soldiers willing to fire on workers were found again. At the same time he supports what "Comms," "Bolshes," and Wobblies do for the sake of workers' conditions in private-capitalist states (not neglecting to note that they too can be extreme nationalists). This ambivalence towards both kinds of capitalist nation-state power stems from the basic anarchism of the gay, sane, and decent attitude: "Where is the true country of men? There where nobody molests me, where nobody wants to know who I am, where I come from, where I wish to go, what my opinion is about war, about the Episcopalians, and about the communists, where I am free to do and to believe what I damn please as long as I do not harm the life, the health and the honestly earned property of anybody else. There and there alone is the country of men that is worth living for, and sweet to die for" (216).

23. The Cotton Pickers.

24. Explicitly stated often enough in The Death Ship (esp. in Chaps. 32 and 43), The Cotton Pickers, and in the Jungle books (most vividly in Government), this principle is dramatized at a most basic level in the scene in Treasure,

when the bandits massacre and rob the train passengers, crying "¡Viva Cristo Rey!" as they do so.

25. Andrés goes to the _monterías_ to redeem his father, Celso to earn the money to marry the girl he loves. The poignancy with which their decisions are imaged is superb (_Carreta_, closing chapters; _March_, opening chapters).

26. Though not posited as moral decisions, each of these crucial moments is instinct with the morality of the sane and decent protagonist, the nonmoralistic morality of soul, spirit, and heart. I suggest this as an amendment to Michael L. Baumann's analysis (op. cit., 40-41) of the ultimately decisive acts in _The Death Ship_ as being "morally neutral."

27. It is not implausible that Traven would have been willing to have his readers entertain doubts about whether Gales really is American, in a world where the American is the most progressive of capitalists and American citizenship is a material disideratum.

28. _The Cotton Pickers._

29. The joy of accomplishment as the true reward of labor (as distinct from wages) is marvelously imaged in _The Death Ship_, explicitly in Chapter 39 where Lavski speaks of the joy of "holding the course straight in dirty weather,"' and Gales of painting the ship, and implicitly in Gales's attitude towards learning the snake-dance and other means of survival. We find this also in _The Cotton Pickers_ (the joy of learning to master picking, baking, and herding skills) and in _The Carreta_ and _March_ (In Andrés and Celso's joy in learning skills).

30. Bakhtin claims, and I agree, that this spirit is also implicit in Plato's Socratic dialogues. (See op. cit. 87-93 and passim.)

31. Hillel said: "If I am not for myself, who is for me? And if I am [only] for myself, what am I? And if not now, when?" Jesus' life and teachings embody this principle and are indeed relevant for our understanding of Traven. (Also see Baumann, 1976, 75-80.)

32. As Plato discerned and pointed out in his argument for the banishment of poets (who he thought were guilty of titillating their audiences) from the ideal republic (_Republic_, Bk. 10, pt. 2, esp. 603-5).

33. Reason or rationality, in this vision, is not the essence of (and can be the enemy of) sanity. Reason cannot answer Ivan's question; the Garcia woman, as Gales shrewdly noted, had to overcome her reason, not her grief, in order to find life worthwhile again (see p.126 above). And rationality is the basis of materialization: The bureaucrats of the legal-rational nation-states and the capital-

ist owners of the great oil companies and the death ships all organize and economize on the most rational principles. For Reason, as Shelley said in his Defence of Poetry, is the distinguishing power; it is Imagination that empowers and informs empathy, the source of sanity and decency.

STILL ANOTHER DEFINITION OF JAZZ LITERATURE

Leo L. Barrow

Jazz literature has more than one creative entity and integrates more than one form of art. Like all literature it cheats and steals with its own grace and charm, integrating its own originality with that of many other creators. It does not distinguish between the creator and the creation: between author, work and character, between life and literature. The poetry of popular songs has a special place in jazz literature because these songs are our most primitive and basic form of literature. They tell everyone's story.

This chapter examines jazz literature in B. Traven's film Macario. In an interview filmed in his home in Mexico City, the director, Galvadón stated conclusively that B. Traven had very little voice in and very little to do with the filming of Macario. He did say, of course, that Traven worked on and helped with the film script. When she was interviewed, Rosa Elena Luján stated that Traven had a lot to do with the filming, was often on the set, and even was instrumental in picking Ignacio López Tarso to play the role of Macario. It was the first major role for López Tarso, who went on to become one of Mexico's finest actors of both stage and screen. It is therefore quite natural for both men to take credit for that excellent choice. This disagreement between the widow and the director, more apparent than real, points to the existence of jazz literature in both the literary and extra-literary aspects of the film Macario.

Traven had many creative entities to help him with his short story Macario. In addition to the Brothers Grimm and their fairy tales, he had the works and songs of generations of Indians who captured the legend of Macario and kept it alive. Besides, there was the original Indian Macario, the healer who must have had some awareness that he told and sang his story, and that his own story helped forge and change the nature of his existence. This protagonist's role as literary character was probably no different from that of El Cid, Amadís de Gaul, and Don Quixote de la Mancha. All of these men must have been aware of their existence as literary heroes and how the legend, oral or written, being created around them altered who they were and what they did. As the protagonist of my novel, The Cookie Monster, I have become keenly aware of how what I write about myself and what other people say and write about me affects who and what I am and do. In a real sense, the person living the legend works hand in hand with other creative entities who paint, dance, tell, dramatize, and write his or her legend.

Macario as a short story is a simple and pure "once upon a time" fable. The narrative is swift and efficient, and the few dramatic moments stand out clearly and achieve a certain cinematographic quality. The writing team for the script, which included Traven and Galvadón, changed a number of the narrative episodes into dramatic ones. In the story Macario is a good man, and the team says this dramatically by having the dead-tired and always hungry woodcutter bring home little presents from nature, such as a pretty feather or a rock. This is cinematic and probably commercial. In the heyday of successful Mexican films, poor people were almost always pictured as good, and rich people as bad--the kitsch attitude--and this cliché was something the filmmakers knew their Mexican public expected and wanted. Macario and his children's hunger is also dramatized, in the table scene where the frijoles disappear before the hunger does, and in the nightmare in which Macario sees the devils eating whole turkeys. In the story the nameless woman saves the money and buys the turkey, but in the film she dramatically steals it.

There are some twenty or thirty examples in the film where the writers have simply dramatized the narrative, but the writing team has gone beyond this. They have added stories and created more literature. The allegory of the cave at the end and the episode in which the children use a bottle of precious water to cure a sick burro provide excellent examples. The sick burro scene never made it into the film, probably because it was too kitsch, and that had already been pushed to the limit in the episode in which the children, frightened by the storm, all jump in bed with their parents. Here Traven might have felt that the abuse of kitsch would detract from the story's philosophical impact--a constant and vital force in all of Traven's novels--and take it too far away from the simple and pure "once upon a time" fable.

Bob Hammond criticizes the use of folk tradition and art in El día de los muertos (All Souls' Day). Perhaps the French mind considers this an exploitation of Mexico's rich cultural heritage in song and dance and popular fiestas, as a kind of filler footage, a hunk of local color to lighten and maybe even distort the serious philosophical message. I consider everything concerned with El día de los muertos an integral part of the film and its success for three reasons. (1) It is thematically appropriate since it deals with the Mexicans' daily lives and their familiarity with death. It also clearly shows that special relationship which exists in Mexico between rich and poor and between the hungry and the well-fed. (2) It lends a rich sense of reality to Traven's simple fable, and helps build a real sentient world around it. At the same time, this celebration of the dead is such an integral part of the Mexican's psyche that instead of taking the film too far away from the simple "once upon a time" fable, it adds its own considerable measure of time-lessness and spacelessness to it. (3) The celebration of the dead on this day is a dramatic work of art. As such it has become an integral part of many hispanic masterpieces, like José Zorrillas's Don Juan Tenorio. It is to this film what Carnaval is to the brilliant French film Orfeo Negro.

The popular feast provides the film with a great wealth of symbols, perhaps the sine qua non of classic films. The candles have their universal symbolic meaning, but they also serve as vertical bars that separate Macario, the "have-not," from the merchant, a "have." These same bars separate Macario and his hungry children from the offering of food for the rich dead, from the seven cooked turkeys, and other nourishment. The bars and the candles are repeated at the end of the film. Everything in the celebration is a symbol, just as everything in life is a symbol. Our computers analyze some of these symbols, like the candy skull given to the children, teaching them to love and live with the sweet taste of death. These candy skulls are also what the rich people give the poor people on this feast day. Most of the symbols in this celebration are felt by our sensibility, but our computers do not analyze them.

The filmmakers use Guadalupe Posada's woodcuts extensively throughout the film; death, hunger, and All Souls' Day were some of his favorite themes. Their liberal use in the credits sets the basic theme and tone of the film. Later they become animated puppets and enter Macario's hungry dream about the turkeys. These puppets are common toys in Mexico, and so their use in the film integrates, once again, childhood innocence and death. Finally, the figure of death, as he is made up and portrayed, seems to be drawn from one of Posada's woodcuts. Thus the plastic art of Posada combines with animation, puppetry, drama and dance, toys, the figure of death, and Traven's masterful fable to help form the cinematic version of Macario.

One cannot become a popular hero anywhere without a song. I don't kow who the author of Macario's song was or whether the corrido (ballad) was written for the film or was written for the legendary Macario during his life or after his death. I do know that Mexico has had many doctors who have preferred to stay in their small villages, curing the sick and accepting turkeys or pigs or anything that these poor people had to offer as payment. These doctors, the exception and not the rule, merit a song and might have inspired one. The ballad, the most popular of all literary forms because it tells one person's story, is essential to the authenticity and success of the film.

The film <u>Macario</u> is an excellent example of jazz literature. It contains many art forms and is the product of many creative entities. The jazz literature phenomenon points to Traven as a sensitive listener, letting every creature tell his own story and become the author of his own work. It is also an indication of Traven's sensitive and liberal perception of reality, letting every creative creature in every genre participate in the big screen of his own life and works. This may be still another reason why so many of us are looking for more than one B. Traven.

B. TRAVEN'S SIX-NOVEL EPIC OF THE MEXICAN REVOLUTION
An Overview

Robert B. Olafson

B. Traven is best known in the United States as the author of the novels The Death Ship and Treasure; both were first published in Germany in the late 1920s, and then in the United States in the 1930s. The international waters plied by derelict tramp steamers are the setting of The Death Ship; the Mexican gulf coast and the rugged Sierra Madre mountains are the setting of Treasure of the Sierra Madre.

Other novels by B. Traven appeared almost annually in Germany from 1926. From 1931 to 1940, Traven published six novels set in southern Mexico. This epic deals with the Mexican Indians and their slow drift into revolt and insurrection, which became a part of the great Mexican revolution of 1910.

The first novel in the series appeared in 1931 with the inauspicious title Der Karren (The Carreta), meaning the ox or bullock cart. The pattern of publication was similar to the five previous publications of B. Traven's novels by the Büchergilde Gutenberg. Nothing was revealed about the anonymous author; the scene was Mexico, and the theme was one of skeptical philosophical anarchism, with sociological and anthropological overtones.

The title of this new novel was less dramatic, less intrinsically interesting, certainly, than Traven's earlier publications with Büchergilde Gutenberg and other German publishers. The words Der Karren were not as inviting to readers as Das Totenschiff (The Death Ship; 1926), Der Wobbly (The Wobbly; 1926), Der Schatz der Sierra Madre (Treasure; 1927), Die Brücke im Dschungel (Bridge; 1929), or, for that matter, Die Weisse Rose (The White Rose; 1929). Yet in retrospect, Der Karren marked a new stage in the art of B. Traven, and eventually it became evident that this was the first of a series of six related novels presenting an epic treatment of the gestation and birth of the Mexican revolution of 1910.

The Carreta is the title of the English language edition. The novel, which is anthropological and social in its documentary and sometimes explanatory prose, studies the peonage system under the dictator Porfirio Díaz, who kept Mexico under his iron heel from 1876 to 1911. Traven's insights into the working man's plight and his penchant for assuming the slave's mentality were keen. It is only after we have read the bulk of the six-novel epic that we are able to grasp the full vision of B. Traven's art, an art that is original, witty, ironic, tender, documentary, sociological, anarchical, and haunting.

This chapter describes each of the six novels beginning with The Carreta. The others are Regierung (Government; 1931-32), Der Marsch ins Reich der Caoba (March; 1933), Die Troza (1936), Die Rebellion der Gehenkten (Rebellion; 1936), and Ein General kommt aus dem Dschungel (General; 1940). These novels are variously called "the jungle novels," "the Mohagony series," or "the Caoba (Spanish for mahogany) Cycle," since they are set in Chiapas, the southernmost Mexican state, where huge mahogany lumber camps existed in the early 1900s. These lumber camps were manned by Indian peon loggers caught in the vicious pattern of debt-slavery, originated and administered by the ladinos, the white elite, who exploited the Indian peons by overwork, cheating, and violence. Many of these logging camps were owned by foreign companies, and all of the labor abuses were winked at by Porfirio Díaz, dictator for some thirty years, whose pockets had been liberally filled with bribes. Andrés Ugalde, an Indian peon boy, moves through a series of debt-slavery conditions in The Carreta (and later in March) to the ultimate hell of debt-slavery, the mahogany lumber camps.

Andrés begins as a farm boy, but is then given to a store owner, who loses him to another ladino, who makes Andrés into a carretero (cart driver). Traven carefully delineates how the peon Andrés is kept in his place by the ladino patrones. Long before terms like "behavior modification," "mind control," and "brainwashing" were made popular, Traven shows with startling clarity their uses and abuses in The Carreta. The philosophical anarchist Traven--the man who wants as few rules in society as possible--shows how the best people, the Indians, are yoked to the lowest level of a corrupt caste system while the worst, the ladinos, hold the reins at the top.

Andrés's story is a bildungsroman, a story of initiation, as he learns the ways of the world as a cart driver and eventually falls in love and takes a common-law wife. Traven also uses the novel to show his readers the mores of Catholic Mexico at the turn of the century. Traven's style is often caustic as he shows how the unexamined customs of Mexico cast all Mexicans into forms of slavery--even the patrones are slaves to customs that dehumanize them. The Carreta then shows how slow the downtrodden are to realize that revolution is their only escape. This first novel in the series says very little about revolt. It shows, rather, how relatively easy it was for the Díaz dictatorship to keep the peon in his place.

The second novel, <u>Government</u>, continues to expose the corruption at the core of Díaz's Mexico and deals in particular with the evolution of the equivalent of the United States' so-called "white trash." Don Gabriel Orduñez is a have-not Flem Snopes type, who by chicanery begins to rise economically, first as the <u>ladino</u> (white) government secretary to a free Indian village and then as a labor-recruiting agent for the <u>monterias</u> (logging camps). The only thing don Gabriel has going for him is that he is a <u>ladino</u>; he is a petty member of the ruling class: To be sure, he is the scum of the earth--but he is not quite as scummy as the free Indians, or so he believes. Traven believes otherwise, of course. The reader sees don Gabriel as a slow-witted slob-- each new method he learns to rob the Indians comes after much head-scratching, screwing up of his features, and fumbling for the words to put the plan into action. He is also henpecked, used by his smarter brother, and fearful of his job and his superiors. Although the tone of the novel is often comic, the pathetic ineptitude of don Gabriel often allows Traven's pen to become savagely sarcastic. It appears that Traven deliberately set himself the task of creating a character with absolutely no possibility of attaining any self-knowledge or any position of economic security anywhere in the world--except in Díaz's Mexico.

Don Gabriel, a sad sack, a born loser, rises only because the payoff system in Mexico is so pervasive at this time that the other <u>ladinos</u> from whom he extorts money have been conditioned to play the nickel and dime game with idiots and geniuses alike. Furthermore, the Indians, to a large degree, are so far removed philosophically from the white man's world of commerce that Díaz's government and don Gabriel, its representative, exist as minor irritants, somewhat like mosquitoes. A sting now and then is accepted and overlooked. If the stings become too frequent, the mosquito is killed; likewise the secretary is killed.

Such acts of resistance were infrequent, however. With the judicious use of a revolver, heaps of doubletalk and mumbo jumbo about the laws of the land, and copious supplies of alcoholic beverages, most secretaries could control the Indians in almost all petty matters. No control whatsoever could be exerted in the truly important matters in the Indian culture. Traven sees well the tragedy of a proud people, paradoxically unconquered and conquered by the Spanish conquest. The Indians' sense of honor and truth is their fatal flaw, and it is the <u>ladinos</u>' total immorality-- total lack of dedication to honor and truth--that allows them to rule.

<u>Government</u> in some ways reminds me of many old "Our Gang"

movies: The plots, scams, and doubletalk of don Gabriel are kid stuff, transparent, lacking even the rudiments of dissembling, and yet these scams work. Don Gabriel and his brother, don Mateo, are "Our Gang" kids who seem to have a perpetual, willing suspension of disbelief from the Indians they work their silly games on. For most of the time in Government, the Indians act as if they are visitors from another planet, perhaps another galaxy. The actions of the brothers are scrutinized, the money is paid to them, the scams are accepted, Indians are killed and sold into slavery—and yet they seem largely untouched. Only once do the Indians rebel, not over money or loss of family, but over loss of a centuries-old form of government. Only once do the Indians see completely through a scam, when a boy returns to tell of being sold into slavery by collusion between don Gabriel and the current Indian chief. The Indians kill their chief, but they do not touch don Gabriel; after all, he is not of their world.

In many ways Traven's Government focuses on the growing problems of "official reports"—manipulation of statistics, influence peddling, and control of the media—which have plagued many countries in the twentieth century. Traven clearly shows that Díaz wanted to convey to the United States and the rest of the world that Mexico was a liberal, progressive country with a well-organized rural school system. Since the hazards of visiting these schools were great, the tourists, bankers, and journalists from other countries visited only the "good" schools in the large urban areas.

The second chapter of Government begins with an indictment of Porfirio Díaz's manipulation of statistics and image-building for the American newspapers. The myth of the benevolent dictator who was leading Mexico into the modern, productive, and enlightened ranks of the best countries of the world was a successful myth for over thirty years. Díaz, at age eighty, was finally exposed, largely by American John Kenneth Turner's Barbarous Mexico, first a series of magazine articles and then a book on the debt-slavery conditions in Mexico. Turner's exposé of slavery began in 1909 in American Magazine and did much to alert the world to the shameful truth about Díaz.

With trenchant irony Traven presents, as Turner did, Díaz's view of himself as "the best Mexican alive and the only Mexican whose life was of consequence." In reality, his dictatorship was one of the most absolute and corrupt in the world.

It is possible that Traven read Turner's Barbarous Mexico, in part or in toto. Although Barbarous Mexico was called the Uncle Tom's Cabin of Mexico because of its appearance shortly before the Mexican revolution, it was not actually published in Spanish until 1955. Traven might have used the book as a source for the Jungle novels. He might have come across Turner's views in American newspapers or in numerous magazine articles in journals such as Appeal to Reason, the International Socialist Review, and Pacific Monthly. Overall, Government leaves a bad taste in the reader's mouth, as he perceives how easily the scams and spoils system worked in Mexico at the turn of the century.

March, the third novel, presents the arduous march to the logging camps. Andrés Ugaldo and Celso Flores are the dupes of labor recruiter-contractors, such as don Gabriel. Both men, and almost all the others in the labor gang being marched through the tropical jungle, have been tricked into assuming fictitious debts owed by others, such as fathers or brothers. Since the Indians seldom can read or write, it is easy to "doctor" debt statements, to trick, cheat, or lend money at huge interest rates. This the recruiters do, as they live off the ignorance and misery of the Indians.

Traven presents great scenes of a naturalistic jungle that tends to augment the dehumanization started by man. The Indians seem unable to escape from this trap. A hint of rebellion comes only when two extremely vicious foremen in the march are killed by the Indians. They do not regard this, however, as a springboard to total revolt, and they subsequently continue their march to almost certain death in the lumber camps.

In Die Troza, the Andrés of the first two novels becomes a boyero (driver of oxen). The oxen pull trozas, mohagany logs trimmed to weigh a ton each. Celso becomes a hachero (woodcutter). Traven begins to focus intensely on man's inhumanity to man, as the foremen, carrying whips and pistols, literally torture and terrorize the workers. Besides the usual kinds of physical beatings, the men who do not work well or meet their huge quotas are hanged on trees by their arms and legs for long periods at night. In this state they are eaten alive by hordes of various kinds of insects. Meanwhile the owners consort nightly with their whores.

The Rebellion of the Hanged, the fifth novel, draws its title from the torture just described. The first part of the novel describes how Candido, a free Indian, gets tricked into debt-slavery and ends up working in the monteria. When his wife develops appendicitis, a corrupt doctor of the ladino class refuses to operate until Candido borrows money to cover the surgery. Candido does this, but by the time he raises the money his wife has died. He then uses some of the money for her funeral and is "hooked" by the labor recruiter for incurring the debt.

At the logging camp, Indians "owe their souls to the company store." They must buy basic necessities at exorbitant prices and often find that after three to five years' work (if they live that long) they are still in debt. Those who are not usually are tricked out of their money by gamblers and prostitutes at a village on their way to freedom, and they end up back on the "hook" of the labor recruiters. Martin Trinidad, called "el professor," ends up working at the camp and gradually motivates the Indians to rebel. This is a painful process, and Traven implies that the majority of men are slow to revolt. The revolt is also Traven's account of the grass roots origins of the Mexican revolution.

General is the sixth novel and completes the epic cycle. Taking Zapata's war cry, Tierra y Libertad (Land and Freedom), the Indian loggers form a ramshackle "army" and begin to fight the dictator Porfirio Díaz's rurales, the owners of the fincas (plantations), and the regular army. The general is a part-Indian ex-army sergeant, who deserts the army of Díaz when his little brother is drowned in a bucket of water by an officer who holds his booted foot on the boy's head--- all because the boy had not obeyed an order fast enough. Andrés and Celso, along with Martin Trinidad, are the general's officers. Some of the battle scenes are horrible, as the pent-up anger of the rebels is released. After the general has won many battles in Chiapas, he learns that the Mexican revolution ended sixteen months before his army was formed. The Indians then form an anarchist commune called Solipaz (sun and peace). Although Díaz has left for London, Mexico City is in a state of chaos, because the winning armies and factions are now contending for total political leadership among themselves.

B. Traven's insights into the Mexican Indian's plight during the Díaz regime reach remarkable fruition in this six-novel epic. Mexican literary critics have praised him highly and even claim him as one of the best of "their" writers. Recognition of his art in these six novels is long overdue in the United States.

Note

I have used the texts of the American editions of these novels, which were published by Hill and Wang in the early 1970s. Since no American edition of Die Troza (The Trunk, or <u>The</u> <u>Mahogany</u> <u>Trunk</u>) has appeared, I have used the German edition and have also relied on Michael Baumann's work, <u>B.</u> <u>Traven:</u> <u>An</u> <u>Introduction</u>.

UTOPIAN ELEMENTS IN THE NOVELS OF B. TRAVEN

Peter Lübbe

Utopianism--the quest of mankind for a perfect society--is a frequent theme in the works of B. Traven. This perfection might be sought in a romanticized past, or in a still more idealized future, yet it is what sustains Traven's characters against the disasters they encounter.

To begin with The Death Ship, with its preface, "The Song of an American Sailor":

Now stop that crying, honey dear
The Jackson Square remains still here
  In sunny New Orleans
  In lovely Louisiana.[1]

These lines take on the character of a leading idea in the novel. The passportless plebeian hero Gales aboard the Yorikke never gives up hope of once more seeing New Orleans and the girl he loves. Yet how is it possible for a man to sustain this claim to the future under the harrowing working conditions on the Yorikke? Traven has the ill-treated Gales cry out, "I spit in your face, Caesar Augustus Imperator-- you and your breed."[2] Behind this attitude lies a philosophy of life, which Gales sums up in sun-drenched Spain in the following words: "You don't live in order to possess, but to desire, to dare, to gamble."[3]

It is the memory of New Orleans which gives Gales the strength to carry on as he stands before the boilers of the Yorikke. Yet at the same time, he is tortured by the feeling that "to think up hope"[4] is more of a curse than a blessing if it prevents a man from rebelling against inhuman conditions.[5]

But this is not hope in any religious sense. Gales has grave misgivings about organized salvation: "Solely through actions which differed from those of the past, through thought processes which differed from those of their fathers, of the saints, of those in positions of responsibility, has mankind created new prospects and the belief that, one day in the distant future, progress will be seen to have been achieved. This distant day will be in sight when mankind no longer believes in institutions, no longer believes in authorities."[6] In 1926 the left wing of the Communist party of the Soviet Union had already lost its struggle against Stalin; and Stalin's opponents were persecuted by the secret police. In the Communist International the supporters of the chairman of the executive committee, Grigori Zinoviev, suffered defeat at the hands of the Stalinists; the anti-Stalinist left wing was eliminated from the Communist party in Germany. In The Death Ship Traven has his hero realize: "The sad thing, the lamentable thing, is that those who yesterday were themselves persecuted are today the bestial persecutors. And among the bestial persecutors of today are also the Communists."[7]

In the novel Der Wobbly the chant of the cotton pickers in the preface to the novel fulfills a similar function to the "Sailor's Song" in The Death Ship. The chant ends with the lines:

Into the sack
Your harvest tip
And smash the scales to pieces.[8]

This proclamation contains two demands: a claim to the harvest the cotton pickers have gathered with their own hands, and the destruction of the instrument the worker feels enslaves him. Their hope for the future is that they may one day be able to bring in their own harvest.

Traven's hymn to the native team spirit of the frugal, fraternal life in the Indio village on the Rio Tamesi in his Bridge occasionally has the effect of the transfiguration of a submerged culture. In the last analysis, however, Traven's bridge leads through the jungle of the American way of life, through the chattels of civilization into "a new world,"[9] a world which man can accept as his home. Together with his Indian wife and their children, the American Sleigh has found this home.

The very motto of Treasure proclaims a message: "The real treasure is the one you do not consider it worth a journey to find, the one your life will seem too short to seek. The glittering treasure you mean lies on the other side."[10] What Traven depicts in Bridge as a completed operation in the figure of Sleigh, he here presents as a process of transformation. Sleigh's social development lies in the past; it belongs to an unwritten prehistory. In Howard, Traven shows why he renounces his original pipe dreams. The difference between the two characters is illuminating. Sleigh surrenders to a state of escapist tranquillity; Howard, on the other hand, finds an active existence among the

150

Indios, away from the restlessness and uncertainty of his earlier daily life, far from the world of Having. His dream of buying a cinema in Tampico having evaporated, he breaks out in Homeric laughter: "The laughter sounded so wholesome that no-one could resist it."[11]

The praise of quiet happiness which characterizes Bridge gives way to a more realistic form of narrative in The White Rose. In spite of all his attachment to the simple Indio life, Traven relates the destruction of the hacienda Rosa Blanca. The downfall of the Rosa Blanca is necessary; it is a "fortunate Fall." Earlier, in Land, his travel guide to Chiapas, Traven had already come to the realization "that this self-satisfaction, this self-sufficiency, this happiness is in its narrowness one of the essential causes of backwardness."[12] Kurt Tucholsky had thought the ending of the novel "somewhat ambiguous."[13] Far removed from any idealization of the simple life, Traven makes it plain that nearly all the former peasants of the Rosa Blanca were employed by the U.S. oil company and "were unlikely to have been prepared to exchange their new life for the old."[14] The "great brotherhood" remains, however, a program, a demand, without concrete form. Traven may well talk of "the first seeds of the idea that all men on earth are a unit"; yet the day on which the loss of the "small-scale homeland" is superseded by the insight that "we are conscious today of being citizens of the world" lies beyond the created realm of the heroes in the novel.[15]

The new complexity of Traven's utopianism is especially striking in the Jungle novels of the following years. There must be change, but it is not simplistic. Traven is not, therefore, concerned with characterization, but rather with circumstantial analysis. The cogwheels of social dependency are laid bare. The author views his creations to a certain extent as pieces of historical evidence; they are closely interwoven with social events. In 1931 the author explained his aims thus: "The author is not writing fairytales for adults, to help them sleep, but documents, nothing but documents, which, in order to make them more readable, he has cast in the form of novels."[16] In these "documentary novels" Traven aims his attack on all forms of rule and of government, since it breeds corruption. And corruption and government are, to the author, largely identical: A state post is not justified by services performed, but rather by the money to be made out of the fatherland. In an essay Traven explains: "Government is everywhere the same, it is always the oppression of one section of the people for the benefit of another section of the same people. What mankind needs is organization and administration. What mankind does not need, and what it must therefore eliminate, is government."[17] Some of Traven's ideas on social self-determination, above all concerning the principle that a political leader should be banned from reelection after one term in office, are incorporated into the features of the independent Indio community Pebvil.[18] Traven recommends this rule of rotation especially to workers' organizations: "Not only in Russia, where it is more necessary than anywhere else, but in all the other European countries where Marx and Lenin are considered stylites."[19]

Traven develops the way in which hatred and the spirit of resistance grow among the enslaved Indian workers of the monterias during the extended rule of Porfirio Díaz. In Traven's treatment of the Indian uprising in Rebellion, he in no way advocates a policy of violence. The author directs the reader's attention to those who are really committing acts of violence: "What happened here, and what, under the same circumstances, happens and must happen everywhere in the world cannot be put down to the muchachos but to those who created these conditions and to whose well-being the conditions contributed."[20] There is no doubt that Traven's target here was the growing power of fascism in Germany. Martín Trinidad, el professor, the head of the rebels, preaches against "the hot air of those who want to be our leaders in order to rule over us."[21] The rebels are fighting for "tierra y libertad" and see themselves as "warriors in the cause of freedom for all those who are not yet free today."[22]

At the start of the rebellion, el professor dreams "that they are on the march to their prized land of freedom and soil."[23] Juan Méndez, el general, the military leader of the "wild bunch," hopes "that the revolution will change not only systems but also mankind's shabby, mercenary pedlar's spirit."[24] It is characteristic of Traven's aims that he does not write a biography of General Emiliano Zapata, even if Juan Méndez embodies many of his traits. The alienation of the real revolutionary leaders enables the author to generalize the events he portrays as well as to create the social model "Solipaz" in the last volume of the cycle. In order to expand beyond the boundaries of the Mexican revolution, Traven abandons his original plan. The author's intentions and his documentary endeavors part company, for the latter had, in fact, been realized in Rebellion. General breaks with the character of the cycle without the author drawing any artistic conclusions. The novel is no longer primarily a document; it is a social model. Traven writes of the savage struggle of the peasant rebels against the police and the army that it is animated by a "natural belief in a justice which must exist somewhere,"[25] filled with a "feeling of longing for freedom."[26]

These rebels prove their military skill and reveal their inner potential and all that has been held down and oppressed within them. Even so, the author acknowledges in the opening chapter "that a revolution alone does not alter a system but merely changes its ownership."[27] Traven does not deceive himself in any way about the revolution in Mexico. It did effect the expulsion of the dictator in 1911, but the people became dependent on new, mutually hostile masters.[28] The victorious rebels in Traven's novel do not, however, want to replace the old political masters or exchange them for more lenient ones; they are in no way interested in effecting a change of ownership.

The author, who is concerned to cast not only the unfinished Mexican uprising, but indeed every wavering revolution, in epic terms, chooses a utopian solution to the conflict. The undefeated rebel army resolves to end its campaign and found a settlement where the Indian peasants can tend their fields and raise their cattle and where their children can be taught to read and write: "To cultivate their land in peace--this was all they hoped for from the world and from life. It was not much. But it was never granted to them."[29] This island of fraternity, "Solipaz," remains, historically speaking, utopian.

A particular twist is lent to the social criticism of the novel's ending by its ironic form. The announcement the traveling teacher Gabino Villalva makes to the rebels--that el cacique had already been deposed at the time they set out from the jungle to force him from the throne--would appear to nullify the whole message. Yet the profound irony lies precisely in the fact that the rebels had to be informed of the pointless revolution. In spite of this revolution, nothing has essentially changed.

As the teacher Martín Trinidad, driven to the montería, sets out from the depths of the forest to free the country from despotism and to win land and freedom, he imagines himself--one day the time will come--teaching "the new generation"[30] at a university. The apparent overthrow of the rebellion signifies the demand for a just world in which "Solipaz"--sun and peace--has been won for all men.

Between General and Aslan Norval (1960) lie the Second World War, the Korean War, and the conflict between the superpowers. Martín Trinidad's dream still awaits fulfillment although the forces working against its realization have naturally taken a different form from those of the thirties. Traven obviously no longer considers Mexico the "country where one can fathom all things, the entire wisdom of the world."[31] Yet in his last novel, Traven attempts once more to create a utopian world. Often clumsy in his characterization, which includes a generous admixture of colportage, Traven devises the story of Aslan Norval, an "American heiress-princess,"[32] who wants to fulfill her childhood dream of building a canal (or a six-track ship-transport railroad) from Texas to California. The worldwide breakdown of mutual fear could free the necessary resources, which would otherwise only be wasted on weapons. The great powers primarily concentrate their energies on ways of "reducing a million people to ashes in half a second," instead of on making the world more habitable, "putting an end to the bitter poverty of millions of people in the under-developed countries,"[33] and taking effective measures against increasing unemployment. The purpose of Aslan Norval's "Atlantic-Pacific Transit Corporation" is to enable Traven to denounce the race to destroy mankind. For "this situation applied not only to one of the two superpowers, but also in equal measure to the opposition."[34]

And so we have come full circle. By taking an appropriate look back at the past and a relevant look around at the present, we increase our ability to set our sights on the future. For Traven, the future is not simply the present carried on into tomorrow. And yet he does not develop a ready-made model of society, an "only-true-path-to-salvation" scheme derived from some "almighty doctrine." From a kind of utopia indiana mexicana, Traven's ideas develop into a utopia humana. Traven shows that the preserving powers of the status quo can be overcome; he makes reality more transparent, brings down intellectual barriers, awakens the silent to speech, and promotes social imagination. He shows what could be.

Notes

1. B. Traven, Das Totenschiff (Berlin, 1926), 8.
2. Ibid., 138.
3. Ibid., 91.
4. Ibid., 149.
5. Cf. ibid., 162.
6. Ibid., 150.
7. Ibid., 86.
8. B. Traven, Der Wobbly (Berlin, 1926), 7.
9. B. Traven, Die Brücke im Dschungel (Berlin, 1929), 178.
10. B. Traven, Der Schatz der Sierra Madre (Berlin, 1927), 7.

11. Ibid., 210.

12. B. Traven, Land des Frühlings (Berlin, 1928), 428.

13. Peter Panter (=Tucholsky, Kurt): B. Traven. Die Weltbühne (Berlin, 48/1930), 795.

14. B. Traven, Die Weisse Rose (Berlin, 1929), 189.

15. Ibid., 190-92.

16. B. Traven, Der Roman "Regierung," in Die Büchergilde (Berlin, 9/1931), 260-61.

17. Ibid., 260.

18. B. Traven, Regierung (Berlin, 1931), 164-205.

19. Ibid., 172; cf. also 178 and 183.

20. B. Traven, Die Rebellion der Gehenkten (Zürich, 1936), 174; cf. 207-8 and 249-50; cf. B. Traven Ein General kommt aus dem Dschungel (Amsterdam, 1940), 15-17, 357-59.

21. B. Traven, Rebellion, 208.

22. Ibid., 248; cf. 288.

23. Ibid., 247.

24. Ibid., 262-63.

25. B. Traven, General, 7.

26. Ibid., 9.

27. Ibid., 32.

28. Cf. ibid., 93.

29. B. Traven, Rebellion, 202.

30. Ibid., 169.

31. B. Traven, Land, 429.

32. B. Traven, Aslan Norval (München, 1960), 168.

33. Ibid., 367.

34. Ibid., 368.

B. TRAVEN'S WHITE ROSE
Regressive Idyll or Social Utopia?

Peter Seibert

I

The White Rose has already been discussed in this collection
of essays, so its outlines will be familiar. It represents
Traven's first venture into the contemporary policies of his
adopted country, referring as it clearly does to the expansion of U.S. oil interests in Mexico under President Calles
--a very controversial topic. Even after World War II the
topic and Traven's treatment of it contained enough political dynamite that it seemed advisable to the American government to intervene (successfully as it turned out) through
diplomatic channels to stop the filming of the novel in
Mexico.

In spite of the "new" topic which Traven had discovered,
thematic references to earlier works abound: There is, for
instance, the fear of losing one's identity in a civilization dominated by bureaucracy and profits. This fear was
probably also the basic reason for Traven's toying with his
own identity. In The Death Ship the threat to identity is
seen in the loss of one's name, which leads to the horrors
of the Yorikke, a secularized Dante's inferno.

In The White Rose it is not an individual who is threatened by the loss of his identity, as in The Death Ship, but
a hacienda, a small world with its own standards and laws:
According to the desires and will of the Condor Oil Company,
it is to be converted from the living organism Rosa Blanca
to "lots 119 through 176" (205).[1] With his signing aboard
the Yorikke the American sailor became an appendage of the
engine, and his own needs and wants were sacrificed to the
smooth functioning of the ship. According to Traven, util-
izing men to further the aims of "Caesar Augustus Capitalism" presupposes the "objectification, the destruction of
man as a whole, as a totality which is consequently followed
by his final physical destruction."

According to the plans of the oil company, Rosa Blanca is
already dead at the beginning of the novel. However, its
fate is portrayed as an agony in which the Mexican-Indian
way of life shines in all its glory and throws deep shadows
on the North American "Gesellschaft" ("Gesellschaft" in the
double sense of Company and of Society). As in Treasure--
and in a different form in The Cotton Pickers--it is the
role of gold and capital to serve as fetishes which bring

156

death and destruction. The conflict between the two cultures is described by an "objective" third-person narrator, a shift away from the "autobiographical" format of The Cotton Pickers. In contrast to the capitalistic ethic, we find the serene world of the Indians. The White Rose actually marks an apex in Traven's literary production, since in his later works the Indian community again loses its utopian character, until at the end of the Caoba Cycle it needs its own utopia, the community "Solipaz."

It is important to note to what extent The White Rose continues the themes of earlier books, notably Land. Although this "documentary" study of 1928 concentrates on the portrayal of the Mexican antithesis to the American way of life, it is the Anglo-Saxon capitalistic counterpoint that is implied. The attacks on the United States are not weakened, but the discourse has changed. The antagonism between the capitalistic federation of states in the north and the Mexican in the south determines—as in The White Rose—the relationship of the two forms of society. The author of Land and of The White Rose sees the Indian communes threatened by American intervention. The effects can be understood much better

if one learns that an American newspaper mogul owns nearly two million acres in Mexico, not to mention the amounts of land and property the great American oil and mining companies have in their hands. Two ministers of the present American government, the minister for foreign affairs and the minister of the treasury, are in a roundabout way through their families principal stockholders of two of the most important American oil companies in Mexico. The American government works not only in the interests of their own big capitalists, but also in the interests of European oil capital, especially the English one.[2]

Both texts address not only the contradiction between the United States of Mexico and the United States of America, but also the solution of this contradiction. In this regard, however, the fictional and nonfictional work seem to differ in a critical manner: In The White Rose the solution of the contradiction implies the destruction of the hacienda, the Indian-Mexican way of life; in Land the antagonism is terminated through a projected American-Mexican confederation, a surprising proposal for a solution and one which does not logically result from Land's basic theses and analyses.

In The Night Visitor, yet another solution seems to emerge: the decline of the "white gods," as the conquered

peoples rise against colonial and imperialist oppression.
This blueprint of the future is very disconcerting for
Gales, since he is a member of the "white" world and this
prophecy therefore applies also to him. By studying Indian
history, he hopes to be able to see the "future of our
race."[3]

Traven's models for the solution of the conflict, presented in his works over a period of only two years, are
contradictory. They are irritating and force us to combine
our analysis of The White Rose with an attempt to define
more exactly the ideological and political point of view of
the author at the end of the twenties.

II

In his contributions to the biography of B. Traven, Rolf
Recknagel highly praises The White Rose: Traven has made it
clear through his descriptions that the chairman of the oil
company "is a typical product of conditions created by
monopoly capitalism." That establishes the strategy for the
attack on the realistic social critic Traven. Since Recknagel assumes that The White Rose presents insights into the
mechanisms of monopoly capitalism, his criticism of the
novel is comparatively mild. He reproves Traven only for
his "linguistic negligence" and the tone which the author
adopts in some parts of the book: "This time Traven is
especially generous with profanities."[4] But even this tame
criticism is implicitly withdrawn when Recknagel quotes
(without comment) Tucholsky, who had interpreted Traven's
linguistic negligence as proof of proletarian authenticity:
"[Traven] is a victim of his class. This proletarian cannot
speak correct German."[5]

Contemporary Communist critics were by no means as favorable to The White Rose, shocked as they were by its "exoticism" and lack of proletarian optimism. Characteristic of
these attacks was a 1932 article by Adam Scharrer in Linkskurve, the journal of the BPRS (Association of Proletarian
Revolutionary Writers). Scharrer had to deal with the clear
popularity of Traven among leftist workers, but this did not
prevent him from writing a stern rebuke,[6] culminating in the
warning, "if he [Traven] does not change his course as
quickly as possible," he will soon find himself "on the
other side of the front lines, on the side of the enemies of
the proletariat."[7] The dichotomy of "realism vs. romanticism" allowed Scharrer such a vigorous classification and
rejection of the author B. Traven. He wrote that in The
White Rose Traven turns out to be a writer who no longer
dares "to jump from romanticism into reality." "Romanti-

cism" is used in this case as a synonym for "exoticism."
With Traven's "exoticism" Scharrer claims to have discovered
the basis for the success of the author of The White Rose.

For the leftist Communist author of Vaterlandslose Gesel-
len, prone to a rather uncritical veneration of the working
class, the success of the "exotic" Traven must not be attributed to the proletariat, however. Consequently, he substitutes a bourgeois reading public for a proletarian one. His
question--"Success with whom?"--Scharrer answers by stating
that Traven's works are no longer the "exclusive publishing
monopoly of the Gutenberg Büchergilde," but that the bourgeoisie now finds its pleasures in reading Traven: "For the
entertainment of the bourgeoisie the dazzling fireworks by
the author suffices to alleviate its fear of the facts.
This is especially so if several thousand kilometers of
water lie between these facts and the bourgeois. This, and
only this, explains the success of Traven."

Rather, the accusation raised here documents Scharrer's
narrow-mindedness with regard to world political events and
contradictions, a narrow-mindedness which was not only an
expression of the sectarian tendencies and attitudes of the
membership of the KAPD (German Communist Workers' party),
but which also had its representatives in the other proletarian parties. Scharrer accused Traven of "only seeing the
many oppressed and deprived slaves of colonialism but not
the approaching and assembling proletariat, the growing
revolutionary wave passing around the world." In retrospect, this optimism naturally seems naive: Germany itself
was only months away from the Nazi seizure of power.

Scharrer's denunciation of Traven's exoticism is coupled
with critical comments on the portrayal of nonexotic facts,
such as the description of the capitalistic world of the
Northern Hemisphere in the United States. But here Scharrer
seems concerned more with questions of literary form than
with subject matter; he speaks derisively of the "instruction in political economy" being provided. The White Rose
tries to discuss monopoly capitalism at some length, but on
a rather skimpy foundation of theory or evidence, so Scharrer's criticism is understandable.

Traven's weakness becomes more evident whenever he speculates about the sources of wealth; he even falls back on the
dishwasher-rags-to-riches fairy tale to explain the accumulation of wealth in the hands of Mr. Collins. Just like
every other millionaire, the owner of the Condor Oil Company
had to work hard to climb to the top. These early struggles
are the ideal preparation for the vigorous competitive
struggle in which the best will be victorious. The rise of
Mr. Collins is accelerated with explosive force when he puts

his "brilliant" idea into action: Instead of destroying
himself in the struggle with the anticapitalistic labor
movement, he uses it for his own interests to make higher
profits, but without undermining its class-consciousness.
On the contrary, he strengthens it. After a cleverly managed overproduction of coal by his combine, Collins provokes
a national strike, and with the help of his stockpile of
coal he manages to cover the market and acquire a coal
monopoly. Unions here are thus seen as virtual tools of the
capitalist order, obeying its "iron laws" (an opinion also
found in Ziegelbrenner). One predictable consequence of
this theory is a tendency to attack such working class
organizations as consider strikes an essential proletarian
instrument for the class struggle, namely, the socialists
and the communists. In this "novel from Mexico" the ability
to vanquish the capitalist system, "if [it] can be overthrown at all," is denied to them.

The ideological tradition which Traven follows is not
difficult to identify; it can be traced to Gustav Landauer's
Aufruf zum Sozialismus (Call to Socialism), which in many
passages is a tirade against Marxism, "the pest of our time
and the curse of the socialist movement." According to this
appeal of 1911, which went through large printings in the
twenties, the workers fight, "they think in a struggle
against their capitalist employers but in reality they are
fighting against themselves in their role as consumers."
According to Landauer, this split of the workers into producers and consumers makes it logically impossible for them
to win a labor struggle: "The so-called capitalist is not a
firm tangible figure: he is a mediator to whom much is
attributed but he is not touched by the beating which the
fighting worker in his role as producer wants to administer
to him. The laborer beats right through this transparent
make-believe figure and only hurts himself." In order to
make things still clearer for the proletarians who advise a
class struggle for the "introduction of socialism": "In
reality this struggle of the workers in their role as producers for the capitalist market is nothing but a turning in
the circle of capitalism."[8]

By a fraudulent business transaction, which he will use
again later and with the same success, and with the help of
objectively collaborating, although subjectively class-
conscious workers, Collins manages to accumulate his capital. This episode also provides--nolens volens--an explanation for the worldwide economic crisis which hit in the year
of publication of The White Rose. In The White Rose the
crisis does not seem inherent in the laws of capitalism, but
it is produced and terminated by individual entrepreneurs,

called "supermen" by Scharrer. This is glossed over by Peter Lübbe when he states that "the business practices of this oil magnate are sometimes explained in a somewhat subjective manner."[9] The strong individual who makes history, especially in capitalism, and the masses without power—this is the ideological construct which Traven presents at the end of the twenties to the German labor movement, which desperately needed weapons in its defense against the social and historical concepts of nationalism-socialism.

Scharrer's reading enjoyment was marred by the "long-winded pornographic excess" in the novel. Indignantly he states, "With true lasciviousness he [Traven] describes the desires of a director of an oil company. One turns one page after another, nearly half the book, to skip over the dirt." Scharrer overlooks that Traven describes here what he interprets as a decisive moving force of history, especially in its capitalistic phase, namely, the sexual drive. Because of his narrow-mindedness, Scharrer fails to see the basis of Traven's concept of history.

In his desire to satisfy his sexual drives, Collins gets involved in many affairs, notably with his favorite, Betty, and he acquires huge debts. To remain in good standing with his banks, in order to get credit, he constantly has to extend his economic empire, and he acquires large parts of Mexico. Traven tells us: "He wanted power only so that he could stand before Betty and appear in her eyes as the most powerful, the most intelligent, the most audacious man in the world. In days of old he would have marched out at this point and vanquished continents" (104). In his philosophical digressions about history in Land, Traven had already demonstrated that the enthronement of the sexual drive as a determining force in history leads to a concept of history which culminates in wild speculations about "female" and "male" epochs[10] and even equates "decadence" and "loss of male virility."

III

But holding out against the depredations of Condor is La Rosa Blanca, a land of abundance where the range of agricultural products contrasts sharply with the monocultural world of the Mexico outside: "Its products were corn, beans, chile, horses, cattle, hogs, sugar cane—and therefore sugar —and finally, oranges, lemons, tomatoes, and pineapples" (5-6). This is quite a variety, which also helps explain the autarky of Rosa Blanca in the middle of oil fields. But not only the variety of products distinguishes the hacienda;

it also produces them in abundance: "The question of feed-
ing the children does not arise, for corn and beans grow on
the hacienda in plenty, and everyone who lives there has a
right to the corn and beans and chickens and hogs" (22).
There are no internal conflicts in this affluent society;
everybody lives in complete harmony, and the enchanted light
of a classless society falls on Rosa Blanca: "Here no
problems existed. Social questions were not raised here.
Here there were neither rich nor poor, neither masters nor
slaves" (22).

Not only do the human inhabitants of the hacienda live in
undisturbed harmony, but the relationship of the people to
their animals is also that of a Franciscan idyll: "From the
huts the smoke of the ovens drifted out through the ever-
open doors and gaps in the walls. In front of several huts
women were kneeling before the metate and grinding corn.
The pigs, chickens, turkeys, burros, birds, and animals of
the woods and jungle that were domesticated and accustomed
to the house, small deer, raccoons, dogs, and cats, ran
loose around the patio and pressed against a woman who was
squatting before a metate" (23).   For the woman it is a
great pleasure "to have all the animals around, and all the
children among them" (24).   Even the animals live in paradise as far as their relationships to each other are concerned. Not force but freedom determines their bond to the
hacienda; the animals of the jungle, like the parrot, stay
voluntarily. Whenever a discordant note is struck, it is
neutralized right away in this communal life. A good example on the hacienda is "a small, fierce, gray, nasty pig.
But Loro the parrot loved it" (24).

In this land a hard conflict of man with nature is totally
superfluous. According to Wolf Reif, a characteristic feature of similar paradisiacal places in exotic novels of the
twenties is that "the work necessary for the provision of
basic needs is minimal and can be taken care of play-
fully."[11]   The women enjoy the baking of the tortillas, the
singing Indios shoe the horses, and under the conditions of
nonalienated work the return of the Indios is transfigured
into a noonday idyll, which blends into the workday idyll:
"From the fields the men were leisurely sauntering home to
dinner. Some were carrying machetes in their hands, and
others mattocks over their shoulders. Several were smoking.
Several were whistling. The youngsters who had been out
with their fathers were squealing and playing tag with one
another. The door of the little chapel was decorated with
fresh flowers for next Sunday's fiesta" (25).   As decoration
for this pastoral setting Traven creates a scene with women
who seem to have stepped right out of paintings by Gauguin:

"Far beyond the huts he saw women coming up the hill with jars on their heads, carrying water home from the stream. The women went barefoot, with their black hair, freshly washed in the river, hanging loose. They were wearing long red-and-green striped dresses twisted round their slender hips, and white blouses with short sleeves and red embroidery on the bodice" (25).

The idyll is complete with the mention of the decorated chapel, although in other novels Traven again and again criticizes and satirizes the church. In the <u>corrido</u>, the ancient song of the hacienda, the harmony of this world is praised in such terms that one suspects an ironic intention: Margarito sings "without noticeable dissonance in a calm melodious way about the beautiful Indian maid who was seduced and deceived by a proud Mexican in a red hat, on a fiery white charger. Discordant notes are foreign to Margarito. Everything goes together, and everything is in harmony" (27). It becomes clear, however, that no irony is intended when we read that the song of Margarito is only a weak prelude to an eternal symphony, which rises to a crescendo in an expression of harmony between man and nature:

> Every noise, every tear, the lowing of the cattle, the grunting of the pigs, the crackling of the chickens, the crowing of the roosters, the gobbling of the turkeys, the shouting of the children, the whimpering of the infants, the occasional barking of a dog, the flapping of tortillas in the huts, the buzzing of the flies, the gossip and chatter of the women in the kitchen, the cursing and abjurations of Margarito as he tended to the mules, the squeaking of the cabin door opening just then, the sobbing of a youngster whose mother had boxed him soundly around the ears because he had smashed a jug, the call of an Indian away off in the fields, the chirping of the locusts and crickets, the soft soughing of the sun-shafted blue air above him--all these blended for him into a single song, the eternal song of a Mexican hacienda. Here it was the inimitable song of the White Rose. (24-25)

The transformation of Rosa Blanca into an oil field must turn this harmony into dissonance. In a foreshadowing, Jacinto Yañez anticipates the end of the "golden age," symbolically indicated by the disintegration of musical harmony: "And the sunlit air once so full of joyful song, would now be full of the moaning and groaning, the rattling and clattering, the stamping and rumbling of machines and pumps" (27).

Obviously, this idyll is far from being an accurate historical picture. The real Mexican hacienda was essentially a colonial or neocolonial form of land ownership, of large-scale (latifundio) agricultural production and management throughout Latin America: "As a social and economic institution it has survived about 400 years. Since the final subjugation of the Indios it has dominated the way of life of the population in the countryside."[12] As a form of ownership and production it has to be differentiated from the callpulli, which indeed is family-based, but also from the rancho on the one hand and the ejido on the other. As a rule, the ejido stood on land returned to the communities in the course of the Mexican agrarian reform, which indicates that the haciendas were heavily attacked by the Indian farm population, who demanded land from the haciendas for their ejidos. Notes in Land prove that B. Traven knew the difference between these forms of ownership.[13] Rosa Blanca has several characteristics of a hacienda, such as its large size, the presence of a mayor domo, and naturally an owner. But Traven has carried out a consistent transfiguration.

Compadrismo, for instance, which according to modern Latin-American scholars is a fossil of "catholic patriarchal family structures,"[14] is seen here as the basis for the internally conflict-free Rosa Blanca. At a time when an ever increasing amount of the work performed on the hacienda consisted of piecework, we find only nonalienating work at Rosa Blanca. The quasi-feudal attachment to the soil is turned into a voluntary and affirmative presence on the estate. The question of land ownership, a central concern of the Mexican revolutionary movements, is avoided: The Indian Yañez is the owner, but he considers himself "nothing but a steward, an advisor" (23) of the Indios living on the land.

Finally, let us look at the chapel decorated for the fiesta and compare this idyll with the description of the function of a hacienda church as provided by the most important and most widely used handbook for hacendados. According to this handbook, the church, which since the time of the encomienda had to be built on the land of each hacienda, where it had "great importance for the identification of the workers with the estate,"[15] should be judged by the hacienda management only, in terms of its utility: "One must examine the taste and the preferences of the workers in order to benefit from their weakness for innocent traditions. If one calculatingly and cleverly uses the religious cult, the priest, for instance, can be used as the ally of the manager and as a mediator respected by everybody. From the pulpit he can present the measures of the management in

the best light even if they look hard."[16] The support of
the chapel and the chaplain should not be the responsibility
of the <u>hacendado</u>, however, but should be assumed by the
Indios themselves.

So how different was the real-life hacienda from the
capitalist economic values which here supplant it? It was
already a neocolonial institution. Luis Vitale considers
the development of the hacienda "conditioned by the ever-
increasing demand of highly industrialized nations for raw
materials."[17] His opinion is shared by André Gunder Frank,
who refuses to see in the hacienda the continued existence
of a special, basically anticapitalistic entity: "The
growth of the <u>latifundia</u> and their seemingly feudal conditions of serfdom in Latin-America has always been and is
also now the commercial answer to a growing demand"; it
represents "not the transferal or the survival of indigenous
institutions which have remained outside the reach of capitalism."[18] Although Traven sees it differently, an integration into the capitalistic economic system was possible
because the hacienda not only does not show any contradictions to the colonial or neocolonial system, but is also an
integral part of it. The denial of the colonial character
of the hacienda takes Rosa Blanca out of history, or at
least it removes its origin into pre-Columbian times. The
stress placed on the <u>Indian</u> nature of Rosa Blanca serves the
same purpose as a pre-Columbian origin: The relationship
between colonists and colonized is turned around; in this
manner it is abolished as a colonial and repressive relationship.

Only after negating the colonial character of the hacienda
can it be given status of autonomy and autarky. In his
<u>Seven False Theories about Latin America</u>, the Mexican-German
sociologist Rodolfo Stavenhagen has challenged the claim
that "those parts of America where the indigenous population
lives are economically self-supporting."[19] This does not
mean for Stavenhagen that individual communities may not be
cut off from the world economy for periods of time, but this
cannot be seen as true autonomy, and the sociologist certainly denies that it brings about the development of an
affluent society among the Indian farmers:

> The economic cycles of colonial America are to a large
> degree determined by the economic cycles of the Western
> world. In Central America many native communities which
> are today cut off, isolated, and thrown back on a subsis-
> tence basis, were not always in this situation. Right
> after the conquest the natives were driven by the colon-
> ists into the barren parts of the country where they

disappeared because of the extremely harsh living conditions. In periods of economic depression those communities which before were relatively integrated into the global economy are cut off from the world and reduced to minimal subsistence.[20]

Traven has built the framework for his utopia from pieces which he has taken from contemporary Mexican realities. By doing this he has glorified the reality itself, since the colonial conditions appear in a distorted and nonalienated form. A closer look reveals that the lament about colonial slavery for which Scharrer rebuked Traven is really a eulogy of the results of colonial repression. The "freedom" on the Rosa Blanca sanctions the colonial conditions in Mexico-- that is, "slavery"--and even shows these conditions as something worth defending.

IV

The idealized Rosa Blanca can also be seen as the culmination of a long anarchist tradition, strongly influenced by Landauer's rejection of Marxist rationalism. These ideas, of course, had played an important role in the Munich Räterepublik, when Marut had cooperated with theorists like Silvio Gesell, Ernst Toller, and Erich Mühsam. The free-state syndicalist thinkers wanted to resolve the basic social contradictions by a reorganization of the relationship between man and soil. They dreamed about the abolition of alienation, an alienation which had been experienced especially by intellectuals, but they lost sight of the question of ownership and production. In his _Aufruf_ _zum_ _Sozialismus_, Landauer underlined the sentence: "The question of ownership will be solved in essence by a restructuring of our spirit."[21] Technical progress is held responsible for social ills, and a demand for a return to agrarian forms of production and an abandonment of all technical development is voiced. While during the early nineteenth century exemplary alternative projects (to use a modern term) such as the Oneida-Farm, profited from technical progress, this movement expected to be saved by a "withdrawal from capitalism," as Landauer called it: "no sort of progress, no sort of mechanization, no sort of virtuosity are going to bring us salvation and grace."[22]

Technical regression becomes a revolutionary program which will restore a natural order and the harmony between man and nature. Gesell calls his economic concept a "natural economic order"; the program of the "Swiss Free Land-Free Money Association" organized by Gesell promises to create the "foundations for a beautiful, free and natural existence for the people by the most simple but effective means."[23] Landauer, on the other hand, offers a definition of socialism which seems to caricature the well-known one by Lenin, which includes an electrification of the young Soviet Republic: "Socialism is a reunion with nature."[24] Reunion with or connection to nature also refers to the creation of a new form of society on an agrarian basis. At another place in the _Aufruf_ Landauer writes no less vaguely: "The struggle for socialism is a struggle for the soil."

Of necessity, these regressive utopias must exclude the proletarian worker as a revolutionary subject to the extent in which they propagate a mystique of the soil, of sowing and harvesting. The proletarians lose their agrarian existence during the process of urbanization, to become mere appendages to machines. Landauer declared, "The social question is an agrarian question"; and the nonhistorical peasant is seen as a revolutionary force. The only chance for the worker to participate at the side of the farmer in the re-creation of the world lies in abandonment of his existence as proletarian. Here Landauer joins the myth of the soil to the myth of the blood: "Much still exists to which we can link up, which is still vibrant with external manifestations of living spirit. Village communities with relics of communal property, with reminiscences of farmers and land-workers of the original boundaries. The farmer's blood is still running in the veins of many city proletarians. They must learn to listen to it again." In short, liberating the workers will be the job of the peasants.

The end of the Caoba Cycle with the establishment of the syndicalistic-anarchistic utopia "Solipaz" demonstrates the extent to which Traven remained a follower of the "free state" advocates and syndicalists even in his Mexican exile. At first glance, however, _The White Rose_, written much earlier, seems to contain fewer ideas propagated by "free state" advocates and syndicalists. Does this represent Traven's "premature" abandonment of these ideas--ideas which he later revised? At one place in the novel syndicalist projects are mentioned directly and shown in a positive light since they are in opposition to the oil company: The Condor Oil Company refuses to grant "credit to cooperatives and unions that build houses to rent at cost" (57). This passage stands isolated in the novel, however, and could be used to support the hypothesis that Traven at times abandoned his earlier ideas.

It seems that in _The White Rose_ the question of land reform is of greater importance. However, in analogy to Landauer's essay, it is not treated as a question of prop-

167

erty except in terms of U.S. expansionism. As long as Rosa Blanca can remain inviolate and repulse the attacks of Mr. Collins, the question of land ownership remains divorced from concrete historical conditions. In the case of Traven and many other writers of the times, we find a preference for "easily understandable miniature spaces,"[25] which led in theory and practice to the establishment of small communal settlements and found its literary equivalent in the portrayal of alternative social island communities. There was also an escape from the present historical stage of civilization and rule over nature, resulting from a desire for simple, intelligible structures. They hold out the promise to revoke the powerlessness of the individual and his feeling that his fate is determined by outside forces. This seemed possible through the reconstruction of a natural state in which nature is neither an antagonistic nor a subjugated force, but in which man and nature live in harmony and form a whole.

B. Traven believed he could reverse the historical process, which Adorno and Horkheimer, in the Dialectics of Enlightenment, describe as a process "in which the power of the system over man grows with every step which takes him out from under the power of nature."[26] However, the revocation of the individual's alienation and powerlessness by negating human history as a continuous process of subjugating nature proves itself to be a dangerous illusion. To quote once more the Dialectics of Enlightenment, "Every mystical union is a lie."[27] It advocates the subjugation of the individual under the laws of nature, which means that the nature mysticism of an engaged fighter for the self-determination of man already implicitly contains his surrender to forces outside of him. The telluric characters of The White Rose do not rise above nature; they subject themselves to nature as its creatures. The Indio "lives in the soil and with the soil. As a product of the soil. Just like a tree."[28] In several passages the narrator approaches nature as "something higher, something holy," and atavistic ideas of nature as Mother Earth and as fruit-bearing virgin break through. In consequence, the celebrations on the hacienda are cultic festivals; the inhabitants do not form a producer's cooperative, but a cult community, which gathers around an altar with a fire resminiscent of a burnt offering.

Because of the upheld mystical unity of man and nature, Rosa Blanca is removed from the historical process and carries all the marks of eternity: Eternal is the corrido, the ranch song, and the hacienda enjoys eternal youth. Already in Landauer's writings the "withdrawal from capitalism" means "withdrawal from history." Landauer considers the "standstill" as the ideal condition of human existence. He maligns "development" and "progress":

Listen, wise and liberal contemporaries, long centuries and often millenniums of relative standstill have been and are still for many nations living beside us a sign of their culture. Progress, or what one calls progress, this continuous wobbling and vacillating, this getting-tired-quickly and this neurasthenic short-breathed pursuit of the new, as long as it is new, progress, these crazy ideas of the advocates of development and their maniacal habit to say good-bye upon arrival, progress, this unsettled restlessness and hurry, this being-unable-to-keep-quiet and this travel-fever, this so-called progress is a symptom of our abnormal conditions, our lack of culture; and we need something else than such symptoms of our decadence to overcome our decadence--as I said, there have been and there are still times and nations with a productive life, times of tradition, of the epic, of agriculture and country manufacture, without much outstanding art, and without much within science.[29]

The inhabitants of Rosa Blanca refuse to participate in historical events: "Of politics there was not a word. Not one of the men here cared whether Don Manuel or Don Justo was President of the Republic; no one cared whether the Americans would march into the Republic or show off their battleships and their guns in Nicaraguan harbors. To these men such matters were of no interest whatsoever" (139). The methods of cultivation have been unchanged since time immemorial. The shelling of corn on the cob is done "with another cob. That was the way corn had been shelled here for five thousand years--more, twenty thousand" (21). The hacienda's withdrawal from history is proven by the unchanging nature of the means of production, which are indicative of the manner in which man deals with nature. In order to preserve the land's prehistoric existence, the purchase of a corn-shelling machine must be foregone: "It's been like this for fifty thousand years. Why, then, did he have to buy one this week? What was the hurry? The machine could wait" (21). Even the introduction of a handmill for the grinding of corn meal is rejected, since with the handmill alienating work would come to Rosa Blanca and revolutionize its life. Progress, as far as the means of production are concerned, would cause a change in the relations among people; it would disturb the rhythm of life and endanger

Rosa Blanca's natural state, since the handmill could do the work in three minutes

> at which the Indian woman sits for an hour and uses all her strength. But a handmill cost fifteen pesos, and what was going to be done with the time left over when the chore was finished in three minutes. It was a much greater pleasure to have all the animals around, and all the children among them. In those three minutes at the handmill, the animals could not gather, the children couldn't scamper about and scream and yell with the animals, nor could one see and experience as much. When the raccoon went at the cat or the dog was annoyed by the turkey, that was life. The handmill wasn't life or laughter. With the use of the handmill it would have been impossible for the wife to tell her husband, when he came home from work, all the comical incidents that happened while she was grinding corn. (24)

The attributes "age old" (<u>uralt</u>) and "eternal" (<u>ewig</u>), used synonymously, place Rosa Blanca outside history. The narrator underlines this absolutely extrahistorical condition with pleonastic word creations such as <u>urewig</u>. In addition, the cartwheel lying in a corner of the patio symbolizes the hacienda's detachment from the historical process. The wheel, robbed of its function of movement and restlessness, has reached the ideal state of standstill and embodies a perfection which knows neither beginning nor end. It resists all change: "Every Saturday it should have been cleared away, and every Sunday morning when Jacinto stepped out onto the portico the cartwheel was still lying in its corner" (19). It survives the death of several <u>hacendados</u> and even resists its own decay: "That cartwheel was rotting away slowly because it was made from good iron-hard wood" (19). The narrator himself feels compelled to interpret the wheel as a symbol for the Indios, or, more exactly, for their extrahistorical existence, so that no uneducated interpreter from proletarian circles should misunderstand him as far as this point is concerned: "Indeed, what Jacinto knew even better was that the cartwheel would still be lying there when he himself was called away. For the wheel was no lifeless hunk of decaying old mahogany. The wheel was a symbol—a symbol of the race that peopled the Republic, a race that was, is, and always will be the same. It could not be moved. The cartwheel had become ageless" (21).
The entrance into history means the abandonment of the unity of man and nature and the revocation of his paradisiacal existence. The destruction of this unity is caused by

outside forces, by those who have been alienated from nature for a long time, namely, the city dwellers. Traven continues Landauer's criticism of the city in all its sharpness and makes the inhabitants of the cities responsible for the destruction of the basic social communities: "Such small people are always disturbed in their order—what seems to us their primitive structure and cohesion—if a clan or tribe of city dwellers, of city builders, makes its appearance. Cities must absorb men en masse in order to survive and flourish. And since these masses inhabit less land than is needed to feed them, they invade the people who are directly attached to the soil. They then construct a system in which the townsman turns into tyrant and the farmer into helot" (23). Classless society is being terminated, and the masses are indirectly held responsible for the establishment of class society.

The classless utopia advocated by Traven is described both in Creation and in the Solipaz community of the Caoba Cycle. In both, humanity has resumed its harmony with nature: "People lived in peace on earth and were happy. They rejoiced about the sun which gave them light and warmth, which gave fruits to their fields, and fragrance and beautiful colors to the flowers."[30] Therefore the end of the Caoba Cycle is not to be interpreted as an unfinished revolution: The revolution has reached its goal; the revolutionaries withdraw again from history and are indifferent to everything else happening in the country. That the demise of Rosa Blanca and the incorporation of its inhabitants in the historical process must result from the rape of nature is indicated already early in the novel. Only so can the contradiction in the following sentence be explained: "But as long as the sun rose and set, Rosa Blanca had work and food" (26). By necessity the liquidation of Rosa Blanca must take on apocalyptic dimensions.

Traven follows Landauer's ideas about the antagonism between the rhythm of life of "people with a productive life" and that of the "great machine 'Our Modern Age'" (56), and he tries to capture these rhythms in his narrative style. The unconnected listing of the activities and results of conferences, such as the meeting of the Condor Oil Company directors, is modeled on the lapidary style of press agencies and conveys an impression of restlessness and bustle. This hectic activity, intensified by an increasing disorder in the listing and a worldwide jumping from topic to topic, is impressed on the reader:

From such conferences, and not from the White House in Washington, there can originate, and have originated: the rejection of foreign ambassadors; the changing of its own envoys; sickness and resignation of secretaries of state; armed intervention in the affairs of Bolshevik Russia; the abolition of freedom of speech for communists; the plotting of a new Mexican revolution; support for the Turks against England; twenty-year minimum sentences for Wobblies; free trade for whiskey smugglers; the dispatching of pocket battleships and Marines to Colombia; the entry of American troops into Peking; the stuffing of starving Greek and Armenian children with trashycanned goods that could no longer be fed to American soldiers because of the precipitate peace; unlimited land and water rights for America in the independent Republic of Nicaragua; lively hope that the Habsburgs and Hohenzollerns would grasp the scepter in their hands again; the replacement by others....(56-57)

Let us stop here, after the first third of the listing. The "wobbling and vacillating" of American society loses in this listing more and more of its recognizable logic, until it ends in activities and directives which seem paradoxical and contradictory:

a glut of anti-Semitic articles in the newspapers, the exchange of professors between Columbia, Chicago, and California universities; the reduction of Bible prices; the granting of more long-term credit to German industries and to Bolshevik Russia; the deportation of pacifists and similar peace-pipe smokers; the building of eighteen new battleships and one hundred fifty submarines; a treaty among all peoples not to make war without first asking Washington's permission; the League of Nations against Mankind and for Profit; congratulatory telegrams to Germany for delivery of military zeppelins; propaganda for the uplifting of morals among the working class; the banning of two-dollar prostitutes; the encouragement of mobile prostitution to revive an auto industry struggling for its life.... (57)

It is naturally not the aim of the author to describe the world as chaotic but to show behind the reigning chaos the logic of capitalism.

From the narrative staccato for the world of capitalism, the narrative rhythm changes to an adagio for the world of Rosa Blanca. We still find a listing, but the items are now connected by conjunctions and by lexical and syntactic repetitions. The flow of narration is not abrupt at all. To illustrate the slow-down in the tempo of narration by simple

means, such as repetitions and parallelisms, we limit ourselves to the scene in the patio discussed earlier:

> Then, once again, the wheel was going to be burnt. Then
> again, with Manuel's help, it was going to be used for
> something. Then, as a young man, Jacinto had sat on the
> wheel in the evenings... (20)

The syntax changes here, but the new sentence must follow on
from the first despite grammatical problems. A break in the
narrative flow must be avoided:

> Sitting on it, he had hummed sweet ranch songs to him-
> self. And many a night he had squatted on it and quietly
> cried to himself because he believed she would not have
> him. Then, a bit later, he had cuddled on it with her in
> the night... (20)

Just like the headline style of newspapers is copied to
portray the sphere of the oil company, we find here reminiscences of the narrative style of oral traditions.

The change in narration on the stylistic level corresponds
to a change in the narrative structure. While the events on
Rosa Blanca are described in linear succession without
changes in linear levels, and the flow of narration is not
disturbed by interpolations, previews, or flashbacks,[31] the
narrative structure becomes complicated when the Condor Oil
Company is the subject of the plot. Then the simple chronology of events is abandoned in favor of a complexity
caused by previews and flashbacks, by insertions of stories
which suddenly disrupt the narrative suspense, and by the
inclusion of independent stories which are necessary neither
for the progression nor for the comprehension of the main
plot. This complexity lacks a strict structure, however, so
that the impression of precipitous events in an anarchistic
world is intensified.

Traven designates the nonhistorical world of Rosa Blanca,
which protects the individual from the modern world, with a
concept that idealized the withdrawal from history and poli-
tics--namely, "homeland" (Heimat). Traven probably agreed
subjectively with Bloch's request not to surrender this
concept of Heimat to their fascist opponents, in spite of
the fact that it was principally used to activate reactionary and chauvinistic feelings. In his Mexican exile Traven
was not able with his mystical program to modify the connotations of the concept as Bloch wanted it. On the contrary,
he uses Heimat, this "affair of the heart and the soul"
(136), to justify irrational political concepts. The real

reasons for historical processes and events are not observed by this concept of Heimat and covered with a mystical darkness. They are explained in a manner which even justifies colonial and imperial wars. In The White Rose the European becomes a pitiable Ahasverus, a wandering Jew. To state it more simply, the hunter becomes the hunted. In his lack of Heimat lies the impetus for the European's desire for world dominion:

> The white man had forgotten who he was and where he came from millenniums ago, flitting about, always harried and chased, never having time, never gaining time, whether he was building railroads and express locomotives or wireless telegraph stations. Always there was the restlessness, the harassment. And the more devices he invented to save time, the less he had. Chased from one continent to the next, from Asia to Europe, from campaigns and world wars-- all to find a homeland. And all his scientists try, and try in vain, to find out where his true homeland is. (137)

Disregarding the fact that Heimat as a counterconcept designates a nonhistorical world devoid of social problems, the concept also revolves around the typical hopes of large parts of the population, which towards the end of the twenties in the United States, in Europe, and especially in Germany were threatened by constant economic problems and lived in fear of a descent into the proletarian ranks actually happening then. "Peace, contentment, security" (137)-- these more petit-bourgeois than farmer's notions of happiness are seen by the Mexican governor in The White Rose as guaranteed by the existence of the Heimat of the hacienda. The advent of civilization puts an end to this natural existence. Rosa Blanca, whose name connotes virginity and innocence, loses this virginity and perishes. It is not the fate of the Indios, the dislocated inhabitants of the hacienda, that is the focus of interest, but the "quaking earth" (27) tormented by "heavy trucks with steel treads" (27). The destruction of the "ancestral home" (Urheimat) (27) happens like a natural catastrophe: The sun darkens, the earth loses its fertility, and all life dies.

In view of the apocalyptic nature of the hacienda's destruction the language of the author assumes a biblical format. Yañez, who has to die for this paradise, appears like Christ weeping over the future destruction of Jerusalem. In imitation of the New Testament, destruction unfolds: "The families would destroy themselves, ancient ties would be ruptured, the son would no longer know his father, the nephew his uncle" (25). Turning to the Rosa Blanca, the

174

prophet Yañez "had talked with the forefathers, with whom he was not acquainted, but who he knew were his forebears. He had talked with his descendants, of whom he similarly knew they were his blood, his race, even though he was not acquainted with them" (26). And he tells his chosen people: "Rosa Blanca would be like the factory in the city where the father works, something necessary, but something to which one has no personal connection. The families would travel from place to place until the father found work that would assure his family its daily bread. Nothing could be more certain than that" (25-26).

As is well known, the history of salvation which Traven uses here, at least as a store of quotations, does not end with the dire prospect that man will have to earn his bread by the sweat of his brow, but it gives an outlook for better times, for a return to paradise. This hope is also presented in the last chapter of Traven's novel. The basis for this hope, however, comes as a surprise.

That the ending of the novel presented difficulties for Traven has been known since the publication of his first novel, The Death Ship. The author himself made several critical remarks about its conclusion. The ending of The White Rose also presents Traven with a dilemma. The prophecy of Yañez establishes the plan of the novel; the tragedy of the Rosa Blanca must be fulfilled or the conclusion would devaluate the novel as a whole. The Rosa Blanca is literally bled dry when "the rich black oil, the pulsing lifeblood of the Mexican soil, could be shipped off in unprecedented quantities" (205). The former Indian farmers, provided they have not been completely evicted from their homeland but are being used as workers for the production of oil, pay a high price besides all the deprivations which they must suffer: Their lives become a nothing, just like those of the sailors on the Yorikke.

The destruction of this whole world is so complete, the eviction from paradise so final, that a restoration of this world, a return to paradise at the end of The White Rose, would not be believable. Yet Traven's political self-conception hardly allows him to end with this apocalyptic vision. The solution he finds not only contradicts other statements expressed in the final chapter, however; the author also retracts central ideas expressed in earlier chapters and risks a break in the overall conception of the novel. Now the loss of paradise is interpreted the other way around and celebrated as an act of becoming human beings for the Indios. The process of becoming conscious and the beginning of self-recognition are results of this loss. The Indios start living consciously in completely different surroundings: "And they were seeing that new world, living in it, understanding it, and feeling almost like members of that wider world" (195). The former inhabitants of the Rosa Blanca say about themselves: "We have become richer than we were, we have become greater than our fathers were. Today we are citizens of the world. What is more, we are conscious citizens of the world, because we understand the earth and the other people in it, and we understand more and more. And because we understand more, our love has become greater. What greater thing can a man gain than a greater love for his fellow man" (196).

Considering Traven's affinity for biblical ideas, it is hardly surprising that he refers once more to the biblical connection between the eviction from paradise and the eating from the tree of knowledge. The reevaluation of the loss of paradise as a distancing of men from nature caused by reflection opens the way for a positive view of mechanization and industrialization, which, in consequence, do not contain the menace of a new alienation for the Indios. Contrary to all expectations raised in the novel so far, men's rule over nature is now seen as a _positive_ force of history and related to the restoration of a harmonious society. However, it is not the newly developed working class, which according to Marxist thought carries out its historic role and effects the restoration of a harmony on a higher level, but "man" who has become conscious. Therefore, it is not proletarian internationalism that promises a better future, but rather an apolitical cosmopolitanism, which is stimulated and carried by man's "greater love for his fellow man" (196).

Traven sympathizes with the oppressed, but he knows the limits of the theory of the decline or even suppression of rural life in the face of change. He interprets the results of the destruction of a Mexican hacienda and the obliteration of its identity by American capitalism as a process of gaining consciousness and as an awakening to the understanding of the historical process which allows the formation of a new identity without having experienced and overcome alienation. His ideological point of view is more diffuse at the end of the novel than at the beginning. The materials for his ideological construction come from different sources. Inconsistencies in this construction do not bother the syncretist author. The use of different ideological elements makes Traven's work acceptable for many. It is possible that this--and not his "exoticism," as Scharrer thought--is one of the reasons for Traven's success during the last years of the Weimar Republic.

V

We don't have to be reminded of the fact that in the years following the publication of The White Rose the accession to power of a usurper was being prepared in Germany. He was going to put in the shade the inhuman features of "Caesar Augustus Capitalism" which Traven had given to the figure of Mr. Collins. This German Führer planned to conquer and suppress not only individual nations, but also the world itself. The slogan of Mr. Collins, "the war fought in the most brutal manner lasts the shortest time and is therefore the most humane" (4), seemed to have become the basis of German politics.

Following this period and the fall of fascism, Traven revised his novel by introducing a new character. In the BT-Mitteilungen No. 2 this character is presented: "The Wolfgang Krüger Verlag, Hamburg, will soon publish a new edition of the novel about oil. It reveals a trait of Mr. Collins which is found in no other chapter. This super-capitalist always appears boasting, shouting and spreading fear. But in this new chapter for the first time in his active life he finds a man whom he can not shout down. And this dynamic Mr. Collins proves to be a trembling nobody as soon as he is pitted against a man who can destroy him with one sleepy nod, him and the millions of his Oil Company."[32] The announcement asks the publishing companies to follow the new version in all future editions.

The inserted chapter is not germane to the rest of the plot of the novel; however, it further modifies the events and Traven's criticism of capitalism. The new character, a "king" (127), calls Mr. Collins to account for his fraudulent practices; he appears as the incarnation of a noble and honest capitalism. Since his age is given as 120 or 130 years, he must be an allegorical version of bourgeois society. As an allegory, he has the attributes of divinity. The bank in which the meeting of the "king" with Mr. Collins is arranged becomes a "church" and "sacristy" (124). The exit of the old man is portrayed as the end of a theophany:

The king stood up and, his shoulders stooped, walked slowly to the door. Without turning round, he said evenly: "Good day, mister."
He touched the door lightly. It opened noiselessly, as if by itself, and let him go out. (128)

With the introduction of this character, Traven retracts his condemnation of capitalism on principle and replaces it with a criticism of the abuses and excesses of capitalism, for which Mr. Collins is in part responsible. The reason that Traven can do this rather easily and without having to rewrite the whole novel lies in the fact that, already in the original version, these excesses were not shown as an integral part of this form of society but as the results of Mr. Collins's traits of character and actions. In consequence, Traven's view of the capitalistic order becomes basically an apologetic one: Following the defeat of Hitler-fascism he maintains that the old system can not only be reformed, but that it can be cleansed through the action of a moral authority, "the king":

> Everyone who was in the game with me had complete confidence of winning as much as I. Those who got plucked were amateurs, usually gamblers, who use all sorts of tricks to cheat the honest players. It is these parasites who deserve their fate. They are trying to make suckers of all the rest of us who play fair and square, and they employ every kind of dirty trick to cheat us. It is these parasites who cause those devastating panics in the domestic development of honest business and hard-working industry....Every era has its own laws. Mine had its laws, by which we lived and worked and did business. Yours has other laws, which you have to obey if you don't want to be considered a criminal. And so, young man, don't forget my warning. I mean it in dead earnest. I'm not repeating it. (128)

In the West German postwar situation, this had to be read as a song of praise for the reestablishment of a capitalism based on free competition, a hymn which, in addition, was sung for the West Germans by an _American_ king, "one whom he [Collins] called The Magnate, The Tycoon, and at times The Really Big Shot, the Greatest of the Great" (124). The theocratic disguise of the economic omnipotence of a "clean" liberal capitalism made the "anticapitalist" Traven also adoptable and acceptable for the West German society of the "economic miracle" years. In 1974, during the social-liberal era of reform, a book was published with the title Vorbilder für Deutsche. Korrektur einer Heldengalerie.[33] One of the new heroes was B. Traven.

Notes

1. B. Traven, _Die Weisse Rose_ (Berlin: Büchergilde Gutenberg, 1929). I am quoting from B. Traven, _The White Rose_, translated from the German by Donald J. Davidson (Westport, Connecticut: Lawrence Hill & Co., 1979). Page numbers

following quotations from The White Rose refer to this
edition. Since the text of the German edition, B. Traven,
Die Weisse Rose (Reinbek bei Hamburg: Rowohlt, 1962), de-
viates in some passages from the English text, several
quotations have been translated directly from the German
text. In these instances, the page number of the German
text is listed in the notes.

2. B. Traven, Land des Frühlings (Berlin, 1928), 24.

3. B. Traven, "Nachtbesuch im Busch," in B. Traven, Abenteuergeschichten (Zürich, 1974), 207-49, 215.

4. Recknagel, 1977, 219-20.

5. Ibid. The Review of B. Traven by Tucholsky is found in
Kurt Tucholsky, Gesammelte Werke III (1928-32) (Reinbek bei
Hamburg, 1961), 606-14.

6. Klaus Bergmann, "Der Kreis schliesst sich. Dossier
über die Entstehung des Mythos B. Traven," in Beck et al.,
34.

7. All references to Scharrer's article are found in Adam
Scharrer, "Traven und sein Erfolg" in Linkskurve, No. 3, 4.
Jg. (March 1932), 29-32.

8. Gustav Landauer, Aufruf zum Sozialismus (Köln, ⁴1923)
52, 75.

9. Lübbe, 1965, 174, footnote.

10. In 1923 Ortega y Gasset had demanded in El Tema de
nuestro Tiempo (Madrid, 1923) the renewal and extension of
the development of historiographic theory in this direction.

11. Wolfgang Reif, Zivilisationsflucht und literatische
Wunschträume. Der exotistische Roman im ersten Viertel des
20. Jahrhunderts (Stuttgart, 1975), 94.

12. Herbert J. Nickel, Soziale Morphologie der mexi-
kanischen Hacienda (Wiesbaden, 1978) (= Das Mexikoprojekt
der Deutschen Forschungsgemeinschaft 14), 1.

13. B. Traven, Land des Frühlings, 21-31.

14. Barbara Beck and Horst Kurnitzky, Preface to the second edition of André Gunder Frank, Rodolfo Stavenhagen, Luis
Vitale et al., Lateinamerika: Entwicklung der Unterent-
wicklung, ed. by Bolivar Echeverria and Horst Kurnitzky
(Berlin, 1975) (=Politik 15), 10.

15. Nickel, 139.

16. J. B. de Santisteban, Indicador particular del admin-
istrador de hacienda (Puebla, 1903), 100 (here quoted from
Nickel, 139).

17. Luis Vitale, "Ist Lateinamerika feudal oder kapitali-
stisch?" in Frank, Lateinamerika, 65-89, 82.

18. André Gunder Frank, "Die Entwicklung der Unterentwick-
lung," in Frank, Lateinamerika, 28-43, 41.

19. Rodolfo Stavenhagen, "Sieben falsche Thesen über Lateinamerika," in Frank, Lateinamerika, 13-28, 15f.

20. Ibid., 17.

21. Landauer, 34.

22. Ibid., 135.

23. Silvio Gesell, Die natürliche Wirtschaftsordnung durch Freiland-Freigeld (Rehbrüche bei Berlin, 1922) (1st edition 1911), 391.

24. Landauer, 145. All references to Landauer's Aufruf in this section are taken from pages 142-145.

25. Wolfgang Reif, 88.

26. Max Horkheimer and Theodor W. Adorno, Dialektik der Aufklärung. Philosophische Fragmente (Frankfurt/M, 1971), 38.

27. Ibid.

28. Die Weisse Rose, 17.

29. Landauer, 10.

30. B. Traven, "Sonnenschöpfung," in B. Traven, Abenteuergeschichten, 322-57.

31. The vision in which Yañez sees the destruction of the hacienda is no exception, since in this preview the world of the Indian has already been transcended and the intrusion of the capitalistic north is prefigured.

32. BT-Mitteilungen No. 2, February 1951, in BT-Mitteilungen No. 1-36 (Reprint Berlin, 1978), 25.

33. Peter Glotz and Wolfgang R. Langenbucher, Vorbilder für Deutsche. Korrektur einer Heldengalerie (München, 1974).

LOVE AND DEATH IN THE EARLY WORKS OF B. TRAVEN

Peter Küpfer

I

At a central point in his book about B. Traven, Michael L. Baumann[1] mentions the astonishing fact that something akin to a love relationship develops between the harassed and tortured stoker Gales and his tormentor, the death ship Yorikke. In fact, in the passage referred to by Baumann, which occurs toward the end of the second book of the novel, Traven carries a contrast to its logical conclusion, a contrast which worries him in all of his novels, namely, the emotional, affective bond of the oppressed to his oppressor. The Yorikke is not simply a concrete, individualized instrument of exploitation, but it is also something like a symbol of the capitalist system of exploitation, a symbol of Western society and civilization, which for Traven is doomed like the death ship. In this sense, Traven touches upon a quite modern and very profound social problem--namely, the problem of psychic dependence, the acceptance of unacceptable conditions.

It is paradoxical that the oppressed and tormented individual not only becomes accustomed to his intolerable situation, but he even defends and justifies it while it persists. In many cases, he does _not_ change an intolerable and unacceptable situation by a spontaneous and desperate attempt at revolt and rebellion, but he accepts his supposed fate and even legitimizes it. In Das Totenschiff this problem is treated again and again, and in an increasingly incisive and urgent manner. In the above-mentioned passage in the novel, Traven finally goes so far as to bring the paradox to a head by having Gales address a hymn of praise to the death ship. After we read about all the insufferable and painful experiences Gales has on the Yorikke, the author then confronts us with Gales's following address:

All right, I cannot pass by you, Yorikke; I have to tell you I love you. Honest baby, I love you. I have six black finger-nails, and four black and green-blue nails on my toes which you, honey, gave me when necking you. Grate-bars have crushed some of my toes. And each finger-nail has its own painful story to tell. My chest, my back, my arms, my legs are covered with scars of burns and scorchings. Each scar, when it was being created, caused

me pains which I shall surely never forget. But every
outcry of pain was a love-cry for you, honey.[2]

We hear nothing but a sadomasochistic perversion of a sincere declaration of love. The obvious exaggeration points
to the paradox, which consists of having the tormented
declare his love for his tormentor. It is a typical stylistic feature of Traven's writings, and it is found in Ret
Marut's earliest stories, as well as in B. Traven's late
novels of the Caoba Cycle. Hyperbole as a figure of classical rhetoric is a favored stylistic feature used by Traven
to denounce hidden or obscured power structures. The mad-
ness which finds expression in the overly subtle statement
of logical opposites is intended by Traven to show the
senselessness and enormity of social conditions.

The relationship between master and slave, which was still
interpreted ontologically by Hegel and seen as historically
and materialistically determined by Marx and Engels, is
given an additional dimension by Traven. The fact that men
exert power over other men is considered by him to be an
essentially sociopsychological problem: What must have
happened to a man like Gales or Stanislawski for him to
"willingly" accept the hellish torments he is subjected to
on the Yorikke? Traven poses the question about the antecedents for such behavior; he inquires after the history and
the process which finally result in this behavior.

In this connection, the first book of the novel acquires
its special meaning and importance in the novel as a whole;
it shows Gales under the tutelage of the state, or as a
victim of bureaucracy--his bodily existence does not prove
anything, and he is therefore eliminated as a human being by
bureaucratic measures. This is the story of a psychic
disposition, which makes understandable Gales's paradoxical
behavior. It is the point of view of somebody who has gone
through the bureaucratic mill, of one who has been destroyed
by physical exploitation, of one who is "dead"; it is the
voice of the "mastered." For Traven, mastery or rule will
exist inasmuch and as long as human beings are accustomed to
slavery and are being educated for slavery.

Against this background, The Death Ship can be considered
a report on this process of acculturation. It describes,
symbolically, the mechanisms by which men slowly become
accustomed to misery. It is the history of a negative
socialization, which Traven considers wrong because it results in the acceptance, even "love," of a principle which
denies human beings their dignity. Therefore, The Death
Ship is the ghastly representation of Western civilization,
in which the shipping company sacrifices the crew to "Caesar

Capitalism"; and Gales's "declaration of love" for the Yorikke can be read as an exhortation to the German working class in the late twenties, people who had suffered through a terrible war, were now victims of an economic crisis, and were being influenced by incresingly perfected mass media used for political indoctrination. Traven posed the question: "German worker, what is your relationship to the ship Yorikke?"

II

Without doubt The Death Ship is a deeply pessimistic book, at least as far as parts two and three are concerned. Based on the results of new research on the biography of B. Traven,[3] we can now imagine the situation in which he wrote this novel. After having escaped from the white terror, he spent years underground on the run, finally parting company with Europe and its war-mongering civilization in the last number of his Ziegelbrenner: He was not going to make common cause with a spirit which here (in Europe) "was debauched and dissolute," according to Ret Marut's own words. Wyatt's research allows the conjecture that parts of the text of Das Totenschiff were written in prison in England or that the episodes in the first part of the novel are based on similar experiences of the author.[4] Rejection of European culture, despair about the failure of the revolutionaries, and impotent rage against "the freest state in the world,"[5] as the young Weimar Republic, the progressive, social-democratic Germany, was wont to call itself in these troubled postwar years--all these things were on Traven's mind while writing Das Totenschiff.

Only a short time later, however, the self-same B. Traven unexpectedly offered to his proletarian German reading public in the Büchergilde Gutenberg--a much more optimistic book, The Cotton Pickers.[6] And the hero of this novel is the same Gales who in The Death Ship desperately denounces and bemoans the spiritual corruption of the oppressed in the face of the oppressor, and their susceptibility to the propaganda of their rulers, which he demonstrates through his own example. But now Gales has become a different person. Carefree, cunning, and audacious, he continues in the picaresque tone and manner--which is a feature of the first book of The Death Ship--and he even enhances this tone without once resorting to the depressing negative approach which is characteristic of the second part of The Death Ship. He is a resurrected jack-of-all-trades, who not only outwits the representatives of authority, but who also objectively weakens them. In all places where he has been, a

strike is started--naturally by pure coincidence--since he
has left a situation in which conditions have been changed
in favor of the workers and to the detriment of the employers. Therefore, the novel ends on a euphoric note, with the
expression of a feeling of cosmic unity of the hero with the
world:

> On the grassy flats, only glowworms and fireflies were
> visible. But invisible life sang with a million voices
> and made music like that of violin, flute, and harp--and
> tiny cymbal, and bell.
>   There lay my herd! One dark, rounded form next to the
> other. Lowing, breathing, exhaling a full, warm, heavy
> fragrace of natural well-being, so rich in its quiet
> earthiness, such balm to the spirit, bringing with it such
> utter contentment.[7]

The general tone of the novel is positive, although even
here death throws its shadow on this expression of enjoyment
of life when the Indian Gonzalo falls victim to white exploitation still existing in Mexico. But the people, the
masses, have started to take their fate into their own
hands. They do it cheerfully and calmly, and in the case of
setbacks, in the secure knowledge of their strength and
their final victory. Gales has also acquired a peace of
mind, which, for Traven, is a genuinely Indian personality
trait. What has happened to him?

Traven's Land is very informative in this respect, since
parts of it were proably written during his early days in
that country. His meeting with Mexico was a decisive experience for him. Here he saw realized what had failed, as far
as he was concerned, in Germany and Russia; here he saw
growing and developing a candor in dealings with the authorities, a fresh revolutionary breeze, a much more firm and
decisive attitude, which would redeem world history from the
course of European ethnocentrism. And Land shows us that
Indian substratum in which Traven places all his hopes: in
the Indian blood, the Indian race, which is fresh and un-
spent; in the Indian mind, which for centuries has withstood
colonial suppression through the same stoic and uncompromising determination; and, finally, in Indian community life,
whose principles are diametrically opposed to Western ideas.
For Traven, the Indian community is based on cooperation and
solidarity. He compares the Western principle of exaggerated individualism, of competition, with the Indian principle of the common use of available resources; and he
places the benefits accruing to the community as a whole
against the outstanding achievement of the individual at the

184

expense of its weaker members. The influence of libertarian thinking on Traven—especially Landauer's opposition to the principle of achievement as a principle which secures privileges—becomes very evident.

His first Mexican experiences, his first information about the Indian roots of Mexican culture, must have heartened and electrified Traven, disappointed and embittered by Europe as he was. A revolution which, like the Mexican, is based on the Indian substratum—and Traven insists upon this point in Land—has therefore much more promising and positive characteristics for him. Here in Mexico it must be successful, although it did not succeed in Germany and Russia. In contrast to the European revolution—and in this connection both the United States and Russia are European—the Mexican revolution, as an Indian revolution, does not have to fight against its heritage, its cultural deadweight. On the contrary, it liberates those forces which have been inactive, which have slept underground during the centuries of European colonization.

In this Mexico in transformation, Gales enters the school of class struggle. In his consciousness are mirrored the experiences of the labor movements in Europe and North America. Stunned and fascinated, he relates to his proletarian readers of these two cultural areas—to readers who think in European terms and are familiar with the European labor movements—the new and unprecedented developments which are happening in this regard in Mexico. And Gales takes the same stance he expects from his Euro-American readers: namely, one of learning. As narrator he demonstrates this stance to his readers: Gales is himself a learner. And Traven is obviously not interested in specific forms or contents of the labor struggle, but in the spirit and consciousness with which the struggling workers are imbued. In his Munich Ziegelbrenner days, Traven had repeatedly attacked the inconsistency and weakness of the German labor movement and its leaders; here in Mexico he rejoices for the firm and incorruptible stance of the workers. He expects that this example will have a positive effect on his audience, especially on his German readers who are exposed to the temptations of political reformism.

A scene from the strike of the waiters in The Cotton Pickers will serve as illustration. The dominating character in this scene is Morales, a militant syndicalist. Even Gales accepts him as leader. When Morales is fired, the other waiters ask for their wages and leave. The effect of this demonstration of solidarity is threatened when two nonorganized, unemployed waiters offer their services to the owner of the café. Gales tries to explain to these two that

185

through their action they are not only hurting their colleagues' interests but also their own. In the German edition of the novel, the two unemployed waiters are not two unspecified characters but a German and a Hungarian who have been stranded in Mexico. In contrast to the militant Mexican workers, they obviously lack class-consciousness, and this can be explained historically. They are representatives of the European labor movement, of the German, to be more specific, and their lack of consciousness is the result of the specific history of the German labor movement. In this scene Gales, with his American name, speaks to the two scabs in fluent German. This demonstrates that he is knowledgeable about German conditions and that he knows exactly to whom he is speaking. He attempts to transmit the results of his own process of learning and to enliven their lack of consciousness with a dash of the Mexican temperament, but without success. He tells the innkeeper's wife, who could not understand the German conversation, with intentional ambiguity: "Incite? I? The two Germans? Certainly not, I am only teaching them a few important Spanish words so that they can get along better in life."[8]

Based on this scene, the novel can be looked upon as an attempt to teach the German proletarian readers from the Büchergilde Gutenberg, who have been influenced by the reform movement, "a few important Spanish words," to impart to them a straight Mexican view of these things.

Against this background, the concept of love acquires a new content for Traven in the first years of his Mexican existence. While in The Death Ship he had principally portrayed the perverse love of the tormented for the tormentor as the result of a misguided socialization, here in Mexico he now fills the concept of love with his newly acquired knowledge. For him love is now the main ingredient of Indian community culture; it now stands in direct contrast to the concept of the rule of men over other men. For Traven the essence of Indian culture, as he understands it, is love as a euphoric feeling of a common bond between people. Love is a natural form of exchange and human intercourse among equals; it is given to all members of the community, to which they belong and contribute through their individuality and personal qualities. Among the Mexican Indians, love is the uncorrupted and incorruptible ability to love; it is the last and authentic bastion of native against Western civilization, the latter based on the authoritarian principle which is artificial and unnatural. That is the starting point of the Mexican Traven, from where he could write the epic of Indian liberation, the six volumes of the Caoba Cycle.

III

The novella The Bridge in the Jungle was written and finished in 1925, at about the same time as The Death Ship and The Cotton Pickers. The Büchergilde Gutenberg hesitated for four years, however, before it decided to publish the novella. The preprint in serial form in the Berlin paper Vorwärts in 1927 had caused a wave of protests among its readers, who maintained that Traven had gone too far with his unappetizingly realistic portrayal of the corpse of a child putrefying under the hot tropical sun.

But Traven's pointed realism in the portrayal of death has a meaning. Especially in Bridge Traven insists that at the end of life stands death and that death is final, the end of conscious life for the individual, of life aware of itself. The revolting word pictures in the description of the process of decay of little Carlitos's body are supposed to place the unchangeable fact of death before the eyes of the reader. Every human being has only one life. The knowledge that life ends in death causes Traven to inquire about the meaning of life. He stresses the pictures of death because Western European culture has repressed the fact of death, primarily through transcendental philosophy, which interprets the world and human existence in view of an afterlife. Traven's detailed description of the process of putrefaction is supposed to overcome this way of thinking and reorient it to this life, to the here and now. Here, as well as in a different manner in The Death Ship, the graphic vividness of the literary means used by Traven has the purpose of shocking the reader and causing him to think for himself. Not only the commentaries of the narrator, but also the text itself is subversive and constantly suggests questions: Why did little Carlitos have to die? What did the Spanish conquerors, the Catholic missionaries, and American civilization actually contribute to the autochthonous Indian culture? How do these Western influences affect the Indian organism, which Traven shows as a microcosm?

The bridge in the jungle should link two worlds, but in actuality it demonstrates their separation. Traven's story leaves no doubt that Carlitos is a victim of Western profit-thinking; he is lured to his death by the deceptive bridge, put in the jungle in order to make money. But the anguished pictures of death which overshadow the first part of the novella are superseded by a new topic, which towards the end of the story gains in importance and allows it to end, in a grotesque manner, in a lighter vein. United by the tragic death of Carlitos, the Indian community forms a bulwark which repulses the influences of Western culture or transforms them in such a manner that they no longer represent a danger. The alien nature and the garishness of the Indian funeral ceremony are an indication of the vitality and validity of the Indian system of values, untouched in its core. The signs of Western colonization have only been superimposed on the Indian culture; they are only a slight veneer, which gives way as soon as the old Indian elements emerge. Although the funeral music is mixed with superficial Western entertainment-music, and although the swollen corpse of the child is pressed into a tight Western store-bought suit, under this surface the Indian life-force re-asserts itself. The ceremony is strange, but in the final analysis it is also moving for the Western observer. Gales is integrated into the community of mourners in spite of the fears which had risen in him because of the strange ritual. From an observer he turns into a participant. The second part of the novella is full of grotesque word pictures, but it ends on the topic of community. The solidarity which the grieving family experiences is genuine; it alleviates their sorrow. This essence of community culture again proves stronger than the basically destructive influences of Western civilization it successfully repels.

IV

It should also be noted that this theme of death confirms the thesis that B. Traven was indeed the later pseudonym of Ret Marut. To illustrate this, let us consider the "Death Songs of Hyotamore of Kyoena," published in Ziegelbrenner.[9] The author examines the death cult of European societies and considers this a false cult--it is an expression of the mis-orientation of an entire culture. His argumentation runs as follows: A culture which honors the dead lacks respect for the living. In our culture, man experiences respect and dignity only as a corpse during his funeral. During this funeral ceremony, feelings are suddenly mobilized--artificial feelings which the deceased had never enjoyed during his lifetime. That is one aspect of our false relationship to death. The other aspect lies in the illusion that our real life begins only after death, in our orientation to-wards an afterlife. Rulers use this metaphysical perspective to justify their rule, and the miserable find consolation in the thought of a life beyond. A further basic statement concerns itself with the baroque paradox that the dead are living and the living are dead:

Verily, I am saying to you: Dead ones are living who are more alive than the living; and there are living among you who have been dead since their first day in school, even though they are telling you: "We are living because we rule."[10]

This paradox is not solved in the baroque manner, with reference to eternity, however, but with reference to the here and now of society. Obviously, the living death as Hyotamore understands it is tied to social institutions--for example, to school as an instrument of socialization--as well as to positions of power and rule, as the above quote proves. To be dead means the same in this instance as it did in The Death Ship: to live in a society in which a hierarchy based on power infringes upon the life of the individual.

For Hyotamore, as well as for Traven, the death and power principle form a unit and show the two sides of a nondeveloped life in the shadow of death, because power can be maintained and legitimized only with the help of a philosophical orientation toward something higher, something metaphysical, to whose greater glory the life of the individual must contribute and is sacrificed in the final analysis. The ruler can rule only because of his metaphysical legitimation; he is ruling "by the grace of God." And the oppressed man finds solace in his misery by looking towards a future, heavenly justice, which will be meted out to him after his death. Only a materialistic philosophy which considers death as the end of conscious life and not as a transition to the "real" life, and which looks upon death as a natural, nonmetaphyical occurrence, as the decay of conscious life to an unconscious state, of living to dead matter--only such a thinking can, according to Hyotamore, give its undivided attention to this life on earth and is in a position to recognize the basic illegality of every hierarchical structure, of every privileged status. That is the classical idea of enlightened materialistic social theory, and the following aphorism of Hyotamore sounds like a summary of Feuerbach:

As soon as you comprehend that death is not the end but only a condition, only one stage in a process which you can exactly observe then there will be no more slaves on earth. And naturally no more masters. The gods have taken leave before...[11]

Cannot this quote be looked upon as an interpretative commentary on Traven's super-realism, which he used in Bridge to describe the decay of the body of Carlitos?

The topic of death finds more varied expression in the

writings of Ret Marut. In a situation in which the social
life of the individual is dominated by a collective death
principle--the principle of rule--the _individual_ death has a
special meaning. As suicide, it may constitute the final
and most extreme act of _refusal_ of power. This is the
central idea of Richard Maurhut's novella _To Fräulein von
S..._, published in 1916. Because of his intention to commit
suicide, the protagonist refuses to allow his military superiors to use his heroism (which they misunderstand) for
purposes of war propaganda. The protagonist does not volun-
teer for dangerous missions at the front in order to sacrifice himself for his country; rather, he wants to commit
suicide because of an unrequited love. At the same time, he
realizes through this act of extreme refusal, his suicide,
the only form of love towards Fräulein von S... that seems
possible to him.

A similarly paradoxical, extreme portrayal of the topic of
love is found in the novella _Khundar_. Only by renouncing
the principle of power and the throne does the princess gain
her freedom for Khundar's love. She dies in the moment of
ecstatic union with Khundar, the prophet of refusal and
poverty. Here, also, love is possible only through a symbolic death.

Now the circle is closed. For Ret Marut/B. Traven, the
principle of power is also the principle of death. Social
exercise of power, in every form and manner, leads to death.
Wherever the power principle rules, life is threatened and
limited by death in its possible forms of development. The
hierarchical principle allows death to determine life; under
this principle, life can develop only under the predominance
of death. Within the borders of its power and influence,
love is not possible in life, but only in death.

As far as Marut is concerned, every individual who grew up
in Western civilization is branded by this principle. He
has drunk it at his mother's breast and he has accommodated
himself to it until it has become second nature; his whole
education has this goal. As editor of _Ziegelbrenner_, Marut
nursed the hope that by enlightening individuals he could
induce them to free themselves from this mark, to become
responsible for themselves and thus to become "Ones," as Max
Stirner called them. After the debacle of the Räterepublik,
this optimism was no longer possible for him, as _The Death
Ship_ indicates. Only through his encounter with a culture
which for him was free of the stigma of the occidental power
principle could he regain his health. From then on, the
Indian race--the Indian blood--was for him a guarantee for a
human existence not influenced by the principle of death.
For him, the Mexicans were immune to the temptations of

Western individualism because, according to his ideas, their thinking and feeling were based solidly on the Indian substratum. They would help propagate the principle of equality, the principle of love. They were going to build a society in which--as was the case with Max Stirner--the common use of available goods and resources and individual enjoyment need no longer be contradictions. For love, as the principle of exchange and association of individuals among each other, is based on their equality and their freedom. Or, in the concepts of Max Stirner: Love as a form of relationship between "owners" presupposes their free association.

Notes

1. Cf. Baumann, 1976, 47. In my dissertation (Küpfer, 1981), I have made some mistakes in regard to Baumann's study which I regret. I would like to take this opportunity to correct these misinterpretations. In my study, I attribute to Baumann an interpretation of Stirner which he did not express. I especially would like to retract my statements that Baumann in his study accepted Stirner-cliches uncritically and that he maintained that Stirner's philosophy leads directly to fascism (cf. Küpfer, 1981, 28ff. and 106).
2. The Death Ship, 250.
3. Cf. especially Wyatt, 1980.
4. Cf. also Baumann, 1976, especially 77ff, and Küpfer, 1981, 176-80.
5. Cf. Der Ziegelbrenner, 3.H. 18/19, 3.12.1919, 9ff.
6. The first part of The Cotton Pickers was published already in 1925 in the Berlin Vorwärts, the official newspaper of the Social Democratic Party of Germany, which later also published Bridge. This indicates that Traven was obviously interested in reaching the German workers organized in the labor unions and in the Social Democratic Party.
7. The Cotton Pickers, 196.
8. Die Baumwollpflücker (Frankfurt a.M.: Diogenes, 1982), 104.
9. Der Ziegelbrenner, 2, H.3, 16.3.1918, 49ff.
10. Ibid., 49.
11. Ibid., 52.

WARS AND RUMORS OF WARS IN THE WORKS OF B. TRAVEN

Armin Richter

The topic of war is very relevant to the study of B. Traven
and his alter ego Ret Marut. Traven deals critically with
war in his novels, articles, and correspondence. Of course,
there are problems here. Only fragments of Traven correspondence are available to the researcher today. Also, Traven dealt with major events such as World War I in only a
peripheral way. He was not as directly concerned with the
subject as were contemporaries like Erich Maria Remarque or
Ernst Jünger. That is not to say that some of Ret Marut's
war sketches or his novel An das Fräulein von S... are not
rather successful, as Peter Küpfer has shown. But the
convincing narrative and touching scenes are primarily found
in secondary plots and events relating to the actual topic
of war. Marut does not succeed in presenting the complex
reality of combat, though perhaps this was not his goal. He
certainly did not have the firsthand experience or observations which' we know he needed as a foundation for his
writing.

What remains are the journalistic pieces he wrote concerning war. These include half of the Ziegelbrenner (which can
thus be regarded as the climax), as well as a large essay
written in 1945, "La tercera guerra mundial" (World War
III). This essay is of special interest today, since it
discusses recurrent issues: the danger of war breaking out
and the necessity of maintaining peace. These two works
alone--Ziegelbrenner and "La tercera guerra mundial"--would
justify studying the subject of war in Traven's work. In
addition, one finds many remarks about war interspersed in
Traven's narrative works. This is especially striking in
his Death Ship, which often parallels Ziegelbrenner.[1]

In order to study the topic of war in Traven's/Marut's
work, one has to consider the themes of revolutionary war,
civil war, rebellion, uprising, mutiny--in general, the
struggle of armed force from below against armed force from
above. As we know, this is a topic in itself in both B.
Traven's novels and Ret Marut's Ziegelbrenner. Traven regarded such insurgency as almost always justified: Liberation justifies armed force. Consider, for example, his
reaction to successive class conflicts, such as the German
crisis of 1918-19: "For decades, the proletariat has hoped
to lead their revolution without violence, especially without bloodshed. This hope has been silenced by Noske, Hoffmann, and the bourgeois prosecuting attorneys and judges.

When one side waits with bayonets and machine guns, behind which stand jail and the executioner's axe, one cannot assume that the other side will carry the stems of white lilies."[2] Compare his letter on the Spanish Civil War, where the Republicans were "heroes" of an "honorable battle."

The theme of revolutionary war will be discussed elsewhere, however. Here we will concentrate on the kinds of international conflict in which governmental and economic power plays a role.

The two expressions "the causes of war" and "the threats of war" are often tied to the same basic situation. But it is important to differentiate between them in order to understand Marut's/Traven's perception of them: One refers to the past and inquires about the causes of finished or ongoing wars; the other asks what could possibly trigger future wars.

An understanding of the consequences of the past often points to future dangers. On the basis of past experiences, Marut must already have seen the danger of another war occurring, for in the first <u>Ziegelbrenner</u> to appear after World War I he warns about a "new world war." B. Traven published his essay "La tercera guerra mundial" right after the end of World War II.

Contrary to chronological sequence, I will deal first with this essay of 1945, which contains a whole series of judgments and predictions which shed light on political situations still relevant to the world today and which should give us something to think about. In hindsight, one can see some political misjudgments, but they were sound opinions given the time of writing. For instance, it made perfectly good sense in 1945 to count Great Britain next to the United States and the Soviet Union as one of the three world powers. Traven saw the threat of a third world war arising from probable conflict between these three superpowers in varying alliances. This might appear strange today, but it was quite possible after World War II.

"There are three possible combinations," Traven speculates, "and everyone of them is plausible:

1. The Soviet Union and England against the United States
   ...
2. England and the United States against Russia...
3. The United States against England while Russia remains neutral, observing the development of events."[3]

"Let's forget about Roosevelt, Churchill, and Stalin shak-

ing hands in Teheran and Moscow. That made a nice picture
for the papers, and many people liked it, including the
communists." So Traven begins his explanation of the various alliances.

It is remarkable that in his discussion of possible enemies in a future world war, Traven also visualizes Russia as
a neutral observer, while he sees the United States as a
certain participant in such a war. In my opinion, this
points to the essential message of Traven's complex essay:
that America would be the most militaristic power after
World War II, and even the future aggressor. This may sound
shocking and provoking to American readers, but it is frequently repeated in his work. Traven felt that the desire
of the U.S. president and the military to establish the
military draft even in peacetime (although it had previously
been in effect only in times of war) was indicative of this
militaristic attitude. Another indication was the U.S.
intention to make the American navy the strongest fleet in
the world within two years.

Traven believed that such a major rearmament was against
common sense and would cause a new war before 1950. With
little delay (precisely, in 1950), his prediction became
reality. The Korean War did not grow into a world war,
however, and therefore did not fully substantiate Traven's
vision.

Traven thought the reason behind the quick rearmament by
the United States and its apparent interest in war lay in
the fact that it had financed two world wars and now, as
creditor to financially weak nations, had to collect force-
fully the outstanding capital. This idea is quite plausible. Since Traven's time, critics have even said that the
United States did not really want to defend freedom in
Vietnam and elsewhere, but instead wanted to protect vital
economic interests.

In addition to the emergence of an influential U.S. military elite connected with the war industry and financial
circles which anxiously anticipated a new war, Traven mentions further danger signals for an impending war: The
United States attempted to withhold the technology of
nuclear weapons from its former partners; a power vacuum
arose on the territory of the defeated Axis powers; the
Soviet Union became a new superpower; and the Western
powers' fear of Communism resulted in the protection of
Western dictatorships, such as those in Spain and Greece.

The specific hazards which combined to create the threat
of a third world war can be divided into three ideological
categories, and these were the same as those which led to
World War II: "nationalism," "capitalism," and "militar-

194

ism." Traven specifies and clarifies the general causes of war through examples in the <u>Ziegelbrenner</u> and reduces them to a shorter formula: the term "capitalism." All wars are economic wars. Nationalism and militarism merge into economic imperialism.

This model, however, disregards a factor which plays an important role in the onset of war: mankind's latent readiness for war, without which war is unthinkable. In the first two issues of the <u>Ziegelbrenner</u> from 1917, Ret Marut addresses two lengthy passages to this phenomenon, which he also feels was a cause of World War I. He mentions there that declining production, together with the deteriorating living conditions which most people have to face, let war appear as a source of liberation. On the other hand, he remarks, "Why are the great artists and industrious researchers never eager for war? That should make one think."[4]

Traven also repeatedly addresses the origin and phenomenon of a people's predisposition towards war in his novels. He believes the nature of the workplace plays a role in this phenomenon, as does a "Gehirnverkleisterung" (clogging of the brain) by a mass-culture, which does not stimulate and explain, but rather distracts and stupefies. This aspect seems to be even more important today, when a far more dangerous leisure and entertainment industry has been established. This industry, which provides almost around-the-clock coverage, numbs people to all their suffering, for it makes no distinction between the war and its horrors for the entire world and the entertainment shows it presents.

How important are Traven's statements about war, and what implications do his texts have for posterity; what do they mean to our age of growing concern about the threat of war? First, war--like love--is a perennial topic in literature. It must be said that war as a symptom, just as love as a symptom, is a theme that does not become obsolete. Only the form of this symptom changes. Therefore, discussions of this subject remain topical.

Second, in a time in which scientific and technocratic literature about war and the threats of war is overly abundant, it seems to be especially important to publish works which are less factual and empirical and which lie outside the realm of science. Such works are still capable of communicating a feeling for the term "war." They create images which evoke mourning, fear, or indignation and can, thereby, eliminate passivity.

To Ret Marut, "the threat of war is only completely overcome, when all the cruelty, monstrosities, and inhumanities of war are so deeply and permanently etched out of the consciousness of mankind that even the slightest possibility of war, even in the deepest unconscious, is no longer imaginable."[5]

Today, we refer to this "etching into the consciousness" as sensitization. Ret Marut's comments on war in the _Ziegelbrenner_ serve this purpose well, for the original text uses powerful language which is not intended to convince, but rather serves as an outlet for frustration.

Marut writes about war from the viewpoint of the home front. He observes the events of war through the eyes of an active civilian who views war as one cause of the already existing human and societal degeneration. By citing the example of how women's hair was collected during the war in order to produce parts for drive-belts and sealing plates for submarines, Marut points out how warring countries value humans only for their material worth and regard them as consumer goods. Under such conditions, infringement upon an individual and countless offenses against human rights and human dignity appear to be only logical. His commentary evokes an image of industry which utilizes human beings as raw material and anticipates the praxis of the Nazi concentration camps:

It starts with hair; this is already something from our body; one could take it a step further and say: If we can take hair from the living people, why can't we take hair from the dead, too? This would only have been a small step, after one had refused to put a black suit on the dead and even denied them their linen shirt. But it would not have stopped there. One step would have followed the next. The last step would not have been further from the first...than the step which had already been taken when we jumped from recruiting young strong twenty-year olds to the re-enlisting of one-eyed veterans and the enlistment of criminals....The militarists would not have had respect for anything. It started with the hair and would have ended in the boiling of the dead and fallen. This sounds so unreal today that it horrifies us. And yet I say: Humanity did not save us from this horror, but rather the revolution which ended the war. Horrible things happened during the war and other things stood ahead of us. War is a continuous horror and no one can tell in advance where such horror will end.[6]

In the _Ziegelbrenner_ emotional commentaries on war such as this one alternate with short, trivial passages:

Bull Market (Boom)
The Wolff-Bureau reports:
  Successes on the Isonzo front have contributed to the
confident mood on the stock market. Amid a generally
positive atmosphere, the value of single stock in the
armament industry has risen.
  Things seem to be in great shape. Why the alarm?[7]

A laconic and ironic style using very few words conveys
the idea to the reader in an unscholarly fashion. This
refreshing, goal-oriented realism lacks the paralyzing alarm
and the apparent optimism which cover the apathy that is so
common in the peace movement. Thus, I believe it still has
the capacity to evoke outrage in the modern reader.
  The time has come to publish a selection of outstanding
passages from the Ziegelbrenner which deal with such critical themes as the role of journalism and the church in war.
This material, in the original and in translation, may be
effective and create new opportunities for change.
  Such a selection of texts from the Ziegelbrenner would
have to include the following comment, in which Marut writes
about American soldiers in the European theater of World War
I. Marut responds to the comment of the American Expedi-
tionary Forces:

Our ranks are getting used to and seem quite happy with
their lives in the trenches. Or...are getting used to and
seem quite happy with hand grenades; or...are getting used
to and seem quite happy with blown-out intestines;
or...getting used to and seem quite happy with death.
Mankind can become accustomed to everything: being born,
dying, and killing. That is the biggest tragedy of mankind. But it is not really to his advantage, as one often
likes to infer....Who knows, perhaps an official report
will some day state: "The troops are getting used to and
seem quite happy with peace." I have to admit, however,
that I am worried about what will happen to mankind before
and during the time in which man is becoming accustomed to
peace. My concern is partly based on the fact that one
could write, "the arms suppliers and war profiteers are
not getting used to peace at all." The failure of the
capitalistic system to become accustomed to peace, could,
under certain circumstances, cause us more misfortune than
World War I caused. But if armament manufacturers and war
profiteers come to the conclusion that they could get used
to peace, then peace is truly on the way.[8]

1. Ziegelbrenner, No. 1, 5; Das Totenschiff (1926), 90 (originally there was no animosity between peoples, but rather war-mongering); Ziegelbrenner, No. 5/8, 150; Das Totenschiff, 36 (meaning of "wars of liberation"); Ziegelbrenner, No. 18/19, 10f.; Das Totenschiff, 86.
2. Ziegelbrenner, No. 23/25, 27.
3. Estudios Sociales, Vol. 15, No. 11-12 (Mexico D.F., 1945), 9-16.
4. Ziegelbrenner, No. 1, 3ff.; No. 2, 9; No. 2, 25ff.; No. 2, 30.
5. Ibid., No. 9/14, 85f.
6. Ibid., No. 9/14, 86f.
7. Ibid., No. 2, 41.
8. Ibid., No. 2, 46.

B. TRAVEN AND THE WOBBLIES

Philip Jenkins

Introduction

I wish to examine the connections of the Traven novels with
the American syndicalist tradition, especially with the
movement of the "Wobblies," the Industrial Workers of the
World (IWW). There are numerous references to the Wobblies
in the novels, especially those narrated by "Gerard Gales"
and the social and occupational settings of the books are
very much those of the real-life movement. Wobblies--like
Traven's characters--tended to be miners, sailors, migratory
agricultural laborers, and workers in the lumber industry.
One can read Traven almost as a commentary on IWW activities, especially in the IWW's years of decline after 1919.

But where did the author acquire his material? Some have
argued that the Wobbly background arose from the real experiences of an American syndicalist, a "bearer of experiences" or Erlebnisträger. This person either played a large
role in writing the books, or at least supplied much of the
material on which they were based. The nature and quality
of Traven's discussion of the Wobblies are therefore of
great importance for understanding the authorship and
genesis of the novels--particularly the early ones.[1]

I will try to show that Traven's discussion of the Wobblies is both accurate and a fine piece of observation,
which makes the novels a notable historical source. In
particular, The Cotton Pickers and The Death Ship have
extensive references to contemporary syndicalist activities.
But I would emphasize that these references are only contemporary: They refer to what the Wobblies were doing in the
mid-1920s, not to their great age of a decade or so previously. I will argue that Traven writes nothing about the
Wobblies that he could not have observed himself. There is
little evidence for the existence of a real-life "Gerard
Gales," a Wobbly whose reminiscences were used by Ret Marut
to create "Traven" and his work. With only one possible
exception--in the ideological outlook of The Death Ship--
there is no need to invoke an Erlebnisträger.

I will begin by sketching the history of the IWW, an organization which has attracted more than its share of romantic legend. The movement was formed in 1905 and exists to this day, although its greatest period can be dated to between 1912 and 1919. Very soon after its foundation, it adopted a strongly syndicalist line based on a curious synthesis of Marx, Sorel, Bakunin, and Darwin.[2] Despite some recent claims to the contrary, the group justifies the term "anarcho-syndicalist" in that it avidly wanted the existing order replaced by a social and economic organization linked to the point of production and founded on the supremacy of the working classes.[3]

As with any anarchist grouping, the union's organization was loose, and it was constantly prone to factional splits. But generally two main subdivisions can be discerned within the IWW, which are of importance for studying Traven's links to syndicalism. In the industrial eastern half of the United States, the Wobblies found their greatest strongholds among immigrant labor in low-wage occupations like the textile trade. Their great moments here come with the strikes in Lawrence, Massachusetts (1912), or Paterson, New Jersey (1913). It is the Western Wobblies who are of greater relevance for our purposes, however. This group bears very close resemblances to Traven's world, especially to The Death Ship and to The Cotton Pickers--a work which was originally called Der Wobbly.

The western United States shortly after 1900 was still very much a frontier territory, without the strict occupational or craft divisions which marked the East. A worker had to be able to turn his hand to anything, and he was likely to move rapidly between jobs. In this context, the only labor organization which made practical sense was that of the IWW--organization at the point of production, not on a craft basis. The Wobblies made considerable inroads into the tramping labor force, both at the workplace and en route. The organization recruited by means of the imaginative tactics which made them legendary--by having their activists wander the country like hoboes, spreading propaganda by popular songs and poems. Widerberg's film of the 1970s, The Ballad of Joe Hill, represented the height of the romanticization of the IWW, but mythmakers already had a substantial basis on which to build.[4]

The Western Wobblies were concentrated in certain industries. First, by 1916 they had a solid base in migratory farm labor, both in California and the Midwest. They were also well represented among ranch populations. But their greatest strength was on what has been described as the "extractive fringe," in industries producing minerals, oil, and timber.[5] In the Rocky Mountain states--notably Idaho and Colorado--they found themselves organizing a mining population in the throes of a virtual civil war. The "war" lasted from 1892 to 1930 and was characterized by bombings, assassinations, mass internments, and deportations.[6] Other storm centers included the lumber camps, mainly of the Pacific Northwest but also of Texas and Louisiana, and the oil fields of Texas and Oklahoma.[7] Each of these industries saw a series of great set-piece battles and strikes between 1905 and 1920; and if the Wobblies lost, they could still win long-term benefits. If a striking labor force was defeated and dismissed, then it simply moved to other "points of production," at which to recommence "missionary" activity. For instance, the great strike in the Louisiana timber industry in 1912-13 was a fiasco. Hundreds of radicalized workers were then sent on their way, however, and most ended up in the Oklahoma oil fields, where new battles began.[8] And if all American states became too difficult, then the Wobblies could use their strength among the maritime proletariat to move to new fields of action--England, Australia, or South America.

The Wobblies nationwide reached their height with about 250,000 members in 1917, but thereafter decline was swift. War and the Russian Revolution provided an excuse for efficient repression. IWW militants soon found themselves in prison or on the run--and now, old links with Mexico and South America proved useful. As early as 1911, Mexican anarchists had attempted to draw Western Wobblies into the revolutionary movement, and the frontier responded enthusiastically. Volunteers may have included the legendary Butch Cassidy--the literary quest for whom in recent years has resembled that for Traven.[9] In the autobiography of Agnes Smedley, the radical, she mentions how, about 1912, many of her cowboy and miner friends from Arizona had "decided to go into Mexico and help in the revolution."[10]

After the repression of 1919, such links helped Wobbly refugees, who found a safe haven where congenial ideas flourished--especially among the Zapatistas of the south. The radicals of the two countries became very close. As early as 1921, there was an IWW local in Tampico, where Traven probably arrived in Mexico; by 1927, there was a local here of the Mexican syndicalist union, La Casa del Obrero Mundial.[11] And as Robert Goss has pointed out, Traven was very interested in the doings of the latter.[12] In Mexico City proper, there was a prominent Wobbly exile called Lin Gale--a fascinating name for lovers of Traven books, some of which include as narrator the near-Wobbly "Gerard Gales."[13]

But it would be wrong to suggest that the IWW simply collapsed in 1919. Indeed, some of the theories which presume that a real-life Wobbly must have influenced Traven are based on a false chronology. They assume that Wobblies were a thing of the past some years before "Marut's" arrival in Mexico, and therefore he would have needed a storyteller, an "experience-bearer." But this is unnecessary. The Wobbly historian Fred Thompson puts the peak of IWW successes as late as 1922, only two years before Traven's probable arrival. In the early 1920s, the IWW led major strikes in Mexico, Chile, Peru, and South Africa, all areas influenced by American exiles or "missionaries." Even after the repression of 1917-19, there were several large-scale Wobbly campaigns in the United States proper between 1922 and 1936. These included, for instance, the mines of Colorado, the ships and ports of California, the farms of Washington state, the lumber camps of Idaho, and the construction industry of Nevada.[14]

Of course, the Wobblies were not what they had been before the First World War. They had suffered from changes in the patterns of migratory labor and from the 1920s boom. Many radicals who would once have helped build the syndicalist dream now turned instead to the concrete achievements of the Soviet Union, and they joined the Communist party. In the 1930s, the Wobblies lost even their base in radical noncommunist labor activism to the new CIO. But I would emphasize that in the mid-1920s, the years of the first Traven novels, the Wobblies were still an active reality.

The Wobblies in the Traven Novels

Even such a brief sketch of the Western Wobblies will show why students of Traven's life and work have so often suggested a link with American syndicalism. The world described for the IWW is very much that of the novels—a world of mines, lumber camps, ranches, and plantations, a world of marginal and migratory labor. Robert Goss has shown that The Cotton Pickers (1926)—or Der Wobbly—is a thorough and accurate depiction of Wobbly life and politics.[15] The novel shows a multiracial itinerant labor force, the workers ready to take any job offered, even when they must pretend to possess a skill they had never encountered. Gales, the hero, varies between jobs as a cotton picker, a baker's assistant, a cowboy, and a worker on an oil-rig. His friend Antonio takes very similar jobs and also spends time as a bandit and a Zapatista revolutionary. Other novels depict Traven's characters in occupations like sailor or gold-prospector and, frequently, worker in the oil or lumber industries. He describes precisely the locales and the social context of the Wobblies.[16]

Resemblances between fiction and reality are even more precise. Gales is often accused of being a Wobbly--usually by employers or bureaucrats--although he consistently denies it.[17] But his accusers have excellent grounds for suspicion. As in real life, they could see a white man living like a native, sharing the lot of the very poor, teaching them radical songs and poems like the "Song of the Cotton Pickers."[18] Confirmation of their suspicion comes when strikes follow in Gales's path: first at the cotton plantation, later at a café. Even his alleged ultimate destination is Argentina, another country where IWW-affiliated sailors' locales were established at this time.[19] Gales is precisely the sort of American who would have been expected to carry a Wobbly red card. His presence in and around Tampico would have been peculiarly chilling. In 1921, the IWW hall in that town had been raided, with the result that a local general strike had been called to secure the right to operate a local there.[20] This may well be what Traven has in mind when he describes local employers and police officials being forced to bow to the wishes of the union. And the union's colors are red and black--that is, the insignia of anarcho-syndicalism.[21]

Gales was in the appropriate jobs in the right area at the right time. Moreover, his whole style of life was very much that of the real-life Wobblies, as will be apparent from accounts of real IWW activists. Many shared the jobs Traven describes, adopted the same romantic and nondogmatic style of propaganda, and--often--were equally mysterious about their true identities. The major historian of the Wobblies wrote of the mysterious origin of one of their founders-- Daniel DeLeon--in a passage which will immediately strike a chord in readers of Traven: "So fully and relentlessly did he distort the circumstances of his birth and early life that little that is historically sound is known about De-Leon's birth. What passes for biography is largely a composite of his own peculiar fictions, the product of what one scholar has characterized as the mind of a pathological liar."[22]

The marginal workers who composed the IWW's militants often found such ambiguous origins congenial. One highly successful agitator was Frank Little--"part American Indian, part hard-rock miner, part hobo"--who was lynched in Montana in 1917. He had spent a decade wandering and spreading propaganda in the West, among miners, harvesters, and construction workers.[23] Perhaps the most celebrated such militant--and another man whose career resembles that of Traven's heroes--was Joe Hill, who was born Joel Hägglund in Sweden in 1879.[24] He was an itinerant laborer in the fields and mines of the western United States, and he acquired Wobbly sympathies in the Northwest. He planned to go to Mexico to help the revolution, but instead remained in the United States, writing songs and poems--which bear a strong resemblance to Traven's "Song of the Cotton Pickers."[25]

Literally hundreds of similar examples could be chosen to illustrate the accuracy of the portrait of Gales--and the reasons, perhaps, why only a very ignorant landowner in 1920s Mexico would hire a mysterious American wanderer. But to conclude this summary, we might examine the life of a revolutionary and syndicalist profoundly influenced by the IWW tradition, to show that we are dealing with an international phenomenon. This was the Scot, John S. Clarke (1885-1959), who briefly became a British M.P. in 1929.[26] But in earlier life, he had enjoyed the wide travel described in his Roughing It Round the World. In 1909, he had joined a tramp steamer destined for Malaya, but he had found this to be a true "death ship" when it foundered off the coast of South Africa. Whereupon Clarke attempted to cross Africa--alone, penniless, and on foot. He was no stranger to the marginal occupations described by Traven, and he spent much of his life as a lion-tamer, or in other circus-related trades. Resemblances to the life of Marut-Traven are many. When in 1919 "Marut" was engaged in attempting to establish a syndicalist republic in Munich, Clarke was involved in very similar efforts in Glasgow. Finally, Clarke's revolutionary journalism and poetry were as humorous and lighthearted in style as they were deadly serious in intent: very much like the poems of Joe Hill, or the novels of Traven. Traven's early novels show a very plausible syndicalist environment.

The Wobblies and The Death Ship

The account of Gales's life as a sailor fits the description of a Wobbly at least as well as his doings in Mexico. Traven was very well informed on the maritime aspect of IWW affairs, and The Death Ship can be precisely fitted into the political context of 1922-23. This is the date for the action of the book that would be suggested by the numerous references to the issue of German war reparations. We also know that Traven was wandering through Western Europe in

1922, and he made a sea journey to Canada in 1923. The dates are important, as this was the time of one of the last great IWW industrial battles on behalf of seamen.

In 1913, the IWW had gained the allegiance of the Marine Firemen, Oilers and Water Tenders Union, which claimed effective control of ships on America's Atlantic and Gulf coasts. For several years, the IWW found maritime workers a prime source for recruitment, and they organized a Marine Transport Worker's group (MTW), which attempted to bring together seamen, engine crews, and stewards, as well as waterfront employees. From 1921 to 1925, the MTW fought a series of strikes, and defections from more conservative unions gave them a strong foothold on the West Coast--especially in San Pedro, the port of Los Angeles. So fearsome did IWW strength become that the law enforcement authorities stepped in to make hundreds of arrests.[27]

That was the political reality, and it is obliquely referred to on several occasions in The Death Ship. For instance, the American consul quizzes the sailor Gales on his political affiliations for no apparent reason. But Gales has just listed the ports he has sailed from, and they were mainly Wobbly centers, which were on strike in 1923: New York, Philadelphia, Galveston, and the Gulf ports. That alone would excite the consul's suspicion and make him ask about Gales's Wobbly sympathies. In particular, he asks:

"But you said you shipped in New Orleans?"
"Yes, sir."
"Never in Los Angeles?"
"No, sir."[28]

But why should Los Angeles be mentioned--except that Traven is almost certainly referring to contemporary events in San Pedro. We can be all the more sure of this when Gales supposes that the "death ship" was in fact an ancient vessel, on which to ask for luxuries would be counted by barbarian rulers as "criminal syndicalism--for which being thrown to the lions was considered a very lenient punishment."[29] It may even be that Gales is lying when he denies having sailed from Los Angeles. At least, he later refers to "Los An" as one port he knows, and we may be meant to believe that Gales knew what the consul was fishing for when he mentioned the city. It often appears that the Gales character is not so naive as he seems. At least, he is aware that the "Wobbly Firemen's Syndicate" is a tough negotiating body, much harder for owners to deal with than the conservative seamen's union, and that Wobbly sailors were usually too sensible to let themselves be found on a

death ship.[30] The novelist is obviously aware of syndicalist struggles in the shipping industry, by the mid-1920s
one of the last successful areas of Wobbly activity.

Bolshevism and The Death Ship

Clearly, Traven knew a great deal about the Wobblies, and it
might be argued that he acquired too much knowledge too
quickly to be explained by anything other than cooperation
with a real-life Wobbly. I will discuss this later; but I
would argue that one of the best pieces of evidence for this
theory is the ambiguous nature of the politics in some of
the novels, particularly in The Death Ship. I mean by this
that we have a serious dilemma, which could perhaps be
resolved by assuming the participation of more than one
creative mind. In summary, the dilemma is this. Marut-
Traven was an anarchist, who in the context of his age had
every reason to hate and mistrust communism in general and
the Soviet Union in particular; but The Death Ship suggests
that the author was a fairly orthodox communist. It might
be that this novel arose, at the least, from a cooperation
between Marut the Stirnerite anarchist, and a real-life
Wobbly, who by the 1920s was following leaders like Bill
Haywood into pro-Soviet stances. Marut came from a European
political culture where anarchism was in full retreat before
the communist challenge; his colleague would have been an
American, for whom such divisions had very different connotations.
    First, let us examine the attitudes of Traven's European
anarchist contemporaries to communism. The Russian Revolution had been a major trauma for anarchism, which until that
point had presented a serious alternative to socialism or
communism. Many anarchist militants had deserted to the new
Bolshevik-inspired parties, while the anarchist "rump" grew
increasingly hostile to Soviet models. In 1919, Marut had
participated in a syndicalist rising in Bavaria, which was
defeated by the Communists even before the coming of the
right-wing reaction. Between 1918 and 1921, the Bolsheviks
had undertaken a savage repression of Russian anarchism--
individualists like Marut, syndicalists, or peasant "Zapatistas." The defeat of the Kronstadt rising was widely seen
as a triumph of the new bureaucracy over a spontaneous
workers' movement.
    After about 1920, radical intellectuals faced a difficult
choice. Most sacrificed some individualist ideals and
joined the communist cause. A few condemned themselves to
political ineffectiveness by maintaining a libertarian oppo-

sition to communism as well as to capitalism. Those who took the communist course included many--like Grosz or Gorky--whose hearts were never as fully committed as they claimed.[31] Those who maintained an anarchist stance are of particular interest for our purposes, as providing the nearest approximations to Traven's work. These included Ernst Toller and also Marut's great friend and colleague Erich Mühsam. He cooperated with the communists in some humanitarian projects, but otherwise he remained a staunch individualist opponent of all governments.[32] Similar views were held by the Prague anarchist circle which included Kafka and Hasek, two authors who provide probably the closest parallels to Traven's individualist attacks on bureaucracy.[33] Traven therefore seems to belong to that tradition of European anarchism which remained loyal to its old ideals and resisted the seductive appeal of Moscow's example. By the 1920s, there were few places in Europe (outside Spain) where a libertarian or individualist revolutionary could find hope. Noncommunist radicalism seemed confined to backward areas like Mexico, and Traven turned with relief to the Zapatista Indians of the Caoba novels.

Most of Traven's novels are anarchist and anticommunist. They concern marginal individuals for whom any state machinery or bureaucracy was anathema, observers of primitive communitarian societies who were resisting the encroachments of capitalism and authority. But one work seems to raise questions about this view. If we look at the overt political references in The Death Ship--rather than the substance of the novel--we seem to find a much more sympathetic attitude to the Soviet Union than might be expected from any anarchist in the 1920s. Also, Traven uses the word "communist" in a very odd sense, which suggests that Bolsheviks and syndicalists were identical and that recent persecutions and controversies had simply not occurred.

The Death Ship is unique in this. In The Cotton Pickers, Traven writes approvingly of the Russian Revolution, but only of the early spontaneous popular risings against authority.[34] Any anarchist could have written this. By contrast, "Bolshevik" references abound in The Death Ship. The novel has a strange duality of attitude towards the Soviet Union. On the one hand, the author mocks American sympathizers who see the USSR as a worker's paradise. The Soviets are bureaucratic despots, and their people are as chauvinistic as "the hurrah nationalists of Germany."[35] But Russian solutions seem to be the ones that the novelist favors. It might not exactly be paradise, but "nowhere on earth except in Bolshevik Russia are deck-hands considered members of the same social class as the skipper."[36] Gales in The Cotton

Pickers is constantly being taken for a Wobbly activist; but in _The Death Ship_, bureaucrats often suspect he is a Bolshevik agent.[37] Gales himself remarks at the beginning of the novel that common seamen had to be kept hard at work, for fear that "they might fall for some dangerous ideas about Russia."[38] These are very strange comments for a supposedly anarchist writer.

Wobblies as Communists

This political ambiguity also becomes apparent if we examine the explicit references to syndicalism or the IWW in _The Death Ship_. First, there are several sympathetic comments on Wobblies, as the feared enemies of all bureaucrats and tyrannical employers. But what is curious is that Traven uses "Wobbly" and "communist" as virtually synonymous, and he makes no obvious distinctions between syndicalists and Bolsheviks. Wobbly sailors are "Bolshes" or "communists"; their union is run by "the Wobblies in particular and the communists"--meaning here that Wobblies _were_ simply communists, rather than that the two groups cooperated.[39]

A striking example of this is the scene in _The Death Ship_ where Gales hears the sound of "communists" being tortured in Barcelona's military prison. But in 1923, these people would almost certainly not be "communists" in the sense of members of a communist party. Rather, they would be anarcho-syndicalist militants of the CNT, the radical labor federation strongly established in Barcelona. In 1923, the city was at the height of a near civil war between syndicalists and rightists, in which a new military regime was intervening decisively against the Left.[40] The prisoners therefore fit a definite political context--but they would not represent Bolshevism, which as yet had made little impact in Spain. So again, Traven is identifying syndicalism with communism and ignoring the recent years of mutual violence and hostility. It is almost as if these passages were written prior to the Russian Revolution.

Why does he subsume all these obvious differences in the broad term "communists"? Technically, he is right. Anarchists and syndicalists believed in abolishing property, in establishing common ownership of goods. But calling them "communists" by the 1920s seems disingenuous. These groups were usually very dubious about the Soviet Union, but Traven must have realized that most of his readership would understand "communist" in a Leninist, pro-Soviet sense. It is a strange usage for a European anarchist, especially for an author as politically conscious as Marut-Traven.

But what of American radicalism—and especially the IWW? The answer is that such a usage would have been very characteristic of a large group of Wobblies. Many American radicals had been attracted by the Russian example, and they had either defected to the new communist party or else tried to incorporate "communist" language and models. American communism was deeply influenced by ex-Wobblies and other syndicalists, like Willliam Z. Foster, Elizabeth Gurley Flynn, and John Reed. In particular, Bill Haywood had caused grave divisions in the IWW in 1921 by his flight to the USSR. There was clearly a danger that communism would win over all the IWW's militants, and the relationship to communism was the key issue in the movement between 1921 and 1927. In particular, should the IWW affiliate to the Moscow-based Red International of Labor Unions? The movement was bitterly divided, and the split was reflected in the loyalties of IWW newspapers and journals. As early as 1919, One Big Union Monthly had created a furor by referring to "industrial communism" instead of "industrial democracy" as the IWW's aim. By the 1920s, the journal Solidarity became a vehicle for communist and pro-Soviet views within the movement. In fact, the alliance with Moscow was defeated, but there is abundant evidence of the existence of Wobblies who felt the necessity of a common front with Moscow. This was a distinctively American position, and one scarcely possible for a European who wished to remain in the anarchist tradition. It was also an issue very much under discussion in the years in which The Death Ship was being written.[41]

Was Traven an American?

Let us examine the idea that Traven's Wobbly material derived from another person—a real-life Gerard Gales—who cooperated with "Marut." The evidence for this is three-fold. First, Traven knows a great deal about the Wobblies, and he reveals this in books written within (at most) two years of his coming to Mexico. Second, it might be that The Death Ship shows evidence of an ideological stance which is not Marut's, but which would fit certain Wobblies. Third, there simply was not enough time for Traven to produce these early books out of nothing in so short a time, and so perhaps we should assume the work of an earlier writer.

The evidence for an earlier Wobbly having contributed to the Traven novels is examined by Michael L. Baumann in his invaluable Introduction to Traven's life and work. The author cites the common biography which Traven gave both for Gales and later for himself, and he asks whether in fact this might be accurate. Briefly, this claims that Gales/Traven was born in the American Midwest about 1900 of Scandinavian parents, had lived as a "farmboy-sailor-oddjob-ber-tramp," and moved to Mexico about 1912. Perhaps from about 1920, he had attempted to sell his books to American publishers, but from 1923-24 he had admitted defeat and translated his books into German--where they had enjoyed their success.[42] Clearly this could not be the whole story. Few would doubt that Traven was in some sense identical with Otto Feige and Ret Marut. But invoking two components of "Traven"--Marut and Gales--would have certain advantages. It would explain the close acquaintance with the Wobblies, and how so much knowledge could have been incorporated so rapidly into the Traven novels in so short a time. It would also solve the puzzle of how Traven seems to refer to events that took place in Mexico in 1920, when Marut was unquestionably in Germany. Marut encountered the Erlebnisträger--who might have been called Torsvan--and the Traven novels were born. In later life, Traven was only maintaining a scrupulous honesty when he resolutely denied being the author of the novels. In fact, he was only the transcriber of several of them.

Only One Traven

I believe this view can be attacked from a number of perspectives. For instance, Traven's comparison of how matters stand in Mexico in the late 1920s with ten or so years previously seems only a matter of supposition on his part, a characteristic attempt to seem an "old hand" in local affairs. Most of his Mexican color seems to derive from personal observation, but also from extensive conversations with local people. We certainly do not need to assume his earlier presence in Mexico. Not until 1931 did Traven feel sufficiently confident to venture into Mexico's history before his arrival, and to begin the Caoba Cycle.

On another point, it does not seem remarkable that Traven should have been so productive during 1924-27. He would always be capable of writing quickly and including contemporary events in his novels, to provide a sense of journalistic immediacy. For instance, the Cristero rebellion broke out in 1926; and in the following year, Treasure includes descriptions of Cristero atrocities.[43] Again, the fierce anticlericalism of The Carreta, first published in 1931, seems to be a product of anti-Catholic campaigns just gathering momentum in that same year.[44] Traven did not need much time to reflect in order to incorporate experiences into his novels.

But it is in the discussion of the Wobblies that the existence of an American collaborator can most probably be discounted. Marut-Traven knew a great deal about the Wobblies, and it would be surprising if he had not carried their distinctive red membership card. He was deeply interested in the IWW, which is portrayed with great sympathy; but it is portrayed as it existed after 1922, and not in its heyday. One would have assumed that the Erlebnisträger would have been in an excellent position to give Traven extensive material on the great age of the Wobblies--enough perhaps to supply a cycle as rich as that of the mahogany cutters. Instead, Traven simply gathered everything he could find about the current reality.

Traven says nothing about the Wobblies that reveals any significant knowledge of events before his arrival. On the contrary, I believe we can explain all his syndicalist material with reference to events in his life that can be dated with fair certainty. Apparently, Marut sailed to Canada in 1923, but he was refused entry. If he came into social contact with any of the ship's sailors or workers, he might well have encountered Wobbly terms and ideas. He crossed the Atlantic for a second time in 1924, so the curious and politically conscious Marut might have become familiar with the IWW even before setting foot in Mexico-- and perhaps The Death Ship was already reaching an advanced stage in his mind. At least, Atlantic shipping was by this time one of the best places to learn about the Wobblies.

If Traven then arrived in Mexico at Tampico, he would find an IWW presence, and sympathetic authorities chastened by the recent general strike. This would have been a remarkable experience for a European refugee--a workers' government which was not attempting to impose Bolshevism!--and it may have impressed the author. At this point, if not before, he would be well aware of the value of an IWW red card. It would help him both with American exiles and with Mexican unions which remembered their debt to the IWW. If Traven then took several marginal jobs on the pattern that "Gales" describes in The Cotton Pickers, he would probably meet Americans or Mexicans who would mention the IWW. Around Tampico, for example, there was always casual work to be found in the oil fields. Here one would certainly meet veterans of oil disputes in Oklahoma a decade previously. Some of Traven's workmates might well have been able to quote Wobbly poems like those of Joe Hill--enough for Traven to create the song he gives Gales.

I would argue that that amount of contact with the IWW is

likely to have been the minimum that an observant and interested Leftist would have encountered at that time and place. Moreover, it is <u>all</u> that is needed to explain the Wobbly references in the novels. Indeed, it might even be argued that the Wobbly material can be explained by assuming even less direct contact, and by supposing that Traven's account of a series of poorly paid marginal jobs was simply another pose. After all, John Dos Passos (born in 1896) gave an excellent and accurate description of Wobbly activities from as early as 1906, although this could not have been from personal observation.[45] And for all their autobiographical color, the Traven books are not memoirs, but novels, in which an experienced writer was inventing characters and situations. It might also be that in attempting to depict a Wobbly setting in <u>The Death Ship</u>, Traven realized that a real-life Wobbly would be more pro-Soviet than himself; and realism required depicting such attitudes.[46] Some credit must be given to a writer's imagination, no less than to his capacity to do research.

We cannot rule out the possibility that Marut had taken a literary interest in the Wobblies almost since their foundation. We know that he frequently claimed U.S. citizenship, from at least 1908, and consistently through the war years; and a man of such omnivorous interests may have read extensively about his supposed homeland. Did he read about the Wobblies? After the Lawrence strike of 1912, the IWW became a source of considerable public interest. A recent bibliography of publications relating to the IWW suggests the vast range of early material available, at least in English.[47] Most celebrated was Paul Brissenden's <u>The IWW</u> (1919), which quoted Joe Hill poems and much Wobbly ephemera. That Traven might have consulted such works is suggested by the odd reference in <u>The Death Ship</u> to a blinkered academic as a "prof of phil at the State U. of [Wisconsin]."[48] This might be Traven simply affecting American color; but in the 1920s, there was indeed a "Wisconsin school" of labor studies, which studied American unions from a moderate and liberal perspective. Had Traven read scholars like John R. Commons?

In suggesting that Traven might have used a distinctly literary imagination for his realistic descriptions, I am attempting to show only that such an extreme position is possible. Traven could have acquired direct knowledge of the Wobblies very easily, and there is no need to invoke a conveyor of syndicalist experiences. By contrast, if there had been such a person, the novels might have been very different. Perhaps the Traven mystery is not quite as complex as it sometimes appears.

First, a general acknowledgment. In writing this paper, I have been greatly helped by the work of Robert Goss, especially by his essay "Der Wobbly und die Wobblies," which is to appear in the essay volume of the Traven Werkausgabe. Goss very kindly lent me a copy of this unpublished article. He also directed me to several leads about Traven's relationship to anarchism, in a letter to me (May 3, 1981). Throughout this paper, I would like to acknowledge the help of Goss, and of Ernst Schürer, with whom I have had some very instructive conversations about Traven's work.

1. For general discussions of Traven's work, see Chankin, 1975; Baumann, 1976; Beck et al., 1976; Wyatt, 1980.
2. This account of the IWW is based on: Renshaw, 1967; Dubofsky, 1969; Thompson, 1977; Conlin, 1969 and 1981.
3. Conlin, 1969, 8-40.
4. Conlin, 1981, 3-24.
5. Ibid., Part Two.
6. Graham and Gurr, 1969, 270-376.
7. Conlin, 1981, 97-166; Tyler, 1967.
8. Conlin, 1981, 144-5.
9. Larry Poynter, The Search for Butch Cassidy (1979). Cassidy apparently faked his death in Bolivia in 1904 and wandered under a series of pseudonyms until his death about 1939.
10. Agnes Smedley, Daughter of Earth (London: Virago, 1977), 121; Goss, "Der Wobbly," 15-16.
11. Thompson, 1977, 135, 232-33; Letter of Robert Goss to myself, May 3, 1981; Marjorie Ruth Clark, Organized Labor in Mexico (Chapel Hill, NC, 1934).
12. Goss letter, May 3, 1981; Goss, "Der Wobbly," 15-17. For Traven at Tampico, see Wyatt, 1980, 134, 163-69, 208-13.
13. Goss, "Der Wobbly"; Beck et al., 1976, 119-45.
14. Thompson, 1977, 139--78; Dubofsky, 1969, 445-84; Conlin, 1981, 167-236; Renshaw, 1967, 234-37.
15. Goss, "Der Wobbly."
16. See The Cotton Pickers, The Death Ship, Treasure.
17. The Cotton Pickers, 37-38, 199 (references to 1969 U.S. edition).
18. Ibid., 38.
19. Ibid., 54; Thompson, 1977, 134.
20. Thompson, 1977, 135, 232-33.
21. The Cotton Pickers, 110. Traven's novels are very sympathetic to syndicalism, and some have argued that this shows the influence of another author besides Marut the individualist. But as Wyatt points out (217), both Marut

and Traven synthesized anarchism and syndicalism in a manner common to their age.

22. Dubofsky, 1969, 133.
23. Ibid., 186.
24. Ibid., 308-13.
25. Brissenden, 1920, 370-80.
26. Ray Challinor, John S. Clarke (London: Pluto Press, 1977).
27. The Death Ship; Dubofsky, 1969, 287, 474; Thompson, 1977, 76, 136-42.
28. The Death Ship, 54-56; Thompson, 1977, 141.
29. The Death Ship, 101.
30. Ibid., 106. In the early 1920s, one of the great political issues in the United States was the release of Wobbly political prisoners like Haywood and Magon, who were usually held in San Quentin and Leavenworth prisons; and The Death Ship refers to both Leavenworth and San Quentin (113).
31. David Caute, The Fellow-Travellers (London: Quartet, 1973), 32-40 for Gorky; 31, 56.
32. Ibid., 44 note; Conquest, 1971, 587; George Woodcock, Anarchism (London: Penguin, 1970), 407-8.
33. Ibid., 407. For early remarks on similarities to Hasek, see Baumann, 1976, 15. Kafka's Trial appeared in 1925--the year before The Death Ship.
34. The Cotton Pickers, 67-68.
35. The Death Ship, 80-82, 169, 235.
36. Ibid., 97.
37. Ibid., 36, 245.
38. Ibid., 8.
39. Ibid., 106, 133.
40. Ibid., 79-80; Woodcock, Anarchism, 354-58.
41. For the contemporary debate, see:
John Gabrial Soltis, "The Bolsheviki in America," One Big Union Monthly, May 1919; and "The realism of the Bolsheviki" in Ibid., September 1919; John Sandgren, "Industrial unionism versus Bolshevism" in Industrial Worker, November 8, 1919.
Brissenden, 1920, 375 also quotes a Wobbly poem in support of the Bolsheviks.
Dubofsky, 1969, 457-63.
Conlin, 1969, 146-47.
Tyler, 1967, 208-10.
E. H. Carr, The Bolshevik Revolution 1917-23 (London: Pelican, 1973), Vol. 3, 394-98, 454-57.
42. Baumann, 1976, 27-37; Wyatt, 1980, 18-19, 59-61, 85-86, 212-18; The Death Ship, 109-10; Max Schmid, "B. Traven und sein Ich-Erzähler Gerard Gales" in Beck et al., 1976, 119-45.

43. Wyatt, 1980, 217.

44. Traven, _Treasure_ (Cardinal, ed., 1961), 138-44; Traven, _The Carreta_ (New York: Hill and Wang, 1970), 127-30, 197-99; Wyatt, 1980, 215-16.

45. Compare Wyatt's remarks (Wyatt, 1980, 216); John Dos Passos, _The 42nd Parallel_ (1930: Signet Classic, 1969 ed.), 115-24.

46. Similarly, in _Bridge_ Traven remarks that the Zapatista agrarian radicals saw themselves as communists and venerated Lenin. Traven knows that they are naive--but he respects their mistakes, and thereafter calls them simply "communists" (159, 200). Presumably, he is paying the Wobblies the same compliment.

47. Dione Wiles in Conlin, 1981, 237-317.

48. _The Death Ship_, 81.

B. TRAVEN: ANARCHIST FROM THE JUNGLE
Anarcho-primitivism in the Jungle Novels

Patrick D. Murphy

Introduction

B. Traven claimed that "there goes one thought like a red thread from the first line of his first book to the last line of his last book," and some have sought this continuity in the anarchist tradition. This alone, it is suggested, unites Feige, Marut, and their "successors." But too much can be read into this suggestion of political homogeneity. Traven's anarchism undergoes a major change at the time of the writing of Land des Frühlings.[1] This new belief is present in The White Rose[2] and is the guiding ideology throughout the Jungle novels. The early Traven novels present an essentially Stirnerite "individualist" anarchism.[3] Anarcho-primitivism replaces this in the Jungle novels. Combined with the basic tenets of European anarchist thought is the philosophical concept of primitivism--the belief that primitive societies constitute the source of the human values and forms of organization that should replace the existing social systems. Anarcho-primitivism moves in the opposite direction from anarcho-syndicalism in discussing the structures that will emerge once the state is overthrown.

This change, a far cry from the type of anarchism promoted in The Cotton Pickers,[4] reflects the tremendous impact of Traven's experiences among the Indians of southern Mexico recorded in Land.

In the earlier novels Traven focuses attention on the psychology of individuals, particularly on Gales's inner conflicts, and these themes continue through The White Rose. In the Jungle novels he necessarily shifts attention from the individual psyche of the alienated white man or a particular Indian to the collective psyche of the primitive--the Indians--depicted through a variety of characters. These characters, to the degree their inner emotions, thoughts, and desires are individually analyzed, primarily represent the way of life of an entire people. Through them Traven presents to his urban audience the collective unconscious-- the traditions, rituals, instincts, and inherent values-- that makes primitive society the beacon for the future.

Two new elements in Traven's anarchism appear in the Jungle novels: the "primitive" component of anarcho-primitivism; and its political implications for a readership based in the industrialized countries, implications which are radically different from those that can be drawn from his earlier works. Of the six novels, <u>Government</u> and <u>General</u> are critical to an understanding of these themes. Although <u>Government</u> was published second in the series, it functions as a prologue in which Traven outlines a just, primitive society and discusses the qualities of primitivism that render it superior to all forms of "modern" government. <u>General</u> concludes the series with the Indian rebels' victory, which rounds out Traven's conception of anarcho-primitivism by presenting it in action.

Anarcho-primitivism

Traven introduces the reader to two Indian communities in <u>Government</u>: Bujvilum, in the first half of the novel; and Pebvil, in the second half. The Bachajontes inhabit Bujvilum, a small and very poor independent village--one that is not part of a Mexican hacienda--deep in the jungle. From the start he contrasts the corrupt, centralized dictatorship of "civilized" Mexico, wholeheartedly supported by the United States and Europe, with the simple honesty and integrity of these "backward" Indians. Through frequent narrative intrusions he argues that not only Mexico, because it is a dictatorship, but also all industrialized countries, capitalist or self-proclaimed socialist, are corrupt, exploitative, and oppressive. Modern capitalism forms an international network whose roots sink so deep that they affect even this isolated village. This emphasis on the idea that civilization cannot be merely ignored by the independent Indians distinguishes <u>Government</u> from earlier Traven works. While a Gales may be able individually to escape civilization--end his alienation through identification with a nonwhite people in the jungle--this is not an option for the communities that exist beyond the Western world's boundaries, such as the Bachajontes, who are <u>in</u> Mexico, but are not <u>of</u> it. However, the Bachajontes also have roots, which run deeper and are far more ancient than capitalism's. The Bachajontes have a chance of withstanding the incursions of capital because they are rooted in an organic relationship with the land that forms their culture and determines their character.

The Indians were far from being ill disposed. They were not warlike. They were tillers of the soil, who are everywhere of a peaceable disposition as long as they are left to go their own way....Agriculture rules out the

217

warlike spirit. Fields and herds go to ruin if men have
to be out on the warpath....Agriculture is no nursery of
adventure. The adventurous and warlike spirit arises only
when his own land no longer supports the agriculturalist.[5]

Bujvilum provides the reader with a graphic illustration
of primitivism: small agricultural communities, politically
organized on the basis of mutually recognized rules of
social order and responsibility developed through tradition
and generated from within the practical life of the community. There is none of the alienation that modern workers
feel even in the midst of society. Traven demonstrates this
through the example of Gregorio, the village member who
commits murder and remains to accept judgment rather than
easily escape:

He might have survived in the jungle as an animal, but
only in communion with his tribe could he live as a being
conscious of human kinship. (88)

The relationship to the land is the essential formative
component of the primitive society. Values and traditions
are not formed on the basis of allegiance to abstract principles, but instead arise out of concrete experience built
up through countless generations. All of the Jungle novels'
major characters gravitate toward this man-land relationship, with even the carreta drivers dreaming of buying land
and settling down. In General Traven finally draws the
conclusion that freedom in its most basic sense, the immun-
ity of the individual from the actions of government, is
inseparably linked with working the land. Only in relation
to the land as its agricultural steward can man become
whole, because then he can be self-sufficient--as an individual and as a community. This organic unity of the individual with the tribe on the land produces the dignity, integrity, and stoic endurance of the Indian.
These qualities of the Indian are contrasted with the
image of modern man, who is fragmented, dissembling, and
avaricious. His identity depends on the cash nexus and the
fetishism of commodities. Land is merely property to the
capitalist and a source of consumer commodities to the urban
dweller. Traven portrays modern man as adrift in the ocean
of countries, swept by the crosscurrents of competing governments, and buffeted by the winds of struggling parasiti-
cal elites. His ship is sinking. In the Jungle novels the
ladinos typify modern man, acting as government secretaries
and as labor agents for the monterías and for reactionary
landowners, who view the Indians as well as the land as

merely property to be exploited. In <u>Government</u> the life of Don Gabriel, the Bujvilum government secretary, serves as a continuous contrast, in its dissipation, parasitism, and hypocrisy, to the primitive way of life.

Gregorio's separation from his wife is the turning point in <u>Government</u>. This scene states two crucial themes: the government will not leave the Indian alone, but through its greed and corruption will continuously seek to rob him not only of his wealth, but also of his dignity, and in the process it will destroy his community; and, in response, the Indian will accept only so much intervention from external "civilization" before he revolts. The seed of that revolt lies in Gregorio's sudden moment of self-awareness:

> He stood in front of his wife for a moment....He looked at her and saw in her, as never before, the whole meaning of his home and his world. He saw this world rise before him for the first time in his existence, and as it rose it fell apart. (96)

After this scene the focus of the narrative shifts to Don Gabriel, who gives up his Bujvilum secretariat--the village is too thin a carcass for him to pick--and becomes a recruiter of contract labor for the <u>monterías</u>, with Gregorio as his first recruit. Just as in <u>The Carreta</u>, the <u>monterías</u> represent the future toward which Traven's Indian characters are being driven by the dictatorship. The <u>monterias</u> become a symbol of the fate of all of the Indians, as they are slowly but inexorably driven from the land by the encroachment of world industry.

In the section focusing on Don Gabriel, Traven makes a direct comparison between <u>finca</u> peons (indentured Indians on the landed estates) and industrial workers in other countries. The basis for revolt (the indignities, alienation, and exploitation dehumanizing peasants and laborers everywhere) and the seeds of revolt (growing self-awareness, desires for a new sense of community, struggles for self-respect and dignity) exist in every country of the world, according to Traven. The basis for revolt nurtures its seeds within the Gregorios of the world, whether in Russia, Germany, or Mexico. The question, then, throughout the Jungle novels is not if but when the oppressed will revolt, and in what direction that revolt will take them.

The Bujvilum inhabitants carry on a type of cyclical revolt in response to the extortion of the secretaries, but it fails to hold its ground against the government. Young men begin to be taken away to the <u>monterías</u>. This act breaks the hereditary link with the land. Unlike the theft of crops or taxes, which take only possessions away from the community, this act begins to take apart the community itself. Don Gabriel is spearheading this attack. He also provides the means of connecting Bujvilum's story with that of the Pebvil Indians. The story of Pebvil demonstrates the need of the oppressed to revolt against efforts to restrict their freedom, and it serves as an example of a successful revolt.

The concluding paragraph of Government returns the reader's attention to the monterías and emphasizes that this story has been told for a very specific purpose: to open the eyes of the European reader, with the goal of promoting action. Traven agitates against the evils of industrialism:

> You cannot have cheap mahogany and at the same time save all those innocent Indians who perish by the thousands in the jungle to get it for you. It must be either one or the other. Either cheap mahogany or respect for the humanity of the Indian. The civilization of the present day cannot run to both.... (229)

The choice is presented to the reader: Western inhumanity or Indian humanity; tyranny at the behest of industry, or freedom in the agrarian relation with the land; alienated consumerism or integrated subsistence; civilization or primitive community. Traven stands in the Jungle novels with the primitive, not only for the Indian, but necessarily for everyone. He presents it as the only road to human dignity and freedom.

The march down this road begins in Rebellion and is completed in General. "Tierra y Libertad!"--land and freedom-- are the first words of General. In these words Traven found the political slogan that represented his own blend of philosophy, and which at the same time was drawn from the experience of Indian rebels within the Mexican Revolution. Freedom cannot be gained without that connection with the land and the establishment of the kind of community identity portrayed in Government

Early in General Traven disassociates this slogan from the revolution in which it arose. He finds it necessary to openly criticize the Mexican Revolution and admit its failure in terms of truly revolutionary goals. The overthrow of Díaz and the dethroning of the Catholic church as the sole arbiter of morality are positive results of the revolution, but in the end--clearly seen by the latter 1930s, when the major land reform programs had been completed--it failed to free the Indian:

What happened at this finca now was exactly the same as
occurred later throughout the whole Republic: the peons,
accustomed for years to masters, tyrants, oppressors, and
dictators, were not in truth liberated by the revolution,
not even where the feudal estates were divided among the
families of peons in little holdings, ejidos. They remained slaves, with the single difference that their masters had changed, that mounted revolutionary leaders were
now the wealthy, and that the politicians now used small-
holding, ostensibly liberated peons to enrich themselves
immeasurably... (60)

Life on the _fincas_ had broken that sense of community still
held by independent Indian villages. Rosa Blanca in The
White Rose is an exception because it is an Indian hacienda
run on different principles than the _ladino_ holdings. The
revolution could not undo that ideological loss merely by
ending Díaz's rule. The land reform movements that produced
the _ejidadores_ also could not succeed because the very
nature of such reform locks the Indian into a capitalist
relationship with the land and a closer political and economic relationship with the national economy.

Is it the case, then, that only the independent Indian
communities have the potential to realize Tierra y Libertad
because they are the only ones which have not had their
traditional community destroyed? Is there really no returning to the natural communion with the land represented by
primitivism? Traven replies with the formation of Solipaz,
the rebel army village, at the end of General. Not only is
there a basis for the continuation of already existing
primitive villages, but there is the possibility of reestab-
lishing that relationship in new villages. The rebel army
realizes this goal, but first the rebels must pass through a
process of purification and resurrection.

From the beginning of The Carreta through Rebellion, Traven chronicles the stripping away of the Indian's identity
with his land, community, family, and traditions--the breaking down of his dignity and humanity. The conscripts for
the _monterías_ are reduced to animal-like survival. Economic
deprivation alone does not lead to revolt--the Indians have
always been poor, with the independent villages often the
poorest of all--but it is the spiritual and psychical deni-
gration added to it that produces rebellions:

When their sufferings, their tortures, their deprivations
under their masters in the jungles...grew so intolerable
that they and, extraordinarily enough, almost all the
others working at that time in the remotest regions of the

tropical forests simultaneously came to the realization that it was better and more worthy of their human dignity to perish in a revolution than to live longer under such humiliations and torments, then they took action.[6]

Even as the revolt was spontaneous in character, so too is the rebel army's march out of the jungle. Their program is the slogan Tierra y Libertad, and their strategy is a tactics-as-process military plan to overcome all opposition. They are not united by a common ideological program but by a commonality of individual yearnings for freedom:

> When they shouted for Libertad, the muchachos hoped that after they had won their battle for freedom they would be allowed to lead their lives in their own ways, untroubled by men in whom they could put no trust....
> ...however unclear in detail the conception of land and freedom might be to the rebels, they nevertheless felt instinctively and rightly what they wanted. And what they wanted was: no longer to be dominated, no longer to be commanded.[7]

Traven establishes three main groups of Indians as examples for the reader: the independent villagers, the finca peons, and the montería rebels. The rebel army is the most heterogeneous group, composed of Indians from different tribes and work backgrounds: peasants, soldiers, carreteros, and even a teacher. The independent villagers struggle to maintain their primitivism, revolting whenever it is threatened. The finca peons seem virtually incapable of revolt, except in rare instances when their impoverishment and brutalization are suddenly intensified.[8] Traven sees their revitalization as a slow, painful process.[9] Such peasants will need the years of chaos that follow a revolution in order to form themselves into a community free from external authority.

The rebels are the most important of the three groups. They are the only example applicable to countries that are more industrialized than Mexico. Unlike the finca peons they quickly regain a sense of community, impose internal discipline, and realize the interconnectedness of land and freedom. They do not accomplish this through philosophical enlightenment, but through the purifying experience of their violent revolt. Their bloody battles with government troops cleanse their spirits, enabling them to regain their human dignity. When they turn their camp into a permanent village at the end of General, they have already developed the relationships and cohesiveness necessary to function as an integrated community ready to withstand the onslaughts of "civilized" government.

Just as at the end of Government the Pebvil Indians' revolt is a temporary resolution of their conflict with the central government, so too is the establishment of Solipaz. But it is a resolution, however temporary, that provides hope for a final resolution of the conflict between humanity and industrial "progress." Implicit in General's conclusion is the eventuality that the Solipazes of the world will have to overthrow all of the world's central governments.

Implications and Conclusion

Perhaps deep in the rain forests of a backward country like Mexico, racked by revolution and with the outlying areas isolated by lack of communication and transportation, small villages of fiercely independent and impoverished Indians might be able to carve out an independent niche for themselves. Such communities would be too small and unimportant to pose a threat to any central government, and so the march of history and industry could safely pass them by. Such groups could make practical use of the anarcho-primitivism espoused by Traven in his novels. However, they were not written for such an audience, but were drawn from the experience of such communities for the benefit of others. The Jungle novels are directed at a European working class audience. What then are the political implications of such an ideology, presented to that audience by a writer whose first concern is clearly not theory but action?

Traven unequivocally supports the righteous violence of the oppressed. Although throughout the series he clarifies that revolt is forced upon the lower classes by the cruelty of the oppressors, and is therefore defensive in character, he upholds such violence as not only justified but necessary. Revolutionary violence is presented as a purifying action, which the oppressed must commit in order to regain their humanity. He suggests no possibilities for peaceful revolutionary or evolutionary change. The necessity of violence as a spiritual cleansing becomes a basic tenet of Traven's message to the laborer in the industrialized countries.

Any form of centralized government is inherently oppressive. The "socialist" state is still a state, just as the revolutionary government of Mexico was still a government and inevitably became an enemy of Indian freedom. All governments must be brought down. Traven emphasizes, though, that the overthrow of governments is not to be accomplished by elite political parties organizing people around abstract programs, or into "one big union," but, rather, will be the result of spontaneous uprisings in response to intensifying dehumanization. It is a fairly classic concept of spontaneous anarchist revolt, but it reveals Traven's continuing departure from Stirner, with the emphasis on group rebellion rather than individual revolt.

Traven warns the oppressed against trying to replace the state with some new entity that copies the old industrialized base and geographical boundaries. Instead, small, decentralized, agrarian-centered communes are suggested as the alternative to the modern nation-state. This stands in direct opposition to anarcho-syndicalism.

The ability of such communes to survive once they are established will depend on the amount of chaos and the extent of destruction of the old governments. A large number of European governments would have to be overthrown with such tremendous economic disruption that they would be unable to rapidly regroup. Such disruption would provide the time needed for alienated workers, like _finca_ peons, to gain a new sense of community identity.

Looking at the devastation of World War I and the cracks that appeared in European governmental authority that enabled such events as the Bolshevik Revolution and the Bavarian Räterepublik, and observing the developing storm of another world war in Europe, it is quite possible that Traven believed or hoped that such devastation--if it must occur--would bring down governments and open the way for the rise of anarcho-primitivist communes. He does not present Solipaz as a blueprint for such communities, but as an example of the direction that man must take in opposition to "the civilization of the present day." If the period immediately ahead would not open such cracks in Europe, Traven appears sadly confident in _General_ that the oppressors will keep pushing until the masses in countries like Nazi Germany are forced to revolt, just as the Indians revolted in the _monterías_.

Is such a notion totally naive? Do the events of World War II and its aftermath render Traven's political philosophy an anachronism to be placed alongside Owen's model communities? I won't pass judgment here on anarcho-primitivism's possibilities for success, but I would briefly comment that it may very well be experiencing a revival. Such interest since the middle 1960s in part accounts for the growth of Traven's audience, particularly in the United States. Turning to the Indian's way of life as a guide or resource for future society can be seen in elements of modern American life, as well as in its literature. Gary Snyder's poetry and essays are one such example; Wendell Berry's are another.

The point of such a cursory mention of avenues for comparative study of Traven's work with themes in contemporary poetry is that Traven's anarcho-primitivism is far from a dead letter. Instead, it may prove to be a precursor of a theme of rising influence in the literature that is being produced on what appears to be the eve of a far more devastating period of economic crisis and military conflagration than the one in which Traven wrote the Jungle novels. In order to be able to make such comparisons, though, we need to more clearly define Traven's anarcho-primitivism. This paper has been an effort to contribute to that clarification.

Notes

1. In discussing Land des Frühlings (Berlin: Büchergilde Gutenberg, 1928), I have relied on Michael Baumann's analysis in "B. Traven: Realist and Prophet" (Virginia Quarterly Review, Vol. 53, No. 1), quoted in Dedria Bryfonski, ed., Contemporary Literary Criticism (Detroit: Gale Research Co., 1979), Vol. 11, 537-38; as well as his analysis in Baumann, 1976. While I disagree with a number of Baumann's interpretations, his exegesis of the Jungle novels provided an excellent starting point for my own analysis, and his discussion of Land des Frühlings was indispensable for the development of my thesis.
2. B. Traven, The White Rose (Westport, Conn.: Lawrence Hill and Co., 1979).
3. Baumann, 1976; see chapter three, "Traven's Anarchism."
4. B. Traven, The Cotton Pickers (New York: Hill and Wang, 1969).
5. Traven, Government, 12-13.
6. Traven, The Carreta, 226-27.
7. Traven, General, 4.
8. Ibid., 7-9.
9. Ibid., 106-8.

B. TRAVEN'S REVOLUTION IN LATIN AMERICA

Jonah Raskin

The emphasis of scholars over the past two decades on solving the mystery of B. Traven has yielded new and important
insights into the man, but in the process the books have
been obscured. And those critics who have focused on the
fiction have tended to analyze the earlier work, leaving the
Jungle novels--the Caoba Cycle--without the recognition they
deserve. That is unfortunate, not only because the Jungle
novels are the maturest expression of Traven's artistic
vision, but also because they are among the very finest
novels in any language to describe the genesis, growth, and
triumph of a revolution. With all of Latin America--from
Nicaragua and El Salvador to Guatemala and Mexico--in varying degrees of revolutionary ripeness, the Jungle novels are
still news, and well worth our attention.

The first indication we have that Traven was at work on
the series is a letter he wrote to the Berlin-based Büchergilde Gutenberg in October 1927. "I regard the Mexican
Indian and the Mexican proletariat...as my deepest friends,"
Traven confided.

> I know the courage, devotion and sacrifice (unheard of in
> Europe) of the proletarian Indian in his fight for deliv-
> erance into the light of the sun. It is a fight for
> liberation that has no equal in human history. Until
> today I was unable to make the European working man under-
> stand a single part of this fight for freedom. It can't
> be done in a simple narrative form. Confronted with the
> immense cultural, economic and philosophical accomplish-
> ments of the Indian, all the tools of the poet and the
> writer fail. I am hard-pressed, both socially and emo-
> tionally, to empathize with this fantastic cultural event,
> and give it form in words and glowing pictures.

That Traven was resolved to give artistic form to the
struggles of the Mexican Indian proletariat must have come
as something of a surprise to the editors at the Büchergilde
Gutenberg since two years earlier, in 1925, referring to
Bridge Traven insisted, "I cease with this work to be a so-
called 'worker's poet.'" A surprising remark for a writer
who had vowed to celebrate proletarian life and "shatter the
cultural hegemony of the bourgeoisie," but given the context
it is clearly understandable.

Having written two proletarian novels, The Death Ship and

The Cotton Pickers, Traven had acquired the reputation of a working-class novelist, and more than anything he hated labels and pigeonholing. Above all he wanted to maintain his individuality. "I would be very unhappy," he wrote, "to be catalogued as a 'worker's poet'...to escape from that category I would immediately write a 'hurrah for capitalism' novel." That threat obviously was idle; Traven was no more capable of writing a novel celebrating capitalism than he was capable of revealing his true identity.

But what was it, then, that persuaded him, after he had threatened not to write another proletarian novel, to turn to the Mexican Indian proletariat as the heroes for his fiction? We know from his diaries of 1926 and 1927--handwritten in English--that he saw Indians used as slave laborers to build roads, cut and haul timber, pick coffee beans, and toil on the large _fincas_. This was a devastating discovery, and doubly so because initially Traven believed that the Mexican Revolution of 1910-20 had transformed the lives of the Indians, that peonage and debt-slavery had been abolished, and that the conditions of the working class had been fundamentally improved. Indeed, that is the point of view that comes across in _The Cotton Pickers_. True, working conditions are depicted as hard, and workers are portrayed as underpaid, but Mexico is presented as a nation that is fast on its way toward being governed by workers and their democratic trade unions, not by bureaucrats or by a new ruling class. What had been crushed in Germany, what had been betrayed in Russia, Traven was convinced had become a reality in the New World.

This illusion of the Mexican Revolution was shattered by the Chiapas experience--the discovery of twentieth-century slavery in the jungle. Concurrently, Traven came to feel that his novels of proletarian life were inadequate, and he was anxious to express his newer, more profound vision. From this point on he ceased to write of the down-and-out white men we meet in _The Death Ship_ and _Treasure_ and concentrated instead on describing Indian peasants and proletarians. Furthermore, he shifted emphasis from writing about workers in trade unions to portraying the guerrilla army, believing that armed struggle, rather than trade union activity, was more likely to bring about liberation for the working class.

By making this political change Traven put himself in touch with perhaps _the_ crucial historical thrust of our time--the revolutionary movements of the Third World. Yet it wasn't only a case of political realignment. It was profoundly personal and artistic, too, as reflected in Traven's remark that the story he wanted to tell could not be told "in a simple narrative form." And so he turned to the epic; he drew upon folktales, legend, and myth, digging more deeply than before into traditional Mexican images and symbols. And influenced by the art of his contemporaries Diego Rivera and David Siqueiros--by their sense of color and form as well as theme--Traven painted his own vast, multi-paneled murals of modern society. In the Jungle novels Traven became a master of pattern and structure, the six self-contained books building into one continuous work of balance and symmetry.

The title is especially appropriate since the jungle is an abiding presence in the work, but "Road to Liberty" would have been equally appropriate since the road is a character in its own right, and one of the leading symbols in a work thick with symbols. In The Carreta, the second novel in the series and the most romantic, we meet Andrés Ugalde, Indian peasant, ox-cart driver, and prisoner of the road. Holding the reins and cracking the whip, Andrés regards himself as free and independent, only to discover that he too is a beast of burden, that like the oxen he has a yoke to bear. When his father falls into debt and has no choice but to toil in the logging camps, Andrés takes his place, surrendering the illusory bit of freedom he possesses. And by surrendering that illusion of freedom, he eventually grasps real, tangible freedom.

In March, the third book in the series and probably the most gruesome, Traven describes the nightmarish journey, on a road paved with terror and brutality, into the heart of the jungle hell. But even here, with oppression at its harshest, there is resistance, as Traven balances the countervailing forces of liberation and tyranny.

In The Troza, the fourth and pivotal book, we learn much about the logging industry. The trees are cut down and carted off, leaving a wilderness of stumps; the overseers cut down the men, leaving them stumps of their former humanity. An escaped worker hiding in the jungle sings verses of defiance and can't be caught. And when one worker dies of a snakebite, his comrades defy their masters and give him a proper burial, affirming their own dignity. The men who survive, including Andrés and Celso. are hard and tough and resistant as mahogany, until, in Rebellion, insurrection breaks out and, in General, the men become soldiers in an army of liberation. Now the road to slavery becomes its opposite, a path to freedom. Marching out of the jungle, the Indians become masters of guerrilla warfare (here Traven drew upon the strategy and tactics of Sandino and Zapata), and masters of their own destiny. Having defeated the dictator's troops, they establish the village of Solipaz, a separate, self-contained utopian community. And so the reader is taken on a road that leads from dictatorship through hell and rebellion to paradise.

In 1935, in a letter to his British agent, Traven explained that the crucial dramatic scene in <u>Government</u> (it occurs in chapter 9 and describes the uprising of the Pebvil Indians) "was based on an actual incident that had taken place on January 1, 1928, a short time before I was visiting that district [but] was placed for certain reasons at a time about twenty-five years ago." Traven did not explain what the "certain reasons" were for lodging that incident in the past, but we may assume they were more political than artistic. By setting the incident in the past, Traven made it appear, at least on the surface, that he was writing a historical fiction rather than a novel of contemporary Mexican life--a shrewd and practical move, since the message of the book was subversive and might provoke a clash with Mexican authorities.

Further insight is provided by a letter Traven wrote in 1950, again to his British agent. The occasion for this letter was a British edition of <u>Rebellion</u>, translated from German into English by a Mr. Duff. When, in the text, Traven referred to "the dictatorship," Mr. Duff added a footnote specifying that it was the Díaz dictatorship. And Traven took him sharply to task. "By doing so Mr. Duff gives the story a time limit which Traven never intended," B. Traven worte, in that habitual way he had of speaking of himself in the third person:

In Latin America dictatorships come and go. Right now there are five or six countries under a dictatorship, and the rest are under a sort of semi-dictatorship. Mexico has only one political party, and only members of that official party are elected to Parliament or any public office, with one or two so-called independents tolerated so as to make the machinery not too obvious...When a paper needs pepping up its circulation a sensational story is published about the cruel conditions in which the Indians are forced to work at the camps. The Government sends a commission of three or four men to investigate. Before that commission arrives everything looks rosy and the commission reports that the paper exaggerated its big story. Before the commission is actually back in the capital, conditions at the camp are worse than ever. And since this is so Traven wanted his story to be timeless and that's why he refrained from mentioning the name of any dictator.

We should also note that when writing the Jungle novels Traven was thinking not only of Latin American dictators and dictatorships, but also of the German government that existed during World War I (when he published _Ziegelbrenner_ under the name of Ret Marut) and the Nazi dictatorship of the 1930s. In the midst of writing this series of books, the Nazis came to power, forcing the Büchergilde Gutenberg into exile and confiscating, burning, and banning Traven's books. That act, as one might imagine, further inflamed his passionate hatred of dictationship, and those flames of antifascist sentiment found their way into the pages of the last three Jungle novels.

Then, too, while writing his epic of dictatorship and revolution in the Americas, Traven's memories of his partici-pation in the 1919 Bavarian insurrection were reawakened, and they came to be expressed in the text through the char-acter of Martín Trinidad. Known to his comrades as "The Professor," Trinidad is the intellectual leader of the lum-berjacks and ox-cart drivers. Through him Traven was able to recycle Ret Marut's anarchist philosophy and view of history. Thus, Trinidad advises, "If you want to make a revolution, then carry it through to the end, because other-wise it will turn against you and tear you to shreds." That, of course, is what had happened in Germany in 1919, and Marut had nearly lost his life. Again Trinidad insists; "If you want to win and stay winners we'll have to burn all the papers. Many revolutions have started and then failed simply because papers weren't burned as they should have been. The first thing we must do is attack the registry and burn the papers, all the papers with seals and signatures-- deeds, birth and death and marriage certificates...Then nobody will know who he is, what he's called, who was his father, and what his father had. We'll be the heirs because nobody will be able to prove the contrary."

Clearly, comments like these derive from Ret Marut's/B. Traven's idiosyncratic preoccupation with his own identity and the mystery of his origins, and not from any crucial ingredient of the Mexican Revolution. Traven's past in Germany came back to haunt him while he was writing the Jungle novels, and it helped to make them a richer, deeper, more complex work--the European experience overlaid with the Mexican experience, the Old World wisdom infused with the knowledge born of the jungles of the New World.

The Jungle novels restate in a more sophisticated form the political ideas of Ret Marut. They also revive the themes of Traven's earlier novels. Death and resurrection, para-dise and hell, rags and riches--these bold threads run

230

through The Death Ship and Treasure, and we see them again in the six-novel epic.

In The Death Ship Gerard Gales wakes one morning to find that his ship has sailed without him, that he is without money, or papers, or the relative comfort he had aboard his mother ship. Deported by the police, kicked from one country to another, he is finally hired by the captain of the Yorikke and descends into a living hell, an inferno of dead souls. But in that hell, in that world of the dead, Gales discovers, for the first time, his own strengh and the humanity of his fellow man.

In Treasure Traven's ragged prospectors strike it rich, but riches bring a hellish existence, a death in life, at least for Dobbs. The real paradise, the genuine treasure, as Howard learns, is with the materially impoverished but spiritually rich Indians.

In the Jungle novels the characters and the settings are different, but the moral patterns are much the same. Things turn upside down and inside out. They turn into their opposites: rags into riches, riches into rags, paradise into hell, and hell into paradise.

Whether it was on the high seas or at the center of a mahogany forest, Traven celebrated the brotherhood of man under the most adverse conditions. And we may safely assume that Traven's own growth, his own deliverance into maturity, came in the wake of his difficult years as a fugitive, vagabond, and down-and-out proletarian. Indeed, hell, death ships, and death camps seem, in Traven's eyes, more desirable than luxury liners, the preacher's paradise, or the fashionable world of the rich. In Traven's world one is likely to find angels, not in heaven, but in hell, and treasure, not in riches, but in rags--eternal life at the brink of everlasting death.

In March Traven describes the jungle as a terrain of constant warfare, and he goes on to say that "Men's strife for existence could hardly be waged more inflexibly than the battle among the plants...Whatever is conceived here and once conceived grows and survives, has to be of a truly heroic nature. Softness and timidity are stamped into the mud to rot. The one that loses the battle serves as fertilizer for the one of greater beauty, strength and nobility."

How Darwinian! And how much like Jack London at his most Nietzschean. Traven, for all his insistence on brotherhood with the Indian proletariat, and the necessity of collective action against dictatorship, could be--as much as Jack London--a believer in the superman, the uncommon hero, the man of "greater beauty, strength and nobility."

Nobility is the key word here, though it may seem odd

coming from the pen of a so-called proletarian novelist. It is nobility that Traven admires. It is the aristocracy that he desires to belong to, though not the aristocracy of the Old World, and not the nobility of the European court. Traven's aristocrats are night visitors at remote bungalows, small boys who fall from bridges in the jungle, and peasants like Andrés Ugalde and Celso Flores. In the world according to B. Traven, the most obscure of men are the most genuinely aristocratic. In the Jungle novels the most plundered of humanity are the most princely. That is news, and always will be. And that is why, as Traven himself recognized, the Jungle novels are "timeless...the essential part of the story is happening all the time."

POLITICAL SATIRE MEXICAN-STYLE
Critique of Proto-Fascist Tendencies in B. Traven's Government

Jörg Thunecke

Although the past two decades have seen the appearance of a vast number of publications in many languages on the phenomenon of fascism, and although enormous amounts of research time and mental energy have been put into the study of it, historians and other social scientists have been unable to reach a consensus on what fascism is or was. Explanations for it and interpretations of it are legion, and they diverge possibly more widely than on any other historical topic. This situation has been brought about to a large extent by the inability of scholars to agree on any general definition of a term which is still in day-to-day political use and which continues to evoke emotional responses--and not simply among historians.

Many general works on fascism begin therefore with a comment on current usages of the word, though it is only fair to state that an investigation of the usage of the word in antifascist and nonfascist circles does not yield anything, save that it is definitely a pejorative term; neither do the opinions of self-confessed fascists provide any useful aid: Whatever their practical political effectiveness, current usages distort more than they explain. Therefore, no short paper can hope to comment on all the questions raised in the vast literature on fascism, or adequately summarize the current state of knowledge in all the various national contexts. The general message of this literature, however, is that fascism cannot be studied simply within isolated national contexts, but that the careful study of specific cases--like the present one--must be the foundation for generalizations.

Since, therefore, the question of what fascism is produces so many discordant answers, the problem of where to begin shall in this instance be solved by taking a shortcut and offering a working definition which takes account of the socioeconomic and political aspects of Traven's novel Government (1931). As Manfred Clemenz's definition facilitates an easy structuring of Traven's comments on these matters, his division of the term fascism into generic, functional, and phenomenological dimensions shall here be adopted.[1]

According to this division the generic dimension of the term, i.e., the social circumstances of its origin, stipu-

lates that a fascist system be preceded by a futile proletarian revolution, followed by a counter-revolutionary reaction, particularly if a recession threatens the interests
of the bourgeoisie and/or big business. In addition, its
functional dimension, i.e., the role of fascism within a
given political entity, calls for the suppression and exploitation of the proletariat, concomitant with the termination of any economic crises, especially through the initiation of new economic programs offering quick returns and
large profits. Finally, the phenomenological side of fascism is characterized by strong military and/or paramilitary
organizations, the use of force/terror as a deterrent, and
the belief in political creeds opposed to humanist and
liberal ideals.

Traven's description of the struggle for freedom by the
Mexican Indians of Maya stock in the period prior to the
overthrow of the Díaz dictatorship in 1911 can best be
illustrated in Government, the second of the five novels of
the Caoba Cycle. It offers "a forceful attack on a system
of government that feeds on the poor, an indictment of a
world that allows—and calls for—slavery."[2] The political
system used by Traven for his novel, the dictatorship of
Porfirio Díaz—a mestizo, who between 1876 and 1911 was
"elected" Mexican president seven times,[3] and who, for over
thirty years, was the undisputed leader of his people—
consequently serves as a powerful example of the functionings of a hierarchical organization which restricts the
rights of the many by elevating a rich, influential oligarchy.
    Thus Traven's novel can be interpreted as "primarily a
study of political corruption and misrule,"[4] the literary
medium of his attack being that of political satire.
Throughout, Traven attempts to diminish his subject matter
by ridiculing it and by evoking towards it attitudes of
amusement, contempt, and scorn,[5] using the literary form in
its most traditional way: as "a corrective of human vice
and folly."[6] Two things are essential to satire, as Northrop Frye has pointed out in his essay "The Nature of
Satire":[7] wit, or humor; and an object of attack. This
latter component of satire presents no problem, since Traven
directed his satire against "the graft and corruption of the
Díaz regime,"[8] the target of his attack being personified in
the character of don Gabriel Ordunez, a petty government
official, "whose mission it is to carry, at the point of the
sword, the light of civilization to a small Indian community.[9]
    It is in the course of his satirical assault on the cor-

234

ruption under the Díaz dictatorship in <u>Government</u>[10] that
Traven uncovers various forms of nascent fascism (proto-
fascism), which--though his style oftens suffers from an
overdose of didacticism, as he writes "about systems and
ideas rather than about flesh and blood"[11]--are proof of his
political convictions and his antitotalitarian stance: "Don
Porfirio Díaz had himself re-elected every four years when
his time as president was up. The gang who waxed fatter and
fatter under his regency did the electing. Whoever did not
wax fat under his government had no vote."[12] Traven quite
plainly "despise[d] straight narrative,"[13] being "always
ready to digress and tell some story which illustrates his
theme,"[14] a feature of his style which can be observed in
the following excerpt, where he ridicules the "art of government":

> The art of governing is only made out to be mysterious in
> order to frighten revolutionaries and to prevent the sim-
> ple subject from knowing how little capacity and knowledge
> is needed for government. How many half-wits and idiots
> have governed their peoples for half a century in peace
> and glory! (178)

Since satire, and above all political satire, imitates a
vice or folly, and since in satire nothing is ever done
without purpose,[15] it should not surprise that Traven repeatedly embarks on long tirades--"jeers, maledictions, or
ironical explanations."[16] This is illustrated, for example,
by his contempt for the political rewards granted to those
who had helped the dictator--who considered himself "the
best and greatest and most intelligent statesman on
earth"[17]--achieve self-aggrandizement. In turn, the dictator guaranteed that "governors, mayors, police chiefs, secretaries and engineers remained in office until death relieved the people of them,"[18] resulting in a "golden age"
for the oligarchy:

> Dreissig Jahre Diktatur und die Folgen eines goldenen
> Zeitalters unter jener Diktatur, die ein stolzes Volk so
> zu unterdrücken verstand, dass in den günstigsten Fällen
> drei Prozent des Volkes sich an den politischen Wahlen
> beteiligten, weil sie hinkommandiert wurden, um den Schein
> eines zivilisierten und konstitutionell regierten Landes
> aufrechtzuerhalten... (GE: 39)

In a typical totalitarian ploy, the outside world was deceived into believing that Mexico had developed a highly
sophisticated democratic system: "This was reported in all

the American newspapers and the world knew that Mexico was
not governed by a despotic dictator. It was an up-to-date
and civilized republic with a highly developed constitu-
tional system" (27). The deception, on the whole was the
result of falsified statistical data:

> One of the most important tasks the dictator set himself
> was to cook up statistics for the benefit of the world at
> large. If he had neglected to do this, the world would
> never have known what a great statesman he was and what a
> debt of gratitude the Mexican people owed him for sacrifi-
> cing himself again and again, bearing the heavy burden of
> dictatorship and wearing the president's crown of thorns,
> in order to be the first and foremost of the servants of
> his beloved people. (28)

Eventually, everybody working inside the system became used
to deception on a small scale, comparable to much larger
deceptions practiced by the dictator himself:

> Statistics and reports assume great importance under a
> dictatorship or a despotism. They are the façade of the
> structure and there must not be so much as a scratch on
> the gilding. And nowhere are people, whether in an offi-
> cial or private capacity, so clever at running up façades
> as under a dictatorship, where everyone who wishes to live
> unmolested, or even to live at all, has at all costs, and
> whatever else he may say or do, to plaster up a stucco
> front in case he incurs the suspicion of not seeing eye to
> eye with the political regime. (40-41)

Nepotism was a sure way of securing one's position within
such a system, while the economic spoils were divided according to strict hierarchical rules.[19]

Understandably, the satirist's purpose is "not to create
something new but to expose the real evil in the existing";[20] i.e., it is not his job to attack institutions as
such and to suggest substitutes of his own choice, but to
attack perversions of existing institutions.[21] Nationalism,
for example, is seen by Traven as one such perversion of the
institution of the state, particularly if used to disguise
the desire to enrich oneself at the expense of the masses of
the people and if practiced by the political leaders themselves: "Like every other jefe politico, don Casimiro
thought first of his own interests. He served his country
not for his country's good, but in order to profit at its
expense" (1). This is especially true if other issues

236

typical of a "système fascistoid" are raised at the same time—for instance, the consolidation of the economic position of an oligarchy intent on dealing with a recession while maximizing profits—issues which explain why such a group of influential people was keen to replace "a president who is hostile to monopolies by one who favours them."[22]

> The dictator, don Porfirio, had astonished the world by showing in a brief space of time that the bankrupt Republic of Mexico was so flourishing that other countries could only envy its bursting treasury. It was proved by the statistics, which also proved that a great statesman had brought the Mexican people to a level of civilization and prosperity which no one would have thought possible. He knew how to keep national expenditure down to a ridiculously low figure. That was easy. Official salaries were in many cases so small that a mouse could scarcely have lived on them; and if a government inspector or a judge wanted to live in a manner befitting his station, he had to find some other source of income as well. It went without saying that he used his power to enlarge this other source to the utmost. The treasury grew richer and richer, the national debt, on paper, smaller and smaller; the poverty of the people, ignorance, corruption, and shameless injustice were, on the other hand, more and more widely diffused. (71)

Thus a dictatorship like that of Díaz succeeded in deceiving the outside world about the true state of affairs in the country. It speaks for the high level of Traven's artistry—as well as his personal integrity, being quite clearly "forced by his conscience to write satire,"[23] though "his passion for anonymity strained against his determination to make himself heard"[24]—that he constantly queried the assumed high level of civilization in Mexico, lending weight to the conviction that—for him at least—"satire mean[t] civilization."[25]

Consequently, the spurious economic miracle, achieved through the exploitation of the native Mexican Indian proletariat, is repeatedly criticized in <u>Government</u>, the plight of the workers being compared to that of their European counterparts. It lends support to Elliott's claim that "satire spreads like a shock wave from an explosion: from local viciousness to worldwide inhumanity..."[26] By characterizing the Mexican Indian as an inferior human being, in terms reminiscent of nineteenth-century racist outbursts,[27] Traven's description of the Mexican situation not only fits the functional dimension of a fascist regime (suppression of

an indigenous proletariat) but also the specific phenomenological criteria stipulating a political creed strictly
opposed to liberal and humanist ideals. In fact, the picture painted by Traven of attitudes towards Mexican Indians
simply abounds with invectives and prejudices of the worst
kind.[28]

Even more to the point, Traven shows, though not without
considerable irony, that this situation is aggravated by the
fact that the exploitation is being conducted in the name of
big business and is openly condoned and encouraged by the
dictator himself, who has no genuine interest in the economy
of his country: "The government was not interested in
Mexicans building up industries of their own in their own
country. It suited it better to make a profit out of the
high tariffs on imported goods and to stand well with Americans, English, and French export houses" (47). Corrobora-
ting evidence can be found in a principle adhered to by most
right-wing regimes, the preaching of economic efficiency as
a means of boosting national prestige: "Don Porfirio, the
president of the Mexican Republic, had, in exchange for hard
cash, given foreign companies licenses to denude the forests
of valuable timber which were one of the great resources of
the country. The more national resources were developed,
the higher was the country's credit on the international
money market. It was therefore a highly patriotic act to
make these riches available to the rest of the world" (133).
Consequently, excesses prevalent in capitalist systems are
condoned by the dictatorship, regardless of the cost in
terms of human lives:

> On the contrary, the government was glad to see debts paid
> off, and even more glad that the companies who paid it
> well for licenses and concessions should be kept supplied
> with labor, so that production could be maintained and
> exports increased. Exports were necessary to the finances
> of the country and kept up the value of the peso on the
> money markets of London and New York. It was therefore a
> highly patriotic activity to supply the coffee plantations
> and the monterías with labor and to keep the supply con-
> stant; it was just as important as dying gloriously and
> miserably for the honor of your country assured the joys
> of paradise. (128)

The Indian, a nonentity--"A worm. A flea. A louse. A
trembling reed broken by the storm...a speck of dust driven
hither and thither by every puff of wind" (129)--is given
the "unique" opportunity to slave in the monterías in the

238

name of national pride and glory, a typical fascist ploy exonerating those in power:

> To deal in cattle was mere self-seeking. To recruit Indian labor in order to put production on a competitive level was, on the other hand, a patriotic activity. As long as there is an unshakable conviction such as this, it is impossible to commit injustice or practice cruelty, to break up family life, to rob a man of all that life means to him. If you find the right formula, any crime can be justified and even sanctified in your own eyes and before the world. (129)

The result was that slave labor was common in the Mexico of the immediate prewar years, and the country was considered a link in the Western capitalist system viciously satirized by Traven.[29] Don Gabriel's description of the treatment of the native labor force, the fact that "a third, in some of the monterías half, of the peons are dead within the year and have to be replaced" (120), permitting anything short of open abduction, makes it abundantly clear for every discerning reader that the capitalist system—in collaboration with a "régime fascistoid"—was to blame for the trade in human lives in Mexico at the beginning of the century. The god "profit" makes no concessions to human dignity, and its followers show little mercy for the plight of fellow human beings[30]—especially not if similar business operations are conducted on a worldwide scale, dwarfing those practiced in Mexico.[31]

It is at this point that the central issues of Traven's political creed are laid bare: the preoccupation of an author "of pure ideals and ingenuous optimism"[32] with the defense of man's dignity in the modern world,[33] his "stand against the poverty of the spirit of the politico-economic age."[34] As a consequence, his verbal attacks on regimes such as the one described in Government—which, since the fiasco of the Bavarian Republic in 1919, were no doubt dictated by the advocacy of force, "if the poor and oppressed of the world were to throw off their chains,"[35] coupled, though, with "an element of self-reproach"[36] at not being able to carry out such actions himself—produced some of the most penetrating insights into the phenomenological nature of fascism, above all the description of the presence of a strong military force prepared to terrorize the local Indian population.[37] Traven also points out the effect of indoctrination, which teaches the natives from childhood onward that rebellion does not pay,[38] with the result that for some time not even the mahogany workers and forced laborers of

southeast Mexico, condemned to work in the monterías for
life, dared rebel against orders given by state representatives:

> If the man failed for any reason to leave his native place
> in time to arrive in Hucutsín on the proper day, he was
> guilty of breach of contract, the worst offense that an
> Indian laborer could commit under the dictatorship of don
> Porfirio. An Indian who had murdered one of his fellow
> men, that is to say another Indian--incurred a smaller
> penalty than for breach of contract. (169)

Neither did the Indian chiefs consider rebellion a feasible
alternative:

> The cacique could not set himself against the orders of
> the government. That would have laid him open to the
> charge of disobedience and landed him in prison for years
> to come. It might even have gone worse than that with
> him, for the judge might have found that disobedience to a
> special decree of the governor was an act of rebellion and
> an open defiance of the power of the State, and in that
> case he would have been shot. (190)

And even if the laws of the land were clearly on the side of
the Indian, the representatives of the state normally managed to interpret them to their own advantage:

> Laws for the common good are all very well. But there
> must always be officials to see that the laws are honored,
> and these officials who have power and authority to see
> that the laws are honored must be strong enough in their
> own sphere to go beyond or to alter or to tighten up the
> laws just as they see fit. Otherwise there would be no
> sense in a dictatorship and you might just as well have a
> democracy. There has got to be some difference, after
> all. (20)

Although it was far more likely that such laws were on the
side of the ruling minority in any case:

> Wie gut aber auch Gesetze sein mögen, in einem Lande wie
> Mexiko können die allgemeinen Landesgesetze immer nur für
> einen geringen Teil der Gesamtbevölkerung gerechte Gesetze
> in ihrer Wirkung sein. (GE: 81)[39]

Also interesting in this context is Traven's description of
the educational system in operation among the Mexican Indian

population--and the sideswipe against his old enemy, the
Catholic church--for he considered it the fault of the
school system that the natives were subdued with such relative ease in later life. Attempts at educating the native
Indians were, as far as the Mexican dictatorship was concerned, merely a means of impressing foreign powers, which
was achieved, on the whole, by publishing statistical data
bearing little or no relation to reality.

For similar reasons, the dictator found it desirable to be
considered ruler over a "civilized" country, and he engaged
in a kind of window-dressing where statistics on educational
matters "were carefully printed on the best of paper and
splendidly bound, and...dispatched to the governments of
every civilized country" (44), regardless of the fact that
normally fascist doctrine was diametrically opposed to Western liberal ideas on pedagogics:

> But the dictator did not want merely to show the iron hand
> of a great statesman who guaranteed peace and security
> within his country's borders; he wanted also to have the
> reputation in civilized countries of being the man who
> educated the people of Mexico. This fame he achieved by
> means of statistics showing the number of schools he had
> opened in the country, in order to provide the children of
> Indians and peons and, indeed, of all the working people
> with up-to-date instruction. (28)[40]

Traven's satire of the political system in question culminates in the ironic contrast of the white Mexicans' claim
that their country has attained a high degree of civilization, with the depiction of the truly civilized indigenous
population, a contrast reminiscent of D. H. Lawrence's description of the Indians of New Mexico in the early 1920s in
Mornings in Mexico (1927): for while "the dictator wanted
to see the country opened up and taking its place in the
ranks of highly civilized nations" (26), the "uncivilized"
Indians, who could not read or write, were far "less easily
led into folly" (192), and never thought of bringing danger
on their people and wasting its wealth and manhood. In both
cases interference from the outside world in the Indians'
internal affairs is the real problem.[41]

It therefore comes as no great surprise that the utopian
model[42] of an alternative political system, proposed by
Traven towards the end of Government, turns out to be one
used by the Mexican Indians, who, with their ancient tribal
traditions, "can escape the greed and irrationalities of
modern government."[43] The ensuing comparison of the electoral system under the Díaz dictatorship with that of the

Indians finds the former to be totally corrupt; and Traven presents a near perfect example of how ridicule can be used as a weapon,[44] as demonstrated in the discussion between Tomás, speaker for the Tsotsil Indians of the Pebvil area, and the government representative, resident secretary don Abelardo, who, with the consent of the regional governor, intends to change the natives' age-old electoral system.[45] In this, don Abelardo is given a lesson in truly democratic government, where everybody has the chance to be elected and to put his ideas into practice during his term of office as "jefe":

> We have found through age-long experience that it suits our people to choose a new jefe every year, to take him every year from a different barrio, and never to re-elect a man who has once been jefe. If we were engaged in a long war and wanted the most experienced man as jefe, or if we were on a long migration to a new territory, then it might be advisable to keep the most experienced man among us in office for a longer time. But the tradition of our people tells us that we have not altered our method of election even in critical times. (188)

Highlighting this electoral ritual is the inaugural ceremony for the newly elected chief, who, while having to sit on a chair with a hole in the seat under which a charcoal fire is lit, endures considerable pain throughout the period of the official speeches, a tradition recommended with biting sarcasm by Traven for general use in totalitarian and democratic systems alike[46] to remind the political leaders of the temporary nature of their appointment.[47]

We therefore arrive at the conclusion that Traven, in his novel Government--despite the sometimes pedantic tone "bristling with explanations of how the 'system' works"[48]-- shows evidence of considerable development of his political awareness, apart from the equally noticeable enhancement of his artistic ability of expressing ideological beliefs within relatively narrow constraints of prose fiction.

Quite evidently, the defeat of the 1918-19 revolution and the failure to establish a Räterepublik in Munich rankled Traven. By 1930 he had familiarized himself with recent Mexican history; and no doubt alarmed at political developments in central and southern Europe, he accepted the challenge of a satirical novel attacking a political entity whose various features, when viewed in their entirety, merge into a "système fascistoïd." Overall, Traven's novel serves as an excellent case study for proto-fascism: Its embodiment, a government sympathetic toward fascism, fits Clemenz's criteria in all vital aspects, so that the conclusion seems inescapable that a totalitarian state stood model for this work by one of the most versatile and underrated writers of modern times.

Notes

1. Manfred Clemenz, "Versuche einer Begriffsbestimmung des Faschismus," in Gesellschaftliche Ursprünge des Faschismus, edition suhrkamp 550, 3rd edition (1972; Frankfurt a.M.: 1980), 205-32.
2. Baumann, 1976, 122.
3. Recknagel, 1977, 252.
4. "Government. By B. Traven," in The Times Literary Supplement, November 30, 1935, 817.
5. Meyer H. Abrams, "From A Glossary of Literary Terms," in Satire: Theory and Practice, ed. Charles A. Allen and George D. Stephens (Belmont, CA: 1962), 43.
6. Ibid.
7. Northrop Frye, "The Nature of Satire," in University of Toronto Quarterly 14 (October 1944): 76.
8. H. R. Hays, "The Importance of B. Traven," in Chimera 4 (Summer 1946): 48.
9. TLS, 817.
10. Arthur Calder-Marshall, "The Novels of B. Traven," in Horizon 1 (July 1940): 527.
11. TLS, 817.
12. B. Traven, Government (New York: Allison and Busky, 1980), 177. Page numbers following quotations refer to this text. Since the English edition significantly differs from the first edition in German in parts—B. Traven, Regierung (Berlin: Büchergilde Gutenberg, 1931)—"GE" following a quotation in the text refers to this German edition.
13. Calder-Marshall, 526.
14. Hays, 51-52.
15. Ronald Paulson, The Fiction of Satire (Baltimore: 1967), 4.
16. Hays, 52.
17. B. Traven, Government, 178.
18. Ibid., 178.
19. Cf. ibid., 1-2, 11-12.
20. Paulson, 5.
21. Elliott, 271.
22. Government, 119: "...in the place of an antimonopolistic president a promonopolist..."
23. Elliott, 265.
24. Wyatt, 1980, 214.

25. Frye, 79.

26. Elliott, 195.

27. Cf. e.g., Thomas Carlyle, "Occasional Discourse on the Nigger Question," in Critical and Miscellaneous Essays: The Works of Thomas Carlyle (London: 1905), 348-83 (first printed in Fraser's Magazine in 1849); and editor Philip D. Curtin's comment in Imperialism (London: 1971), 135, calling this essay "one of the most vitriolic pieces of racist writing."

28. Cf. GE: 83-84.

29. Cf. Government, 133.

30. Cf. GE: 126 and Government, 228-29.

31. Cf. Government, 218-19.

32. Wyatt, 1980, 202.

33. Cf. Hays, 54.

34. Ibid.

35. Wyatt, 1980, 202.

36. Ibid.

37. Cf. Government, Chapter 10.

38. Ibid., 33-34.

39. Cf. GE: 29.

40. Cf. Government, 35-36.

41. Cf. GE: 197-98 and D. H. Lawrence, Mornings in Mexico (1950) (Harmondsworth: Penguin Books, 1975), 89-90.

42. Cf. Chankin, 1975, 92: "Government is a simple statement of anarchist antipolitics."

43. Ibid., 92.

44. Abrams, 43.

45. Cf. note 6 and Government, 187-90.

46. Government, 177.

47. Cf. ibid., 175-76.

48. Baumann, 1976, 122.

B. TRAVEN'S LAND DES FRÜHLINGS AND THE CAOBA CYCLE AS A SOURCE FOR THE STUDY OF AGRARIAN SOCIETY

Friederike Baumann

Chiapas has attraced the attention of social scientists from Mexico, Europe, and the United States for more than three decades. Like the adjacent regions in Central America, it has a predominantly agrarian economy, and the majority of the population consists of Indians who live in villages, speak different languages, and wear distinct dress. In no other region has the Mexican government made such a concerted effort to develop strategies and institutions in order to integrate these Indian communities into Mexican society. More research has been done on the Tzotziles and Tzeltales of the Highlands of Chiapas than on any other Indian group in Latin America, and the majority of studies concentrate on the communities of Zinacantan and Chamula. In the last ten years, anthropologists alone have published more than thirty books on these Indians.

Recently, historians too have been discovering the people and institutions of Chiapas as an object of research. Unlike anthropologists, who collect the bulk of their data through personal interviews and personal observation, historians have to work with written documents. This presents problems for social historians interested in the fate of rural people, since rural people were and are mainly illiterate. They have few written records from which we can learn how previous generations perceived their world, their problems, and their options, and only for the most recent past can we tap the information stored in their minds. Sometimes we get glimpses of their points of view from such sources as court records or documents of the agrarian reform, as in the case of Mexico. Mostly, however, historians have to work with information on rural conditions left by the upper classes and on reports by outside observers.

Consequently, it is not surprising that Traven's works on Chiapas, which are known by social scientists, are of particular interest to historians. Traven is one of the few writers on Latin America who described the lives of rural people, who was interested in Indians as human beings and workers, and who had Indian protagonists in his novels. For information on the monterías, the mahogany lumber camps in the southeastern lowlands along the Usumacinta River, he is still the only significant source.

Traven's writings on Chiapas consist of the nonfiction work Land des Frühlings and six novels, the so-called Caoba

Cycle. In Land he tells about his travels in Chiapas from May to October 1926. He journeyed from Huixtla, on the Pacific, across the Sierra Madre to the Highlands, stayed seven weeks in San Cristobal de las Casas and Chamula, returned to the train station Arriaga via Tuxtla Gutierrez, and explored the country along the tracks of the Pacific railroad to Mapastepec on horseback during the last few days before the rainy season. He informs the German reader about Indian customs and values, about their way of life in the communities, and about the greatest yearly social event of the Chamula nation, the Fiesta of San Juan. Indians, landscapes, flora and fauna are seen through the eyes of an unusually perceptive and compassionate outsider, an unconventional anthropologist and naturalist. He demonstrates deep respect for the dignity, physical strength, diligence, and moral virtues of the Highland Indians. He intersperses his observations with anecdotes, historical and linguistic information, and his theories and opinions on a wide variety of subjects, from the male sex drive to U.S.-Central American relations. Despite the wealth of objective information contained in Land, however, it is richer as a source for the writer Marut-Traven than for Chiapas. It is a fascinating document of his philosophical, political, and historical reflections, ʼgrowing out of his confrontation with revolutionary Mexico and his discovery of Indian community life, which, unlike the life in Western countries, seemed to him free from individual ambition and greed. Land also shows his passionate endorsement of the policies of the revolutionary government and his belief in the future greatness of Mexico and of its Indian citizens.

In the Caoba Cycle, unlike in Land, Traven explores the complexities of Chiapan society. The novels deal with the conditions of life in the Highlands during the dictatorship of Porfirio Díaz: the exploitation of Indian peasants and laborers (The Carreta, Government, and March); the suffering of workers in monterías (The Troza); and, finally, their progression from slave-workers to revolutionaries and their successful military encounter with the defenders of the old regime on their way back to the Highlands (Rebellion and General). In a series of life stories we get to know Chiapan society and socioeconomic relations in this society from different perspectives, those of peasants, workers, traders, shopkeepers, labor contractors, officials, administrators, and owners of monterías. And we meet Indians from different economic groups within Indian society: members of free communities, peons on haciendas, owners of small ranches, and persons earning a living outside agriculture. In these novels, Traven does not focus on the lives of Indians within their autonomous communities, as he does in <u>Land</u>. Instead, he concentrates on relations between the Indian and non-Indian (<u>ladino</u>) society of Chiapas, and on the conditions of integration into <u>ladino</u> society encountered by individual Indians.

No other source equals the Caoba Cycle in its wealth of information on work processes, and no one teaches us respect for manual laborers as Traven does. We learn what it means to earn a living as <u>carreteros</u>, mule drivers, or as workers in the lumber industry. We find out about the workers' strenuous physical labor and their constant struggle against a forbidding environment. And we learn about the skills, mental agility, and endurance workers need in order to do their jobs well--and often in order to survive. We are informed in minute detail about the price that has to be paid by men and animals to bring civilization, in the form of imported material goods, to underdeveloped regions and to provide raw materials for foreign markets. No one who has read the Caoba Cycle will be able to look at a piece of furniture made of mahogany without an acute awareness of the blood, sweat, and pain that went into providing the wood.

The Caoba novels, furthermore, instruct the reader on how the Porfirian dictatorship was translated into a system of economic exploitation of the majority by members of the local elite--policemen, judges, and political officials. Traven also deals extensively with a universal problem in rural Latin America before the population expansion and the accompanying rural underemployment: the recruitment of rural workers in a labor system called "debt-peonage." Journalists like John Kenneth Turner had reported on the horrors of forced labor in the <u>henequen</u> plantations of Yucatán and in the tobacco plantations of Oaxaca, but no one has given as much attention as Traven did, not only to the sufferings of workers, but to the mechanisms of this labor system.

How did Traven get all these insights into conditions in Chiapas before the Revolution? Earlier, it had simply been assumed that the Caoba Cycle was based on Traven's personal observations of Chiapan society during years of residence in the region. According to Traven's widow, Traven-Croves did spend considerable time in Chiapas in his later years, and he loved Chiapas well enough to want his ashes dispersed over its jungles. But before the publication of the first three novels of the Caoba Cycle, we know of only three trips he took to the region. Marut-Traven arrived in Mexico in the summer of 1924. He traveled to Chiapas in the summer of 1926; diaries show that he also took trips there in 1928 and 1930. Unless Marut had been in Mexico before 1907, Marut-

Traven was in Chiapas for the first time in 1926. Land, published in 1928, reflects the enthusiasm of a newcomer to this region, showing Marut-Traven's fascination with Highland Indians and their village society and with plant and animal life. It does not demonstrate any familiarity with the structure of ladino society or any awareness of ladino-Indian conflicts. The only reference to local revolutionary policies is a glowing account of the success of the Industrial School in Tuxtla Gutierrez and its Indian students. Marut-Traven discusses debt-peonage on haciendas in prerevolutionary times, but he makes no mention of the monterías. He also discusses problems with the agrarian reform in general and theorizes about economic development without any reference to regional conflicts. He only touches on the subject in an anecdote about his own clever escape from a potentially dangerous encounter with white guards on hacienda lands who mistook him for a land surveyor. And this at the moment when the institutional revolution had begun in earnest: Governor Vidal—for whom Traven shows admiration—had begun to implement major land reforms; agrarian workers became organized; and labor contracting had come under state control.

For The Carreta and Government, published in 1931, and March published in 1933, Traven already had a wealth of information on every aspect of life in Chiapas at his disposal. One marvels at how he managed to gather the raw material for these books in such a short time and in a few trips, while he was also getting ready for publication Treasure (1927), the 429-page Land (1928), Bridge (1929), The White Rose (1929), and many short stories (1928 and 1930).

It is probable that he was able to collect some information from books and newspaper articles in libraries. Discussions of debt-peonage on haciendas in Chiapas appeared in Mexican newspapers as early as the 1880s. Before 1910, articles in Chiapan newspapers deplored the excesses of "slave trade," that is, the labor contracting for monterías and coffee plantations. In 1907, the governor of Chiapas had issued laws that were supposed to regulate labor contracting. In 1911, there was a report on the depletion of the male population of Bachajon because of forced recruitment for the monterías. Government takes place in a community of Bachajones.

Even if Marut-Traven came to know Chiapas only during the 1920s, he could still observe many remnants of the prerevolutionary period at first hand. For one thing, physical conditions had not changed greatly. Now, sixty years later, airplanes, paved roads, and trucks have revolutionized travel and transportation. But during the 1920s, despite road-building and the appearance of some automobiles, travelers rode on mules or horses, and goods were transported by carreteros, mule drivers, and Indian carriers. In Land, Traven reports at length on the skills and strength of these men and on the horrendous road conditions. As Marut-Traven found out in 1926, the rainy season transformed roads into quagmires, so that automobiles had to be abandoned and travelers could be stranded for days or even weeks until the roads dried up again. It was also still possible to study at first hand the organization of monterías and the work done on them. Agua Azul, for example, which Traven describes as a model montería, was still producing mahogany in the late 1930s. And workers continued to be held against their will in some monterías. As late as 1939 one can find telegraphic appeals for help by montería workers in the presidential papers of President Cárdenas.

Most important, however, in the 1920s Traven would have had access to excellent informants. With a good command of Spanish—though better still, with a good knowledge of Indian languages—and with tact, patience, and sensitivity, Traven could have found Indians who told him about their lives and their experiences in the monterías, and he could have learned their point of view. He could also have made valuable contacts with a number of foreign residents, most probably with Germans or German-Americans, but also with Americans, and he would have profited from their insights into and analyses of local conditions. Some of these people, planters or businessmen, were articulate and observant men, and some had lived in Chiapas since the 1890s.

However Traven may have collected the raw material for his novels, we must ask: How accurate was his description of prerevolutionary economic and social conditions in the Highlands, of the world of the monterías and of revolutionary events?

The historian Thomas Benjamin did research on the monterías and verified the historical accuracy of Traven's account of working conditions, labor recruitment and retention, and the torture of hanging. He thinks that the uprising described in Rebellion and General was based on an uprising on the montería Las Tinieblas in 1904. Unlike the revolt Traven describes, this rebellion was crushed by rurales. The administrators were prosecuted in a district court for their abuses of workers, but the result of the trial is unknown.[1] The Mexican historian García de Leon thinks that Rebellion is based on uprisings in 1912, particularly on monterías belonging to Romano & Cia., which were repressed by troops from Tabasco and Ocosingo.[2] Benjamin shows that most monterías were liberated from the outside between 1913 and 1915 by General Luis Felipe Domínguez and his legendary Usumacinta Brigade from Tabasco, although some owners were able to move their work force across the border to Guatemala. Domínguez then decreed the first reform labor laws, and in October 1914 the Carranzista government of Chiapas canceled all debts of workers. Nevertheless, work on the monterías was resumed in 1915, stimulated by the demand for mahogany for warships in World War I.

It would be misleading to conclude from General that the success of the revolutionaries there stands for the actual course of the revolution in Chiapas. Traven clearly deals only with the successful rebellion of one small group of men against their immediate oppressors and their victory over the first military detachment sent against them. His account breaks off before their return to their homes in the Highlands, before their confrontation with the dominant groups we got to know so well in Government. Traven's revolutionaries settle in an isolated community, Solipaz, after learning that rebellions like their own had occurred in many parts of the nation and that Porfirio Díaz had fallen from power. The future of Traven's revolutionaries is left open, but having proven that they could be masters of their own destiny, they seem confident of being able to find solutions to any further problems. Knowing from the works of Thomas Benjamin and other historians about the course of the revolution in Chiapas, one cannot help but worry about the fate of the inhabitants of Solipaz. Unlike in northern Mexico, the revolution was imposed on Chiapas by outsiders, by a Carranzista military government sent from the north in 1914. It decreed revolutionary legislation, such as the cancellation of all workers' debts; and, in some instances, it removed peons from haciendas by military force. But the government was unable to enforce its laws; it was not even able to gain effective military control over the state. In most districts, except for the coffee region on the Pacific, a bloody civil war raged for several years—it was worst in the regions adjacent to Tabasco. The rural population suffered bitterly from mistreatment by the warring factions, including the revolutionary government forces. They suffered from famine and from the "pacification" of the countryside by the Carranzistas, who forced them to move to large settlements. Reactionaries calling themselves "Villistas" fought the revolutionary government. They came to power in elections in 1920 as "Obregonistas." Only after the election of Governor Vidal, in 1924, did a revolutionary government install itself successfully.

So far, relatively little is known about economic condi-

tions in the Highlands or about Indian-_ladino_ relations
before 1930, since most anthropologists have tended to study
Highland Indians as members of ahistorical, isolated communities. The works of researchers like Henri Favre, Robert
Wasserstrom, and Jan Rus, who deal with economic issues in
their historical context, confirm what Traven describes:
the vital role of Indians in the regional economy and the
complex ties between _ladino_ and Indian societies.[3] In my
own ongoing research on the agrarian export economy in
Chiapas, I am uncovering data from many sources which support Traven's insights. Let me give an example dealing with
labor recruitment, the so-called _enganche_.

Until recently, historians considered debt-peonage a form
of slavery in everything but name; it was universally used
by landowners and entrepreneurs in order to secure cheap
labor after the abolition of slavery and forced Indian labor
following Latin American independence from Spain. The standard account of _enganche_ is as follows: Labor recruiters
would entrap ignorant, illiterate Indians during fiestas by
advancing money to them and having them sign contracts while
the Indians were getting drunk. When sober, Indians found
themselves in debt that had to be worked off. From that
moment they were "hooked" for life, since employers made
sure that their debts increased rather than diminished and
that they never earned enough wages to pay off their debts.

Only recently has a more complex picture of debt-peonage
emerged. Mounting evidence shows that debt did not invari-
ably mean lifelong exploitation of rural workers and that
Indians were not always defenseless victims. In my own
research on the coffee industry in Chiapas, for example, I
found that most indebted Highland Indians came to the coffee
fincas for a limited time, worked off their debts, and
returned to their villages. Planters needed a large number
of workers only during harvesttime; to keep workers against
their will and to feed them for the whole year were not in
the economic interests of the planters, many of whom were
Germans. There is also evidence that Indian villagers considered money advances (debt) a customary right, without
which they refused to come to work in the coffee harvest.

Traven makes a strong case that Indians were not simply
passive victims of exploiters, although they were surrounded
by greedy labor contractors and a repressive social system.
They knew the difference between work on the _monterías_ and
work in the coffee region, and they considered work on the
coffee plantations, as hard and poorly paid as it was, a
desirable option to earn money. They did earn cash there,
they were free to return after having paid off their debts,
and they did return to the Highlands with cash in hand--like

Celso in <u>March</u>. The Indian chief in <u>Government</u>, in whose
community land had become scarce, considered employment for
his young people as peons on new plantations a desirable
opportunity, even though he was aware of the danger of their
being detained for life. According to Traven, Indians also
knew that to sell their labor was the one option they had to
obtain cash for a marriage, for the purchase of a pig, or
for an emergency, whether it be illness, death, or a jail
fine. Traven makes it clear that in a corrupt system there
was ample opportunity for <u>ladinos</u> to create emergency situations for Indians, such as doctors' charging high fees for
medical services or court officials sentencing Indians to
jail on phony charges. Traven also points to yet another
problem for Indians, which was the periodic contractions in
the labor market. Indians could not always find wage labor,
even if they looked for it. Celso was forced to seek work
on the <u>monterías</u> because there were no jobs on the coffee
plantations; he ended up with the worst exploiters, the
Montellanos, because no new workers were needed in the well-
administered <u>monterías</u>.

Traven explores the complex role of <u>enganche</u> in the society of Chiapas. He makes the case that employers and
labor contractors were far from being the only exploiters of
workers. Celso was cheated of his earnings not by coffee
planters, but at home in the Highlands by local <u>ladinos</u>.
Exploitation in connection with the <u>enganche</u> system involved
the entire <u>ladino</u> society. Not only landowners, entrepreneurs, labor contractors, and their assistants, but government officials, professionals, alcohol producers, and
tradesmen as well stood to gain from the work of Indian
laborers. Labor recruiters played a strategic role in the
regional economy—that of bankers. As long as there was a
demand for workers, they would advance money even to the
poorest man, since he was able to pay off his debt with
labor. Consequently, landowners in financial difficulties
could get cash by making their peons pay off their debts;
corrupt policemen and judges could collect money fines from
destitute Indians; and the state could collect fees for
labor contracts from workers. Although some of Traven's
assertions have yet to be tested with data from other
sources, his analysis of <u>enganche</u> already forces researchers
to formulate new questions about this labor system.

Even if Traven's information on Chiapas should not always be
correct, and even if he should not have been able, after
all, as an outsider and non-Indian, to understand the Indians' mentality and to present it correctly, the Caoba
Cycle is still an important source for social scientists.

As a matter of fact, it is an important source for anyone interested in the fate of rural people in the Third World. The importance lies less in the description of past events and previous social conditions in Chiapas than in Traven's general approach to his subject and in the issues he raises. He forces us to consider problems in Latin America—universal problems like poverty, exploitation, dictatorship, modernization, or revolution—from his perspective.

Traven relates the eternal story of human suffering and the exploitation of man by man within the framework of rules imposed by an economic system that controls us all—a world economy dominated by capitalism. In this system, the exploiters of Indian workers are oppressed too. Even the Montellanos, the prototypes of exploiters, are haunted by creditors and live in fear of losing their investment, the fruit of their lives' work. Traven illustrated with the story about the mahogany industry what consequences the inclusion of a developing nation in the world economic system had. He connects us, the consumers in the industrialized nations, directly with the debt-slaves in the _monterías_, and he spells out our involvement: As long as we buy products made from mahogany, Indians will have to do dangerous, backbreaking work to produce it, unless machines can be developed which do the work for them. Benjamin's research confirms Traven's analysis. Not the labor legislation of revolutionary governments, but the demand for mahogany in the world market and technology determined the fate of the Indians. Whenever the world demand for mahogany or the price of wood sank, fewer workers were recruited in the Highlands. The hard labor of _montería_ workers did not cease with revolutionary laws; it ceased only when machines, which could do the men's work in the jungles, were introduced in the 1930s. If our consciences as consumers seem clear because we do not own mahogany furniture, we only have to think of tropical products like bananas, cheap textiles, industrial minerals, diamonds, and even fruits and vegetables from California. The basic issue remains the same, and so does our direct link with the most lowly worker in developing nations.

Yet Traven is far from making a case against economic development. What he does is show how unevenly the benefits and costs of modernization are distributed. He has no romantic illusions about traditional agrarian society. In _Land_ he warns readers against idealizing Indian communes, and he considers conditions even in the worst industrial slums preferable—for everyone but the Indians themselves— to the harsh living conditions in Indian villages. In _Land_ he also argues that not the agrarian reform but only industrialization could offer a better future to rural Mexicans. In the Caoba Cycle, Traven makes us aware of how difficult it was in traditional agrarian society to scrape together a living that would mean more than having the sheer necessities for survival. He looks at the problems people had in making a living from the perspectives of members of different classes. The limitations of poor soil forced Indian peasants of independent communities to seek an income outside their villages, as artisans, mule drivers, carriers, and seasonal laborers. Small traders braved week-long journeys through jungles in search of meager markets. Members of the middle class attached themselves to the few who controlled political power in order to secure a livelihood from patronage and the spoils of government. It was a system of crude exploitation in which all groups lived off the small surplus produced by the peasantry. They extracted their surplus by fair and foul means, through high prices for consumer goods, low wages, fees, fines, taxes, unpaid labor, and simple cheating. The account of don Gabriel's career shows that as government official in Bachajon he was able to extract only a small income from the villagers in his control, even though he had political patronage and used every possible trick or opportunity. Don Gabriel's opportunities to make money from Indians increased radically with the development of the export economy. He collected taxes for the right-of-way from groups of workers on their way to the plantations, and he became a labor recruiter himself, getting off to a good start by calling in the debts of villagers.

The increased demand for labor in the export economy opened a whole new field of profitable economic endeavor--enganche--for members of the small rural middle class like don Gabriel. All groups, including Indian peasants, had greater economic opportunities. But economic development also widened the range of possibilities for the exploitation of the peasantry by the dominant groups. Knowing that debt-peonage is a thing of the past, at least in Mexico, does not mean that we can put our minds to rest and assume that exploitation disappeared with it. In the modern world economic system, developing nations are still assigned the role of producers of raw materials for the industrialized nations. Exploitation of the lower classes is widespread in Mexico today, even if it no longer takes the form of debt-peonage. Exploitation is far worse in Central America, and the present governments in El Salvador and Guatemala surpass the worst excesses of the Porfirian dictatorship, with advice and financial assistance from the current United States government.

Traven also raises the issue of racism as an additional
factor in the exploitation of Indians. In the Caoba Cycle
we get to know the Indian protagonists first and foremost as
human beings with whom we can identify, whose motives and
perceptions of reality we learn to understand. Only then do
we get to know them as Indians. Still, we are always made
aware of their specific difficulties as Indians in their
relations to non-Indian society, to the world of the ladinos. Double standards based on race have not only been
accepted by ladinos as a fact of life, but by Indians themselves. Since physical racial differences between the two
groups are minimal, the main distinctions are in language,
education, and mental attitudes. An Indian like Andrés, who
becomes literate, speaks Spanish, and works as a carretero,
turns into a ladino in the eyes of everyone but himself--
since he remains Indian in his own consciousness. Here
Traven touches on the issue of integration, and he sketches
some ways in which it could be achieved. In Land, he has a
vision of racial integration, the mixing between Indians and
non-Indians to create a new race. This new race would
inherit some of the Indians' attitudes towards life--herein
lay Traven's greatest hope for the future greatness of
Mexico. In General, he points to a different method, that
of education, combined with political and economic revolution. Literacy would allow the Indian villager to gain an
awareness of the world outside the constraints of village
culture and an awareness of a wider range of choices. Economic and political revolution would make those choices real
and desirable. Each individual would have to gain an awareness of his choices by himself, on his own terms. The terms
of integration could not be prescribed; the choices could
not be made for him. Is Traven here putting his finger on
one reason for the consistent failure of even the most well-
meaning Indian agencies to achieve integration, in Mexico as
well as in the United States?

Another course of action that cannot be prescribed or
imposed is revolution. Traven shows by the example of
montería workers what changes in mental attitudes have to
occur to make slave-workers rebel against their oppressors
and for them to become revolutionaries. In his discussion
of revolution, Traven raises perhaps the most crucial--and
certainly the most relevant--issue in Central America today.
He also alludes to a fundamental problem in agrarian revolutions.

The revolutionary goals of Traven's peasants turned montería workers turned rebels is "tierra y libertad." As
Traven explains, for them this means enough land to grow
crops in peace to make them self-sufficient and freedom from

outside interference. He makes clear in General that these goals might not have universal appeal to rural people: They might not be shared by peons. Most peons might consider themselves better off than peasants in independent villages, since they would enjoy the relative security of the haciendas--sufficient land to grow food or food rations. John Womack's study of the "classic" agrarian revolution, that of the Zapatistas in Morelos, confirms Traven's interpretation of the cry "tierra y libertad" and the attitudes of peons. Zapata's revolution was that of independent villagers robbed of their lands by expanding sugar producers. They were not interested in gaining control of the Mexican state, but in having their lands returned to them, in being self-sufficient, and in arranging their lives as they saw fit in their own region. By and large, peons on sugar haciendas refused to join the Zapatistas and instead sided with their employers.[4]

The problem in agrarian revolutions is that, despite the peasants' minimal demands for material comfort, it is very difficult indeed for them to reach their goal of self-sufficiency and the freedom to arrange their own affairs as they see fit. Land and water are limited resources, and even revolutions and agrarian reforms cannot resolve basic conflicts over their use. Not everyone in society can be a self-sufficient peasant. To feed nonpeasants, peasants have to produce a surplus for the market, or some land has to be used for large-scale agriculture, and workers are needed for the crop production. Either option prevents peasants from having "tierra y libertad." Either as producers or part-time workers they are drawn into a market economy and become subject to economic and political forces they cannot control. Or oil might be found one day on their land, as is happening in Chiapas today, and they might have to give their subsistence base to PEMEX in the national interest--as a source for much needed foreign exchange. And then we are back to the conflicts Traven discusses in The White Rose. Only now the part of the villain is not played by an American Oil company, but by the Mexican government. The most arduous tasks of any government concerned with the plight of the mass of its rural people are: (1) the creation of desirable economic and social alternatives to subsistence agriculture; and (2) the protection of peasants against a new, more complex but equally vicious system of exploitation. The results of the agrarian reforms in Mexico show that very often the price paid by those communities which received enough land to support themselves was a strong dependence on the state and its officials. But many rural people in Mexico never got sufficient land to satisfy their most basic needs, and they were--and are--unable to find sources of income outside of agriculture. The urban labor market cannot absorb them. Their last, desperate option-- emigration to the United States in search of work--is becoming increasingly difficult. Many U.S. citizens favor policies that would prevent the entry of these economic refugees, although most of their own ancestors had come from Europe for the same reasons.

Another aspect of these agrarian conflicts concerns us, as American citizens, directly. Traven's interpretation of "tierra y libertad" can be applied to current events in Central America. People in Guatemala and El Salvador are struggling against oppressive regimes. The people of Nicaragua have done what Traven's revolutionaries set out to do, namely, to defeat an oppressive dictatorship, and now they are wrestling with the problems of how to build a better society. They have been searching for a social system that would fit their particular needs without outside interference. But, as all of us who follow current events in Central America know, a good deal of interference does come from the United States.

In short, Traven's works on Chiapas are not only a most valuable and stimulating source on Chiapas and a challenge for researchers, but they are also a key to a better understanding of the problems of rural people in Latin America. One could wish that the Caoba Cycle were made required reading in high schools and colleges in the United States. Why should the next generation of Americans not learn about human suffering and human dignity from Traven--and at the same time learn to become more sensitive to the problems of their Latin cousins south of the border? Perhaps reading Traven would make young Americans more indignant about injustice than the present generation is, and, as citizens of a democracy, more courageous and insistent in their protests against policies of their own government whenever these policies ignore the plight of the majority of people in our hemisphere and their needs and aspirations.

Notes

1. Benjamin, unpublished manuscript. See also Benjamin, 1981.
2. García de Leon, 1979, 57-87.
3. Favre, 1971; Favre, 1965, 63-134; Wasserstrom, 1983; Rus and Wasserstrom, 1980, 466-78.
4. Womack, 1968.

THE RECEPTION OF B. TRAVEN IN THE GERMAN DEMOCRATIC REPUBLIC

H. D. Tschörtner

The novels and short stories that were published under the name of B. Traven in the years 1925 to 1955 have found a widespread and varied reception in the German Democratic Republic. They were issued by several publishing companies in forty different editions and numerous reprints. Traven's epic work is regarded as that of a progressive writer of international rank who addressed his works to repressed proletarians. At its best, it belongs to the permanent collection of world literature.

Traven's first Collected Works, consisting of thirteen volumes, was based on the texts of the first editions. It included critical commentaries and appeared in the GDR from 1964 to 1972. The Berlin company Volk und Welt became the author's regular publisher, and the first three Traven novels were published by them in 1954. Since then, this company has continued to take editorial care of his works in a diligent and meticulous manner.

The publishing business in the GDR for the most part had to be built up anew after the destruction of fascism. The material devastation was great, and only a few older companies could resume production. Numerous new companies were founded. A large task had to be accomplished with modest means: German and international literature outlawed by fascism had to be published, as well as the fiction written in exile and the current literary production.

So it was no wonder that Traven's books were initially put aside. They had already found a large circulation in the Weimar Republic through the Büchergilde Gutenberg, which was controlled by trade unions, and they were best remembered for their effect on proletarian readers. One book that was not put aside was The Carreta, an excerpt from which appeared especially for children in 1946 and 1950.

It was understood, however, that Traven's works were to be made available to the working people in the GDR, although the majority of this new audience hardly recognized the author's name any longer. Thus, the publication and distribution of Traven's ideas to this audience did not occur without difficulties and resistance.

When in 1954 it became known that two companies planned to publish Traven's books, the response was less than enthusiastic. In B̲ö̲r̲s̲e̲n̲b̲l̲a̲t̲t̲ f̲ü̲r̲ d̲e̲n̲ d̲e̲u̲t̲s̲c̲h̲e̲n̲ B̲u̲c̲h̲h̲a̲n̲d̲e̲l̲, the trade journal of publishers and booktraders, the plans to issue Traven's works were regarded simply as a mistake, and people were warned about "the controversial works of the even more controversial B. Traven" (32/1954). A letter about this controversy was turned down for publication by the editors, as it would have caused a discussion about Traven that was regarded as "unnecessary and not productive." As a result, the daily newspapers kept silent after the publication of the first volumes, which consisted of the novels T̲h̲e̲ C̲a̲r̲r̲e̲t̲a̲, M̲a̲r̲c̲h̲, and T̲h̲e̲ T̲r̲o̲z̲a̲ (Verlag Volk und Welt), as well as T̲h̲e̲ C̲o̲t̲t̲o̲n̲ P̲i̲c̲k̲e̲r̲s̲ (Verlag der Nation). Thus, the author B. Traven burst like a flash of lightning into the consciousness of the literary public of the GDR.

Of course, one couldn't avoid a discussion about these books or this secretive author who produced so much that was contradictory and puzzling. The well-known author Ludwig Renn, who had lived in exile in Mexico, first tried to promote Traven's work with his epilogue to T̲h̲e̲ C̲o̲t̲t̲o̲n̲ P̲i̲c̲k̲e̲r̲s̲. Renn showed great understanding of Traven's peculiarities and emphasized the strongly progressive effect of these books on the Western world and on Mexico. Traven's undeniable anarchist tendencies would have only minimal effect, Renn felt, and could hardly impair the value of the novels. Renn stated that he had met the author in Mexicoo but had respected his anonymity. Later he retracted that statement.

In D̲i̲e̲ B̲u̲c̲h̲b̲e̲s̲p̲r̲e̲c̲h̲u̲n̲g̲, a monthly book review, Helmut Topp introduced all four volumes in detail (1/1955), mapping out their anarchist-syndicalist tendencies and ideological weaknesses from the Marxist point of view. But he also underlined the "point of view of the proletarian class" and declared that the positive qualities predominated. The distinct reference to the dictatorship of Porfirio Díaz, and also to the time period of the action in the Caoba novels, was remarkable.

A proper Traven discussion, which proved itself to be necessary and productive, developed in S̲o̲n̲n̲t̲a̲g̲, the weekly magazine of the Kulturbund. The discussion started with an article by the author Wolfgang Joho: "Traven--Insights and Errors." A vehement polemic followed: "Traven--Polished Anew?" Written by a militant young critic, this article is more or less characterized by dogmatic accusations and name-calling, including "pacemaker of cosmopolitanism" and "spoiled enemy of socialism." His literary objections to Traven's work include its "decentralized composition" and "overweight of the descriptive."

Next came a "Critique of Two Critiques" by Joachim Lutz, who also dealt with Traven's nationality and the context of his text; then a series, "Readers Give Their Opinion"; and, finally, another contribution by Wolfgang Joho, "Traven, Capitalism and the Critics" (Sonntag, 1955, no. 10-12, 15, 24). This extensive discussion, which was carried on with expert knowledge, found great approval with friends of literature and the participating institutions. Thus, the foundation for additional Traven editions was created.

Verlag der Nation published Treasure in 1955; Volk und Welt presented the final volumes of the Caoba Cycle, Rebellion and General, in 1956 and 1957, respectively. A third company, the union publishing house Tribune, contributed two books in 1957: one of Mexican short stories, Der Banditendoktor; and Traven's first novel The Death Ship, his early, worldwide success.

One year later Volk und Welt published a first edition, the volume of short stories Der dritte Gast, which had impressive illustrations by Rudolf Strzelczyk. This volume was published at the same time and in the same format in the Federal Republic of Germany and in Switzerland. Up to that time, ten books by Traven had been rapidly made available to the reading public. The most important works were issued, which meant that the publishers had caught up to the international edition. So the first stage of Traven's reception in the GDR could be considered ended.

When publication was interrupted, Rolf Recknagel, assistant professor of literature at Leipzig, started his research for a biography of Ret Marut. Bit by bit he collected the material proving that Marut was identical with Traven. His statements were at first heavily disputed. The distribution of the so-called American biography by the BT-Mitteilungen and the authorized representative of the author, Josef Wieder, irritated the critics. Aslan Norval, offered as a recent Traven novel, seemed to be suspect. The topic was astonishing, and the manuscript was rejected by different publishers because it lacked literary quality and included rather graphic eroticism.

Rolf Recknagel also doubted the authenticity of this book at first, especially after it was revealed that the former proofreader of the Büchergilde, Johannes Schönherr, who was living in Leipzig at the time, had worked on the manuscript and had contributed the essential Traven elements. Recknagel did not let himself become irritated. He checked, corrected, and expanded his material continually.

Through a long series of publications, Recknagel made a breakthrough in the early sixties, starting with "Secrecy and Business" in Neue Deutsche Literatur (1961, No. 1 and 2) and "Swallowed by the Jungle: Tracing the Life of B. Traven" (1962, No. 9). Six extensive articles appeared in 1962 in the popular magazine Wochenpost under the title "The Secret of B. Traven" (No. 28-33). Finally, the magazine for literary history Weimarer Beiträge published his study "The Rebel B. Traven: An Evaluation of His Most Important Works" (4/1963). Anna Seghers expressed her admiration for Recknagel in a letter and congratulated him on his effort. Recknagel received the Heinrich Heine Award of the Ministry of Culture for the book B. Traven: Contributions to His Biography, which was published by Reclam in Leipzig in 1966. It is now in its third edition and has been enlarged and revised. Later Recknagel's book was accepted as his dissertation.

In the meantime, the dissatisfaction of the Verlag Volk und Welt with the texts of its editions had continued to grow. Recknagel had proved in detail how the author or his representative was obliterating the traces of his identity through deletions and changes. The accusation of text manipulation had been raised already in the Sonntag discussion. It could be said, however, that text revision was an author's right, and that it was definitely not unusual for an author to make changes and corrections with each new edition. Also, the publisher contacted the author and agreed on occasional changes. More and more, however, the opinion was growing stronger that these books should be published with the exact text of the first editions--perhaps as volumes of an edition of collected works. In 1962 Verlag Volk und Welt also took The Cotton Pickers into its series. It was, however, continuing its preparations for an edition of collected works with reliable texts.

This edition would be started with the epic chronicle of the Caoba Cycle, which undoubtedly constitutes the author's main work. Five of these novels had already been published; the only volume missing up to this time was the second one, Government. To bridge this gap and give the action continuity, the last chapter of Government was added to the first edition of The Carreta. And so, the second volume of that series was simply dropped at first.

Within the Caoba Cycle Government has a very specific and important function. It not only shows the development of the montería agents, but, most important, it describes in detail the political circumstances during the dictatorship of Porfirio Díaz, on which the whole action of the book is based. In the other Caoba novels the time of the action is only hinted at. (The exception is General, which clearly reveals itself as a historical novel.) Traven could exclude time-specific facts from the other Caoba novels because they had been sufficiently described in <u>Government</u>. Thus, the grotesque situation arose that several attacks against the conditions under the dictatorship of Díaz in these volumes were (so to speak) hanging in a vacuum and appeared to represent general situations. This was especially so since the publisher did not give any hints to the time of the novels' action on the inside covers of the books.

The Selected Works in Single Editions, based on the texts of the first edition, was started in 1964 with the first GDR publication of <u>Government</u>. It contains an epilogue that shows the context of the series, outlines the historical foundation, and deals with the creation of the first two novels. In the following years, the other volumes appeared. Since two novels form a closer thematic unit, further commentaries were included in the fourth volume, <u>The Troza</u> and the sixth volume, <u>General</u>. Epilogues were also written for <u>The Cotton Pickers</u>, <u>Treasure</u>, and <u>Bridge</u>, when they were published in the Collected Works. By 1967 nine volumes had been presented with the original texts of the first editions.

Also due was an edition of the short stories, which presented a more difficult task. Here the second, expanded edition of the collection <u>Der Busch</u> from 1930, as well as the first edition of <u>Sonnenschöpfung</u> and <u>Macario</u>, proved to be valuable sources.

But immense problems arose for a series of later stories. They could be found scattered in magazines and anthologies, and some had not been published in German at all. At last, seven additional prose texts were successfully combined under the title <u>Mexikanische Geschichten</u>. Four of these appeared in German for the first time; previously unpublished was <u>Der Silberdollar</u>. <u>Feierlichkeit etwas verzögert</u> had to be translated from the English.

The division of the stories into two volumes had an internal and an external reason. The external reason had to do with the amount of the textual material (which included an appendix of variant readings, an epilogue, and a bibliography with detailed information about all of Traven's short stories). This would have led to a very extensive volume not in keeping with the format of the previous editions. More important was the internal reason, i.e., the ten-year break beginning after the Indian legend <u>Sonnenschöpfung</u> from 1936. <u>Macario</u> or <u>Der dritte Gast</u> is the most extensive and most important. In comparison, all others are clearly inferior and can be regarded only as entertaining literature that is fairly well written.

In 1968 there appeared a rich appendix of variant readings

with the enlarged version of The Night Visitor, which also
included some translations of changed Spanish and English
versions. These features and the careful commentaries make
this edition (published by Werner Sellhorn) unsurpassed.

The Collected Works was concluded in the following year
with two major works. The Death Ship, first published in
the GDR in 1957, had been present in a slightly adapted and
shortened version until the Reclam edition appeared in 1967.
It then appeared in 1970 with the text of the first edition
and a larger epilogue in both the Collected Works and the
Library of World Literature. The last gap was closed in
1972 with the novel The White Rose, which was published as
the seventh book by the Büchergilde Gutenberg. It also
stood in the center of Tucholsky's essay about Traven.

The White Rose was the last work before the Caoba Cycle
and was already foreshadowing it. Traven's previous books
were set in the present or, at least, the recent past, but
this work we can date as dealing historically with the time
after the overthrow of the dictator Díaz. This was exactly
what had not been noted, not even by Tucholsky. Traven's
exciting portrayal of a great economic crisis pointed to the
Great Crash, which suddenly developed at the end of 1929
(i.e., after the book was finished). Some objections and
reservations concerning The White Rose could be settled by
the historical classification and contemporary information
that were given in an epilogue. Also, the astonishing
realism of this book cannot be overlooked: the fight about
crude oil, the relations between workers and capitalists,
and between a highly developed nation and a weak, developing
country. The effectiveness of this book can be seen in the
story of the film based on it.

With this publication an important editorial undertaking
was concluded, as was the second stage of Traven's reception
in the GDR. Altogether, eleven novels and two volumes of
short stories, including eight commentaries, appeared with
the authentic texts of the first editions and in the same
format, designed by Professor Werner Klemke, one of the
GDR's leading artists. The name "Selected Works" for this
undertaking appears to be almost too modest; in reality it
is doubtless a "Collected Works."

Unfortunately, the editorial situation does not allow Volk
und Welt to offer these volumes constantly. The demand is
so high that each new edition, each reprint, is sold out
immediately. As the central company for international literature, Volk und Welt has to consider the whole breadth of
world literature in this century. So it is difficult for
the company to make decisions about favorite authors who
have written a large number of books of relatively equal

value. The "competition" between books already published
and new books means that only one title of an author can be
reprinted each year. In regard to Traven this means that,
with equal consideration for all his works, each volume
could appear only once every twelve years. Therefore, a
collector would have to wait twelve years to acquire the
whole Collected Works--undoubtedly an unpleasant situation.

Other publications with large circulations have helped to
satisfy the high demand for Traven works. A book company,
Buchclub 65, so far has published four Traven novels for its
members: The Cotton Pickers, General, The White Rose, and
Treasure. We have already mentioned the edition of The
Death Ship published in Reclams Universal-Bibliothek. In
addition, a reasonably priced series of paper-back books
called Roman-Zeitung had a wide effect. Similar to a pocket-
book series, it is published monthly, and the price is only
eighty pfennigs. In this series four Traven titles were
published: General, Treasure, The Carreta, and Bridge. The
edition of Bridge was No. 279 of 1973. It was a special
interest to the friends of the author as it was not the
text of the first edition that was published in the GDR, but
it was the translation of the (so-called) American original
edition, which contained a hundred pages more. The translation was done by Werner Preusser and authorized by the
author. So an interesting variant reading was presented.

At this point it should be mentioned that Traven's work is
also available in braille and on tapes. In 1975 the German
Central Library for the Blind at Leipzig published a large-
letter edition for the visually impaired. This was a photo-
mechanical reprint of the Volk und Welt edition of The White
Rose. The Cassette Catalogue of the Louis Braille House at
Leipzig contains eleven Traven titles spoken on tape, and
apparently only The Cotton Pickers is a shortened version.
The length of these tapes and cassettes, which are read by
well-known actors, extends from 268 up to 756 minutes. The
short stories are missing, as they always come up in a
series of international prose. There is, however, an edition in braille of the two volumes of short stories that
were published in Volk und Welt's Collected Works. Also,
six novels were published in four to six braille books each.
Visually impaired and blind people can borrow these tapes
and the braille books at the Central Library at Leipzig.

The most recent edition of Traven was the result of dissatisfaction with the state of existing versions. There was
also the wish to satisfy the high demand for Traven's books.
Eleven volumes of the Collected Works were printed together
in five large-format paperbacks. A fairly high number of
copies were printed within a short period of time, and the

collective title given to this series was <u>Romane</u>. Commentaries were neglected; included was only a short text "about the author." The first volume, consisting of <u>The Death Ship</u> and <u>The White Rose</u>, was followed by a volume containing the three Mexican books: <u>The Cotton Pickers</u>, <u>Bridge</u>, and <u>Treasure</u>. Each of the last three volumes contained two novels of the Caoba Cycle.

Such a division could also be the model for a new edition of collected works that Volk und Welt is envisioning. In preparation is a supplement with excerpts of <u>Land</u>; this one cannot be edited as a whole. This supplement would also include essays from the magazine <u>Die Büchergilde</u>, parts of the manuscript <u>Die Kunst der Indianer</u> (The Art of the Indians), a selection of letters by Traven, and a supplement of fictional texts or excerpts (also from <u>Aslan Norval</u>). Volk und Welt also wants to publish a selection of letters to the Büchergilde Gutenberg. Here they are, however, dependent on the publication by the addressee or his successor, i.e., the Büchergilde Frankfurt/Main.

An overview of Traven's reception in the GDR would be incomplete without mentioning the facsimile print of Ret Marut's magazine <u>Der Ziegelbrenner</u>. This was published in 1967 by Verlag Edition Leipzig with an epilogue by Rolf Recknagel, who made this important source available for the first time. The short story <u>Khundar</u>, published in 1920 in the last number of <u>Ziegelbrenner</u>, was included in the anthology <u>Die Traumflöte: Märchen, Grotesken, Legenden und andere nicht geheure Geschichten</u> (1900–1945). This anthology was published by Ruth Greuner and the company Der Morgen in 1979. Verlag der Nation prepared a selection of Ret Marut's stories and essays under the title <u>Zeitrechnung</u> for publication; Rolf Recknagel made the selection and wrote the accompanying commentary.

Of course, the discussion about Traven's nationality and language was not neglected in the GDR either. It had already played a role in the <u>Sonntag</u> discussion mentioned previously, when Wolfgang Joho was asked how he could be so sure as to include Traven's works among German literature. With reference to the <u>BT-Mitteilungen</u> Traven was called an English author of North American ancestry. As we can see on the inside covers of the first edition of <u>The Carreta</u>, the publisher at the time still called him the "Great Unknown" of Anglo-Saxon literature. Rolf Recknagel came into conflict with the copyright owner because of his statements about the identity of B. Traven and Ret Marut. Volk und Welt strictly kept out of this conflict in order not to endanger relations with the contractual partner. So in the index of countries in Volk und Welt's catalogues and in its

bibliography, Traven could be found under "Nationality Unclear." After his death, he was listed under Mexico, since
he had become a Mexican citizen in 1951 and so many of his
works had Mexican themes. Basically, Volk und Welt always
had the opinion that all bibliographical research, all known
dates and those yet to be known, could impair neither the
quality nor the literary value of the books published under
the name of B. Traven.

It was Volk und Welt's aim from the beginning and it will
be their aim in the future to take editorial care of Traven's books and thus make his works available in various
reliable editions to new readers in the German Democratic
Republic.

B. Traven's Work in the German Democratic Republic
Bibliography of Editions

1. Der Karren. Berlin: Volk und Welt, 1954. 352 S. Lw.
   6,40 M - Nachauflagen: 1955, 63.
2. Der Marsch ins Reich der Caoba. Berlin: Volk und Welt,
   1954. 402 S. Lw. 6,40 M - Nachauflagen: 1955, 63.
3. Troza. Berlin: Volk und Welt, 1954. 369 S. Lw. 6,40 M
   - Nachauflage: 1955.
4. Die Baumwollpflücker. Nachwort Ludwig Renn. Berlin:
   Verlag der Nation, 1954. 274 S. Lw 6,40 M - Nachauflage: 1956.
5. Der Schatz der Sierra Madre. Berlin: Verlag der Nation,
   1955. 317 S. Lw 6,40 M.
6. Die Rebellion der Gehenkten. Berlin: Volk und Welt,
   1956. 422 S. Lw. 6,80 M - Nachauflagen: 1957, 58, 58,
   60.
7. Ein General kommt aus dem Dschungel. Berlin: Volk und
   Welt, 1957. 398 S. Lw. 6,90 M - Nachauflagen: 1961,
   64.
8. Der Banditendoktor. Mexikanische Erzählungen. Berlin:
   Tribüne, 1957. 210 S. Lw. 6,25 M.
9. Das Totenschiff. Die Geschichte eines amerikanischen
   Seemanns. Berlin: Tribüne, 1957. 305 S. Lw. 6,50 M.
10. Der dritte Gast und andere Erzählungen. Illustrationen
    Rudolf Strzelczyk. Berlin: Volk und Welt, 1958. 184
    S. Lw. 5,40 M.
11. Ein General kommt aus dem Dschungel. Berlin: Volk und
    Welt, 1960. 159 S. Br. 0,80 M = Roman-Zeitung 133.
12. Die Baumwollpflücker. Berlin: Volk und Welt, 1962. 353
    S. Lw. 6,80 M.
13. Das Totenschiff. Die Geschichte eines amerikanischen
    Seemanns. Berlin: Volk und Welt, 1962. 368 S. Lw.
    7,40 M - Nachauflage: 1964.

14. Regierung. Nachwort Werner Sellhorn. Berlin: Volk und Welt, 1964. 387 S. Lw. 7,80 M = Ausgewählte Werke in Einzelausgaben - Nachauflagen: 1965, 76.
15. Der Schatz der Sierra Madre. Berlin: Volk und Welt, 1964. 126 S. Br. 0,80 M = Roman-Zeitung (Sonderheft).
16. Der Karren. Berlin: Volk und Welt, 1965. 337 S. Lw. 6,40 = Ausgewählte Werke in Einzelausgaben - Nachauflage: 1975.
17. Der Marsch ins Reich der Caoba. Berlin: Volk und Welt, 1965. 387 S. Lw. 6,40 M = Ausgewählte Werke in Einzelausgaben - Nachauflage: 1978.
18. Die Troza. Nachwort o.N. Berlin: Volk und Welt, 1965. 367 S. Lw. 6,40 M = Ausgewählte Werke in Einzelausgaben - Nachauflage: 1979.
19. Die Baumwollpflücker. Der Wobbly. Nachwort Werner Sellhorn. Berlin: Volk und Welt, 1965. 282 S. Lw. 6,80 M = Ausgewählte Werke in Einzelausgaben.
20. Die Baumwollpflücker. Der Wobbly. Nachwort Werner Sellhorn. Berlin: Buchclub 65, 1966. 282 S. Lw. 7,00 M.
21. Die Rebellion der Gehenkten. Berlin: Volk und Welt, 1966. 422 S. Lw. 6,80 M = Ausgewählte Werke in Einzelausgaben - Nachauflage: 1969.
22. Der Schatz der Sierra Madre. Nachwort Peter Lübbe. Berlin: Volk und Welt, 1966. 312 S. Lw. 7,20 M = Ausgewählte Werke in Einzelausgaben - Nachauflagen: 1969, 72.
23. Die Brücke im Dschungel. Nachwort Peter Lübbe. Berlin: Volk und Welt, 1967. Lw. 5,80 M = Ausgewählte Werke in Einzelausgaben.
24. Der Karren. Berlin: Verlag Volk und Welt, 1967. 158 S. Br. 0,80 M = Roman-Zeitung 222.
25. Das Totenschiff. Die Geschichte eines amerikanischen Seemanns. Leipzig: Reclam, 1967. 316 S. Br. 2,50 M = Reclams Universal-Bibliothek. Bd. 346 - Nachauflagen: 1972, 76, 79.
26. Ein General kommt aus dem Dschungel. Nachwort Peter Lübbe. Berlin: Volk und Welt, 1967. 427 S. Lw. 6,80 M = Ausgewählte Werke in Einzelausgaben - Nachauflage: 1971.
27. Erzählungen. Herausgabe, Nachwort und Bibliographie Werner Sellhorn. Bd. 1. 2. Berlin: Volk und Welt, 1968. 366; 372 S. Lw. 15,60 M = Ausgewählte Werke in Einzelausgaben - Nachauflage: 1969.
28. Das Totenschiff. Die Geschichte eines amerikanischen Seemanns. Nachwort Peter Lübbe. Berlin: Volk und Welt, 1970. 383 S. Lw. 7,80 M = Ausgewählte Werke in Einzelausgaben.
29. Das Totenschiff. Die Geschichte eines amerikanischen

Seemanns. Nachwort Peter Lübbe. Berlin: Volk und Welt, 1970. 383 S. Lw. 7,80 M = Bibliothek der Weltliteratur.
30. Ein General kommt aus dem Dschungel. Nachwort Peter Lübbe. Berlin: Buchclub, 1965. 1971. 427 S. Lw. 7,00 M.
31. Die weisse Rose. Nachwort H. D. Tschörtner. Berlin: Volk und Welt, 1972. 327 S. Lw. 7,40 M = Ausgewählte Werke in Einzelausgaben: - Nachauflagen: 1973, 74.
32. Die Brücke im Dschungel. Vom Autor genehmigte Übersetzung der amerikanischen Originalausgabe. Deutsch von Werner Preusser. Berlin: Volk und Welt, 1973. 108 S. Br. 0,890 M = Roman-Zeitung 279.
33. Die weisse Rose. Nachwort H. D. Tschörtner. Berlin: Buchclub 65, 1973. 327 S. Lw. 7.00 M.
34. Die weisse Rose. Nachwort H. D. Tschörtner. Berlin: Volk und Welt, 1973 (2. Auflage). Fotomechanischer Nachdruck: Deutsche Zentralbücherei für Blinde zu Leipzig 1975 (Grossdruckausgabe) 327 S.
35. Das Totenschiff. Die weisse Rose. Berlin: Volk und Welt, 1979. 303 S. Pb. 9,60 M - Romane 1.
36. Die Troza. Nachbemerkung o.N. Berlin: Buchclub 65, 1979. 367 S. Lw. 7,00 M.
37. Die Baumwollpflücker. Der Schatz der Sierra Madre. Die Brücke im Dschungel. Berlin: Volk und Welt, 1980. 309 S. Pb. 10.40 M = Romane 2.
38. Der Karren. Regierung. Berlin: Volk und Welt, 1980. 311 S. Pb. 9,60 M = Romane 3.
39. Der Marsch ins Reich der Caoba. Die Troza. Berlin: Volk und Welt, 1981. 320 S. Pb. 10,40 M = Romane 4.
40. Die Rebellion der Gehenkten. Ein General kommt aus dem Dschungel. Berlin: Volk und Welt, 1981. 357 S. Pb. 10,80 M = Romane 5.
41. Aus dem Land des Frühlings. Auszüge, Aufsätze, Auskünfte. Herausgabe und Nachwort H. D. Tschörtner. Berlin: Volk und Welt, 1986. 497 S. Lw. 12,80 M.

Auszug:
Karrenreise durch die Sierra Madre (Aus: Der Karren). Illustrationen von Willem Hölterer. Berlin, Leipzig: Volk und Wissen, 32 S. Br. = Unserer Welt.
dass. Berlin, Dresden: Kinderbuchverlag 1950.

B. TRAVEN FROM A CZECH POINT OF VIEW

Rudolf Vápeník

According to the well-known bibliography by Rolf Recknagel, Czechoslovakia was one of the first Slavic-speaking countries to translate B. Traven's books. But considering the widespread knowledge of German at the time, some Czech readers may also have read the original German Büchergilde Gutenberg editions. The Czech translations began to appear only five years after the publication of Traven's early works, and they continue to this day, except for the forced hiatus during the Second World War. On the other hand, according to the BT-Mitteilungen, it is said that the original edition of Rebellion "was a favourite object," which "was smuggled especially from Bohemia by brave freedom fighters into Nazi-Germany." A few publication figures will show that in view of the fact that Czechoslovakia is a country with only fifteen million inhabitants, printings of Traven's works have been comparatively much larger than in other countries, which means that there is a tremendous amount of Czech interest in Traven.

It is noteworthy that, except for Land des Frühlings and Aslan Norval, all of Traven's works have been translated into Czech. It might interest those who study Traven in detail that in 1949 I received a 235-page English manuscript entitled "Mercedes Ortega Lozano. The History of a Biological Instinct Miscarried. Screen Script by B. Traven, 1947." In an accompanying letter Traven's European literary agent, at that time Josef Wieder, described it as "the first version" of Aslan Norval, "which was subsequently thoroughly revised" and "the sexual passages were considerably toned down."

Eleven of Traven's novels and all of his short stories have been translated into Czech. The Cotton Pickers was published in three editions, one before the war. (The number in parenthesis for the following publications indicates editions before the war.) The Death Ship was published in five (one) editions; Treasure in six (one); The White Rose in four (one); Bridge and The Carreta in three (one); Government, March, and The Troza in two; Rebellion in four (one); General in one; and all of Traven's stories, under various titles, in six (three) editions. The total circulation of all of these editions is impossible to determine today, since before the war the number of copies printed was not mentioned in the books. However, according to information from one of the first Czechoslovakian publishers of

270

Traven's books, about 10,000 copies per book were printed. The number of postwar copies surpasses one million books; The Death Ship (240,000, Treasure (180,000), The White Rose and Rebellion (150,000 each) had the largest printings.

It should be noted that these numbers refer only to Czech editions. Czechoslovakia, of course, is a state in which two nations--namely, the Czech and the Slovak--live, each with its own language. Translations of foreign writers generally appear in separate editions, even though the differences between the two languages are not extensive and can be mastered by readers without great difficulty. In determining the total of Czechoslovakian editons of Traven, we must therefore add thirteen Slovak editions to the forty-one aforementioned Czech editions, which adds up to fifty-four editions with a total circulation of 1.5 million copies. This number alone speaks for Traven's popularity with Czech and Slovak readers.

If one looks for the reasons why this particular writer was one of the most widely read foreign authors in his literary genre, the decisive factors for his popularity might include his progressive social stance, the exotic nature of his topics (which fascinated Middle European readers), and the vernacular style in which his books were written. One should also not overlook the fact that many of his works were enhanced by illustrations from first-rate Czech artists, such as Antonín Strnadel, František Tichý, and Karel Teissig. Worth special mention are František Ketzek's illustrations for The Troza, which were approved by the author himself, as indicated by a letter from his agent, Wieder, in 1956: "B. Traven wants to let you know how extremely delighted he is that the artist has captured the Mexican milieu; even a native artist could not have done it better."

Among the translators of Traven's works before World War II one finds Ivan Olbracht, one of the greatest Czech writers of this century, who translated two of Traven's books. If one compares his translation of Treasure with the German Büchergilde Gutenberg edition, one discovers that--even considering the language differences--Olbracht's version is surprisingly shorter, by about one-quarter. Looking into this discrepancy, one finds that Olbracht made a rather free translation, not without errors, and with many omissions, which are the main reason for its short length. After consulting Olbracht about these discrepancies during the planning for a postwar edition, it was learned that he had only signed for the Czech version but had not done the translation himself at all; the writer Helena Malířová was responsible for it. This deception shows the helping hand extended by an established artist towards his struggling companion, who, unfortunately, because of her untimely death could not be questioned about the reasons for her omissions. Olbracht, by the way, also translated Jakob Wassermann, Thomas Mann, and Lion Feuchtwanger, and edited Prescott's History of the Conquest of Mexico.

An article which appeared in 1936 in the magazine Čin documents that Helena Malířová was also responsible for introducing Traven to Czech readers. In this article she not only comments with expertise on Traven's main works documenting her opinion with many lengthy quotes, but she also speculates about the reasons for his departure from Europe, surprisingly arriving at the correct conclusion-- that it might have been a conflict between Traven's opinions and those of the ruling classes which forced him to leave the Old World. The conclusion of her article shows how much she appreciated Traven's writings:

"The Land of Springtime" is Chiapas, the most southerly and least explored of the 30 united Mexican states. Traven arrived here not as a scientist, but only as a human being who took the land and the people to his heart. He discovered in them his brothers, even humanity and the whole world, and realized that we all possess the same characteristics and that we are different only because of the color of our skin, because of environmental factors, our blood, education, and conditions. And there in Chiapas his work was written. In it we read about the ancient Indian cities with their high cultural level, about untamed nature, the jungle and primeval forests, about the forgotten past and the unknown present. And we listen because it is not only our author but also a human being from the other side of the world who is speaking to us on a very intimate level.

Perhaps it should be added that it is possible that direct contacts between Helena Malířová and the Büchergilde Gutenberg played a role in introducing Traven to Czech readers, especially since it is known that after 1933 the publisher not only transferred operations from Berlin to Switzerland, but also had branch offices in Vienna and Prague.

It is not surprising that this early and continuing interest in Traven's works in Czechoslovakia piqued the curiosity of the reader in the author himself, as it did elsewhere. Understandably, the worldwide attempts to uncover the secret of Traven's human existence did not stop at the Czech border, and readers tried to discover his roots in Bohemia. One of the first attempts to trace Traven's past had specu-

lated that Jack London faked his suicide in order to escape
his creditors, and that he assumed Traven's identity to
continue his literary production undisturbed. Why should it
be so absurd to identify in the same manner a writer of
Czech origin with Traven? In 1964, the author of such an
experiment, a certain Ivan Růžička, tried to prove in an
article, titled "Traven Unmasked" (Traven demaskovany") and
printed in the well-known publication Kulturní tvorba, that
Traven could be none other than Arthur Breisky, a very
promising writer of the Czech decadence.

Breisky, a great admirer of Baudelaire, Verlaine, Nietzsche, Wilde, and Hamsun, tried to affect an aristocratic
manner, although he was only a minor customs official;
blagueur and dandy, he became notorious because of his
temporarily anarchist leanings. He considered himself a
poète maudit. At the age of twenty-five, he suddenly and
surprisingly left his Bohemian homeland in order to escape
the constraining conditions of the Czech Parnassus, which he
had just climbed with his first publication, a collection of
fictional portraits of famous personalities. Early in 1910,
Breisky showed up in the United States, but even in the New
World fate did not favor his plans: Although talented and
fluent in several languages, Breisky could land a job only
as an elevator operator in a German hospital in New York,
where he was found on the morning of July 10, 1910, with his
skull crushed beyond recognition. Naturally, this led many
of his friends to believe that the deceased was not really
Breisky, but that this had been just one of the many disap-
pearing acts Breisky engineered in order to create a new
identity for himself. This theory was further reinforced by
the autopsy results, which showed signs of a Jewish ritual
which was improbable in Breisky's case.

In short, Ivan Růžička revived the theory that Breisky
continued his life under a new name, and he connected it in
an ingenious manner with the mystery of B. Traven. He tried
to prove, in fact, that the pseudonym B. Traven was only an
anagram derived from shuffling the letters NEF ART B = NEW
ART Breisky. The theory naturally fell out of favor when
new discoveries were made about Marut's similarities to
Traven.

Eight years later, a second hypothesis was advanced by
several Traven experts who contended that there might be a
connection between Traven and a certain theology student
from St. Louis, Charles Trefny, who had studied at the
University of Freiburg in Breisgau in 1902/1903 and was
expelled for practicing medicine without a license. In this
instance, another writer, Marcel Mareš, tried to trace Traven's local roots in the journal Svět práce in a somewhat

different manner from Růžička. Since the town records in St. Louis showed that a family named Trefny from Bohemia had actually lived there since 1864, Mareš connected this name with the pseudonym B. Traven. Since some Mexican Indian tribes are supposed to pronounce "e" as "a" and usually add an "e" between two consonants, Mareš argued, Trefny would become Trafen, or Traven. The initial B was meant to stand for Trefny/Traven's roots in Bohemia.

These are the Czech contributions to solving the riddle of Traven's identity. It is not known if these imaginative assumptions about the author's connections with Czechoslovakia are supported by any facts.

It is interesting to note, however, that in 1974 Rosa Elena Luján mentioned to Theo Pinkus that in fact Traven, alias Ret Marut, while escaping from the liquidators of the Bavarian Räterepublik, made his way from Berlin to Vienna by way of Bohemia. There are also instances of writers with good reputations who tackled the Traven problem. One example is E. E. Kisch, who had succeeded in 1913 in cracking the spy case of the Austro/Hungarian Chief of the Military Staff Redl. During his exile in Mexico, Kisch was less successful in tracing Traven, although he contacted the woman Traven was living with, as well as Oskar Maria Graf, who had been a fellow revolutionary of Ret Marut during his Munich days. According to eyewitness accounts, the failure to solve the Traven riddle caused outbursts of rage by the world-famous "rasende Reporter."

In this connection it might be of interest to note that Traven's writings had a visible effect on the literary work of the internationally known Czech writer Norbert Frýd. After World War II, Frýd was the Czech cultural attaché in Mexico; and he later wrote not only reports but also novels which dealt with Mexican themes in a style not unlike Traven's. His book Studna supů (The Buzzard Well), written in 1953, deals with the struggle of the local proletariat for land. In a new edition in 1972, the author asserts in a postscript that he is "describing the time of upheaval in Mexico during the forties and fifties as accurately as Traven portrayed the Mexico of the twenties." Parallels are also visible in his novel Prales (The Jungle), written in 1965. Václav Šolc, a Czech scientist, whose field of specialization is Mexican Indians, has stated that Frýd had the same knowledge of the life of the Caoba-Macheteros "as depicted in such a suspenseful manner by the mysterious B. Traven." But there is more to it. The main topic of Frýd's novel "the expedition of an American professor to the ruins of a Mayan temple in the jungle of Chiapas"—the members of the expedition include the Czech amateur archaeologist and photographer Zelinka--resembles an episode in Traven's <u>Tors-van</u> Mexican adventure: the author's participation in the 1926 Palacios expedition, which brought him into Chiapas and acquainted him with the settings for his novels in the Caoba Cycle.

Even in Czechoslovakia, Traven's anonymity encouraged plagiarism; in a letter from 1948, his Swiss literary agent, Wieder, asked for assistance in the following matter:

> The publisher Škubal, Bartolomějská 14, Praha 1, has illegally published three of Traven's novels. He bases these publications on a contract with the literary agency Jiřina Vaněčková, Praha 10, Rokycanova 22. Mrs. Vaněčková claims to have received the authorization from a literary agency Weiss in Amsterdam whose owner perished during World War II in a concentration camp. Neither Mr. Weiss nor Mrs. Vaněčková have ever had authority to confer Traven's copyright. After corresponding with Mrs. Vaněčková for some time, she has finally conceded that she is responsible for royalty payments to Traven. She has demanded Traven's address from me so that she can send the royalties directly to him even though she knows that this is impossible since Traven will never consent to revealing his address to anyone, and that it is impossible for a proletarian writer to engage in a legal suit in a foreign country because of lack of funds. Mrs. Vaněčková has no intentions whatsoever to pay royalties; in fact, she belongs to that species of literary agents who shamelessly exploit poor, defenseless authors who dedicate their life to the struggle of the proletariat.

It should be mentioned that Mrs. Vaněčková did not only own Traven copyrights but also acted as Traven's translator. This matter was solved only after Mr. Wieder produced an authorization from the author in which the Swiss Banking Corporation confirmed Traven's signature.

In summary, Traven had some impact in Czechoslovakia, but it should be noted that the echo in the literary press was minimal. The public's interest always focused on the various sensational revelations surrounding Traven's legendary life, rather than on serious scholarly reviews of his books (which were only noted and seldom reviewed). The reaons for this might also be found in Traven's use of conventional literary forms and structures which were considered of mediocre literary quality, and his eschewing of all formal experiments. Certain literary genres, such as the <u>colportage</u>, the adventure and detective novels, were also underrated. In general, the critics only listed briefly the positive and negative aspects of Traven's writings. His political activism, his espousal of social justice against all forms of exploitation and oppression, and his suspenseful and readable style were praised on the one hand. But the critics condemned Traven's tendency toward anarchism (and sometimes nihilism), his glorification of ancient Indian society, and his tendency to interrupt the flow of his story through the inclusion of unrelated materials of a historical, folkloristic, or anthropological nature. In addition, Traven's depiction of human cruelty and sexual details was considered too graphic.

Finally, Czechoslovakia has made its contributions to the current state of Traven scholarship. Besides my own article in the periodical Světová literatura (World Literature 1956, 5), a study by the Germanist Karel Krejčí, published in a collection of essays by the philosophical faculty of Brno University in 1960, is one of the few studies to extensively examine the life and writings of Traven from a Czech point of view. Krejčí sees Traven as a pioneer of the period of New Objectivity in German literature, and he tries to prove through a structural analysis of Traven's writings that he was of German descent. It seems impossible to him "that a native American, one who had never set foot in Germany, could have this tremendous vocabulary and this unique artistry which presupposes a consciousness of literary form and style which a stranger who studied German only as a foreign language, could never acquire."

From recent times one might mention various commentaries on editions of Traven's works by the main Czech publisher, Svoboda. Among them are an attempt at a chronological summary of Traven's life and works, in a selection of his stories under the title Noční návštěva (Night Visit) from 1977, and an epilogue to a 1982 edition of Diktatura (Government), which discusses the biography and artistic development of this unique literary phenomenon of our century.

B. TRAVEN IN SWEDEN

Helmut Müssener

The sources and materials available for a study of Traven's reception in Sweden are far richer than one might initially suppose. All Traven's works (except for Land) have been through numerous Swedish editions, as will be clear from the appended bibliography. Traven was a popular and widely read author in that country, and some of his works have been translated into Swedish more than once.

Traven's reception in Sweden began in 1929 with the appearance of The Death Ship and Treasure, published by Axel Holmström. For the next decade, until 1939, Traven's books continued to appear with the same publisher, in many cases even in original translations. In fact, General was already published in Swedish in 1939, a full year before the German first edition. Later, in the forties and fifties, a clearly noticeable decline in publication of Traven's works occurred. When Traven's publisher, Holmström, died in 1947, the rights to Traven's works were handed over to the publishing house of the Social Democratic labor party of Sweden, Tiden, and the associated Folket i Bild Publishing Company, which published Traven's books sporadically. From 1954 to 1957, Tiden brought out the Caoba Cycle—unfortunately, incomplete and in an order different from the one the author had in mind.

For this period, one cannot speak of a deliberate cultivation of Traven's work; rather, it was utilized in order to benefit the book club associated with the publishing company. It was at the end of this period, in 1960, that Traven's late work, Aslan Norval, was published in the only translation I know. The book was received without enthusiasm, was never republished, and was relegated to oblivion, where it seems to belong.

In 1970-71, a Traven boom began when Folket i Bild published the complete Caoba Cycle in the correct order and at a low price. The 15,000 copies per volume which were printed were sold even at newspaper stands. In 1975, The Cotton Pickers followed in an edition of 10,000 copies.

The two Traven works that are undoubtedly considered classics in the Swedish book market and seem to be immune to the seasonal fluctuations of book sales are The Death Ship and Treasure. The Death Ship appeared in 1978 in three new editions: in a special, revised translation from the English in a series called "A Book for Everybody," which is supported by several national educational organizations and reaches a wide audience thanks to a greatly reduced price and imaginative marketing techniques; in an illustrated, single-volume, hardback edition put out by the private publishing company Atlantis; and in a limited collector's edition for bibliophiles, which boasts original woodcuts and drawings by the famous Swedish proletarian painter Torsten Billmann.

In 1980, the most frequently published of all of Traven's books, Treasure, appeared in a new translation from the English in two editions, including one for the book club Bra Böcker (Good Books), which gave Traven the status of a classical author by including his work in their classics series. Traven's audience had already awarded him this status much earlier, but Swedish literary scholars have in general ignored him. This is not surprising, since Traven is a revolutionary author who attacks not only the Latin American establishment. In a review in the Social Democratic newspaper Arbetet from November 12, 1934, Eyvind Johnson, who was later awarded the Nobel Prize, calls him a writer who "is much read in our country but hardly ever mentioned in so-called literary circles." I shall elucidate this distinction later.

Traven's popularity and the circulation of his works in Sweden are primarily the achievement of one man who single-handedly fought and won the battle for Traven's recognition. Axel Holmström, born in 1881, was a baker and, since the age of sixteen a member of the labor union. He belonged to the radical wing of the Swedish labor movement, and he was, according to his obituary in Brand of January 3, 1948, "one of Sweden's best known anarchists." Even before 1914 he espoused an independent socialism of an anarcho-syndicalist nature, and all of his life he was a decided anticapitalist, anticlerical, and, later, antifascist. He remained true to his convictions without making compromises to the left or right.

Holmström's political views also guided his publishing house, which he founded in 1913 and which remained a one-man operation until his death. Names like Bakunin, Herzen, Kropotkin, and Stirner, as well as the bibliographies of these authors and Rousseau which he published, characterize his publishing politics better than any political manifestos. "The last independent Socialist Publishing Company" (Brand, 1/3/1948) and its founder tried to reach those readers who had little money, as evidenced by the number of pages and the price of Holmström's publications. Although Holmström marketed his books in the traditional manner through booksellers, he also advertised and sold them by making speeches at union meetings and at the labor movement's political events, and by placing advertisements in their newspapers and other publications.

Unfortunately for Traven, Holmström's sales pitches brought little success, for the publishing company's record of sales clearly shows that none of Traven's books had become a bestseller; in fact, most were gathering dust on the shelves. Holmström explained the reasons to Traven in a detailed letter of May 5, 1934, written in English with minor mistakes. First of all, he laconically points out: "Sweden is a little country and too many books are published each year. Only a few books become bestsellers; the rest is neglected by the people."

Holmström goes on to describe for Traven how the literary critics in Sweden are divided into two camps. One groups consists of "the old influential critics, [they] were frightened by the radical tendency of your books; they... kept silence." In the opposing group are found "the young, radical critics. They at once in you saw a strong author. But they have no influence." The reading public is similarly divided into two groups according to Holmström: On the one hand, there is "well-to-do public," which disregards the recommendations of the radicals; on the other hand, there are the proletarians "who read your books, but they do not buy them." Holmström leaves no doubt about the reasons for this: "They are without employment, they starve, they can not buy books. But in the public libraries they are battling for your books."

In concluding, the publisher expresses his undying belief in Traven's books and their message. His words are an indication of the political background of his interest in Traven: "Time must change, the proletarians must win sooner or later, and then they will buy your books. Meanwhile your books will help them to win."

Unfortunately, this positive belief in the future did not influence sales, which remained low into 1939 (see Appendix). On July 2, 1938, Holmström wrote, quite resigned: "Your books are still much liked by the people who read them. But owing to the conservatism of the booksellers, they do not sell very good. The great newspapers are silent."

The publisher offers the same pessimistic evaluation shortly before the outbreak of World War II in a letter from July 21, 1939, to Traven's Swiss representative, Wieder, who had once again requested the payment of royalties. Holmström points out that "all books by radical writers have had poor sales during the last few years in this country." He also again expresses his publishing company's creed, which certainly did him credit, but which did not turn him into a successful businessman: "In spite of the fact that it is not good business to publish Traven's books, I shall not stop doing this. It is my duty in life to publish good revolutionary books."

The quotations cited reveal the dilemma of all research into reception. The differences between public praise and reader interest, between book buyers and book readers, between publishing house policy dictated by political and ideological motives on the one hand, and by business considerations on the other, are as difficult to gauge and evaluate as are the underlying factors such as (in this special case) the differences between the content-oriented "young radical critics" without influence on sales and the aesthetically-oriented "old influential critics" who could negatively influence the sale of books simply by remaining silent, between effect and success as revealed by sales statistics and possible influence on the readers.

In spite of the limited number of editions, neither Traven nor his publisher could complain about lack of public interest and praise. Both came, at least until the beginning of the forties, so consistently and emphatically from the left wing of the political and literary spectrum that one could use Traven to divide two basically different spheres of intellectual and ideological reception in Sweden, as pointed out by Holmström in the letter quoted above. In any case, most of the positive reviews are found in the press of the labor movement and the "left" in the most general sense of the term. Traven's critical social involvement and his revolutionary pathos are praised again and again and in the same words as his superficially defined realism, his humor, his irony, and his ability to create suspense, while aesthetic and purely literary questions are never asked. Often parallels are drawn between Traven's work and current European or Swedish politics. Thus, Traven's works are used to illustrate points in a political debate.

These detailed and lengthy reviews appeared in the social-democratic, communist, and syndicalist daily papers, which also printed Traven's novels in installments. In weekly or monthly publications, which occasionally create the impression of a near self-contained "proletarian public," Traven is one of a few authors, sometimes even the only author, of belles lettres reviewed. This is another indication of his importance, which, however, has to be considered in the light of the publication statistics and the remarks of his publisher already quoted.

The critical praise which focuses mainly on the content of Traven's books is generally exuberant. Only a few typical examples will be given.

The writer, and later confidant of Brecht, Henry Peter Matthis gives panegyrical expression to his feelings in a review of Traven's Rebellion in the Social Democratic party organ Socialdemokrat of February 11, 1938:

Yes it is history and an adventure novel, but above all, it is the gripping and stimulating work of a real poet. Passion burned in his heart, as he wrote: passion for freedom and humanity as well as for truth--but his intellect has quietly formed the vast and dangerous material. The plot is lean, it is great art, every chapter is structured with great skill...The novel is characterized by simplicity and naiveté...but it is glowing with hate for the enemies of humanity, the tyrants...and thus it is turned into great literature. Naturally proletarian literature.

This "naturally proletarian literature" refers to the already alluded to opposition between "conventional" and "new" literature that was of such importance in 1930s Sweden. For the left, Traven was, and remains, "a new important writer who is worthy to be listed among the outstanding social authors," as noted by Bokstuga (Study, 1930, 224), the collective literary organ of the Swedish Workers' Educational Association and the Temperance Organization. Furthermore, in the journal of the powerful agricultural labor union--to mention at least one publication of the labor unions' large and influential presses, which are hardly ever considered in investigations of this kind--several reviews, as well as a detailed description of all of Traven's works are found, although belles lettres played only a very minor role, and foreign writers are mentioned only occasionally and in passing (except for Upton Sinclair, who seems to pale in comparison with Traven).

In a review in Lantarbetaren of 1933 (wr. 43, p. 3), its chief editor, Ture Blom, characterizes Rebellion as a "great revolutionary novel which probably has no counterpart in our literature in translation." He calls on every worker to acquire the volumes of the Caoba Cycle: "Agricultural laborers, read the novel, form reading circles and buy the entire cycle! It deserves it!" A reference to the immediate present is characteristic and worth mentioning; it stresses the relevance and appeal which Traven's works undoubtedly had for the Swedish labor movement: "It is amazing how one recognizes the Germany and Italy of our days. Anyway, the almighty dictators are not very creative in their manner of governing."

But in spite of this realization, the reviewer offers

words of consolation which reveal his immovable faith in a predestined course of history: "Every dictatorship carries with it the seeds of its own destruction, Traven notes...because of its ever-increasing pressure it drives people to despair." Therefore, it is probably no coincidence that Traven's Rebellion was printed in 1941 in a second edition of 12,000 copies in the book series of the Swedish Workers' Educational Association, at a time when Sweden was surrounded on all sides by Hitler's armies and when the last hour of Swedish democracy and the Swedish labor movement seemed close at hand. Here Traven serves as an example of Swedish "emergency literature," a technical term for a type of literature which was supposed to bolster the spirit of resistance of the Swedish people and their readiness to defend themselves.

In small-scale publications with little influence for a leftist-oriented, intellectual, and mostly academically educated reading public, positive adjectives and general praise for Traven also abound. This holds true for the Marxist-oriented student magazine Clarté, as well as for the first weekly culture magazine, Fönstret (The Window), which was the only Swedish magazine committed to the ideals of New Objectivity (Neue Sachlichkeit) and which espoused these ideals in a radical, humanistic, socialist spirit with a liberal tinge. Fönstret printed several of Traven's stories as Swedish first editions (see Appendix) and reviewed his books as long as it existed. He was the most popular foreign author and even surpassed other writers preferred by the magazine, such as Ernst Toller, Lion Feuchtwanger, and Ilja Ehrenburg, whose names represented a trend. As far as the reviewers for the publications of the labor movement were concerned, Traven's books undoubtedly held first place among the literature in translation published between 1929 and 1939. They were presented to the readers as great didactic reading experiences.

All these reviews state the same arguments and points ad nauseam. They refer mainly to plot and content, and only seldom to the form, style, or language of the book reviewed. The author's "unadorned portrayal of reality" is praised more than anything else, as in a review by Edwin Eriksson in Bokstugan (1930, 274). The reviewer is attracted by the realism of Traven's "brusque and inconsiderate love of truth," sees embodied in his work "bitter and pointed irony, but also humor," and welcomes the "fresh revolutionary spirit" (Ibid., 1935, 15).

The reviewers especially praise Traven's veracity in his portrayal of the "grandeur of nature, the primitive instincts of men, the lushness and sweltering force of tropical vegetation and the insecure life of the poor struggling proletarians" (Ibid., 1930, 224). Also praised is Traven's exciting technique in telling a story. It is agreed that the strange, exotic, primitive milieu in Traven's works is to a certain degree responsible for their effect, but Traven "is not the usual tourist or travel author" as H. A. observes in Clarté (1933, H2, p. 32). It is also characteristic of these reviewers to look at the authors associated with Traven; Upton Sinclair and Jack London are most frequently mentioned. Direct comparisons are generally in Traven's favor. Possibly of equal importance at this time were the Rumanian Panait Istrati and the Dane Martin Anderson-Nexö.

In light of all this praise, it is hardly surprising that various reviewers repeatedly demanded that the Nobel Prize be awarded to Traven. At the same time, however, they polemicized against the Swedish Academy and its criteria for evaluation and pointed out that a realistic, relevant, and socially engaged (even socialistic) author, as Traven was viewed, would never receive the Prize.

Bridge even caused one critic to make a direct attack on the Academy. In his review in Arbetaren of December 6, 1933, C. E. Englund initially writes about Traven's book: "From soft dreams and hard reality the veil is woven which he wraps around his characters. No anemic school teachers or nagging bags of bones wander through Traven's world. His people are primitive and healthy." But these highly praised characteristics will prove an obstacle to Traven's acceptance according to the reviewer: "However, these characters have too much flesh and blood, too much true individuality to satisfy our prejudiced culture apostles. Therefore, Traven will never get the Nobel Prize, although he is one of the few who has earned it and has distinguished himself. He has done this without being a senile old man sitting at the side of the road and trying to blow away the fog from his youth."

When the Academy did not award the Nobel Prize in 1935 and stated that no suitable candidates could be found, still more reviewers attacked the Academy's calcified aesthetic spirit and demanded, "The Nobel Prize for Traven." One of these critics assumed that in spite of Traven's "outstanding literary artistry" he would be ignored; he considered him the "God Blessed writer, whom one couldn't simply ignore among the best contemporary poets" because he probably could not behave properly among finer people and would have ruined the ceremony. Nils Beyer contemplates in Socialdemokraten of December 18, 1935: "He probably would not have had enough style to put on a coat tails. Maybe he even would have shown up in a Mexican Indian blanket and crouched on the floor in some corner of the hall, smiling a smile so full of irony that the lamps in the hall would have lost their brightness. The disgrace might have been truly catastrophic."

Without a doubt, Traven and his world assumed almost symbolic importance for the press of the labor movement and its "young radical critics." He was one of the great examples for those who, in the thirties, started their attack on outdated education and society. In general, they had reached their objective a decade later.

In contrast to this united front of support and approval for Traven and his work by the labor movement and its press, there stands his reception by the bourgeois publications. The already quoted statement by Holmström--"the great newspapers are silent"--holds true for them, but not exclusively. But even when they aren't silent, the reviews are mostly very short and refer in general only to the content of Traven's works; they are also printed in the back pages and are lost in a wealth of similar notes. In addition, they are often unsigned or only initialled. Famous critics are almost completely missing. These reviews have no advertising value; more often one even finds negative reviews, which are intended to discourage readers from buying the book.

Above all, these critics attack Traven because of his political views, which are now as detrimental as they were positive in the press of the labor movement. "The Marxist in Mexico," reads the alliterative title of a review by E.A.M. in Dagens Nyheter of December 9, 1934. Traven is primarily classified as a "talented fellower in the footsteps of Upton Sinclair," who is "at his best when he forgets about being a class-conscious Marxist." He is often reproached for being too political and one-sided, and his strong involvement in political issues is condemned in literary groups.

In the rare positive reviews, Traven's social and ideological intentions are not mentioned. In reviews of Bridge, for instance, the politically castrated writer is called "an artist in the truest sense of the word" by T. Skoglund in Sydsvenska Dagbladet of December 23, 1933. According to J. O-v in Svenska Dagbladet of November 27, 1922, Traven "excels in milieu descriptions." The selfsame reviewer also naively and apolitically extols Traven's closeness to primitive people: "Through his descriptions we experience the emotions of the people of the jungle in such a way that we believe ourselves to be one of them." Without the political background all that remains of The Carreta is a "description

of the country people in Mexico,' who are "no less entertaining because of their social pathos," as E.M.A. writes in
Dagens Nyheter of December 9, 1934

It is also noteworthy that, with on exception during those
years, Traven is completely ignored in the literary and
cultural journals of the bourgeoisie, and not one of his
books is reviewed. Thus, the impression that at this time
in Sweden there existed two cultures, two book and reading
societies without contact except for occasional polemics, is
in Traven's case qualified only by the journal Bonniers
Literarische Magazin (BLM), which began publication in 1932.
This journal became the mouthpiece of a generation which at
that time was trying to gain influence and power in Sweden
and which would soon play a major role in public discussion
and debate. It was their representatives who reviewed all
of Traven's works in BLM--and (without exception) positively. It is true that many of these generally short
reviews are lost in the multitude of reviews of other books,
but their importance is not diminished by this fact, if only
because of the quality of the writers, who included Eyvind
Johnson, Artur Lundkvist, Josef Kjellgren, and Per Meurling
(who wrote a long essay on Traven for BLM--the only one in a
purely literary journal). They belong, stated roughly and
in a simplified form, to that group of worker writers and
leftist intellectuals equally influenced by Marx and psycho-
analysis, who, since around 1930, first participated in the
cultural and literary debates in the press of the labor
parties and trade unions. They rebelled against the bourgeois literature which they saw embodied in the members of
the Academy and the reviews of the great newspapers, and
slowly they began to dominate literary debates. Afterwards
many of them were domesticated and assimilated by the establishment, as is usually the case.

They came, almost without exception, from the city or
country proletariat, were born after 1900, and had little
formal schooling; either they had continued their education
through independent efforts, or they had gone to sea. Politically, they sympathized at this time (the early 1930s)
with unorthodox Marxism. They considered themselves members
of the labor movement and were leftist-socialists, anarcho-
syndicalists, or communists by reasons of their origin,
their biography, and their feelings ("left, where the heart
is"). Thus, their sympathy for Traven was understandable.
However, their unanimous praise for and clearly noticeable
interest in the author and his work were surprisingly diverse as well as unified. Their involvement with his person
and work is quite detailed and well documented, and, for
some, it was of influence for their own writing.

The same holds true for the members of an informal literary circle called De fem unga (The Five Youngsters). They attracted public attention in 1929 when they published a literary almanac by the same name which initiated a new period of Swedish literary history. Without exception they are numbered among the important writers in Sweden in the thirties, up until World War II and the postwar era. Harry Martinson, a former sailor and tramp, lyric poet, and novelist, who became a member of the Academy in 1949 and was awarded the Nobel Prize in 1974, praised the work of Traven by stating, "Not to have read a book by Traven is nowadays an indication of insufficient familiarity with contemporary literature." (The quotation is from a blurb in the 1975 Cotton Pickers edition; its exact origin could not be ascertained.) In a review of The White Rose in the Torshälla Kuriren of December 27, 1930, the novelist and "primitivist" Gustav Sandgren calls Traven "a social critic along the lines of Upton Sinclair, but with far greater artistic means of expression and a unique bitter sense of humor." He recommends the book as "well worth reading" for all libraries. The novelist Erik Asklund, famous for his portrayal of Stockholm, sees Traven's position strengthened by the publication of Bridge and finds his opinion reconfirmed "that he is a great writer. Every new book by him is an experience" (Fönstret, 1933, Nr. 12, p. 8).

Of this literary circle, Artur Lundkvist and Josef Kjellgren deal with Traven in reviews and essays which cannot be discussed in detail at this point. Ake Runnqvist, in his study Arbetarskildrare from Hedenvind till Fridell (Proletarian Writers from Hedenvind to Fridell, Stockholm 19, p. 149), calls Lundkvist a novelist and a lyric poet, "one of the most influential and original Swedish literary critics," and "a travel author with an eye for social injustices and without a rival in Sweden when it comes to capturing the atmosphere of foreign countries." Lundkvist was awarded the Lenin Prize for Literature in 1958, and he has been a member of the Academy since 1968, occasionally being referred to as its "strong man" or "secret leader." He has continually praised Traven's realistic representation of nature and people, and their artistic characterization, as well as Traven's psychological understanding and social involvement. Finally, there is Josef Kjellgren, sailor, ship's boilerman, and journalist, described by Ake Runnqvist (p. 152) as "our most consistent proletarian writer" and "pioneer for a socialist realism"; Kjellgren is the author of the novel Människor kring en bro (People Around a Bridge) and the four-volume cycle about the fate of the steamship Smaragd. He writes about Traven in various reviews and short essays, which clearly reveal how much he was impressed and influenced by him.

Unfortunately, the question of influence cannot be pursued in detail, but it should be assumed in the cases of Lundkvist (who describes distant, exotic countries in a critical manner) and the former sailor and tramp Martinson. Traven's influence can be taken for granted with Kjellgren, the author of four novels about the steamer Smaragd. It is of special importance in this connection that Kjellgren praises Traven as the "Unknown European" in a poem written in 1930, and places him alongside writers such as Gorky, Barbusse, Hedenvind-Erikson, Whitman, and Toller. Traven's presence in this distinguished company shows his position not only for Kjellgren himself, but also for his friends and the members of their generation in Sweden. Also obvious is Traven's relationship to these "Five Youngsters," who found expressed in his works their own ideas and who felt supported by his writings. It is highly likely that they learned from him and through him.

Traven's significance and renown were not limited to this circle of authors, however, but reached others as well. Many of them, although young at the time, are known today as famous writers and literary critics; and their numbers include people like novelist Eyvind Johnson, who at that time was an anarcho-syndicalist. In 1957, he was elected to the Academy, and in 1974 he received the Nobel Prize together with Harry Martinson. To this list of Traven enthusiasts belong the lyric poet, Erik Lindegren, member of the Academy since 1962; famous proletarian writers like Rudolf Värnlund and Moa A. Martinson; the Finnish-Swedish lyric poet and novelist Elmer Diktonius; and Rabbe Enckell, who, in a review in Hufvudstadsbladet (Helsingfors) of October 31, 1935, compares Traven to Tolstoy. The Marxist literary critics Erik Blomberg, Nils Beyer, Henry Petter Matthis, and Stellan Arvidsson (also a Social Democratic member in the Swedish parliament) should be mentioned. Other politicians influenced by Traven include Hinke Bergergren, one of the "Grand Old Men" of the left wing of the Social Democratic party; Gösta Netzen, who was later appointed; and C.-H. Hemansson, who was later elected chairman of Sweden's Euro-Communist party. This company of literary enthusiasts is appropriately led by Per Albin Hansson, Premierminister of Sweden for many years. According to a review of Traven's Government by Eyvind Johnson in Arbetet of October 14, 1935, Hansson praised The Death Ship and characterized it as useful: "Overall it certainly is a good combination in the struggle against dictatorship which should be read by many people."

Everything I have discussed here should demonstrate how relevant Traven's books were at that time for leftist reviewers, which arguments they used in his support, and the role which Traven played in the Swedish debate about the function and importance of literature. I have further given an example of the eternal dilemma of all reception research, namely, that critical success and favorable recommendations by reviewers are not necessarily reflected in book sales. Until conclusive evidence can be offered, we have to rely on the figures and explanations offered by Holmström: "The proletarians read your books, but they do not buy them." This statement is indirectly confirmed in one of the Stockholm novels by Erik Asklund, a member of the group De fem unga. In his novel Bröderna i Klara (The Brothers of the Klara-Quarter, Stockholm 1962, 322), one of the characters, a janitor and former sailor, when asked whether he reads books, answers, "Yes, there are libraries in the sailors' hostels in many ports. I have read Jack London...and Upton Sinclair. Maybe also Traven." These three names stand for a whole literary program, which is read by the proletarian public but which is usually not mentioned in academic histories of literature, as I have shown in the case of "Traven in Sweden."

After 1940, little is said about Traven's books, but more about the author. It is at this point that there begins the great discussion about his identity, which was followed closely by Swedish papers. Because of Traven's supposed Norwegian or possibly even Swedish descent, they hoped to claim him as one of their own literary giants and thus enrich Sweden's national literary history. All new information was fully reported in numerous articles and in all newspapers, regardless of their political leanings. For advertising reasons, the question "Who was B. Traven" was posed even on the covers and in the blurbs of new editions of Traven's works. The question was usually discussed in detail and then disregarded as unimportant by reference to Traven's well-known dictum that it is not the author as a person who is important, but his works.

A contribution in Dagens Nyheter of October 15, 1967, by the journalist Jan Olof-Olsson (Jolo), in which he discusses the results of research done by Judy Stone on the identity of Traven, is characteristic for this time. Olsson is perfectly correct in stating in his introduction that "in the 30's it was generally accepted that Traven's identity was a mystery." He then assesses the consequences which he believes have resulted from Traven's game of hide-and-seek: "At the present time he is known because of the fact that he is not known. He has succeeded in covering up what he wrote. Traven's name does not refer any longer to his books, but to the 'Traven mystery' The most interesting fact about him has become the question of his identity."

Only very occasionally do we find articles in the forties and sixties that concern themselves with Traven's works, or reviews of the new editions which came out sporadically in the fifties. It should not come as a surprise that this was just another indication of old social considerations. After 1968, Traven fell in step with the spirit of the times when student revolts and the reaction to the Vietnam War made revolutions popular again and interest in underdeveloped countries was growing, especially in Latin America, which was supposedly exploited by interested U.S. imperialism and by their own governments. It is thus small wonder that the publishing company of the Social Democratic party, Tiden, took this opportunity to have the entire Caoba Cycle reprinted in 1970/71 by its subsidiary Folket i Bild. Its marketing strategy addressed the general consumer, and the printing of 15,000 copies of each volume shows that they expected good sales.

The reprinting of the Caoba Cycle had been preceded by an appeal from the Euro-Communist writer Sven Wernström, who demanded in a detailed article in the liberal daily paper Dagens Nyheter of June 4, 1970, a new edition "for the politically active youth of our times." For him, Traven's work is principally a means to a revolutionary end: He considers Traven "considerably more important than many classical writers who are so avidly advertised in editions for our young people," since Traven, as "an undogmatic revolutionary who is distrustful of all dictatorships, fascist as well as communist, is more relevant and more interesting today than ever before." Over 15 years have passed since then. Times have changed; the Caoba Cycle is not available in bookstores at the present time and will most probably not be reprinted in the near future. But thanks to Treasure and The Death Ship (see Appendix), Traven has not been forgotten. These two books are examples of successful adventure novels; however, they are not limited to this genre of literature, since, according to reviews, they manage to escape strict classification. Their author was and remains--despite fancy bibliophile editions and his status as a classical writer--a fomenter of unrest who, according to Bo Magnusson in Göteborgs Sjöfarts-och Handelstidning from July 7, 1979, "takes shots at all sides," and "is a free spirit" and "conscious author" who "is completely on the side of the underdog." The Death Ship is indeed "a book for everyone"--in 1978 as well as in 1929.

The Swedish people have had the opportunity to learn to

know Traven. The mixture of exciting adventure and social criticism, of foreign and exotic jungles with familiar human issues, of suppression and revolt, of the individual and the collective--all have managed to retain their explosive force until today. In an essay on the occasion of the publication of the Caoba Cycle in 1971, the author Björn Nordenborg wrote in <u>Arbetaren</u>, Nr. 26/27: "The confrontation within him between General Emilio Zapata of Mexico and the anarchist Erich Mühsam of Munich, fascinates us. The result of this confrontation, its explosive mixture, is as dangerous, relevant, and valuable as ever."

Note

The author is preparing a lengthy essay on the reception of Traven in Sweden which will appear in the "Schriften des Germanistischen Instituts der Universität Stockholm." The connection between the Büchergilde Gutenberg, Traven's German publishing house, and Axel Holmström was established by the German anarcho-syndicalist Augustin Souchy, who lived in Sweden during World War I and who spoke Swedish (see Augustin Souchy, "Wahres und Falsches über Bruno Traven," in <u>Geist</u> <u>und</u> <u>Tat</u>, 4, pp. 117-20, Frankfurt/Main, 1958).

Appendix

1. <u>Traven's</u> <u>Books</u> <u>in</u> <u>Swedish</u> <u>Translation</u>--<u>Bibliographical</u> Overview

<u>Bomullsplockarna</u> (<u>The</u> <u>Cotton</u> <u>Pickers</u>)

Trans. by Eugen Albán Stockholm 1930	Axel Holmström's Förlag 241 pages
Trans. by Roland Adlerberth Stockholm 1975 Published as Vol. 8 in the series "Arbetarberättare"	Tiden's Förlag 221 pages (Proletarian narrators...)

<u>Bron</u> <u>i</u> <u>djungeln</u> (<u>Bridge</u>)

Trans. by Arne Holmström Stockholm 1933	Axel Holmström's Förlag 142 pages

De hängdas revolution (Rebellion)

Trans. by Arne Holmström
Stockholm 1938

Axel Holmström's Förlag
376 pages

Trans. by Arne Holmström
Stockholm 1941
(Published as a second edition 3-15,000 copies printed in "A.B.F.'s" book series [book series of the Workers Educational Association])

Axel Holmström's Förlag
346 pages

Trans. Arne Holmström
Stockholm 1954

Tiden's Bokklubb
380 pages

Trans. Arne Holmström
Stockholm 1971
(15,000 copies in this edition)

Folket i Bild's Förlag
380 pages

Dikatatur (Government)

Trans. Arne Holmström
Stockholm 1935

Axel Holmström's Förlag
332 pages

Trans. Arne Holmström
Stockholm 1956

Tiden's Bokklubb
319 pages

Trans. Arne Holmström
Stockholm 1970
(15,000 copies in this edition)

Folket i Bild's Förlag
319 pages

Djungelgeneralen (General)

Trans. Arne Holmström
Stockholm 1939

Axel Holmström's Förlag
365 pages

Trans. Arne Holmström
Stockholm 1955

Tiden's Bokklubb
380 pages

Trans. Arne Holmström
Stockholm 1971
(15,000 copies in this edition)

Folket i Bild's Förlag
380 pages

Djungelnatt (The Troza)

Trans. Arne Holmström
Stockholm 1937

Axel Holmström's Förlag
300 pages

Trans. Arne Holmström   Folket i Bild's Förlag
Stockholm 1970   300 pages
(15,000 copies in this edition)

Dødsskeppet (The Death Ship)

Trans. Eugen Albán   Axel Holmström's Förlag
Stockholm 1929   342 pages

Trans. A. Forsström   Tiden's Förlag
Stockholm 1951   302 pages
(Also published in the bookclub Tiden's Förlag; translation from the English)

Trans. A. Forsström   En bok for alla/Littera-
Stockholm 1978   turfrämjandet 380 pages
(Revised translation from the English; the publishing house "A Book for Everyone" is a public foundation by various educational organizations and trade associations which publish books at greatly reduced prices)

Trans. A. Forsström   Atlantis Förlag
Stockholm 1978   415 pages
(Revised translation from the English; illustrated with woodcuts and illustrations by Torsten Billman)

Kärran (The Carreta)

Trans. by Arne Holmström   Axel Holmström's Förlag
Stockholm 1934   288 pages

Trans. Arne Holmström   Tiden's Bokklubb
Stockholm 1957   288 pages

Trans. Arne Holmström   Folket i Bild's Förlag
Stockholm 1970   288 pages

Marschen till Caobans rike (March)

Trans. Arne Holmström   Axel Holmström's Förlag
Stockholm 1936   336 pages

Trans. Nils Holmberg   Folket i Bild's Förlag
Stockholm 1970   333 pages
(15,000 copies in this edition)

Miljarder på spel (Aslan Norval)

Trans. Arne Holmström   Tiden's Bokklubb
Stockholm 1950   252 pages

Sierra Madres Skatt (Treasure)

Trans. Eugen Albán   Axel Holmström's Förlag
Stockholm 1929   276 pages

Trans. unknown   Tiden's Förlag
Stockholm 1949   314 pages
(Also offered by the bookclub of Tiden's Förlag in a new
translation; the translator is not named)

Trans. unknown   Folket i Bild's Förlag
Stockholm 1953   314 pages
(In the series "Travels and Adventures"; this translation is identical to the translation of 1949. 50,000
copies in this edition.)

Trans. Eugen Albán   Prisma Förlag
Stockholm 1969   216 pages
(Paperback edition--translation identical with the edi-
tions of 1949 and 1953, but not with that of 1929)

Trans. Ingrid Berglöf   Komet Förlag
Stockholm 1969   224 pages
(Translation from the English; appeared in the series
"Film-bibliotek")

Trans. Eugen Albán   Tiden's Förlag
Stockholm 1977   217 pages
(Translation identical with the editions of 1949, 1953,
and 1969, but not with that of 1929)

Trans. Gunilla Berglund   Trevi Förlag
Stockholm 1980   331 pages
(Translated from the English)

Trans. Gunilla Berglund   Bra böckers Förlag (Book-
Höganäs 1980   club) 331 pages
(Translated from the English; bookclub edition in the
series "Klassiker")

Urskog (Jungle)

Trans. Arne Holmström   Axel Holmström's Förlag
Stockholm 1932   147 pages
Contains the following stories: Uppväckandet av en död (Reviving the Dead); Indian dans i urskogen (Indian Dance in the Jungle); En guds födelse (A New God Was Born); Historien om en bomb (The Story of a Bomb); Dynamitpatronen (Dynamite); Sjukhuset (On Welfare); Vaktposten (The Guard); Asneköpet (Purchase of a Donkey); En hundaffär (Selling a Dog); Medicinen (Medicine); Ett Nattligt besök (The Night Visitor).

Vita Rosen (The White Rose)

Trans. Eugen Albán   Alex Holmström's Förlag
Stockholm 1930   288 pages

A list of stories individually published in Swedish journals to date:

Dynamitpatronen	Fönstret 1930 #14
Sjukhuset	Fönstret 1930 #15
En guds födelse	Fönstret 1930 #17
Familjeära	Fönstret 1930 #28
Indianer i urskogen	Fönstret 1932 #25
Den uppfångade blixten	BLM 1936 p. 189ff.
Medicinen	Folket i Bild/Kulturfront 1958 #51

2. Traven's Books in Swedish Translation (chronological order)

Death Ship	1929			1951	1978	1980
Treasure	1929		1949	1953	1968	
Cotton Pickers		1930			1975	
White Rose		1930				
Jungle		1932				
Bridge		1933				
Carreta		1934		1957	1970	
Government		1935		1956	1970	
March	1936				1970	
Troza	1937				1970	
Rebellion	1938	1941	1954		1971	
General	1939		1955		1971	
Aslan Norval				1960		

3. Copies Printed and Number of Copies Sold
(Source: Axel Holmström's unpublished works; letters to B. Traven)

	Printing	31.12.1933	31.12.1938
Death Ship[1] (29)	3,000	1,907	2,250
Treasure[1] (29)	3,000	1,256	1,365
Cotton Pickers[1] (30)	4,000	2,274	2,400
White Rose[1] (30)	3,300	1,571	1,700
Jungle (32)	2,000	576	800
Bridge (33)	3,000	610	1,000
Carreta (34)	3,000	–	1,280
Government (35)	3,000	–	1,300
March (36)	3,000	–	1,450
Troza (37)	3,000	–	1,400
Rebellion	2,000	–	800

[1]These works also were published in installments in the papers of the labor movement; exact details cannot be given at the moment.

295

B. TRAVEN AND THE GERMAN EXILES IN MEXICO

Wulf Koepke

It should be emphasized from the beginning that this chapter will concern itself only with the literary influences of Traven on the German exile community in his adopted land.[1] As far as we know, there were no direct contacts between the author and his compatriots--a separation quite in keeping with Traven's rejection of anything German, even to the point of claiming American parentage.[2]

But the literary connections were strong. It is obvious that writers like Anna Seghers, Bodo Uhse, Ludwig Renn, and Gustav Regler knew Traven's works. His early novels, especially The Death Ship, had caused a sensation in leftist circles, since they were both progressive and immensely popular--a rare combination. In 1933, Traven had naturally rejected the Nazis and followed the Büchergilde Gutenberg to Zürich. When he finally quarreled with the Büchergilde editors, he published the last of the Caoba novels, General, with the emigré firm Allert de Lange in Amsterdam, shortly before its end in May 1940 when German troops occupied Holland.[3] In the very partisan climate of the exile, the German writers knew that Traven was on their side. It can be assumed, then, that they knew his works in general, and the books relating to Mexico in particular.

This needs to be stressed because Traven is rarely mentioned in exile literature. Gustav Regler, for instance, the renegade communist who made an effort to live among Mexicans and apart from the exile circles, mentions Traven neither in his autobiography, Das Ohr des Malchus, nor in his book on Mexico, Verwunschenes Land Mexiko.[4] There are some--very few--words from the group of Alemania Libre, but they are very significant because they are words of high praise. Anna Seghers maintains in her essay "Volk und Schriftsteller," which appeared in Freies Deutschland of October 15, 1942, "Since Volk is not only nature, not blood and soil, it impresses itself upon a writer not as a natural phenomenon, but as a social one."[5] Therefore, foreign-born writers can very well be "volkstümlich" (popular) even if they write in a language other than their own, or in translation. Her first example is Joseph Conrad, the next one B. Traven: "Traven is a writer who portrays in an exemplary fashion by means of the German language events among the Mexican people (Volk)."[6] Ludwig Renn reports in his autobiographical writings that Rebellion was adapted for the stage by students in Morelia while he was teaching there, and that it was performed with great success, a report restated in his Nachwort to a 1954 East German edition of The Cotton Pickers: "The Mexicans were thrilled by the power of the revolutionary play. That is the effect Traven intended."[7] Renn mentions that the students in Morelia, mostly Indians, were sad because they had to turn to a foreign author for a play on the Mexican Revolution.[8] Ludwig Renn's report, confirmed by Anna Seghers,[9] shows that the exile admired--and possibly envied--Traven's power over the minds of the Mexican people: He knew how to write for "das mexikanische Volk" and to reach the masses, to be "volkstümlich" (popular) in a foreign country and in a foreign language. Even more, he was "vorbildlich"--a model to follow, someone who showed the others how to do it. The term "vorbildlich" has added significance given the ideological context of the Communist party: Anna Seghers and Ludwig Renn integrated Traven's Mexican fiction into the history of revolutionary proletarian literature.

This is most remarkable, since they could not help noticing the anarchist tendencies in Traven's books, while they were loyal party members during the period of Stalinism. Traven/Torsvan certainly did not like party communists and the system of the Soviet Union. However, the very name of Freies Deutschland stood for a popular front, a Volksfront orientation, which welcomed all "democratic" antifascist allies, just as the Spanish anti-Franco coalition had been a popular front--and most of the Germans in Mexico had fought in Spain. Attempts at a German Volksfront under the leadership of Heinrich Mann had been made since 1934. It was fitting that the Mexican Freies Deutschland was eager to secure the support of Heinrich Mann, who was by then a forgotten old man living in isolation in the Los Angeles area.[10]

The concept of Freies Deutschland demanded that first and foremost all energies should be concentrated on the antifascist struggle, which included building up a popular front of the Germans in Latin America, fighting against German Nazis on the continent, convincing the wavering German communities to choose the correct side, and convincing the Latin American governments to take a stand against Hitler. This is reflected in the program of the Heinrich-Heine-Klub in Mexico City[11] and also in the publications of El Libro Libre, which in the area of German fiction were concentrated on topics of resistance against Hitler's Germany: Anna Seghers's Das siebte Kreuz and Bodo Uhse's Leutnant Bertram are among the best-known examples.[12]

And yet the exiles did not forget their second duty, which was solidarity with the masses of the Mexican people and

support of their revolutionary struggle. The Germans were
in a somewhat delicate position, since they owed gratitude
to a Mexican government that called itself revolutionary;
they could not help noticing, however, that the Mexican
revolution was far from completed from a communist point of
view. They also had ties with the Mexican communists--
although these were badly split--who were of course in
opposition to the government.

It is therefore significant that Freies Deutschland includes quite a few contributions on various aspects of
Mexican life and culture, and that El Libro Libre published
Kisch's Entdeckungen in Mexico, with its harsh indictment of
the continuing exploitation of Indios, very much in the vein
of Traven's Caoba Cycle.[13] Generally speaking, the German
exiles were quite open to the Mexican environment around
them, although they lived in a close-knit group and rarely
left Mexico City. Latin America proved to be more attractive for exile writers than most other exile environments,
with the possible exception of France. There was so much
more interest in pre-Columbian art, Indian folk-art, the
Indian way of life, the scenery of the various parts of the
continent, and the present and future problems of its societies, than in the history and traditions of North America.
This is also true for writers in other Latin American countries, such as Paul Zech in Argentina, Erich Arendt in
Colombia, or Ulrich Becher in Brazil.

Writers like Anna Seghers and Bodo Uhse were on the "liberal" side during the period when the party wanted to impose
Soviet Socialist Realism on the exile writers. This is
shown by Anna Seghers's correspondence with Georg Lukacs and
by other writings of the period, such as "Volk und Schriftsteller."[14] Seghers's first writings had coincided with
Traven's sudden appearance on the German book market. Traven's direct impact on German writers was possibly even
greater in the genre of the short story than in the novel--
at least, the story is the one genre in which the German
exiles in Mexico have related their experiences. Traven's
first collection of stories, Der Busch, had appeared in
1928, and individual stories were of course reprinted several times.[15] These stories were very timely because they
combined several attractive elements. They were mostly
"Indianergeschichten," a genre introduced by James Fenimore
Cooper, whose stories were mostly read in abridged versions
for youngsters, and whose noble savages had been kept alive
by Karl May's noble Apaches. Thus, exoticism proved to be a
fascinating ingredient.[16] These Indians and white men were,
however, described in the matter-of-fact way of the American
short story, and even the incredible events were told in a

factual way, the narrator usually appearing as a firsthand witness to the events or even as a first-person participant. Thus, the strong element of authenticity was mixed into the exoticism, with a narrative stance of mere reporting, not psychological "Einfühlung" (empathy). The narrator emphasizes that the mentality of these Indians is very different, and he questions fundamental beliefs and attitudes of the white man by contrasting him with the Mexican Indians. This fits into the period of Die neue Sachlichkeit "New Objectivity"--which replaced Expressionism and its high rhetoric of "der neue Mensch" (new man) with a factual but critical view of present society, and a generally favorable attitude towards modern civilization. This is one point where Traven seems to differ, although his Land contained a plea for a more progressive agriculture. The apparently simple reporting technique of the narrator, however, frequently brought about new narrative strategies and new types of "heroes," as in such diverse works as Döblin's Berlin Alexanderplatz, Feuchtwanger's Erfolg, and Remarque's Im Westen nichts Neues, or, more pertinent still, Anna Seghers's Die Fischer von St. Barbara and Ludwig Renn's Krieg.

Traven's stories, in spite of their Hemingway-style factuality, still preserve essential features of the German Novelle. They not only present an exciting event, a good dose of humor and irony, and a narrator who seems to stumble into the events accidentally, but they also describe a turning point in a person's life, and in spite of the abstraction from psychological analysis they probe the depth of the human personality. There is a Leitmotiv, and even the atmosphere of romantic mystery traditional since the stories of E. T. A. Hoffmann and Edgar Allan Poe. Traven's forte is to explain a person's character in the context of his social and cultural environment, the interdependence of the individual and the group, and of man and nature.

In the fierce struggle within the Communist party about the right concept of a revolutionary proletarian literature, the victorious trend was the conservative concept that prescribed an adherence to the tradition of the nineteenth-century realist writers, like Balzac and Tolstoy, and a rejection of modernist narrative or stage techniques and strategies. This struggle had begun around 1930, was continued during the exile period--chiefly in the so-called debate on Expressionism--and had its effects after 1945 in the German Democratic Republic (GDR). Traven did not fit into the prescribed form. He was realistic, and his heroes were average people; he presented popular movements, but he did all of this in a somewhat romantic spirit, with clear anarchistic tendencies and with a clear predilection for the individual who manages to survive, and not for heroes of the class struggle. He did not reduce social conflicts to class struggle either, since he insisted on the significance of the racial differences in Mexico.

Considering Traven's stance and type of literature, it is surprising how closely Anna Seghers's or Bodo Uhse's Mexican stories follow Traven, who was evidently a role model "vorbildlich," for them. Except for Ludwig Renn's children's book Trini, an adventure story of a Mexican boy at the time of the exploits of Pancho Villa and Zapata, no narrow partisan spirit or didacticism emanates from the Mexican stories of the exiles. Most of them were written after the return to Germany and were aimed at a German audience as Anna Seghers stresses at the beginning of Crisanta;[17] and they had that fascination with exoticism which was part of Traven's success in Germany before 1933 and after 1945. The stories also reveal a certain amount of nostalgia, understandable enough in the case of aging writers struggling in the trying conditions of the early years of the GDR. Both the subject matter and the style of these stories present an atmosphere of freedom, of the wide-open world, which is part of Traven's nature, but which is absent from most of the earlier GDR literature. The distance in space and culture serves not so much to draw parallels between the readers' living conditions and those of the books' characters, but to stress the differences. Thus, the Mexican stories brought back by the writers from their exile could serve as a diversion, as a true entertainment, for the Germans on their road to socialism.

Socialism and the class struggle were of course not absent from the exiles' writings. Egon Erwin Kisch in Entdeckungen in Mexiko and Ludwig Renn in Morelia provide detailed accounts of oppression and exploitation.[18] Bodo Uhse's Sonntagsträumerei in der Alameda is set against a background of a railroad strike and police brutality. Efraim in Der Weg zum Rio Grande experiences a process of awakening class consciousness and hope for a change. Miguel, one of Crisanta's lovers, takes advantage of an adult education program and is on his road to advancement. However, this theme of class struggle and technical progress—also prominent in Gustav Regler's Verwunschenes Land Mexico which deals at length with irrigation and reforestation—pales in comparison with the emphasis on conditions that will never change: the landscape, the character of the Mexican people, their mentality, and their truly human and humane way of life. Fundamental issues of human existence emerge as their preoccupation.

There is a strange fascination with death in Mexico.
Regler's Verwunschenes Land Mexiko devotes one of four chapters to the theme of death; it is echoed in Bodo Uhse's
diaries[19] and even more distinctly in his stories, especially Reise in einem blauen Schwan or Sonntagsträumerei in
der Alameda. The closest parallel is Traven's Macario, with
its roots in Grimm's and Bechstein's Gevatter Tod. Death
and unreality surround the pre-Columbian ruins covered by
the Mexican jungle, where it may seem that the past is alive
and the present is dead. Traven's "Der Nachtbesuch im
Dschungel" tells us how the first-person narrator is caught
by this jungle atmosphere in his lonely cabin, until he
meets the dead Aztec prince emerging from the ruins in the
jungle, when he is frightened by brutal hogs.

This strange intermingling of past and present, of fantasy
and reality, is re-created in a different way in Anna Seghers's story Der Ausflug der toten Mädchen, written during
her Mexican days. Here, a hot afternoon in a Mexican village inn is magically transformed into the scenery of the
German Rhineland, and the middle-aged and sick exile becomes
the teenager on a school excursion. Past and present,
Mexico and the Rhineland, become transparent; the flow of
time is transformed into a simultaneous moment in which the
isolated exile can see in one glimpse the lives and deaths
of her former friends and teachers from World War I to the
Nazi era. Time rushes forward and turns life into death,
and yet it stands still: The Mexican innkeeper sits as
motionless at the end as he was sitting at the beginning.
The one-directional time flow of the European mind is replaced by nature's cycles and a feeling of duration above
change, as Alfred Döblin--who never went to Latin America--
described it in his trilogy Amazonas.[20] Questioning the
reality of the present, reliving the past, traveling in
time--all these are, of course, attitudes typical of the
exile, the person who is waiting for a return to a home that
may not exist anymore. The timeless and yet unreal landscape and culture of Mexico, as they are presented in "Der
Nachtbesuch," therefore have a curious affinity to the exile's condition, and they are also suitable to question the
European concepts of time, progress, and history.

Traven's Mexican stories are characterized not only by a
frank description in convincing detail of the abject poverty
and exploitation of the Mexican Indians, but also by the
presentation of a mentality quite different from that of the
white man. The behavior of the Indians is very consistent
and reasonable under their conditions and in the framework
of their beliefs, but it strikes the European reader as very
strange, as in "Die Geschichte einer Bombe," where one is

struck by the sudden alternation of murder and life-saving; the Indian blend of Catholicism is exposed in "Der aufgefangene Blitz" and "Der ausgewanderte Antonio." The Indian way of doing business, incomprehensible to a capitalist, finds its expression in "Der Eselskauf" and "Der Grossindustrielle."[21] Such is the world of Anna Seghers's Crisanta, although Seghers intentionally refrains from the anecdotal structure of Traven's stories; and such are the human relations in Uhse's Der Weg zum Rio Grande, where an exciting plot also develops, without the happy ending of most of Traven's stories. (Efraim, who is trying to cross the Rio Grande to become an illegal migrant worker in Texas, barely escapes when the guides not only take the money of the men in the group, but also murder them one by one in cold blood.) Traven, Seghers, and Uhse tell the incredible and inexplicable events in this strange country in a matter-of-fact way, with a good dose of irony, humor, and even sarcasm, but without raising their voices. While Traven seems to relish the taming of the shrew in "Bändigung," Uhse is clearly appalled by the cruelty of a Mexican millionaire towards his wife in Gespräch beim Regen, in which the millionaire chooses not to clear his wife of a murder he knows she did not commit, so that her conviction will leave him free to live with a dancer in Paris. Uhse and Regler point out the divided self of the Mexican in the manner of Octavio Paz, and the exiles are more shocked by the brutality and the extremes of human nature in this country--which also haunted Spanish exiles like Max Aub--than Traven seems to be, at least in his stories: Traven clearly puts the burden of survival and improvement of one's condition on the individual's shoulders, whereas the exiles partly view the characters of their stories as victims. Crisanta may be closest to Traven in this respect, as well as in its point of view, which is to tell Crisanta's story from her own, Indian perspective.

There is again and again a development which blurs the borderline between reality and imagination, as in "Der Nachtbesuch" or "Dennoch eine Mutter," where the girl Mercedes is frustrated because her lover does not show up for the wedding, and she invents the rest of her life--marriage, the birth of a son, his upbringing--so convincingly that her friends are searching for the son after she dies. Uhse's Reise in einem blauen Schwan concentrates the imaginary happiness of Miguel and Carmela in a ride in the blue swan of a merry-go-round, a ride for which Miguel knows he will have to pay dearly; and he is in fact murdered by Carmela's husband, Sanchez Cristobal. Here, just as in Sonntagsträumerei in der Alameda, love and death, poverty, anxiety, brief happiness, fantasy and brutal reality are blended together in touching exmples of human existence. The color blue has special meaning, both here and in Seghers's stories, as in <u>Das wirkliche Blau</u> and at the end of <u>Crisanta</u>.[22] In contrast to literary conventions, it does not indicate infinity or religious dimensions, but the human condition and the wide land of human dreams and imagination.

This is a world where miracles indeed occur, but they are "Wunder der Wirklichkeit," miracles of reality as Anna Seghers called them, and Traven did his best to so portray them, both his religious "miracles" and the miracle healings of his "doctors." Thus, Mexico becomes this strange mixture of everyday reality and incredible events, just as time and timelessness blend into one another. This view of the Mexican people and of their "simple" life revolving around life and death, love and hate, poverty and wealth--the incomprehensible mentality of Mexico's people, which is at the same time so deeply human and "normal"--was transmitted by Traven to the exiles. Whereas the exiles were unprepared for most of the cultures and peoples where they went, they came prepared to Mexico, prepared by the world of Traven; and one might even ask if he did not shape their image of Mexico too much, so that they followed his perspective to the exclusion of other possible ones. He certainly was "vorbildlich" for them in the essential ingredients of the stories. They knew the same authors that Traven knew: Joseph Conrad, Jack London, James Fenimore Cooper, Ernest Hemingway. In spite of their struggle for progress, they integrated themselves, as Traven had done, into the tradition of the antipioneer, the anticivilization story, the story which praises man as part of a natural environment, and as respecting nature, not destroying it. This is in harmony with Traven's view of the Indians and the general idea of the "people," the lower classes, among these socialist writers: the <u>Volk</u> (people) is genuine, human, and leads a meaningful life, as opposed to the artificial life of the upper classes in Mexico and the capitalists in the United States. The humanity of the people prevails in spite of oppressive living conditions and under any social and political system. This somewhat idealized image of the people fits, on the one hand, into the politicl context of the GDR; on the other hand, it contradicts the socialist concept of progress. The stories of Traven and the exiles are reminders of a timeless humanity, basic human values and conditions that may transcend specific historical and social circumstances. This ambiguity of work for better living conditions and praise for "primitive" man may be quite plausible in Traven, but it is rather surprising in the work of communist exiles. It was certainly reinforced by their experience of the Mexican people and environment. From this aspect as well, the exiles' Mexican stories transcend specific ideological requirements and differ from most of what was written in the GDR at that time. Although none of their stories is located in the jungle of Chiapas, which they did not know firsthad, they followed Traven in their emphasis on the interdependence of man and the natural environment.

If the comparison of the exiles' works with Traven's stories helps to bring into focus the exiles' experience of the relativity of European civilization and values, involving a different notion of time, human existence, and the natural environment--although they tried to stay loyal to their political beliefs, which included the Western idea of progress--a look back from their works to Traven might also reveal frequently neglected features in his work. Traven may have felt at home in Mexico, but he was still a stranger, just like the exile in Der Ausflug der toten Mädchen. The frequent switch to fantasies in Traven's works, his dreaming about the Mexican past, the fairy-tale-like atmosphere of stories like Macario, and the re-creation of Indian legends as in Sonnen-Schöpfung--all of these elements make him far more than a realist writer who recorded his autobiographical experiences. The element of imagination, of sheer fantasy, of romantic storytelling ought not to be overlooked in Traven's work, and it was certainly carried on by Anna Seghers and Bodo Uhse, not to mention Paul Zech in Argentina.[23]

It would be far too much to claim an exclusive influence of Traven's works on the German exiles in Mexico. They came from similar traditions and were marked by comparable experiences. Their political views were as different as their intentions while writing. However, Traven provided them with a model of how to write not only about the Mexican people, but also about experiences of alienation, of feeling oneself lost in a strange country, of a blending of dream and reality, which found such powerful expression in Der Ausflug der toten Mädchen and Sonntagsträumerei in der Alameda. Rightfully or not, they discovered in Traven the representation of the exile's condition, and Die neue Sachlichkeit blended with Romanticism. This blending may be revealing for both Traven and the exiles. Traven encouraged and legitimized the exiles' flights of imagination as much as he directed them to a careful observation of the life of the Mexican people. The comparison of Traven and the exiles therefore may also serve as a help in placing Traven in the context of the history of German literature.

304

Notes

1. El Libro Libre, Mexico City, 1945. Traven's life could have made a fascinating chapter in Entdeckungen in Mexico by Egon Erwin Kisch, who was also later one of the first reporters to track down the identity of Ret Marut and B. Traven. 2. Recknagel, 1982, 22, 303.

3. Raskin, 1980, 29.

4. München: List, 1954; original title Vulkanisches Land. Ein Buch von vielen Festen und mehr Widersprüchen (Saarbrücken: Saar-Verlag, 1947). Das Ohr des Malchus. (Köln/ Berlin: Kiepenheuer & Witsch, 1958), English ed. The Owl of Minerva (New York: Farrar, Strauss, 1959).

5. Anna Seghers, Woher sie kommen, wohin sie gehen. Essays aus vier Jahrzehnten (Darmstadt/Neuwied: Luchterhand, 1980), 53; "Volk und Schriftsteller" also in Wolfgang Kiessling, Alemania Libre in Mexico (Berlin: Akademie Verlag, 1974), II, 120-27.

6. l.c.; Recknagel dedicated his biography of Traven to Anna Seghers.

7. Morelia. Eine Universitätsstadt in Mexico, in Gesammelte Werke (Berlin: Aufbau Verlag, 1968), VI; Recknagel, 247.

8. Morelia, VI, 455.

9. Recknagel, 1982, 247; the confirmation is based on a letter of Anna Seghers to Recknagel (369).

10. Kiessling, Allemania Libre II, 361-431.

11. Kiessling, Allemania Libre I, 103-17, and II, 183-96.

12. Kiessling, Allemania Libre I, 220-43, and II, 249-51.

13. Besides the "Vanille-Indianer," Kisch also deals with conditions in the mines and other agricultural sectors.

14. "Zwei Briefe an Georg Lukacs," Woher sie kommen, wohin sie gehen, 29-45, also "Aufgaben der Kunst," op. cit., 70-75; cf. Die Expressionismusdebatte. Materialien zu einer marxistischen Realismuskonzeption, ed. Hans-Jürgen Schmitt (Frankfurt: Suhrkamp, 1973).

15. Recknagel, 1982, 406-9.

16. Wolfgang Reif, Zivilisationsflucht und literarische Wunschträume. Der exotistische Roman im ersten Viertel des 20. Jahrhunderts (Stuttgart: J. B. Metzler, 1975).

17. "Ihr fragt, wie die Menschen in Mexico leben?--Von wem soll man erzählen?" Erzählungen (Neuwied/Berlin: Luchterhand, 1964), II, 141; she goes on to say why she does not want to tell about famous Mexicans, but about the girl Crisanta.

18. Uhse's Mexican stories from Sonntagsträumerei in der Alameda und andere Erzählungen (Frankfurt: Röderberg, 1979).

19. Reise- und Tagebücher I, Gesammelte Werke V (Berlin: Aufbau Verlag, 1981), 487-530.

20. The two volumes in the edition of the Walter-Verlag need to be supplemented by the third part, Der neue Urwald, which makes the white man of today disappear in the jungles of South America. Nature has the last word.

21. B. Traven, Erzählungen (Zürich: Limmat Verlag, 1968), 2 volumes.

22. Kurt Batt, Anna Seghers: Versuch über Entwicklung und Werk (Frankfurt: Röderberg, 1973), 175-77.

23. Arnold Spitta, Paul Zech im südamerikanischen Exil 1933-1946, Bibliotheca Ibero-Americana vol. 24, (Berlin: Colloquium, 1978); also Wolfgang Kiessling, Exil in Lateinamerika (Frankfurt: Röderberg, 1981), 324-52; neither of them mentions B. Traven.

THE PRIMITIVIST AS ANARCHIST
Two Novels by B. Traven in the Mexican Literary and
Political Context of the 1930s

Cynthia Steele

Although B. Traven's critics often study his novels within the U.S. and German literary traditions, many critics of Mexican literature have also included certain of his novels within an important subgenre of Mexican literature, indigenista fiction. In Mexico and other Spanish American nations, this subgenre is a variant of the realist novel which deals with the conflicts between Indian groups and the dominant, nation-building society. The decade of the 1930s, when Traven published his cycle of Jungle novels in German, was an era of extensive social and economic reform in Mexico which culminated in the presidency of Lázaro Cárdenas (1934-40); a key element of Cárdenas's policy was Indian reform. During this decade, three important Mexican novels about the Indian issue were published, constituting the first flowering of indigenista fiction in Mexico.[1] They were El indio (1935), by Gregorio López y Fuentes; El resplandor (Sunburst, 1937), by Mauricio Magdaleno; and Canek (1940), by Ermilo Abreu Gómez.

The first two Spanish-language editions of Traven's works were also published in Mexico during the 1930s: Bridge in 1935; and Rebellion, in 1938. The possibility that the Mexican indigenista writers influenced Traven is remote, since the original, German edition of Bridge antedated all three Mexican novels, and Rebellion antedated all but one, El indio. It is very probable, however, that, in writing about the Mexican Indian, Traven was influenced not only by his personal experiences in Chiapas during the 1920s, but also by the sensitivity to the Indian issue in Mexican politics and letters during the 1930s. Surely this climate was in part responsible for the publication of these first Mexican editions of Traven's works during Cárdenas's presidency. Moreover, it is probable that Traven's novels influenced Mexican writers of the 1940s and 1950s.[2]

In this chapter I will analyze Traven's portrayal of Indian society and its interaction with the dominant society in these two novels that were published in Mexico during the

Cárdenas era.[3] In so doing I hope to determine to what extent this portrayal coincides with Mexican indigenista literature of the 1930s, and with the official Mexican Indian policy that this literature interprets.

While both Bridge (1929) and Rebellion (1936) focus on a group of Indian characters, the two groups serve very different fictional purposes. Bridge features an anonymous Indian village called simply "Huts by the River," which is located somewhere along the fictitious Huayalexco River. The Indian group inhabiting the village also remains unidentified, so that the village can represent the thousands of such hamlets which exist in the Mexican jungle. The novel explores the reactions of the villagers to the disappearance of a small boy and the eventual discovery of his body, with particular attention to the grief of the boy's mother, who becomes the archetypical mater dolorosa. Traven's interest in Bridge is to portray the heartfelt reactions of a so-called "primitive" or "natural" people to a tragedy, and in so doing to contrast "primitive" to "civilized" society.

In Rebellion, on the other hand, Traven employs Tzotzil Indian characters to illustrate one particularly cruel form in which the Mexican rural proletariat has been exploited by the ruling classes in Mexico. In view of this political purpose, the use of Indian characters is quite appropriate, since the exploitation of Indian laborers by Mexican landowners has been and continues to be a particularly serious problem, involving both class exploitation and caste or racial discrimination. Traven's choice of Tzotzil Indian characters is particularly effective, since they belong to a Mexican Indian group that, on the one hand, has maintained the strongest cultural identity and group solidarity in the face of oppression and, on the other hand, has continued to be among the most exploited by the Mexican ladinos (i.e., non-Indians). At the same time, since in this novel Traven's purpose is to expose the sufferings of Mexican rural workers as a class, he takes noticeably fewer pains than in Bridge to differentiate the Indian characters culturally from members of ladino society.

Several critics have noted in passing the primitivism underlying Bridge,[4] but this aspect of the novel has yet to be analyzed in detail. Since Bridge was written several years before the first Mexican indigenista novels, we can discount Mexican literary portrayals of the Indian as an influence on Traven. It would seem more likely that, in his early treatment of Mexican Indian culture, he was influenced by the primitivism of D. H. Lawrence's The Plumed Serpent (1926). For Traven during this early period, the Indian is the natural man, the child of nature, living a simple, instinctual, authentic life uncomplicated by intellectual issues or by the consumerism of capitalist society. He is characterized by innocence, honesty, courtesy, dignity, and tenderness.

Although in his essays Traven rejects James Fenimore Cooper's portrayal of the Indian,[5] in Bridge he has recourse to two types of imagery that draw on Cooper's quintessential paradigm of savagism, i.e., of the Indian as at once a noble and an ignoble savage.[6] In the first place, Traven repeatedly compares his Indian characters to animals. The cries of the Garcia woman are described as resembling "the howl of an animal...[an] almost savage howl" (72). Moreover, her eyes resemble those of an animal in danger (53). Perez's eyes reveal "that pitiful sad look which only animals and primitive people possess" (113). Furthermore, Traven repeatedly compares the Indian characters to Aztec priests and gods. Carrying the body of his little brother, Manuel seems to be offering a sacrifice to the gods. He looks like a bronze god, while the dead boy is compared to the son of a dethroned Aztec king (119 and 125-26). The old man who uses witchcraft to find Carlositos's body looks like an Aztec priest: dignified, aloof, and mysterious (98).

The frequent use of imagery involving animals and pre-Columbian gods has the effect of dehumanizing the Indian characters, making them seem at once subhuman and other-worldly. Moreover, the comical situations and events of the novel, including the ludicrous funeral music and the school-teacher's drunken graveside speech, emphasize the Indians' childlike naïveté and ignorance, and thus reveal the author's paternalistic attitude toward the society he is describing.

Primitivism often appears in literature as a reaction against what the writer perceives to be the alienation and corruption of industrialized, urban civilization. In Bridge Traven reveals this attitude both through editorial comments and through descriptions of the intrusions of Western culture into Indian society. One such intrusion is the cheap clothing that has been mass-produced in New York sweatshops and is sold to the Indians by dishonest Syrian peddlers. The Indian women's natural beauty is marred by "the heavy odor of the strongly perfumed soap bought from Syrian peddlers" and by "dresses from modern sweat-shops," which contrast pathetically with "the simple and natural clothes of the men" (42 and 104). The sailor suit, also bought from the peddlers, in which the Indian mother lays out her son's body, horrifies Traven's narrator and mouthpiece, Gerald Gales: "In his torn and patched-up pants and in his dirty shirt with half a hundred holes in it...the kid was very pretty in his way.   In fact he was a real and natural-looking child of the jungle.   He belonged here.   But in that cheap sailor suit he no longer looked like a son of his native land" (126).   The ultimate symbol of the destructive effect of U.S. capitalist society on the Indian is, of course, the shoes that Carlositos's brother has brought him from the oil fields of Texas, and which cause the boy to slip to his death.   The shoes are "unnatural" products of technological, consumer society, and are therefore danger-ous: "Carlositos...was not fully himself.   Accustomed to stand, walk, and run barefooted since he was born, he now felt unsure on his feet...All the flexibility and lightness of his feet, which heretofore had made him feel like a young antelope, he had suddenly lost without knowing why" (21). These slippery new shoes function in conjunction with the bridge built by the U.S. oil company, which saved money by neglecting to install railings.   Thus, the inhumane policies of U.S. imperalists also contribute to the boy's tragedy.[7]

In addition to manufactured clothing, Traven uses North American popular music to symbolize the degrading influence of commercialized, mass culture on the Mexican Indians. During the funeral march, the narrator notes the incongruity of hearing the song "Taintgonnorainnomo" sung by a group of people "who for nine months had had no drop of rain and by whom rain was considered God's greatest blessing" (192). For Gales, this and the other American dance tunes that the Indians play during the procession exemplify our "faked civilization," in contrast to the Indians' "genuine culture" (192).   While he sees the use of these frivolous tunes for a death march as proof that Indian culture has not altogether assimilated "this vomit of our culture," he notes ironically that "[o]ver this trail blazed by our dance songs, there would soon arrive Fords, vacuum cleaners, electric refriger-ators, air-conditioned grass huts, jungle-colored bathrooms, windmill-driven television, canned alligator stew, and pul-verized hearts of young palm trees" (191).   In other words, North American capitalists will soon expand their market to the remote Mexican jungles, attempting to sell the Indians commercialized, inauthentic versions of their own, natural culture, thereby corrupting and degrading primitive society. In this same vein, the narrator notes elsewhere in the novel that the Indian race "has a great future, provided it is not taken in by installment plans for buying things they can do without" (196).

Thus, Bridge conveys a peculiar blend of primitivist and anti-imperialist thought.   The U.S. oil companies and manu-facturers are evil because they are motivated by profit rather than by humanitarian principles; but they are also evil because they are introducing bad taste into a society with innate good taste. This assumption leads Traven to ludicrous assertions, such as the one regarding Carlositos's sailor suit; however ragged, worn, and dirty the boy's peasant clothes may be, they are preferable to a clean, new sailor suit that was mass-produced in the sweatshops of New York. While one might sympathize with the respect that Traven feels for Indian folk culture, in this novel one has the sense that his blanket rejection of mass-produced products and culture leads him to idealize poverty.

An interesting aspect of the characterization of Gerald Gales in Bridge is his ambivalence toward his Indian hosts, an ambivalence that Traven probably shared. At one point Gales argues with Sleigh, the North American inhabitant of the Indian village, that members of Western society see the Indian as mysterious because they don't understand his culture. Here he seems to be arguing against the tendency of primitivists to stereotype and mystify Indian culture. Generally, however, Gales himself views the Indian within the stereotyped framework of noble savagism, with its dark corollary of ignoble savagism. In most situations he regards the Indian villagers with a mixture of respect and benevolent paternalism. After Carlositos's death, however, he succumbs to an irrational fear of the Indian as "other": "I am alone," he thinks, "I am on another planet...with creatures I do not know,...whose souls and minds I can never fathom." He goes on to speculate that, should the villagers suddenly decide to blame him, the outsider, for the boy's death, they might "become infuriated and hammer...[him] into a pulp." In this eventuality, Gales fears that Sleigh would stand by passively and allow it to happen (105-7). This fantasy recalls the fear of Indian mob violence that permeates both nineteenth-century U.S. literature about the Indian, including the novels of Cooper, and twentieth-century Mexican indigenista fiction. The portrayal of Sleigh also brings to mind the image of the "white Indian" so prevalent in the earlier U.S. fiction; that is, the man of European descent who has lived so long among Indians that he has adopted their characteristics or nature, including callousness toward savage violence. Gales avoids being "sacrificed" by his Indian hosts by demonstrating scientific knowledge that they interpret as magical; he thus successfully appeals to Indian superstition, a further component of the literary paradigm of savagism.[8]

Although six of Traven's other novels have been translated into Spanish, Rebellion is by far the most familiar of his works to the Mexican public. In part this is due to the wide circulation of the novel itself, but in addition, the

311

book has been staged theatrically and made into a popular movie. Moreover, the Mexican Secretary of Education recently issued a comic-book version of the novel as part of a federal project to make the classics of Mexican literature available to the masses.

As I noted earlier, Rebellion is clearly a different type of novel from Bridge. The principal strength of Bridge lies in its detailed re-creation of living conditions in an Indian village, and in its evocation of the emotions of grief, tenderness, and solidarity. The principal defect of the novel is its paternalistic attitude toward the Indian characters. In Rebellion, on the other hand, Traven concerns himself with neither anthropology nor psychology; rather, he limits his narrative focus to the inhumane working and living conditions in the mahogany lumber camps of Chiapas at the beginning of the century, and to the revolt that occurs as an inevitable human response to oppression and cruelty. Just as the narrative purpose is more narrowly defined, the narration is more direct, with a third-person omniscient narrator replacing the more subjective--and more interesting--first-person narration of Bridge.

As Joseph Sommers has noted, the weaknesses of Rebellion stem from "the narrator's lofty posture of omniscience, eliminating irony or subtlety in characterization, from the limited mono-institutional setting in which the narrative is developed--a setting which fails to account for the advent of mahogany-based investment, its contradiction with the agricultural patterns of both Indian and ladino communities, and its cultural impact on the Indian."[9] On the other hand, the novel was the first work to treat the issue of the exploitation of the Indians of Chiapas, an issue that would resurface in the works of a minor novelist, Ramón Rubín, at the end of the 1940s, and that would be most fully explored in the words of Rosario Castellanos at the end of the 1950s. Moreover, Traven is the only indigenista novelist writing in Mexico who has ever posited proletarian revolution as the solution to the so-called "Indian problem." While Mexican writers of the 1930s portrayed the Mexican Revolution as incomplete and called for drastic reforms to the political system, Traven depicted the beginning of the Revolution in Rebellion as a prototype for the total anarchist revolution of the future, which would eliminate all forms of authority and bureaucracy in Mexican society.

This difference between reformism and anarchism is the fundamental difference between Traven and the Mexican writers of the 1930s. Gregorio López y Fuentes, the author of El indio (1935), belonged to Cárdenas's National Revolu-

tionary party, later to become the Party of the Institutionalized Revolution that still rules Mexico. El indio, which
was awarded the National Book Award of 1935 and was hailed
as the official novel of cardenismo, shared the cardenistas'
benevolent paternalism toward the Indian, and it espoused
their official policy of incorporating the Indian, through
education and economic improvements, into all aspects of
national life. The Indian protagonists of El indio are
portrayed as degraded noble savages who are incapable of
helping themselves, but who can be redeemed by benevolent
ladino intellectuals.

Mauricio Magdaleno, the author of El resplandor (Sunburst, 1937), and Ermilo Abreu Gómez, the author of Canek
(1940), were Marxists who were aligned with the left wing of
cardenismo. Like Traven, both of these novelists present an
interpretation of Indian oppression that is fundamentally
economic, and, like Traven, they are both extremely critical
of what they see as a corrupt and oppressive social structure. Unlike Traven, the two Mexican authors nevertheless
advocate incorporating the Indian into the existing socioeconomic system, which they view as potentially benevolent,
once it is extensively reformed.

Of the Mexican authors, Abreu Gómez is the closest in
spirit to Traven. His portrayal of Mayan Indian characters
in Canek reveals a strong strain of primitivism of the sort
that predominates in Bridge. At the same time, Abreu Gómez
describes torture and exploitation similar to those portrayed in Rebellion, and the Mayan characters, like the
historical figures after whom they were modeled, also rebel
against their oppressors. Canek is a nontraditional novel
composed of a series of brief anecdotes and lyrical fragments; this structure leads Abreu Gómez to oversimplify the
issues, making his characters unidimensional heroes and
villains not unlike those in Rebellion.

As Joseph Sommers has observed in his analysis of Magdaleno's novel El resplandor, Magdaleno was unusual among
indigenista writers of the 1930s in his complex portrayals
of Indian and ladino psychology, and of the workings of the
social system.[10] Whereas other writers, including Abreu
Gómez and Traven, lapsed into stereotype and oversimplifica-
tion, Magdaleno created a fictional world whose subtlety
would not be matched in indigenista fiction until twenty-
five years later, with the publication of Rosario Castellanos's novels.

Traven and the Mexican writers of the 1930s coincided in
viewing the Indian's miserable condition as resulting from
contact with the dominant society. For the cardenista writers, as for Mexican politicians of the era, the solution lay

in increased contact between the two societies, with a view toward fully incorporating the Indian into Mexican national life. Traven, however, favored more radical solutions. On the one hand, in Bridge, he seems to favor increased isolation, which may fail to alleviate the Indian's poverty, but would prevent the destruction of Indian culture, including the values of simplicity, authenticity, and solidarity. These values are still intact in the remote community that Gales visits in Bridge, as well as in the isolated, primitivist paradise to which Howard and Curtin escape at the end of Treasure.

On the other hand, in Rebellion, Traven posits increased contact between Indian and ladino society, but of a different sort than the Mexican writers advocate. Rather than become citizens of a capitalist society in a reformist phase, the Indians should join forces with all other Mexican workers to make the total proletarian revolution that will eliminate all bosses, replacing capitalism with an undefined anarchistic structure. The liberation of the Indian would thus mean the liberation of all Mexican workers, in a process that would change both the infrastructure and the superstructure of Mexican society, that would "change not only the system but also the narrow spirit of man" (246).

Notes

1. The second flowering of the literature occurred during the 1950s and early 1960s.

2. For instance, the father of the anthropologist and writer Carlo Antonio Castro collaborated in translating the first Mexican edition of Rebellion. While he was working on the translation, he read it to his young son, who would later write his own novel about the Indians of Chiapas, Los hombres verdaderos (The True Men, 1959). (Personal interview with Carlo Antonio Castro, Xalapa, Mexico, May 1978.)

3. B. Traven, The Bridge in the Jungle (New York: Hill and Wang, 1967); The Rebellion of the Hanged (New York: Hill and Wang, 1952). Subsequent references are to these editions and will be cited in the text.

4. For example, see Kazin, 1938, 6; Chankin, 1975, 64-78; and Ruffinelli, 1978, 19-64.

5. B. Traven, "Der Romman Regierung," Die Büchergilde, No. 9 (1931), 261 (cited by Chankin, p. 93).

6. See Pearce, 1965, 202-3.

7. It was Charles H. Miller who first posited this ideological reading of the novel in Miller (1968).

8. The biographical source of this episode, and of the

novel as a whole, was a frightening experience in the Lacandon jungle of Chiapas in 1926. Traven rode his horse across an Indian bridge, thus causing the bridge to collapse and breaking his leg. The collapse of the bridge brought upon the author the wrath of the Indian villagers, who thought that Traven was a demon come to destroy the village. Raskin, 1980, 213 and 187.

9. Sommers, 1979, 26. The translation is from the unpublished English manuscript of the article.

10. Ibid., 31-32.

"SAILING WITH SEALED ORDERS"
Herman Melville's White-Jacket and
B. Traven's The Death Ship

Pattie Cowell

Some years ago, as a graduate student in the final stages of
preparing for comprehensive examinations, I read Melville's
White Jacket and B. Traven's Death Ship on successive days.
Such a large number of similarities--coincidental, I thought
then--emerged from my reading that I determined to investigate further the possibility of Melville's influence on
Traven. The problems presented by such an investigation are
quickly summarized: if one can determine and list many of
the books which Melville read, annotated, owned or borrowed,
no such listing is possible for Traven.[1] The difficulties
of determining even basic biographical information for Traven have been overwhelming; tracing his reading is well-nigh
impossible. We are forced to pursue his literary influence
by inference, by engaging in a process of observation and
study curiously analogous to that employed by White-Jacket
and Gales within their respective fictive worlds. Our
study--like theirs--is destined to be inconclusive, but also
like theirs, it can be illuminating.

This study has two emphases: a tentative historical argument that Traven knew Melville's work and textual comparison
of Melville's White-Jacket and Traven's Death Ship.[2]

I

Suggestions of Melville's influence on Traven are almost
inevitable. Their shared imagery of the sea and their
explorations of shipboard life as microcosms of the larger
world have led scholars to look for other parallels as well.
But are these similarities mere coicidence? Did Traven read
Melville?

We know from Michael Baumann's research that Traven was
familiar with some of Melville's American contemporaries.[3]
He read at least the Cooper of The Leatherstocking Tales,
and perhaps of the sea stories as well. He was familiar
with the works of Longfellow and of Whitman, and with such
later American writers as Jack London and Upton Sinclair.
We know, then, of Traven's general interest in nineteenth-
century American literature.

Further, we know that Traven was in England for several
months in 1923 and 1924, just two years before the publication of Das Totenschiff in 1926, and that he may have

316

visited the United States in 1929 before his much expanded English translation appeared as The Death Ship in 1934.[4] Those visits fall during a period--roughly from 1917 to 1932--of enthusiastic Melville revival in both England and the United States. Work by Carl Van Doren for the Cambridge History of American Literature and as an editor for The Nation encouraged Raymond Weaver to prepare the first biography, Herman Melville: Mariner and Mystic, published in 1921. Several essays of reappraisal were printed in such periodicals as the London Athenaeum, the Review, the London Bookman, the London Nation, the London Spectator, and the Freeman for the Melville centennial in 1919 and in the early 1920s.[5] Some of these periodical pieces appeared during Traven's stay in England, as did D. H. Lawrence's provocative discussion of Melville in Studies in Classic American Literature. Much of this early attention was addressed to Moby Dick, of course, but Lewis Mumford's biocritical study in 1929 expanded the focus to lesser works as well, among them White-Jacket.[6]

Excitement was so great that new editions of Melville's works appeared regularly in England and the United States throughout the twenties. Significantly for my argument, reprints of White-Jacket appeared in London in 1923 and 1924, during Traven's residence there. Other editions were printed in Boston in 1919 and 1923, in London in 1922 and 1929, and in New York in 1924.[7] Melville was in the air; Melville studies were creating a stir; White-Jacket was available again, and not just to antiquarians. It is difficult to imagine a man engaged in writing a sea story, a man who admired nineteenth-century American literature, a man who lives at the geographic center of Melville's rediscovery, not reading Melville.

II

This historical argument is given its greatest corroboration in close textual comparisons of Melville's sea fiction and The Death Ship. Michael Baumann, John Reilly, Donald Chankin, John Fraser, and Charles Miller have already noted several Melvilleian influences on The Death Ship, most frequently from Moby-Dick.[8] They discuss character similarities (e.g., Ishmael-Gales and Pip-Gales), sea imagery, the conspicuous absence of women, the attacks on bureaucracy and hierarchy, the multinational crews, and the cataclysms which end both novels, leaving only the narrators alive. They compare such analogous scenes as the hellish "tryworks" aboard the Pequod with the stokehold of the Yorikke. Donald Chankin's discussion of The Death Ship as "an escape fantasy" opens parallels with The Confidence-Man and Billy Budd as well.[9]

Extending these comparisons, I suggest that close readings of The Death Ship and of White-Jacket reveal a far more fundamental kinship between Melville and Traven. Thematic and structural parallels remain, of course. Melville's first-person narrator--like Gales--is nameless; he is called White-Jacket, identified only by the garment he wears. White-Jacket's vessel, the USS Neversink, becomes--like the Yorikke--a microcosm of a multinational world corrupted by bureaucracy and abusive power structures. Each of these similarities may place Traven in Melville's debt, but the particular debt I wish to explore is more complex: Both White-Jacket and The Death Ship embody a similar epistemological structure; they explore parallel ways of knowing. The narrators--White-Jacket and Gales--undertake a common journey into a way of knowing which is so terrifying that both finish by denying their discoveries.

Both White-Jacket and Gales are philosophers by nature; they apply their considerable education and their close observations of shipboard life to metaphysical inquiry. Gales articulates that inquiry most explicitly. He has been subjected to repeated interrogation about his identity, or, more narrowly, his papers. After refusing to answer an entire battery of questions, he confides to the reader in disgust:

> Yet who is he that could stand a hundred questions and answer none? An unanswered question flutters about you for the rest of your life. It does not let you sleep; it does not let you think. You feel that the equilibrium of the universe is at stake if you leave a question pending. A question without an answer is something so incomplete that you simply cannot bear it....The word "Why?" with a question mark behind it is the cause, I am quite certain, of all culture, civilization, progress, and science. This word "Why?" has changed and will again change every system by which mankind lives and prospers... (DS, 75-76)

Gales understands the scope of that "why." He understands that previous answers--culture, religion, technology, science, political systems of all sorts--are not adequate. But most important, he sees that traditional ways of knowing have deprived us even of tools for answering fundamental questions.

Like Gales, White-Jacket is obsessed with the meaning of his voyaging. He uses metaphor rather than direct statement to outline his search, but what he searches for is as basic

318

as Gales's question:

> As a man-of-war that sails through the sea, so this earth
> that sails through the air....Outwardly regarded, our
> craft is a lie; for all that is outwardly seen of it is
> the clean-swept deck, and oft-painted planks comprised
> above the waterline; whereas, the vast mass of our fabric,
> with all its store-rooms of secrets, forever slides along
> far under the surface. (WJ, 398-99)

Whatever the "craft," be it ship or cunning or art, it is
White-Jacket's business to detail "the interior life of a
man-of-war." In like manner, it is Gales's business to
plumb the mysteries of the Yorikke's dark stokehold, its
unseen chamber of horrors, its unknown age and origins:

> I felt sure--and to this very day I still feel the same
> way--[recalls Gales] that if I had broken open the crusted
> filth and mud, layer by layer, I would have found Phoeni-
> cian coins and medals near the bottom. I still feel
> excited when I speculate on what I might have found if I
> had gone still deeper. (DS, 128)

Both Gales and White-Jacket seek the depths, literally and
metaphorically. Why hierarchy? Why states? Why war? Why
law? Why officers?

White-Jacket and Gales are, then, worker-philosophers,
with a common voice and common questions. But even more
important, they share a common vision: Both narrators suc-
cessively abandon ways of knowing which are not true, ways
of knowing based on authority and on reason. Fundamental
questions cannot, after all, be explored with such faulty
tools.

Initially, White-Jacket and Gales probe answers provided
by authority. Both, for example, describe the carefully
structured shipboard hierarchies. Relations between crew
and officers and relations among crew members are prescribed:

> ...every man of a frigate's five-hundred-strong [says
> White-Jacket], knows his own special place, and is infal-
> libly found there. He sees nothing else, attends to
> nothing else, and will stay there till grim death or an
> epaulette orders him away. (WJ, 8)

And the "places" aboard the Yorikke are no less rigid.
Traven's narrator knows that his shift will be longer than
those of others because he must haul the ashes from the

stokehold. He knows that he must serve an officer's meals, however tired he may be. "I second mate? No, sir. I was not mate on this can, not even bos'n. I was just a plain sailor," says Gales, and that label infallibly assigns him to his place (DS, 4). Whatever the circumstances, a "plain sailor's" failure to be at his post carries severe penalties, the threat of flogging for White-Jacket, the loss of pay or other abuse for Gales.

But if the power of authority is physically inescapable, both novels thoroughly undermine it as a valid epistemological tool. Authority offers no answers to White-Jacket's and Gales's fundamental questions. The rationale for officers' power is presumably their fitness for command, but neither White-Jacket nor Gales can find a single authority figure worthy of office. White-Jacket's skipper is Captain Claret, an alcoholic whose drunken orders nearly result in the loss of the Neversink during a storm off Cape Horn. The commodore of the fleet, who White-Jacket thought was writing weighty memoranda about military strategy, or perhaps his memoirs, is really jotting down notes to the cook about when to serve pickles with the evening meal. The Neversink's midshipmen, "the jelly of youth" (WJ, 346) in training to become officers, are merely errand-boys.

Nor are the officers aboard the Yorikke more fit for command. The skipper, a healthy, handsome, well-dressed, and educated man, cares for his stockholders but not for his crew. He is a gunrunner; he shanghais his crew and then brutalizes them; he will not even remove his hat when a coal-drag who had saved the ship from exploding is buried at sea.

Gales is somewhat better prepared than White-Jacket for the corruption of the ship's officers because he has seen their counterparts ashore. Although Gales refers to them as "high priests," they are by turn inhumane, cowardly, whimsical, and absurd. The guards Gales encounters during his frequent prison stints provide cases in point. During a stay in a Paris jail, Gales is assigned to sew strings on aprons; in ten days he is given time to sew on a single apron string, and it is promptly ripped off for resewing. The authorities during a second prison sentence provide no more meaningful work. Gales must count the items in "a pile of very peculiar-looking nameless things stamped out of bright tinned sheet iron" (DS, 79). No one knows what these nameless things are for, but the official seems so afraid of an error in the counting that he forces Gales to count the pile over and over. Gales leaves prison knowing that the inmate who replaces him will count the same pile.

When the people who represent authority prove incompetent,

White-Jacket and Gales turn to authority itself--the law--
for answers to their metaphysical questions. And here
again, authority is found wanting. Consider White-Jacket's
account of sleeping arrangements aboard the Neversink.
High-ranking officers have quarters and spend "all night in,
just as if they were staying at a hotel on shore" (WJ, 84).
The crew, those individuals responsible for the hardest
physical labor, are packed into a small space and are assigned to watches that dictate four hours on and four hours
off continually. Nor can a crew member let down his hammock
for a nap during daytime off-hours. Why? White-Jacket
explains:

> ...the chief reason is this--a reason which has sanc-
> tioned many an abuse in this world--precedents are against
> it; such a thing as sailors sleeping in their hammocks in
> the daytime, after being eight hours exposed to a night-
> storm, was hardly ever heard of in the navy. (WJ, 84)

In short, it cannot be done because it has not been done--
the weight of tradition.
As Gales attempts to cross the border from France into
Spain, he encounters a similar tradition. He is charged
with spying:

> The officer took a book, opened it, looked for certain
> chapters, read them, and said, when he was through: "You
> will be shot at sunrise. Sorry. On account of being in a
> fortification near the Spanish border. Since the Span-
> iards and we ourselves are still at war with the African
> colonies, the war regulations have not been cancelled.
> Nothing else for me to do but shoot you." (DS, 89)

Never mind that the war is far away. Never mind that Gales
obviously has nothing to do with that conflict. The regula-
tions--White Jacket's "precedents"--direct, and the officer
obeys.
White-Jacket and Gales have to abandon at least one conventional way of knowing: Authority figures and even authority itself are useless tools for seeking answers to
fundamental questions; they become little more than sources
of black humor. When authority--that is, tradition, prece-
dent, regulation, law--fails, White-Jacket and Gales turn to
what they expect to be surer guides. Perhaps reason and
science will provide sound bases for inquiry.
Melville provides two men of science aboard the Neversink,
a surgeon and a professor. But in a grimly hilarious series
of chapters, Surgeon Cuticle reveals himself to be sadistic,

incompetent, and more concerned with scientific experimentation than with his patients. He amputates the leg of a crew
member simply to display his skills to other surgeons in the
fleet; it is never determined that the amputation is medi-
cally necessary. The patient dies, of course, and Cuticle
is delighted to perform an autopsy before those same fellow
physicians. He is more interested in exploring the anatomy
of a cadaver than in saving the life of a fellow being.

Melville's professor is no more promising as the voice of
reason. Although he had trained at West Point in gunnery,
the army found him unfit for duty. Instead he joins the
navy. The professor teaches navigation, never having
learned it himself, and he uses a tactical manual on fleet-
fighting written by a military strategist who had never been
to sea.

Gales's world also questions human reason as a tool for
knowing. How many papers must Gales submit, after all, to
prove that he exists? As one official tells him:

I doubt your birth as long as you have no certificate of
your birth. The fact that you are sitting in front of me
is no proof of your birth. Officially it is no proof.
The law or the Department of Labor may or may not accept
my word that I have seen you and that, as I have seen you,
you must have been born. (DS, 67)

Even the official admits that his reasoning is "silly," is
"nonsense." But he does nothing about it. Or recall the
nameless iron things Gales counted and recounted during one
of his prison sentences. Neither prisoners nor guards knew
what they were; therefore, they concluded that the objects
were top secret military supplies: "Whenever something was
made that nobody knew anything about, everyone concluded
that it was to be used in the next war to end war" (DS, 80).
Out of ignorance, knowledge. And that seems typical of the
application of reason in the worlds of the Yorikke and the
Neversink.

For both Gales and White-Jacket, the conventional ways of
knowing are bankrupt. Neither authority nor reason provides
adequate tools for metaphysical inquiry. But both narrators
desperately need to explore the question "Why?" Both need
to penetrate the interiors of their crafts. Otherwise, as
White-Jacket speculates, "We continue to sail with sealed
orders, and our last destination remains a secret to ourselves and our officers..." (WJ, 398). The Yorikke seems
equally lost: "Perhaps the skipper knew exactly what he was
doing and what his orders were. From [the crew's] point of
view, however, it looked as if the Yorikke had no schedule

whatever" (DS, 288). To unseal the orders, White-Jacket and Gales must create their own tool of inquiry: They build stories. If answers cannot be discovered in authority or discerned by reason, they must be created by art.

Both novels are written from a retrospective point of view. Both narrators are consciously creating a story, a coherent version of their experiences. That is so obvious it needs little development. But its significance is clear only when we note that the whole story is a series of stories, of stories within stories. White-Jacket structures his tale as a series of vignettes, character sketches, and lectures. He records others' stories as well as his own: Jack Chase's desertion, old Ushant's refusal to shave his beard, the publication of Lemsford's poetry. Several of "the people," as the crew is collectively known, come forward with their stories, suggesting that THE STORY is a composite, not White-Jacket's alone.

Gales is even more conscious of his responsibility to tell the whole story. After all, as he points out in the opening chapter:

> All the romance of the sea...died long, long ago....I don't believe it ever existed save in sea-stories....the song of the real and genuine hero of the sea has never yet been sung. Why? Because the true song would be too cruel and too strange for the people who like ballads. (DS, 4-5)

It is the missing "true" story that Gales attempts to tell.

It would be impossible to catalog the number of significant stories contained in The Death Ship in the space allowed here, but let me suggest some representative examples. The Yorikke embodies a story; the rumors about her origins, her structure, and her past cannot be checked for accuracy, but they imbue the craft itself with meaning. As Gales points out:

> ...stories remained on the Yorikke. The crew may leave a ship, their stories never leave. A story penetrates the whole ship and every part of it. (DS, 131)

Like the skeletons in the chamber of horrors, the Yorikke's stories "had fallen apart and had mingled with each other" (DS, 131). And that is how the truest stories are created:

> From the stories about the Yorikke in the ports where we put in, we picked up here a word and there a word, and eventually we put the whole story [of the chamber of horrors] together." (DS, 132)

It is that process of story-building which provides the missing epistemology for both White-Jacket and Gales. In individual stories that carry collective force, the crews aboard the _Neversink_ and the _Yorikke_ create meaning, build a world. And it is a world that White-Jacket and Gales cannot participate in fully until they create their own stories, the novels themselves. In a dramatic scene near the end of _White-Jacket,_ the narrator falls from the masthead into the Atlantic. The jacket that visibly separates him from his fellows threatens to be his death. White-Jacket recalls the experience vividly: "I whipped out my knife...and ripped my jacket straight up and down, as if I were ripping open myself. With a violent struggle I then burst out of it, and was free" (WJ, 394). The alienating garment is cast aside, and the story that has been building can be told. In like manner, Gales experiences what he refers to literally as his "rebirth": "The time came, though slowly, when I began to get my own ideas again....No longer did I stagger about the bucket in a dazed and unconscious state. I began to see and to understand" (DS, 213). Gales and White-Jacket understand that if authority and reason are inadequate epistemological tools, multiple stories with shared resonance create true answers. The appropriate tools for inquiry have been theirs all along: White-Jacket concludes that "sailing with sealed orders, we ourselves are the repositories of the secret packet, whose mysterious contents we long to learn" (WJ, 398). Our stories become the orders, and like voyages, they do not end.

Notes

1. Several articles discuss Melville's indebtedness to individual writers, but the most comprehensive summary of Melville's literary sources and influences is found in M. M. Sealts's _Melville's Reading_ (Madison: University of Wisconsin Press, 1966).
2. The following editions are the basis for my discussion: Herman Melville, _White-Jacket, or The World in a Man-of-War,_ ed. Harrison Hayford, Hershel Parker, and G. Thomas Tanselle (Evanston and Chicago: Northwestern University Press and the Newberry Library, 1970); and B. Traven, _The Death Ship: The Story of an American Sailor_ (New York: Lawrence Hill and Co., 1973). Quotations from these volumes will be identified parenthetically in the text by the initials WJ and DS, respectively, and page references.
3. Baumann, 1976, 91-92.
4. Wyatt, 1980, 355-56.

5. Many of these reappraisals are gathered in The Recognition of Herman Melville: Selected Criticism Since 1846, ed. Hershel Parker (Ann Arbor: University of Michigan Press, 1967), 151-203.

6. Lewis Mumford, Herman Melville (New York: Literary Guild of America, 1929), esp. 114-18.

7. National Union Catalog, Pre-1956 Imprints (London: Mansell, 1975), Vol. 375, 39-40; British Museum General Catalogue of Printed Books (London: Trustees of the British Museum, 1962), Vol. 157, 684-85.

8. Baumann, 1976, 103-5; Reilly, 1977, 112-15; Chankin, 1975, 16-41; Fraser, 1973, 69-92; Miller, 1968, 114-133.

9. Chankin, 1975, 35-36.

LEGEND, STORY, AND FLASHBACK IN THE TREASURE OF THE SIERRA MADRE AND NOSTROMO

Peter Glenn Christensen

In her provocative book, The Mystery of B. Traven, Judy Stone records a conversation with Hal Croves about Joseph Conrad which includes the following passage:

> I asked him to explain his feelings about Conrad. He replied, "I like Lord Jim. It's been so long since I read it. I don't want to give an opinion. Conrad was a great writer. Just consider he was born in Poland and wrote such great novels in English! For that I admire the man. The difference between the two writers, in my opinion, is that Conrad just wanted to write good novels, entertaining novels. Traven always wanted to write books. They came out novels perhaps more accidentally. Some novels don't make you happy as novels. Conrad told a straightforward story which, in my opinion, Traven doesn't. That might be why books by Traven may last longer than books by Conrad. They have already forgotten about Conrad. I think Traven will last longer."[1]

Traven's humorous debunking of Conrad's complicated novels may be an attempt to confuse readers as to how much his own work was indebted to Conrad's. Both Judy Stone and Michael Baumann point out an analogy between Traven's first novel, The Death Ship, and Conrad's sea fiction.[2] In addition, I think we are entitled to look for comparisons between Conrad's extraordinary novel of South America, Nostromo, and Traven's Treasure.

Both novels exist in two forms. Nostromo was first published in installments in P.T.'s Weekly in 1903-1904, before appearing in somewhat altered form in hardcover in 1904. I shall be using the 1951 Modern Library edition based on the hardcover version. The textual history of the "Sierra Madre novel" is more complicated. It was first published in German as Der Schatz der Sierra Madre by the Büchergilde Gutenberg in Berlin in 1927. A second version of the novel, known as The Treasure of the Sierra Madre, was published by Alfred A. Knopf in 1935, and it contains various changes from and discrepancies with the earlier version. These alterations have been described in detail in an article by Inge Kutt.[3] Since today's readers are probably familiar with only one of the two versions of this novel, I shall try to base my arguments on both versions, indicating adjustments which have to be made for each version as I go along. The similarities between <u>Nostromo</u> and the "Sierra Madre novel" hold for both of Traven's texts, but they are somewhat more apparent in the American version. This American version is readily available in the 1967 hardcover reprint by Hill and Wang. Diogenes Verlag has issued a 1978 paperback reprint of the German original. Subsequent textual references pertain to these two editions.[4]

<u>Nostromo</u> and <u>Treasure</u> have three major plot motifs in common. First, characters are examined in terms of their relationship with a treasure from a mine. Second, social, religious, and political customs in Latin America are explored through the use of white, Indian, and mestizo characters. Traven uses the real country in which he lived, Mexico, whereas Conrad developed the mythical country of Costaguana mostly from his readings.[5] Third, capitalism and its effects on developing countries are presented in an unflattering manner. In <u>Nostromo</u>, capitalism is called "material interests," and it is used with reference to the San Tomé silver mine. In <u>Treasure</u>, the oil boom at the beginning of the novel is the most obvious representation of capitalism.

Using these thematic similarities as a background, we can further compare and contrast the two books in terms of structure. The most interesting narrative device in <u>Trea-sure</u> is the three inserted stories which interrupt the chronological progression of the prospecting adventure. These narratives are Howard's story of La Mina Agua Verde, Lacaud's history of the railroad bandits, and Howard's tale of doña Maria's sudden disappearance. In <u>Nostromo</u>, a novel with many intricate digressions that function as types of flashbacks, there are also three insertions which stand out: the legend of the miners of Azuera (Part I, Chapter 1), the story of the group meeting aboard the <u>Juno</u> (Part I, Chapters 5-8), and Martin Decoud's letter to his sister about the Monterist uprising (Part II, Chapter 7). Other background material in <u>Nostromo</u> (which shall not be discussed here) may also be considered insertions by some readers.[6]

In both novels the inserted narratives are essential in guiding the reader's attention toward the relationship between the individual and the group and toward the parallels between past history and current events. Conrad manipulates the insertions for a pessimistic conclusion about social change. Traven, on the other hand, uses them for a more optimistic view. From this standpoint, <u>Treasure</u> is not one of Traven's most typical novels.

Both Traven and Conrad provide a legend as a backdrop for further actions: the story of the miners of Agua Verde on the one hand; the story of the miners of Azuera on the other. The legend of La Mina Agua Verde is told by Howard to Dobbs and Curtin at the Oso Negro Hotel before they have made plans to go prospecting together. Howard begins with the following claim to veracity:

"Ever heard the story--I mean the real true story--of La Mina Agua Verde, the Green Water Mine? I don't think so. Well, here it is for your benefit. I got it at first hand from Harry Tilton. He was one of those who made their pile in that mine." (T, 3, p. 53)

Howard's statement that the narration is "for your benefit," turns out to be highly ironic.[7] Instead of discouraging his listeners from prospecting for gold, his words have just the opposite effect, as the beginning of the next chapter indicates, when Curtin asks Dobbs whether he believes the story is true or not:

"Of course it's true," Dobbs maintained, "What made you think it might be a weak magazine tale?" He was surprised that anybody could doubt the truthfulness of the story, which Dobbs thought the prettiest he had heard.
Yet Curtin's question with that glimpse of doubt had a strange effect upon the mind of Dobbs. Last night, when Howard had told the story in his slow convincing tone, Dobbs had felt that he himself was living the story; he could not detect any fault in it. Everything had seemed as clear and simple as if it had been the story of a man who had made good in the shoe business. But the slight doubt of Curtin had raised the apparently plain story to that of high adventure. Dobbs had never before in his life thought that prospecting for gold necessarily must carry some sort of mystery with it. (T, 4, p. 67)

Once again, dramatic irony will overtake Dobbs, for he will eventually relive the story as a person corrupted by the desire for gold. Although Donald Chankin is correct in comparing Treasure to Chaucer's "The Pardoner's Tale," we could also say that the story of the Agua Verde mine itself functions as a type of "Pardoner's Tale," in the light of which we should examine the whole novel.[8]
Unlike the narratives about the railroad bandits and doña Maria's treasure, Howard's story of the Agua Verde mine is presented in its entirety in the American edition, with quotation marks to indicate the speaker. The other two inserted narratives are lacking the quotation marks, and the reader begins to feel that what he has before him is the

author's presentation with commmentary of the stories initiated by Lacaud and Howard, respectively. The German edition is much better in this respect, and the reader feels confident that the stories are appropriate to the narrators. In any case, in both editions Howard's ideas on exploitation seem similar to Traven's, as in this excerpt taken from the first insertion:

> All the gruesome tortures were committed for the love of Christ and the Holy Virgin, because there was never a torture without a monk holding out a crucifix before the victim, and the greater part of the gold was to go partly to the Spanish king and partly to the Holy Father in Rome. As the Indians were not Christians, but wretched heathen, it was no sin to get hold of their gold by robbing them. (T, 3, p. 54)

Howard's hostility toward institutionalized exploitation gives us a better perspective for understanding his generosity toward Dobbs's memory at the end of the novel, when Curtin finds such an attitude confusing. Howard tells Curtin not to blame Dobbs:

> You see, I think at bottom he's as honest as you and me. The mistake was that you two were left alone in the depths of the wilderness with almost fifty thousand clean cash between you two. That is a god-damned temptation, believe me, partner. (T, 26, p. 301)

We can see that Howard believes in extraneous circumstances even though he does not believe in fate. He knows that the Church and the Spanish government were really the "curse" on the mine.

In _Nostromo_ there is no individual character to relate the legend (which is only four paragraphs long) and provide guiding commentary. The unparticularized narrator of the novel indicates that it is a tradition known to everyone in the community:

> This is the peninsula of Azuera, a wild chaos of sharp rocks and stony levels cut about by vertical ravines. It lies far out to sea like a rough head of stone stretched from a green-clad coast at the end of a slender neck of sand covered with thickets of thorny scrub. Utterly waterless, for the rainfall runs off at once on all sides into the sea, it has not soil enough, it is said, to grow a single blade of grass--as if it were blighted by a curse. The poor, associating by an obscure instinct of

consolation the ideas of evil and wealth, will tell you that it is deadly because of its forbidden treasures. (N, I, 1; p. 4)

In Conrad's legend we have, in effect, only one-half of the story told by Howard. There is no equivalent to the adventures of Harry Tilton and his band to bring the story to the present day. Thus, Conrad's story serves less as a moral point of reference than as a symbol of inherited evil:

Tradition has it that many adventurers of olden time had perished in the search. The story goes also that within men's memory two wandering sailors--Americanos, perhaps, but gringos of some sort for certain--talked over a gambling, good-for-nothing mozo, and the three stole a donkey to carry for them a bundle of dry sticks, a water-skin, and provisions enough to last a few days. Thus accompanied and with revolvers at their belts, they had started to chop their way with machetes through the thorny scrub on the neck of the peninsula. (N, I, 1; pp. 4-5)

For the two gringos and the mozo even success is futile, since the major part of the enterprise turns out not to be locating a treasure, but transporting it away from difficult terrain, a subject which is even more important in the second interpolated story of the novel. Conrad presents the results of the three-man expedition with mock detachment:

The sailors, the Indian, and the stolen burro were never seen again. As to the mozo, a Sulaco man--his wife paid for some masses, and the poor four-footed beast, being without sin, had been probably permitted to die; but the two gringos, spectral and alive, are believed to be dwelling to this day among the rocks, under the fatal spell of their success. Their souls cannot tear themselves away from their bodies mounting guard over the discovered treasure. They are now rich and hungry and thirsty--a strange theory of tenacious gringo ghosts suffering in their starved and parched flesh of defiant heretics, where a Christian would have renounced and been released. (N, I, 1; p. 5)

In *Nostromo* the three most important characters--Gould, Decoud, and Nostromo--suffer estrangement from their better selves and live out the corruption of the legend. Obviously, in *Treasure* only one character, Dobbs, ends up as degraded as they do.

Howard's second story (the third insertion) has two parts.

First, it tells how don Manuel received a silver mine in payment for restoring the sight of a blind Indian boy. He subsequently exploited the Indians working the mine to such a degree that they revolted and killed him. Second, it describes how, years later, his widow, doña Maria, reopened the mine in order to finance her triumphal return to Spain, where she was born. While the story is being told, it appears that it may also be another reminder of moral corruption, but Howard presents a different conclusion to be drawn from it:

> When Howard had ended his story, he added: "I wanted to tell you this tale to show you that to find gold and lift it out of the earth is not the whole thing. The gold has to be shipped. And shipping is more precarious than digging and washing it. You may have a heap of it right before you and still not know if you can buy a cup of coffee and a hamburger." (T, 16, p. 210)

Nevertheless, Howard most likely has some consideration of the moral dimensions of the account, since he prevents Lacaud from telling a gold mine story which is two years old rather than one hundred years old like his own:

> "Tell it to your grandmother," Dobbs said. "We don't want any of your good stories, even if they're only a week old. They're stale already when you open your mouth. Better not say a word. What is it you are? Oh, yes, an eterner, isn't it?" (T, 16, p. 211)

Howard fears that any legend of a mine told by Lacaud will fail to be an exemplum, but will be instead an incitement to Dobbs, and perhaps Curtin, to foolhardiness. Howard's talks contain important social indictments. He gives a detailed account of the policies of the Inquisition in Mexico:

> Against such power what could a plain citizen do? A bishop or a cardinal only needed to get word that a certain citizen was in possession of a very rich mine and it would not be long before witnesses would appear and swear that the mine-owner had doubted the purity or the virginity of the Lord's Mother or that he doubted the miracles of Nuestra Señora de Guadalupe or uttered blasphemous speeches or said that Luther had been just as right as the Pope. If he denied the charges, he was torturned until he not only admitted that the witnesses had told the truth, but added anything else that he was asked to admit. (T, 16, p. 198)

The difference in emphasis between Howard's two stories concerns the role of the state. When doña Maria disappears, it is obviously the viceroy who has done away with her in order to get the wealth. He symbolizes the governmental policy of unwarranted appropriation. In short, we are presented with a trail of events following the discovery of a mineral deposit.

In *Nostromo* an analogous story of snowballing corruption occurs in the second half (Chapters 5-8) of the first section of the novel, "The Silver of the Mine." These four chapters constitute a flashback of the months previous to the riot in the city of Sulaco only partially glimpsed in Chapters 1-4 as the first event of the book. In the flashback, the newly installed progressive dictator of Costaguana, don Vincente Ribiera, comes to Sulaco for a meeting aboard the *Juno* to celebrate the turning of the first sod for the new railroad. This railroad is to convey the silver from Charles Gould's San Tomé mine to the coast for shipment to cities such as San Francisco. Also present at this meeting are Gould's wife, Emilia; General Montero, the minister of war, who leads the revolt against Ribiera eighteen months later; don José Avellanos, an elderly statesman who is suspicious of the role of the mine in the republic; Sir John, chairman of the railway board from London; and the chief railroad engineer.

The difficulty in transporting the silver has led to an influx of ambitious European capitalists. Their activities alter the social and economic conditions of the country, leading to a very complex series of revolts and military confrontations.

The insertion of the events aboard the *Juno* also contains within it many initially confusing references to the San Tomé silver mine, including how it had become an unhealthy obsession for Charles Gould when he reopened it after his father's death. Activity at the mine is described, in part, as follows:

> The string of padlocked cars lengthened, the size of the escort grew bigger as the years went on. Every three months an increasing stream of treasure swept through the streets of Sulaco on its way to the strong room in the O.S.N. Company's building by the harbor, there to await shipment for the north. Increasing in volume, and of immense value also; for, as Charles Gould told his wife once with some exultation, there had never been seen anything in the world to approach the vein of the Gould Concession. For them both, each passing of the escort under the balconies of the Casa Gould was like another

victory gained in the conquest of peace for Sulaco. (N, I, 7; p. 127)

Not many years go by before it becomes apparent that Charles Gould's viewpoint is invalidated. The mine causes division between classes and between the different provinces of the republic. Just as dinner with the viceroy marked the end of fortune's favor for doña Maria, the get-together aboard the _Juno_ spells out the beginning of disaster for Charles. "I drink to the health of the man who brings us a million and a half of pounds," is the toast offered by General Montero to Sir John (N, I, 8; p. 133). Montero wants the mine for his own faction and leads a revolution to obtain it. Thus, the unsavory history of the mine continues in a new political context, as Mrs. Gould and a few others realize:

> Mrs. Gould knew the history of the San Tomé mine. Worked in the early days mostly by means of lashes on the backs of slaves, its yield had been paid for in its own weight of human bones. Whole tribes of Indians had perished in the exploitation; and then the mine was abandoned, since with this primitive method it had ceased to make a profitable return no matter how many corpses were thrown into its maw. Then it became forgotten. (N, I, 6; p. 57)

Certainly this type of abuse of the Indians at the San Tomé mine follows the same scenario as at don Manuel's mine. Unlike the Indians, don Manuel did not understand that since gold can't be eaten, it is of no real value:

> Although the mine gave him great riches, he treated the Indian laborers worse than slaves. He hardly paid them enough to keep them alive, and he made them work so hard that often they broke down. Day and night he was after them, whip in hand, and using his gun whenever he thought it necessary. Indians, particularly those of the North American continent, cannot be treated in this way for long. (T, 16, p. 198)

In _Treasure_ Howard indicates that many early mines run by religious orders were voluntarily turned over to the state because it was economically impossible to run them. In _Nostromo_ a perpetual concession is granted to Charles's father by the Costaguana government for similar reasons. Charles is a type of "eterner" like Lacaud, only on a more complicated level. Both are caught up in their obsessions. Don José Avellanos is the character who, like Howard, understands what the others do not. Describing the mine, he would say to Mrs. Gould, "Imperium in imperio. Emilia, my soul" (N, I, 8; p. 123). In the third and final part of the novel, "The Lighthouse," Mrs. Gould hears the same message from Dr. Monygham, a weary survivor of the atrocities of Guzman Bento's regime:

"Will there be never any peace? Will there be no rest?" Mrs. Gould whispered. "I thought that we—"
"No!" interrupted the doctor. "There is no peace and rest in the development of material interests. They have their law and their justice. But it is founded on expediency, and is inhuman; it is without rectitude, without the continuity and the force that can be found only in moral principle. Mrs. Gould, the time approaches when all that the Gould Concession stands for shall weigh as heavily upon the people as the barbarism, cruelty, and misrule of a few years back." (N, III, 11; p. 571)

At this point, late in the novel, Nostromo, the supposedly incorruptible capataz de cargadores decides to "grow rich very slowly" (N, III, 10; p. 562) on the silver he has hidden on the Great Isabel Island. He had gone there with the revolutionary journalist Martin Decoud to take the silver ingots away from Sulaco so that they would not fall into the hands of the Monterists. Like Dobbs, Nostromo double-crosses his friends in the revolutionary (i.e., separatist) cause, who think the treasure has been lost. Decoud, the only other person who knew the treasure had been saved, had committed suicide on the island.

The remaining insert story in each novel chronicles an uprising. Lacaud's account of the railway bandits who believe themselves revolutionaries (the Cristeros) plays a role similar to Decoud's letter to his sister in Europe telling her of the Monterist uprising and his plan to save the silver. Like the railway bandits, the Monterists think they are real revolutionaries, but their bloodthirstiness is simply clouded with ideology. Decoud writes to his sister:

"I declaimed for five minutes without drawing breath, it seems to me, harping on our best chances, on the ferocity of Montero, whom I made out to be as great a beast as I have no doubt he would like to be if he had intelligence enough to conceive a systematic reign of terror." (N, II, 7; p. 261)

Whereas politics motivates the Monterists, it is religion which spurs on the railway bandits:

The bandits in this case made it quite clear that they
were fighting for their king, Jesus. Fighting on behalf
of the Roman Catholic church, for religious liberty. The
fact is that they had only a very vague idea as to who
Christo was. It would have been quite easy to make them
believe that Bonaparte, Columbus, Cortes, and Jesus were
all identical. (T, 12, p. 143)[9]

The reader is asked both to believe and sympathize with
Lacaud's narrative, for like Decoud's letter to his sister,
his account contains elements of the political vision which
centers the book.
   The three insert narratives in each novel indicate the
curse, the conflict between individual and private ownership
of mineral resources, and the social conditions leading to
rebellion. However, Conrad's use of the insertions confirms
a cyclic and mythical fatality by linking the story of the
gringos and the mozo to Nostromo's death in the last paragraph of the novel:

Dr. Monygham, pulling round in the police-galley, heard
the name pass over his head. It was another of Nostromo's
successes, the greatest, the most enviable, the most sin-
ister of all. In that true cry of love and grief that
seemed to ring aloud from Punta Male to Azuera and away to
the bright line of the horizon, overhung by a big white
cloud shining like a mass of solid silver, the genius of
the magnificent capataz de cargadores dominated the dark
gulf containing his conquests of treasure and love. (N,
III, 13; p. 631)[10]

The references to the clouds, Azuera, silver, and the
treasure from the first chapter of the novel indicate that
we have come full circle and that recent events will again
become the stuff of legend. The narratives of the history
of the San Tomé mine and the adventure with the cargo of
silver thus come to a temporary conclusion with the death of
the character who symbolizes the continuing corruption of
the common man.
   In Treasure there is no equivalent mythical or symbolic
ending. Howard sets the tone of the conclusion. He does
not see Dobbs's actions as a fulfillment of his own stories.
Instead, he is struck by the cosmic absurdity of his recent
adventures:

"So we have worked and labored and suffered like galley-
slaves for the pleasure of it," Howard said to Curtin when
he finished his story. "Anyway, I think it's a very good

335

joke--a good one played on us and on the bandits by the Lord or by fate or by nature, whichever you prefer. And whoever or whatever played it certainly had a good sense of humor." (T, 26, p. 305)[11]

The reason why Howard can laugh is because the fates of all the partners are individual fates. In Nostromo all the characters are inseparable from their political situations in Costaguana, and no individual fates are possible. In this light, we should continue and examine the relationship of Traven's six Jungle novels of the 1930s with Nostromo, since these works also distance themselves from the idea of an individual fate apart from a political context.

Notes

1. Stone, 1977, 63.
2. Baumann, 1976, 94-96, 106.
3. Kutt, 1979, 315-31.
4. B. Traven, The Treasure of the Sierra Madre (New York: Alfred A. Knopf, 1935; rpt. New York: Hill and Wang, 1967); B. Traven, Der Schatz der Sierra Madre (Berlin: Büchergilde Gutenberg, 1927; rpt. Zurich: Diogenes Verlag, 1978). All subsequent references to the novel in English will refer to the Hill and Wang edition. Chapter numbers precede the page numbers, and the title is abbreviated by the letter T. All subsequent references to the novel in German refer to the Diogenes edition. Chapter numbers precede the page numbers, and the title is abbreviated by the letter S.
5. For Conrad's sources see Norman Sherry, Conrad's Western World (Cambridge: The University Press, 1971), 147-204.
6. All references to Nostromo are from the following edition: Joseph Conrad, Nostromo (London: Harpur & Bros., 1904; rpt. New York: Modern Library, 1951). The letter N stands for the novel. Part and chapter are both given.
7. The German edition dispenses with the phrase "for your benefit," but a similar message is conveyed by a passage at the end of the story: "Aber da kann man vielleicht sein ganzes Leben lang suchen, und man findet nichts" (59).
8. Chankin, 1975, 52.
9. Not in the German edition.
10. The passage is different in the serialized edition. This has been pointed out in Raskin, 1971, 188.
11. The German edition tells us, "Dieser Witz ist zehn Monate Arbeit wert" (230). ("This job is worth ten months of labor.")

SLAVES OF PROPERTY
A Comparison of B. Traven's The Treasure of the Sierra Madre and Ilf-Petrov's The Twelve Chairs

Helmut F. Pfanner

A comparison of two works of literature can be based upon a wide array of stylistic and thematic elements. While questions of style are particularly important in determining literary connections between two authors, it can be just as interesting to observe thematic parallels in works dealing with the same human problem under different geographical and social circumstances. Perhaps there is no greater disagreement in today's world than the way in which material property is conceived by the two major ideological systems. While the followers of capitalism defend the right to personal possession as a means to economic and industrial growth, the advocates of socialism want all property to be state-owned for the same purpose. What divides the social theorists of the East and the West is thus not so much the question of wealth as such, since it is deemed necessary for progress on both sides, as the problem of its distribution and ownership. But there is also the belief, almost as old as mankind itself, that the quest for material possessions enslaves the will of man and his power of moral action. The positive as well as the negative aspects of this question converge in the highly ambivalent position of Jean-Jacques Rousseau, who both approved of wealth and condemned it in different parts of his books.[1] The seeming contradiction in Rousseau's thinking can be resolved if his once positive, once negative judgment of property is applied not to the material goods themselves but to man's way of handling them. Being basically "a product of human convention and devising," property, like other products of human artifice, has a two-sided edge for good or evil.[2] If this premise of the French philosopher is accepted, one will see that man's enslavement by wealth depends on the greediness of the individual character; and if this assertion is universally applicable, it must be valid under any historical and geographical condition. The basic truth of Rousseau's belief can be traced in two literary works which, though set in different social environments, share the same theme: how the accumulation of property can affect man's moral action.

The works in question are two novels, which were first published in such close succession that they could have been written at the same time: Treasure by B. Traven, published in 1927; and The Twelve Chairs by Ilya Ilf and Yevgeney

Petrov, published a year later.³ In each case, pen names
were used by the authors, B. Traven standing for Otto
Wienecke/Feige/Marut, and Ilf-Petrov for Ilya Arnoldovich
Faynzilberg and Yevgeney Petrovich. All three of these
authors lived and wrote outside their native environments,
the German-born Traven in Mexico, a major Latin-American
country, and the two Ukrainian-born writers in Moscow, the
capital of Russian culture. What makes a comparison between
the two novels particularly interesting, however, is the
fact that their common theme is connected to the same literary motif, the search for a hidden treasure, and that the
literary situation in both works is that of three protagonists taking part in the search. It is the purpose of this
paper to investigate the similarities between the two novels, focusing at first on the chief characters and then on
their social environment. Finally, I shall attempt to draw
some conclusions about the worldviews of the authors.

    In Traven's novel, the protagonists are three Americans
living in Mexico whose livelihood is threatened by their
countrymen's exploitation of the natural and human resources
of that country. In order to overcome the insecurity of
their periodic unemployment and intermittent dependency upon
fraudulent industrial bosses, they decide to go prospecting
for gold. For this purpose, they pool their financial
assets, as well as their practical knowledge. As real
partners in a joint business venture, they divide their
earnings equally after each day's work, regardless of differences in responsibilities and success. This arrangement
is not indicative of friendship; on the contrary, it is made
clear by the author that they "gathered together solely to
gain riches" and that "they had in common only business
relations." Traven goes on to say that this "proves to be
to the advantage of their work. Friends, really good
friends, kept together by business and forced upon each
other without any contact with other people, more often than
not part the bitterest of enemies."⁴ These words reveal an
author with a deep understanding of basic human interaction.

    The relationship between the protagonists in Ilf-Petrov's
novel is much more complicated from the onset. Only two of
the three treasure hunters work together, though not as
equals, but--to use the author's own term--as "concessionaires." One of them is an old Russian aristocrat named
Ippolit Matveyevitch Vorobyaninov, who has heard from his
dying mother-in-law that she sewed her family's diamonds
into the seat cushion of a chair during the Russian Revolution, which took place ten years before the story unfolds.
The chair was part of a dining-room set of twelve chairs,
which were confiscated as state property and sent to dif-

338

ferent locations. Vorobyaninov undertakes his search with
the help of Ostap Bender, a young rogue and "smooth operator," whom he has met by pure chance in the basement room of
one of his former servants. According to their initial
contract, Bender is to receive forty percent of the spoils;
but Vorobyaninov is soon brought to the realization that he
would never even get close to his goal without Bender's
help, and he therefore must agree to a reversal of their
terms. The element of fierce economic competition is also
present in the third protagonist, a Russian Orthodox priest
named Fyodor, who conducts his own search for the hidden
treasure. Whenever his path crosses that of the two "concessionaires," an outright battle occurs between the two
rival parties. In line with this aggressive and mutually
distrustful atmosphere among the three protagonists, Bender
frequently compares the treasure hunt with a court trial,
as, for instance, in these sentences: "Things are moving,
gentlemen of the jury. Things are moving," or "The hearing
is continued. Do you hear? You, members of the jury."[5]
Like Traven, Ilf and Petrov are experts in human psychology.
Their satire on the laws and practices of free enterprise
also shows their insight into socioeconomic problems.

In The Twelve Chairs, it is undoubtedly the young rogue
who, better than the two other protagonists, manages to keep
his emotional bearing during the many failures of their
fortune hunt. Thanks to his intellectual initiative, the
two "concessionaires" track down eleven of the missing
chairs in different parts of the Soviet Union, and eventually they also find the last chair, which has to contain the
jewels, in the chess room of a newly opened railroad-
workers' club in Moscow. But shortly before their scheduled
pillage, Vorobyaninov cuts Bender's throat with a razor
blade, thus enacting a figure of speech which one frequently
hears applied to capitalistic business practices. It may
seem ironical that not the homeless vagabond, but the one-
time aristocrat and later official of a Soviet vital statistics bureau carries out the murder. Vorobyaninov's action
is paralleled by Dobbs's attempted killing of Curtin in
Treasure, and, as in the case of Traven's chief protagonist,
the worsening of Vorobyaninov's character is frequently
suggested in the novel. At one point, the literary image of
a man's breaking through a surface of ice into a wild tor-
rent of water is used to express Vorobyaninov's greed getting out of control;[6] and at a later stage of this development, the reader's attention is called to changes having
taken place in the old man's physical appearance which
reflect his moral collapse: "...his gait was different; the
expression of his eyes had become wild and his long mustache

was no longer parallel to the earth's surface, but drooped almost vertically like that of an aged cat."[7] Dobbs undergoes a similar physical transformation in Treasure, a fact which has been emphasized in John Huston's film adaptation of the novel;[8] but Vorobyaninov's changes occur more dramatically and are the direct result of his "gold fever."[9] Early in the novel, he has his scalp shaved after having made an unsuccessful attempt at dyeing his hair; and at a later point in the plot, he pulls his jacket through the street dust in order to be able to play the role of a beggar. Almost the same changes take place in the subplot of the novel, since Fyodor cuts off his long beard before setting out on his search for the chairs; and later, in a letter to his wife, he complains that his coat has spots both from the oily waters of the Caspian Sea, into which it had accidentally fallen, and from the spittle of a dromedary in Baku.

The physical and moral decline of these two characters culminates when Fyodor becomes insane following his realization that his long search for the treasure has been futile and Vorobyaninov utters an "insane, impassioned wild cry" upon discovering that he has come too late to salvage the treasure from the last chair. The old man's cry of despair can be compared to the outburst of laughter with which Howard responds to the news about the loss of his gold sand in Treasure. But the meanings of the two reactions are opposite. While the futility of his fortune hunt has driven Vorobyaninov to insanity, a fate not unlike the mortal fear which Dobbs experiences at the moment of his impending death and robbery by the mestizo bandits, Howard's laughter, accompanied by tears rolling down his cheeks, expresses the wise man's inner satisfaction at recognizing the futility of his search for wealth and in knowing that the balance of nature has been restored. His knowledge is shared by Curtin, who joins Howard in his laughter and thus confirms the strength of his own character, which was severely tempted during his lonely hike with Dobbs across the Sierra Madre. Nevertheless, on the scale of moral character, Howard would stand above Curtin, since he was constantly aware of the great danger to their consciences and since he had joined in the search for gold more from a sense of adventure than from a true desire to become rich. In this latter trait he can be compared to Ostap Bender, for whom the ongoing treasure hunt was of greater interest than the financially secure existence of a well-to-do man.

The authors of both works reveal quite similar positions in social matters. For example, they take a rather sceptical view of their heroes' plan for the future. The three

men in Treasure want to become the joint owners and opera-
tors of a Mexican movie theater, but it is finally Curtin
alone who accepts Howard's advice to invest the two remaining bags of gold sand (overlooked by the bandits) in a
grocery store. The plans of the three men in The Twelve
Chairs are even more unrealistic. Bender talks of damming
up the Nile River. Vorobyaninov dreams of a return to his
aristocratic life-style, and the priest Fyodor fancies himself as the owner of a large candle factory. In this latter
case, the antibourgeois attacks of the Russian authors are
obviously directed against religious hypocrisy, since
Fyodor's materialistic ambitions are in keeping with his
having become a cleric in the first place: He had seen it
as a means of avoiding the draft. If one compares the
attitude of the authors towards organized religion in both
novels, however, it is Traven who criticizes the Church
directly, namely, as an institution which took part in the
colonial exploitation of the Mexican Indians.

It may already have become apparent that the female sex
plays no major role in either of the novels. The few women
who are present in The Twelve Chairs are treated in a degrading manner by the male protagonists--for example, when
Vorobyaninov tries to win Liza Kalachow, the young woman who
has a quarrel with her husband, for a one-night affair, or
when Bender decides to marry the widow Gritsatsyeva for no
other purpose than that of getting hold of one of the
chairs. Similarly, the three gold-seekers in Treasure think
of women only as means for satisfying their own sexual
needs. The egocentric character of the male protagonists is
also revealed in their lack of appreciation for nature.
When the two "concessionaires" in The Twelve Chairs walk the
Georgian Highway together, they could not care less that
this is, as the authors say, "the most beautiful highway in
the world."[10] The Caucasian Mountains, with their glisten-
ing ice caps, serve only as a reminder of the diamonds for
Vorobyaninov, while to Bender they are simply useless. The
mountains of the Sierra Madre are, of course, quite useful
to the three prospectors in Traven's novel, but their use
does not extend beyond the level of materialistic exploitation. When the time has come for the three partners to
return to civilization, they get into an argument over
whether they should or should not close up the mine and
restore it to its natural state. It is finally Howard who,
as a mouthpiece for the author himself, succeeds in talking
the two others into helping him with his clean-up operation.
In Ilf-Petrov's work, too, the environmental question is
treated from a critical position. Here one of the most
repelling acts occurs on the beach of the Black Sea, where

Fyodor hacks to pieces a set of twelve chairs under the erroneous assumption that one of them contains the jewels. In another scene, Vorobyaninov and Bender are reminded of the environmental consequences of their actions when a strange object floating down the Volga River turns out to be the same chair whose cushion they had torn to shreds and which they had thrown overboard one day earlier. Bender also defaces the scenery without any cause, however, when he smears on a rock along the Georgian Highway: "Kisa [his nickname for Vorobyaninov] and Ossy [his first name] were here." Despite this similar concern about social and environmental problems, the two works differ in their suggestions for an alternative to the rapacious accumulation of possessions. In The Twelve Chairs, the answer is given at the end when it becomes known that Madam Petukhova's jewels have provided the funds for the new railroad workers' club in Moscow, reflecting a socialist stance. In Treasure, the gold sand collected by the three Americans is spread in the Mexican wilderness by the wind after Dobbs's murder by the bandits, who can see no value in his bags' contents, revealing the position of a political anarchist and romantic nature lover.

Despite their different answers to the question of wealth and property, the authors of both books share the same degree of scepticism towards any kind of political solution to the given problem. The state-controlled communism in which the plot of The Twelve Chairs unfolds provides no more protection against man's greed than does the capitalist system of a liberal democracy and of free enterprise in Treasure. This fact comes to light through the many minor characters and episodes that embellish the Russian novel—for example, when the official recordkeeper of Stargorod (a fictitious name for a small Russian city) sells false information about the ownership of the twelve chairs to Fyodor after he has been cheated by Bender; or, on a much larger scale, when the inhabitants of Vasyuki (another fictitious name) fall prey to Bender's stirring up their hopes for quick economic growth and great wealth with his talk about an international chess tournament. The satirical portrayal of large segments of the Russian population whose bourgeois values have survived the Bolshevik revolution serves a similar function, as do the parabolic tales strewn into the plot of Treasure. In each case, greed is seen as a universal human trait which swells with the amount of material goods coming into a person's reach; and the slaves of property which Traven and Ilf-Petrov have depicted are timeless human characters who exist under any form of government. Despite this basic agreement, the authors of the two novels differ in their various degrees of belief in man's strength to withstand greed's temptation. Traven appears more optimistic than his Russian counterparts. Not only have the Mexican Indians, with the exception of those corrupted by the whites, developed a way of life in which no other "business on earth" is more important than "to live and be happy,"[11] but one of the three prospectors allows himself to be converted to their ways, and one of the two others confesses a certain respect for the simple life of the Indians before he expresses his intention of returning to the civilization of the whites. No such contrast is offered in The Twelve Chairs, since even the watchman who has found the jewelry boxes and immediately reported his find to a Soviet official seems to have been prompted in this act primarily from a sense of duty, if not ignorance; and the one of the three treasure hunters in this novel whose greed is combined with a sense for life's adventures is brutally slain by his accomplice. The "ambiguously poetic justice" of this killing shows that, in the last analysis, Ilf-Petrov's worldview is bleak,[12] in any case more pessimistic than Traven's outlook. This point becomes clear at the end of the novels when the two surviving protagonists in The Twelve Chairs must face either prison or an insane asylum, while the two surviving heroes in Treasure may try their luck in new ventures.

Summarizing, one can say that the thematic parallels between Traven's Treasure and Ilf-Petrov's Twelve Chairs provide a useful basis for a comparison of the two works. In each novel, the literary motif of a treasure hunt points to man's inclination to become enslaved by property. While the two plots unfold in different social settings, the authors see greed as a universal trait which is not connected to any political system. Although, in his judgment of man's ability to control his greed for material possession, the German-Mexican author is slightly more optimistic than the team of Russian writers, it is the conviction of both sides that the problem is not one of politics, but of the individual human character.

Notes

1. Cf. J. MacAdam, "Rousseau: The Moral Dimensions of Property," in Theories of Property: Aristotle to the Present, eds. Anthony Parel and Thomas Flanagan (Waterloo, Ontario: Wilfrid Laurier University Press, 1974), 181-201.

2. N.O. Keohane, "Rousseau on Life, Liberty and Property: A Comment on MacAdam," in Theories of Property, 203-17; the quotation is from p. 204.

3. I am quoting from the English edition, The Treasure of the Sierra Madre (New York: Hill and Wang, 1968). Ilf-Petrov's novel was published in Russian as Dvenadtsat' stul'ev: Roman (Moscow: Tip. Gosizdata "Krasnyi prole-tarii," 1928); it was published in English translation as Diamonds to Sit On: A Russian Comedy of Errors, trans. Elisabeth Hill and Doris Mudie (London: Methuen and New York: Harper, 1930). I am quoting from The Twelve Chairs trans. John H. C. Richardson (New York: Vintage Books, 1961).

4. Treasure, 88.

5. The Twelve Chairs, 43 and 204.

6. Ibid., 243.

7. Ibid., 386.

8. Cf. Kaminsky, 1978, 59.

9. The term "gold fever," which applies literally to all three protagonists in Treasure, is also used, though in a more figurative sense, for Vorobyaninov in The Twelve Chairs, 308.

10. The Twelve Chairs, 364.

11. Treasure, 228.

12. Cf. David A. Lowe, "Ilf," in Columbia Dictionary of European Literature, Second Edition (New York: Columbia University, 1980), 382.

THE MAKING OF TWO GUERRILLA GENERALS IN AZUELA'S THE UNDERDOGS AND TRAVEN'S JUNGLE NOVELS

Lydia D. Hazera

B. Traven's six Jungle novels in the Caoba Cycle center on the exploitation of the Indians of southern Mexico during the last years of the Porfirio Díaz regime. Landowners, contractors, overseers, and government representatives all conspire to dispossess the Indians of their land and to uproot them from their culture in order to subject them to a life of servitude on the mahogany plantations. In reaction to their desperate condition, a group of mistreated Indians revolts against the overseers and organizes into a small band which marches from the jungles to fight the rurales, Díaz's feared rural militia. The leader of this group is Juan Méndez, known in the last novel as General. In contrast to this group of motivated revolutionaries, Mariano Azuela, in his masterpiece The Underdogs[1] depicts a small revolutionary band under Demetrio Macías, a group whose initial motives may be a reaction against injustice, but who end up fighting for the sake of fighting. The group is disorganized and at times undisciplined, becoming nothing more than a band of pillagers. Azuela's view is pessimistic because the peasants involved in the struggle do not understand the causes of the rebellion. The contrast between the two perspectives is particularly evident in each author's approach to the subject. Traven admires the Indians' way of life and deplores the Díaz dictatorship's disregard for the Indian traditions. Azuela also feels empathy for the peasant, but his view is shaded by his immediate experiences in the events and battles of the Mexican Revolution and by his intimate and close relationship with some revolutionaries from his native state of Jalisco.

In an essay on the biographical antecedents[2] of his novel Andrés Pérez, maderista (1911), Azuela reports that his decision to take part in the revolt initiated by Francisco I. Madero was more a matter of the heart than of reason. He admits to never having had an inclination or sympathy for militant politics. Even more revealing as an insight into his professed apolitical stance is his description of the last decade of the Díaz regime as a period that flowed "quietly, like a river of tame waters."[3] As an example of this tranquility, he cites the atmosphere in his native town, Lagos de Moreno (Jalisco), whose inhabitants expressed great surprise upon reading the report of a North American newspaperman which described prevailing slave labor conditions of the workers on plantations in Yucatán and Tabasco. In 1910, Lagos de Moreno was a small town essentially made up of rancheros (owners of small farms) and professional men. Among Lagos's small group of professionals, Azuela, who was a doctor, and his friend José Becerra, a lawyer, were among the best informed and up-to-date on events taking place outside Jalisco. Azuela and Becerra, who shared a common interest in literature, were locally known as dissidents during the Díaz regime. According to Stanley Robe, they "kept their political beliefs to themselves in order to discuss literature freely."[4] These antecedents to Azuela's later active role in the revolution belie his avowed apolitical position and reveal a restless man, who, cognizant of social conditions and political events outside his immediate environment, responded positively and actively to the call of revolution.

During the final years of the Díaz regime, Azuela and Becerra became active supporters of Madero. Azuela credits the Madero uprising with being instrumental in shaking the peaceful and boring atmosphere in Lagos. According to Azuela, Madero was the hope of all persons between the ages of fifteen and forty who sought the social renewal of Mexico. There is no doubt that, to Azuela, Madero was a sincere, honest man; it was the opportunists and political extremists who discredited Madero's pure intentions.

Azuela lived the revolution on two levels, politically and militarily. His political experience centered on his election (by acclamation) as Jefe Político in 1910. In 1911, when he went to take possession of his office, he found his way blocked by a group of "false" maderistas. Ironically, he had to call on a detachment of Federalist soldiers (holdovers from the Diaz regime) to oust the "false" maderistas from the building and allow him to enter. These "false" maderistas are the tejones (badgers) of his novels: "The term is used in contempt and obviously refers to the qualities of craftiness and cunning shared by these animals and politicians who take advantage of every possible opening."[5] This disappointing experience in local politics led him to withdraw from all political activities and devote himself to writing the first of a series to be called Cuadros y escenas de la revolución mexicana, one of the early titles of the book which would become known as Los de abajo (The Underdogs).

Azuela was not destined to devote himself to his medical practice and the quiet task of writing. His good friend José Becerra, who, at the age of forty-nine, went away to join a local revolt led by Julián Medina, an anti-Huertista, wrote to him describing his activities. Azuela visited

Becerra and Medina in Irapuato. He was so impressed with Medina's sincere conviction about the revolution that he became a part of his general staff in October of 1914. Medina appointed him Chief of Medical Service, with the rank of lieutenant colonel. He remained in Irapuato for a month and had ample opportunity to chat with Medina. Azuela found him to be genuine, generous, rowdy, and brave. He explains that the rank of general was not conferred on Medina by any higher authority, but by the brave men who rebelled with him in an armed uprising in the prison of Hostotipaquillo, where they had been incarcerated for subversive activities. Julián Medina was the first revolutionary to inspire Azuela's characterization of Demetrio Macías.

Azuela sought to create his own version, however, and for that reason he continued to live and converse with other revolutionaries. Later he met Manuel Caloca, a young man of twenty whose intrepid fighting and bravery greatly impressed Medina. Caloca took the rank of colonel, a rank later recognized by Medina. When Caloca was gravely injured in battle, Azuela, with eighty other men, escorted him to a hospital in Aguascalientes, where he operated on him. The route followed by Azuela to Aguascalientes partly coincides with that of Demetrio Macías and his men after they leave Juchipila.

Demetrio Macías, the protagonist of The Underdogs, is a composite of the revolutionary leaders Azuela knew intimately. Other rebels who formed part of Macías's band were also patterned in part after men Azuela met during his time as medical officer with Medina. He also had ample opportunity to "dispassionately" observe other aspects of the revolution. Very soon his first favorable impression of these men became a picture of somber disenchantment and sorrow.

Azuela took faithful notes of his conversations and encounters, and he later constructed his novel from those notes. In 1915, having finished most of the novel and finding himself in El Paso with only ten dollars in his pocket, he accepted a proposal from the editor of the newspaper El Paso del Norte to publish his novel in installments. Nine years later, Mexican critics Rafael López and Francisco Monterde, among others, discovered the novel and called it the best account of the revolution. Azuela revised the original text, and in 1924 the present version was published.

The gloomy, pessimistic view of the revolution which Azuela projects in The Underdogs is principally conveyed through the protagonist, Demetrio Macías, a humble, hardworking campesino. Because of an altercation with a local political boss, Macías is falsely accused of conspiring with the

347

maderistas. He is hunted down by the Federalist soldiers,
who rob and burn his house. Demetrio, along with other
peasants with grievances, rises up against the Díaz regime.
Demetrio's initial revolt may be explained as a reaction
against injustice, but his continued participation in the
revolution is never fully explained. Azuela's protagonist
never verbalizes his own ethical values, though he impresses
the reader with his bravery in battle and occasional demon-
strations of kindness. It may be that these natural men
respond more to intuition than to principles.[6] They react
to circumstances without ever giving any serious thought to
the reasons for their actions. Azuela views these men
through a naturalistic lens: In the setting of war, it is
violence, an endemic evil of all men, which dominates their
behavior. This is confirmed by the author's objective presentation of battles and pillaging to underline the actions
of his characters. The rebels do not fight for any ideal;
they are obsessed and dominated by the whole environment of
war.

The insertion of such historical guerrilla leaders as
Natera and Villa into the fictional framework of The Underdogs, and the presumed participation of Macías and his men
in such well-known battles as Zacatecas and Celaya, endow
Macías and his band with epic grandeur.[7] Their victories
and defeats, which coincide with those of the legendary
Villa, thrust the novel's protagonist into the period's
historical framework to make him a part of the revolutionary
epic. Although Azuela denies the rebel leader an explanation for his action, he does confer on him the status of a
hero.

The circular structure of the novel is congruent with the
rebels' odyssey. The first two parts deal with the rebels'
victories and the spoils of war; the third, with their
defeats and with Macías's death in the same place where he
attained his first victory. This circular structure, composed of sketches and episodes of fighting men and their
movements in a limited area, is the novel's most noteworthy
feature.[8] The apparently chaotic composition reflects the
disorderly nature of the revolution and the aimless, futile
quality of the fighting and its leaders.

Interspersed with the fighting and episodes of the rebels
are the perceptions of three characters who act as mediators
for Azuela's concept of the revolution. The poet Solís sees
it as a hurricane of cosmic beauty; Luis Cervantes is the
opportunist who takes advantage of the revolution; and the
unbalanced Valderrama voices the author's most intimate
sentiments: "Villa? Obregón? Carranza? X, Y, Z? What
difference does it make to me? I love the Revolution the

348

way I love an erupting volcano. The volcano because it is a volcano, the Revolution because it is the Revolution. But the stones left above or below after the cataclysm, what do they matter to me?"[9]

Whereas Azuela stresses the immediate impact of the revolution on leaders, rebels, and intellectuals, Traven examines the working conditions of the Indian and his evolution from an exploited worker to a rebel conscious of his rights. His six Jungle novels consistently develop his central theme: the effects of exploitation on a group of people whose traditions and customs are rooted in the communal system. The Indian's uncomplicated and uninhibited way of life, his closeness to nature, is contrasted with the complicated, impersonal, and profit-dominated life of industrialized society. The novels serve as Traven's outcry against all institutions that deny man's freedom and his condition as a human being. Centering on the development of the Indian from a stoic, downtrodden beast of work to a man who finally makes a decision to rebel against his masters, Traven expresses his conviction that men must take a stand against any institution or tyrant that denies them their right to be free and independent.[10]

The evolution of the Indian is presented in several stages. First, the Indian attempts to use cunning and deception to adapt and survive in the world beyond the commune. But since his attitudes and culture differ so much from the ladino's, he is unable to aggressively react, and the resulting ambivalence and confusion make him an easy victim of devious foremen and labor contractors. After experiencing endless incidents of injustice and physical torture, the Indians rise in a rage against their foremen. Their individual actions of rebellion are significant because they represent the victims' exercise of will to redeem their dignity as free men. The final step is to act in solidarity, as part of a group whose protest is aimed at an institution, government, or dictator.

The sly behavior that the Indian considers indispensable for survival in the alien culture is a quality attributed by Traven to defeated and downtrodden races. Traven observes that they have an inborn cunning which serves to avert and ward off the blows of the master. Despite this innate cunning, Andrés, the carretero of the first novel, and Celso Flores, the woodcutter of the third novel, are incapable of fathoming the deviousness of the labor contractors who trap them into working in the mahogany plantations. Andrés is recruited to finish paying debts his father had been unable to pay. Celso, a coffee plantation laborer, voluntarily goes to work in the mahogany plantation and through toil and frugality ultimately succeeds in saving the 80 pesos he needs to marry his village girlfriend. He is then assaulted by three men and accused of starting a brawl. When the police chief, who is in cahoots with the recruiting agent, fines him 125 pesos, he is quickly relieved of his 80 pesos; and because he cannot pay the balance of the fine, he is sentenced to six months of hard labor in jail. The recruiting agent appears out of nowhere and convinces Celso that it is better to work in the plantation than to spend six months in jail. Even acculturated Indians like Andrés and Celso seem unable to cope with the devious methods used to impress them into a life of servitude in the forests.

Andrés and Celso soon are swapping stories about the adventures they had before being recruited into the gang of workers. They are joined by two other Indians, Santiago, an old friend of Andrés, and Paulino; the four develop a sense of solidarity, and they support each other in their daily confrontations with the overseers. Unfortunately, the author observes, "The four of them, just like the rest of the troop, had fallen under powers which were stronger than they were and over which they had no influence whatever."[11] The weakness of the enslaved workers is lack of organization. They individually protest against the foremen, but it "never occurred to a single one of the peons to eliminate the capataces by a combined attack on the system of which a capataz was but a tool."[12] The combined attack on the system will be the final stage in the evolution of solidarity among the Indians.

Comradeship and stoicism among the workers enable them to endure cruel treatment. One form of torture, however, was greatly feared: being hung by the wrists and ankles from a high tree in the middle of the hot tropical forest and subjected to the bites of mosquitos and red ants. Traven explains that it was not the physical torture that frightened the Indian so much as the "unspeakable, inexplicable horror, the instinctive and unconquerable fear that the Indian feels of phantoms and specters--his superstitious belief in ghosts, which he sees arising on all sides in the darkness."[13] Hanging and this inordinate fear of specters drive some of the Indians to defend themselves against the owners and overseers of the plantations. For instance, Urbano, whose fear and pain were still fresh in his mind, knew that he could not survive another hanging in the forest. It was this fear, "matched by desperation," which was "transformed into courage, courage such as he had never felt: a fury unknown to him and seeming to possess someone else who was not he."[14]

The Indian as described by Traven is inherently peaceful,

stoic, and capable of enduring great cruelty. To rebel is a reaction brought about by desperation. This is why Urbano is stupefied when he strikes the owner of the plantation: "But immediately he came to and realized that now he could not retreat. He had just rebelled, and he would expiate that involuntary blow with death after terrible sufferings."[15] Consequently, after gouging out the owner's eyes, the Indian throws himself into the river to drown. This one rebellious act is the turning point. It reveals to the other submissive workers that it is possible to rebel, that they can exercise their will to reclaim their freedom and dignity as human beings. Urbano's individual act of revenge is witnessed from a hidden place by Martín Trinidad, one of three men who had joined the caravan after it had started on its journey into the forests. The three are fleeing from the rurales for different reasons. Trinidad is a teacher whose vocal protests against the dictatorial tyranny of Porfirio Díaz have earned him the fury of a local political boss, who attempted to detain him. Juan Méndez and Lucio Ortiz are army deserters. Together with the four seasoned Indian workers, they become the leaders of a group that will emerge from the jungle to engage the rurales in a series of skirmishes.

Traven has brought together an able group to formulate the reasons for the rebellion and to plan the tactics and strategies for the fighting. Martín Trinidad, the former schoolteacher, articulates the ideology of the protest, telling his fellow insurgents that they were born to be free and that they must fight for land and liberty. The Indians agree that what he says is what they want but have been unable to put into words. The men who prove able to plan the fighting strategy are the two army deserters. In Chapter 12 of the fifth novel, Traven completes his description of the organization of the rebel band into a group of sixty resolute men armed with a handful of pistols, who set out to attack owners and overseers in their camps using the same cruel methods they had experienced: "...when the slave begins to be conscious that his life has become like that of animals, that it is in no way better than theirs, it is because the limits have been reached. Then man loses all sense of reason and acts like an animal, like a brute, trying to recover his human dignity."[16]

By the end of the fifth novel, the leadership has organized into a council of war and given the title of Supreme Chief to the teacher Martín Trinidad. Juan Méndez, the former sergeant, is made general "because of his military background." The rebel army has now increased to eight companies and begins to make plans for attacking and meeting the rurales quartered at the haciendas.

The last novel of the series, General, deals mainly with the skirmishes and encounters between the rebels and the rurales. The first chapter, which opens with the rebels' battle cry, "Land and Liberty,"" sets forth Traven's explanation for the uprising:

When their sufferings, their tortures, their deprivations under their masters in the jungles...grew so intolerable that they...came to the realization that it was better and more worthy of their human dignity to perish in a revolution than to live longer under such humiliations and torments, then they took action.[17]

This novel also provides details on the background of the General, Juan Méndez. It seems that he had fled from the army after killing his immediate superior, a colonel who had punished Méndez's younger brother (who had joined the army at the same time) by immersing his head in a bucket of water and keeping it there until he drowned. The dread of persecution had driven Méndez to seek shelter in the mahogany plantations. His army experience had acquainted him with the rurales and their modus operandi, knowledge which he was now putting to good use in formulating plans and strategies for battling against them. His acquaintance with the topography and geography of the region was another tool for developing tactics suited to the nature of his ragtag army: "He proved, by what he now propounded and arranged, that, although he was only the son of a poor Indian peasant, he deserved to be a general."[18]

In his introduction to Guerrillas in Latin America, Luis Mercier Vega observes that the word guerrilla "signifies a type of warfare that is expressive both of a people's natural hostility to the state and its representatives, and the inability of that people to confront the state openly. The 'small war' reflects an incompatibility between rulers and ruled, a basic refusal of an important section at least of the inhabitants of a region to accept a position of subordination to a de facto authority...."[19] This contemporary definition of guerrilla may be applied to the confrontations between the rebels and the government's militia, the rurales. After years and years of mistreatment, the Indians have no alternative but to express their hostility in violent uprisings. Cognizant that the rurales are better trained, disciplined, and armed, the General resorts to ambushes and surprise attacks. His only edge is the spirit of his men, who know no obstacles and press forward even at the height of the rainy season: "The men were proving that

they were not just simple strikers but authentic revolutionaries, because real revolution does not recognize obstacles."[20]

Comparing Traven with Azuela, Jorge Ruffinelli remarks
that Azuela narrates events to exemplify barbarism, with the
intention of arousing the reader with images of revolutionaries burning books, breaking pictures, and destroying valuable objects, while Traven uses similar events to imply that
bourgeois values have no meaning for those who have never
possessed them.[21] There is no question that Azuela was
intent on emphasizing the savagery of war; however, it was
part of his broader perspective: that men lose sight of
human values when involved in a war situation in which
violence and the division of the spoils are a common day-to-
day occurrence. The main difference lies in their presentation of the events. Azuela's objective presentation creates
a distance between the writer and his work. The events and
actions as they appear on the written page are the only
source of evaluation for the reader. At no moment in the
novel does Azuela intervene directly to articulate his ideas
on the conflict. As observed previously, he uses three
mediators to voice his ideas: the cynical intellectual
Cervantes and the poets Solís and Valderrama, who ironically
praise the beauty of barbarism.

Traven, on the other hand, consistently interrupts the
flow of his narrative to inform the reader of his ideas on
government, bureaucracy, capitalism, the Church, social
injustice, and the workers. Traven's main interest lies in
expressing his opposition to all institutions that deny
man's freedom and dignity and in criticizing the Díaz regime
for supporting a policy that did not recognize the Indian as
a human being: "The golden age of the dictatorship had been
able to produce an unheard-of increase in productivity. But
in doing that it had forgotten the human being and the
individual..."[22]

Traven's narrative is shaded by an empathy for the Indians' culture and communal life, developed during his
visits to Chiapas from 1926 to 1930. As a member of several
scientific expeditions, he was able to closely observe the
Indians' way of life and their exploitation on the mahogany
plantations. Despite the promises of the revolution, the
situation of the Indian in Chiapas had not changed: "In
1927, on his second trip to Chiapas, Traven discovered that
debt slavery still existed, that the extermination of the
Indians was a thriving business."[23] In the Indians' communal life and exploitation, Traven found subjects which he
could use to illustrate and represent his philosophy of the

dignity of the individual and his protest against all institutions.

The fates of the two guerrilla leaders clearly express the differences in the writers' perspectives. The protagonist of Azuela's novel, Demetrio Macías, whose circular odyssey ends in death from a bullet during battle, is the prototype of the intrepid guerrilla leader. Although initially Macías's actions are motivated by protest against injustice, the atmosphere of war and battle obscures the causes of his uprising, and he becomes a part of the circumstances of violence. Azuela is intent on demonstrating how the revolution affected well-intentioned men like Macías, the exploited peasant, and intellectuals like Solís and Valderrama, and how opportunists like Cervantes used the revolution to enrich themselves. Traven, on the other hand, sees the rebel uprising as a success, because its leader, General, and his band of men personify the downtrodden who rise against the tyranny of the dictator to claim their rights as human beings and avenge injustices committed against them. Despite the differences in presentation and focus, both writers identify with the cause of the underdog and protest social injustice and the dehumanization of the individual.

Notes

1. Mariano Azuela, The Underdogs, in Two Novels of the Mexican Revolution, trans. Frances Kellam Henricks and Beatrice Berler (San Antonio, Texas: Principia Press of Trinity University, 1963), 163-261.

2. Sources used for information on Mariano Azuela's participation in the Mexican Revolution are: Mariano Azuela, "Andres Perez, maderista y Los caciques," and "Los de abajo," in Mariano Azuela, Obras Completas (Mexico: Fondo de Cultura Ecónomica, 1960), vol. 3, pp. 1065-1100; Stanley L. Robe, Azuela and the Underdogs (Berkeley: University of California Press, 1979), 1-55.

3. Azuela, "Andres Perez, maderista...," 1066.

4. Robe, 6.

5. Ibid., 7.

6. Portal, 1977, 76.

7. Ibid., 75.

8. Luis Leal, Mariano Azuela (New York: Twayne Publishers, 1971), 110.

9. Azuela, The Underdogs, 252-53.

10. Baumann, 1976, 57 and 68-69.

11. Traven, March, 159.

12. Ibid., 162.

13. Traven, Rebellion, 75.
14. Ibid., 99.
15. Ibid., 101.
16. Ibid., 175.
17. Traven, General, 4.
18. Ibid., 31.
19. Vega, 1969, 1.
20. Traven, Rebellion, 213.
21. Ruffinelli, 1976, 47.
22. Traven, General, 141-42.
23. Raskin, 1980, 171.

CHRONOLOGY OF THE LIFE OF B. TRAVEN (1882-1969)

This chronology is heavily based on the work of Wyatt (1980) and Recknagel (1982). As will be clear from the Preface, many of the events and dates here cited are speculative or controversial--not least Traven's identity with Feige and Ret Marut.

1882, February 23	Born in Schwiebus, Pomerania, as Hermann Albert Otto Maximilian Wienecke. Illegitimate son of Hormina (Hermine) Wienecke, worker in a textile factory, and Adolf Rudolf Feige, a potter by trade, who at that time is doing his military service in the Germany army.
May	Legitimized on his parents' marriage, becoming Otto Feige.
1882-1888	With maternal grandparents in Schwiebus.
1888-1896	With parents in Schwiebus, Stäpel, and Grünberg. Father works as janitor and in a brick factory.
1896	Confirmed.
1896-1902	Apprenticed as locksmith with Firma Meier in Schwiebus. After passing the journeyman examinations, he stays with firm.
1900	Family moved to Wallensen, Lower Saxony, where his father has found a better position in another brick factory.
1902-1904	Military service in Bückeburg, with 7th Jäger Batallion, the "Bückeburger Jäger."
1904	With family in Wallensen. Interest in socialist and anarchist writings.
1904-1906	Otto Feige disappears from home and is never heard of again.
1907	Ret Marut appears as actor in Essen.

1908-1909	Acting in Suhl, Ohrdruf and Crimmitschau. Meets actress Elfriede Zielke. "Marut's" police registration card issued at Ohrdruf.
1910	In Berlin with Elfriede Zielke.
1911	Acting in Pomerania, East and West Prussia, Posen, Silesia, Danzig.
1912, March 20	Daughter Irene Zielke born. First story published. Establishes himself in Düsseldorf as actor. Also works for the theater journal Masken.
1913, August	Vacation with Elfriede Zielke in Tangermünde.
1914	Break with Elfriede Zielke. First known portrait of Marut, by F. W. Seiwert. Meets actress Irene Mermet. Moves to Munich. Corresponds with Hans Frank on proposed Hochschule für Bühnenkunst Düsseldorf.
1915	Leaves Düsseldorf Schauspielhaus, and never again works in theater. Thereafter, lives from writing and journalism. Applies to San Francisco for copy of birth certificate.
1916	"Richard Maurhut" publishes An das Fräulein von S... in Munich.
1917, March	Marut applies for U.S. passport in Munich (refused in April).
September	First issue of Der Ziegelbrenner.
1918, November	Bavarian Republic established, under Kurt Eisner.
December	Ziegelbrenner-Evenings with readings by Ret Marut.
1919, April	Räterepublik in Munich. Marut is censor of press. Toller, Landauer, Mühsam also active.

358

1919, May	Collapse of Räterepublik. Marut arrested, but escapes and flees to Vienna. Accused of high treason. Goes underground.
June	Marut with Irene Mermet in Berlin.
1920	Ziegelbrenner published from Vienna (January), and from Nippes, near Cologne (April).
1921, June	Marut in Berlin.
December	Last issue of Ziegelbrenner.
1922	Marut in Switzerland, Czechoslovakia, Belgium, and Holland? Marut's postcard to Erich Mühsam, from Rotterdam.
1923	Leaves Germany with Irene Mermet. Irene Mermet emigrates to the United States.
July	Sails to Canada but is turned back. Returns to Britain in August.
November	Arrested in London.
December	In Brixton Prison.
1924, February	Released, and living in Britain.
March	Applies for U.S. citizenship in London.
April	Sails from London on Hegre.
June/July	At Tampico, Mexico
1925, February	First "Traven" articles sold to Vorwärts.
June	Vorwärts begins serial publication of Cotton Pickers. By the end of the year, manuscripts of Bridge, Busch stories, Death Ship, and others almost complete. Traven at Tampico, Tamaulipas. Irene Mermet to Mexico. Traven's letters to Ernst Preczang at Büchergilde Gutenberg.
September	Manuscript of Death Ship arrives at Büchergilde Gutenberg.

1926		Death Ship published in Germany. Irene at Tampico, hence to the United States. "Traven Torsvan" on expedition to Chiapas and Vera Cruz as "Swedish photographer."

1926   Death Ship published in Germany. Irene at Tampico, hence to the United States. "Traven Torsvan" on expedition to Chiapas and Vera Cruz as "Swedish photographer."

August   Der Wobbly appears in book form.

1927   Traven Torsvan in summer school at National University of Mexico. Treasure published in Germany.

1928   To Chiapas and Guatemala. Bridge and Land published in Germany. In Mexico City. Book publication of Busch and Cotton Pickers (Der Wobbly).

1929   To Yucatan. To United States? White Rose published in Germany. Letters to Professor Strasser in Switzerland.

1930   To Chiapas. In Mexico City and Acapulco. Working on Caoba Cycle.

1931   Carreta and Government published in Germany.

1933   March published in Germany. Bernard Smith works on English MS of Death Ship.

1934   First English language publication of Traven work--Death Ship appears in London and New York.

1935   Corresponds with Herbert Klein.

1936   Troza, Rebellion, and Sonnen-Schöpfung published in Germany. After 1933, Büchergilde Gutenberg remained Traven's publisher, but they were now based in Zurich, Vienna, and Prague, rather than in Germany proper.

1939   General published in German, from Stockholm. Esperanza López Matéos writes Knopf in relation to the film rights of the Traven novels.

1941   Esperanza translates Bridge into Spanish.

1942	Esperanza as Traven's representative and Spanish translator.
1943	In Mexico City. Members of U.S. "Author's Guild."
1945	In Mexico City. Visits New York and San Antonio, Texas.
1946	John Huston corresponds with Traven.
1947	Appearance of "Hal Croves," meeting John Huston and visiting set of filming of _Treasure_. Josef Wieder of Zurich as Traven's European agent.
1948	Traven in Mexico City and San Antonio. Luis Spota's investigations into Traven's identity.
1950	_Macario_ published in Zurich.
1951	_BT=Mitteilungen_ begins to be published. Last number, 36, appears in 1960. Death of Esperanza López Matéos. Becomes a Mexican citizen as Traven Torsvan.
1952-1953	First appearance of Rosa Elena Luján in connection with Hal Croves/Traven Torsvan.
1954	Hal Croves at filming of _Rebellion_ in Chiapas.
1956	Irene Mermet dies in New York.
1957	Traven married Rosa Elena Lujan in San Antonio, Texas.
1958	Hal Croves in Mexico City, Calle Durango (until 1964). (1958-1964 Adolfo López Matéos, brother of Esperanza, President of Mexico.)
1959	Hal Croves/Traven Torsvan (with Rosa Elena Luján) in Germany for premiere of film of _Death Ship_.
1960	_Aslan Norval_ published in Germany.

1962	Filming of <u>White Rose</u>.
1964	Hal Croves moves to Calle Rio Mississippi 61, Mexico City.
1966	Judy Stone interviews. Canessi working on bust of Traven.
1969, March 26	Death of Hal Croves/Traven Torsvan. His ashes are scattered over the jungle of Chiapas. Rosa Elena Luján announces to the press that her late husband Hal Croves/Traven Torsvan was B. Traven, who had called himself Ret Marut in Germany.

SELECTED BIBLIOGRAPHY

What follows is in no sense a complete Traven bibliography (for which see Recknagel, 1982). It merely represents a select list of some of the works frequently cited in this volume.

Baumann, Michael L. B. Traven: An Introduction. Albuquerque: University of New Mexico, 1976.
_____. "Land des Frühlings." In Neue B. Traven Mitteilungen No. 1 (1978).
_____. "B. Traven: Realist and Prophet." Virginia Quarterly Review 53, 1 (1979).
Beck, Johannes, Klaus Bergmann, and Heiner Boehnke, eds. Das B. Traven Buch. Reinbek: Rowohlt Taschenbuch Verlag, 1976.
Benjamin, Thomas. "Labor in the Monterías of Chiapas and Tabasco, 1870-1945." unpublished manuscript. "Passages to Leviathan: Chiapas and the Mexican State, 1891-1947." Ph.D. dissertation, Michigan State University, 1981.
Bergmann, Klaus. "Der Kreis schliesst sich." In Beck et al., 1976.
Berman, Paul. "B. Traven, I Presume," Michigan Quarterly Review, Ann Arbor, Winter 1978.
_____. "Weimar in the Sierra Madre." New Republic 184, 9 (Feb. 28, 1981), pp. 24-27.
Blum, Mary. "Clearing up the mysteries of author B. Traven." Los Angeles Times Calendar, July 19, 1970.
Borges, Jorge Luis. "Kafka and his Precursors." In his Labyrinths, edited by Donald A. Yates and James E. Irby. New York: New Directions Publishing Corporation, 1964.
Brissenden, Paul F. The IWW. 2nd ed. 1920.
Calder-Marshall, Arthur. "The Novels of B. Traven." Horizon 1 (July 1940).
Campbell, Joseph. The Hero with a Thousand Faces. Cleveland: World Publishing Company, 1964.
Caute, D. The Fellow Travellers. London: Quartet, 1973.
Chankin, Donald O. Anonymity and Death: The Fiction of B. Traven. University Park: Pennsylvania State University Press, 1975.
Clark, Marjorie Ruth. Organized Labor in Mexico. Chapel Hill, NC, 1934.
Conlin, Joseph R. Bread and Roses Too. Westport, CT: Greenwood, 1981.
_____. ed. At the Point of Production. Westport, CT: Greenwood, 1981.
Conquest, Robert. The Great Terror. London: Penguin, 1971.

Cordan, Wolfgang. "Ben Traven--Ende der Legenden." Frank-
furter Allgemeine Zeitung No. 147 (June 29, 1957).
_____. Geheimnis im Urwald. Düsseldorf, 1959. (Translated
as Secret of the Forest. London: Gollancz, 1963.)
Croves, Hal. "The B. Traven Mystery." Letter to the
editor, Time, March 15, 1948, p. 13.
Dubofsky, Melvyn. We Shall Be All. Chicago: Quadrangle
1969.
Ertl, Eric. "Heimatlose unterwegs: Eine Welt zu gewinnen."
In Beck et al., 1976.
Essbach, Wolfgang. "Das Prinzip der namenlosen Differenz.
Gesellschafts- und Kulturkritik bei B. Traven." In Beck
et al., 1976.
Fähnders, Walter, and Martin Rector. Linksradikalismus und
Literatur. Untersuchungen zur Geschichte der
sozialistischen Literatur in der Weimarer Republik. 2
vols. Reinbek: Rowohlt, 1974.
Favre, Henri. Changement et continuité chez les Maya du
Mexique; contribution a l'étude de la situation coloniale
en Amérique latine. Paris, 1971.
_____. "Le travail saisonnier des Chamula." Cahiers de
l'Institut des Hautes Etudes de l'Amérique Latine 7
(Paris, 1965), pp. 63-134.
Fraser, John. "Rereading Traven's The Death Ship."
Southern Review 9 (1973), pp. 69-92.
García de Leon, Antonio. "Lucha de clases y poder politico
en Chiapas." Historia y Sociedad 22 (1979), pp. 57-87.
Goss, Robert. "Der Wobbly und die Wobblies." To be pub-
lished in essay volume of the Traven Werkausgabe.
Graham, D. C., and T. R. Gurr. Violence in America. New
York: Signet, 1969.
Green, Martin. Dreams of Adventure, Deeds of Empire. New
York: Basic, 1979.
Grunberger, Richard. Red Rising in Bavaria. London: Arthur
Barker, 1973.
Guthke, Karl S. "Das Geheimnis um B. Traven entdeckt"- und
rätselvoller denn je. Frankfurt am Main, Wien, Olten:
Büchergilde Gutenberg, 1983. Also in Karl S. Guthke,
Erkundungen. Essays zur Literatur von Milton bis Traven.
Frankfurt am Main, Bern, New York: Peter Lang, 1983.
Hagemann, E. R. "A Checklist of the Works of B. Traven and
the Critical Estimates and Biographical Essays on Him,
together with a Brief Biography." In Papers of the Biblio-
graphical Society of America 53 (1959).
Hays, M. R. "The Importance of B. Traven." Chimera 4
(Summer 1946).
Heidemann, Gerd. "Wer ist der Mann, der Traven heisst?"
Stern, Hamburg, May 7, 1967.

Heidemann, Gerd. _Postlagernd Tampico. Die abenteuerliche Suche nach B. Traven._ München: Blanvalet Verlag GmbH, 1977. Also Wilhelm Goldmann Verlag, 1983 (Goldmann Taschenb. 6604).

Henricks, Frances Kellam, and Beatrice Berler, trans. _Two Novels of the Mexican Revolution._ San Antonio, TX: Principia Press of Trinity University, 1963.

Hetmann, Frederik. _Der Mann der sich verbarg. Nachforschungen über B. Traven._ Stuttgart: Ernst Klett, 1983.

Humphrey, Charles Robert. "B. Traven: An Examination of the Controversy over His Identity, with an Analysis of His Major Work and His Place in Literature." Dissertation, University of Texas, Austin, 1965.

Jacobs, Dan N. _Borodin: Stalin's Man in China._ Harvard University Press, 1981.

Jannach, Hubert. "B. Traven--An American or German Author?" _German Quarterly_ No. 36 (1963).

Johnson, William W. "Who is Bruno Traven?" _Life,_ March 10, 1947.

_____. "The Traven Case." _New York Times Book Review,_ March 10, 1947.

_____. "A Noted Novelist Dies in Obscurity." _Los Angeles Times Calendar,_ April 13, 1969.

Kaminsky, Stuart M. "Gold Hat, Gold Fever, Silver Screen." In _The Modern American Novel,_ edited by G. Peary and Roger Shatzkin. New York: Ungar, 1978.

Kazin, Alfred. "_The Bridge in the Jungle_ & Other Works of Fiction." _New York Times Book Review,_ July 24, 1938.

Klein, Mina C., and Arthur Klein. Introduction to and translation of Ret Marut's "In the Freest State in the World." In _The Kidnapped Saint and Other Stories._ New York and Westport: Lawrence Hill, 1975.

Klotz, Volker. _Abenteuer--Romane._ Munich: Carl Hauser Verlag, 1979.

Knopf, Alfred A. "B. Traven." _The Borzoi Broadside._ September, 1935.

Küpfer, Peter. "Aufklären und Erzählen. Das literarische Frühwerk B. Travens." Dissertation, Zürich, 1981.

Kutt, Inge. "Facts and Guesses." _Papers of the Bibliographical Society of America_ 73 (1979).

Landauer, Gustav. _Erkenntnis und Befreiung. Ausgewählte Reden und Aufsätze._ Edited by Ruth Link Salinger. Frankfurt am Main: Suhrkamp, 1976.

Lübbe, Peter. "Das Revolutionserlebnis im Werke B. Travens." Dissertation, Rostock, 1965.

Luján, Rosa Elena. "Remembering Traven." Introduction to _The Kidnapped Saint and Other Stories._ New York and Westport: Lawrence Hill, 1975.

Lynn, D. "The Works of B. Traven." Arena 1, 1 (1949-50), pp. 89-95.

Marut, Ret. Der Ziegelbrenner. Berlin: Verlag Klaus Gruhl, 1976.

Merker, Paul, and Wolfgang Stammler. Reallexikon der deutschen Literaturgeschichte. Berlin: Walter de Gruyter & Co., 1958.

Miller, Charles H. "B. Traven, American Author." Texas Quarterly 6 (1963).

_____. "B. Traven, Pure Proletarian Writer." In Proletarian Writers of the Thirties, edited by David Madden. Carbondale: Southern Illinois University Press, 1968.

Pearce, Roy Harvey. The Savages of America: A Study of the Indian and the Idea of Civilization. 2nd ed. Baltimore: The Johns Hopkins Press, 1965.

Pogorzelski, Winfried. Aufklärung im Spätwerk B. Travens. Eine Untersuchung zu Inhalt, formaler Struktur und Wirkungsabsicht des Caoba-Zyklus. Frankfurt am Main, Bern, New York: Peter Lang, 1985.

Portal, Marta. Proceso narrativo de la revolucion Mexicana. Madrid: Ediciones Cultura Hispánica, 1977.

Preston, W. Aliens and Dissenters. New York: Harper and Row, 1963.

Raskin, Jonah. "In Search of Traven." In The Radical Reader, edited by Stephen Knight and Michael Wilding. Sydney: Wild & Woolley, 1977.

_____. My Search for B. Traven. New York: Methuen, 1980.

_____. The Mythology of Imperialism. New York: Random House, 1971.

Recknagel, Rolf. "B. Traven und Ret Marut. Eine literarische Untersuchung." Die Kultur (Munich), December 1, 1959.

_____. "Marut-Traven. Ein Stilvergleich." Die andere Zeitung (Hamburg), July 12, 1962.

_____. B. Traven. Beiträge zur Biografie. Leipzig: Verlag Philipp Reclam, 1966, ²1971, ³1982.

_____. Beiträge zur Biographie des B. Traven. Berlin: Verlag Klaus Guhl, 1977.

Reif, Wolfgang. Zivilisationsflucht und literarische Wunschträume. Der exotische Roman im ersten Viertel des 20. Jahrhunderts. Stuttgart, 1975.

Reilly, John M. "The Voice of The Death Ship." Minnesota Review 9 (1977).

Reinecke, Helmut. "Abenteuer und Revolution." In Beck et al., 1976.

Renshaw, Patrick. The Wobblies. New York: Anchor, 1967.

Richter, Armin. "B. Traven als Feuilletonist. Frühe unbe-
kannte Arbeiten unter dem Pseudonym Ret Marut aufgefun-
den." In Zeitschrift für Deutsche Philologie 91, 4
(1972).

_____. "B. Traven (1882-1969)." In Vorbilder für Deutsche.
Munich: Piper, 1974.

_____. Der Ziegelbrenner: Das individualanarchistische
Kampforgan des frühen B. Traven. Bonn: Bouvier, 1977.

Rodriguez, Antonio. "Esperanza Lopez Mateos fue B. Traven?"
Siempre! (Mexico), April 1, 1964.

Ruffinelli, Jorge. El otro México: México en la obra de B.
Traven, D. H. Lawrence y Malcolm Lowry. Mexico:
Editorial Nueva Imagen, 1978.

_____. "Traven." Texto Critico II, 3 (1976).

Rus, Jan, and Robert Wasserstrom. "Civil-religious hierarchies in Central Chiapas. A Critical Perspective."
American Ethnologists 7 (1980), pp. 466-78.

Schmid, Max. "Der geheimnisvolle B. Traven." In Tagesan-
zeiger, Zurich, November 1963-January 1964.

_____. "B. Traven und sein Ich-Erzähler Gerard Gales." In
Beck et al., 1976.

Smith, Bernard. "B(ashful). Traven." New York Times Book
Review, November 22, 1970.

Sommers, Joseph. "Literatura e historia: Las contradic-
ciones ideólogicas de la ficción indigenista." Revista de
Crítica Literaria Latinoamericana 5, No. 10 (1979).

Spitzegger, Leopold. "Wer ist B. Traven?" Plan (Vienna),
Vol. 1, August 1946.

Spota, Luis. "Mañana descubre la identidad de B. Traven."
Mañana, Mexico City, August 7, 1948.

Stone, Judy. The Mystery of B. Traven. Los Altos, CA:
William Kaufmann, 1977.

Suarez, Luis. "y Presenta al mundo a. B. Traven." Siempre!
Mexico City, October 19, 1966.

_____. "Siempre desentrana al fin, la misteriosa actividad
de Traven en la selva de Chiapas." Siempre! Mexico City,
May 7, 1969.

Taylor, Paul S. The Sailors Union of the Pacific. New
York, 1923.

Thompson, Fred. The IWW. Chicago: IWW, 1977.

Tyler, Robert L. Rebels of the Woods. The IWW in the
Pacific Northwest. University of Oregon, 1967.

Vega, Luis Mercier. Guerillas in Latin America. Translated
by Daniel Wessbort. New York: Praego, 1969.

Wasserstrom, Robert. Class and Society in Central Chiapas.
Berkeley: University of California Press, 1983.

Womack, John, Jr. Zapata and the Mexican Revolution. New
York: Alfred Knopf, 1968.

Woodcock, Georg. "On the Track of B. Traven." <u>The</u> <u>Times</u>
<u>Literary</u> <u>Supplement</u>, London, August 27, 1976.

Wyatt, Will. <u>The</u> <u>Man</u> <u>Who</u> <u>Was</u> <u>B.</u> <u>Traven</u>. London: Cape,
1980. (U.S. title: <u>The</u> <u>Secret</u> <u>of</u> <u>the</u> <u>Sierra</u> <u>Madre</u>. New
York: Doubleday, 1980.)

_____. <u>B.</u> <u>Traven</u>. <u>Nachforschungen</u> <u>über</u> <u>einen</u> "<u>Unsicht-</u>
<u>baren</u>". Hamburg: 1982.